# FROM NOON TO STARRY NIGHT

# From Noon to Starry Night

## A LIFE OF WALT WHITMAN

# Philip Callow

*Elephant Paperbacks*

IVAN R. DEE, PUBLISHER, CHICAGO

FROM NOON TO STARRY NIGHT. Copyright ©1992 by Philip Callow. This book was originally published in 1992 by Ivan R. Dee.

First ELEPHANT PAPERBACK edition published 1996 by Ivan R. Dee, Inc., 1332 North Halsted Street, Chicago 60622. Manufactured in the United States of America and printed on acid-free paper.

Library of Congress Cataloging-in-Publication Data:
Callow, Philip.
    From noon to starry night : a life of Walt Whitman / Philip Callow — 1st Elephant Paperback ed.
        p.    cm.
    Includes bibliographical references and index.
    ISBN 1-56663-133-5 (alk. paper)
    1. Whitman, Walt, 1819–1892—Biography. 2. Poets, American—19th century—Biography.   I. Title.
[PS3231.C25    1996]
811'.3—dc20                                                              96-24768
[B]

*To the memory of my parents*

Man, as yet, is less than half grown. Even his flower-stem has not appeared yet. He is all leaves and roots, without any clue put forth. No sign of bud anywhere. . . .

Blossoming means the establishing of a pure, *new* relationship with all the cosmos. This is the state of heaven. And it is the state of a flower, a cobra, a jenny-wren in spring, a man who knows himself royal and crowned with the sun, with his feet gripping the core of the earth.
>                    —D. H. Lawrence,
>                      *Reflections on the Death*
>                      *of a Porcupine*

From having been born so often
I have salty experience
like creatures of the sea
with a passion for stars
and an earthy destination. . . .
>                    —Pablo Neruda,
>                      *Extravagaria* (trans
>                      Alastair Reid)

Immanuel Kant recognized two wonders in creation: the starry sky above his head, and the moral law within him.
>                    —Primo Levi,
>                      *Essays*

Tell all the Truth but tell it slant.
>                    —Emily Dickinson

# Contents

*Acknowledgments*     xi
*Foreword*     xiii

1    The Unfinished Country     3
2    Mothers     15
3    Pupil-Teacher     37
4    "This Is the City"     48
5    Reunion in Brooklyn     78
6    South     152
7    Life as an Art     195
8    Birth of Rainbow     226
9    Lilac and Star and Bird     286
10   The Descent     322

*Chronology*     365
*Notes on Sources*     369
*Selected Bibliography*     381
*Index*     385

# Acknowledgments

BEHIND THOSE POETS who gave me the essential clue to free verse—and to what Lawrence called the instant moment— stands Whitman, our archetypal modern poet. Utterly modern, his authenticity leaps straight in. My respect and love for him has grown immeasurably since that first indirect encounter. His sheer size still amazes me. I can only measure his stature by the debt I owe him.

My sincere and warm thanks go to all those who have helped to make this book possible: the friends who encouraged me with letters, books, and articles, and my publishers in London and Chicago who met every one of my requests without a murmur. I am grateful to the Authors' Foundation for their award of a grant toward my research expenses, and I am of course indebted, as is every student of Whitman, to the pioneering work of Gay Wilson Allen, whose biography *The Solitary Singer* remains unsurpassed since its publication in 1955. I was also stimulated by Justin Kaplan's more recent book, and most of all by the late Paul Zweig's brilliant and fascinating study of the crucial years 1840–1865.

To my wife Anne goes, as always, so much grateful love.

# Foreword

THE FIRST THING to confess is that we can't believe in the legendary Walt Whitman. Some essential darkness is missing. We have learned to expect secret corners of the self, out of which emerge the dark moods, excesses, failures, the preoccupation with death. We want a shadow; we need substance.

The actual person, if we can only find him, smiling evasively in his thicket of identities, is another matter entirely. Mixed in him seems to be an uncanny element: the salt sea. He is curious, a great puzzle. Backing away just beyond our reach he has a curious appeal, half animal, which makes us feel we are in touch with something different. At our too hasty approach he slides off. He is on the margin, a beach creature, hankering after the sea as if compulsively. On land he never feels quite sure, or quite clean enough, always washing and bathing. He has a thing about water, about cleanliness. He lumbers awkwardly and looks clownish, sensing a loss of grace. The poetry of his lost grace, if it is ever to break and run, has to be in submission to the ancient rocking of the sea, slithering out in long pulses across the page in a sea-language, advancing broadly like the sea.

He lives on so many levels: learns a trade, lives with mates as a skilled man, and then in the heavy weather of buccaneer journalism, the daily politics of local issues. A psychological oddity, he loves the ebb and flood of crowds, yet is fundamentally a solitary, with a weird sexual fluidity that remains a riddle to this day, carefully hidden from others as it is from himself. Fearing intimacy he becomes an enchanter, a stubborn innocent branded an obscene immoralist, shocking contemporaries with his candor. His health shattered by the "butcher" wards of the Civil War hospitals, he experiences transactions of love there which are the most satisfying of his life. We seem to know everything and yet nothing about this baffling subject. Contradictory to the last, he affirms life and is inspired by death.

If Emerson is, in John Dewey's words, the philosopher of democracy, "the one citizen of the New World fit to have his name uttered in the same breath with that of Plato," then Whitman is indisputably its poet. Emerson's conviction that life is an ecstasy and the moment a miracle is like one of Whitman's lines in "Song of Myself." In Whitman we have a democrat who set out to imagine the life of the average man in average circumstances changed into something grand and heroic. He is a poet who can make the present concrete and exhilarating, and he has a vision of perfectibility and new brotherhood which, absurd though it may seem to us as an ideal as we near the end of our century of horrors, can no more be abandoned than can democracy itself. And democracy is Whitman's great subject.

It is ours too, more now than ever before. To draw close to Whitman is to come to grips with our own doubts and dreams and absurdities. At the point of death he is as relevant as he is at the point of growth. If we are to believe in a future, in democracy, in individual regeneration as the measure of the world's worth, we should look again at a poet who wanted his poems to circulate as a "coarse but warm blood" and be a testament to our common humanity.

He claimed that he had never been given a proper hearing, and spent his whole life trying to publish himself. A hundred years after his death, the strange fate of his book is known. He said often enough that it had been a financial failure, signing it and himself over to posterity, "a candidate for the future." He has yet to be properly understood. The message of his democracy is that modern life has not even begun. Modern man waits in the wings. A savage and blind medieval drama, sunk in the mire and dreaming nightmares, speaking the language of misery we have come to accept as the only one possible, still occupies the stage. From ages back, churning in blood, these phantoms have represented us. Then comes a book without an audience to tell us the earth is beautiful and man is free, that a world full of joy resides in the breast of each person and can be made available at once. Want it and it is yours.

We are inclined to look on Whitman as the poet of his longest poem, the exultant and robust new morality he called "Song of Myself," and of little else that need bother us. A great mistake, but understandable. There has never been a more remarkable poem. As well as being his longest, it is easily his richest single work. Nothing he did afterward surpassed it. Roofless, at one with the cosmos, it is pagan through and through.

It could have been called Song of America. Yet in fact the United States celebrated so daringly in it is not the one Whitman had actually experienced, any more than its title's "myself" was in reality him. There never was, or has yet been, such an America. Perhaps for that very reason his country—which he never left—is unnamed. More than likely, for all his early nationalism and democratic fervor, he was keeping well in mind the words of one of his heroes, Thomas Paine: "My country is the world, and my religion is to do good."

He might have called his strange poem Song of My Soul, or Song of the Experimental. Its itinerant "I," a prototype for the American soul, is seen in the act of taking the whole universe for its body. The vast land it travels over and surveys, a loose weld of nations forming one enormous Union under its "dense-starred flag," is at once an experiment fraught with risks and a realm bursting with the possibilities for growth, wealth, power. This great dream, which may materialize or fall apart in the dreaming, is the New World in the West with its limitless prairies and its high new sky, new air, new sun, confined only by its oceans.

Here is its first poet. The life-throb of this gigantic melting pot of a nation-to-be is to be given its first genuine voice, owing nothing to Europe with its kings and masters. The sheer certainty of this voice can still astonish us—the passage of time has done nothing to dull it. Sounding so wild and strange to our ears it runs into us direct, or so it seems, without even the intermediary of art. Yet it achieves the magical, that alliance between body and soul which is the aim of the highest art. Also it is comic. It falls silent, laughs, owns up to its own perplexity, mocks the inadequacy of speech. Honesty gives way to rapture, to hot dazzles of contraries. We are urged to take the poet's word on trust—but why should we?—and walk down the open road of his beguiling creation—which he assures us is our creation too. Such is the spell he casts on us that we feel tempted to say yes, to suspend disbelief in spite of ourselves and all the evidence. Where has he sprung from, this blend of seer and insurance salesman, with—in Lorca's loving phrase—"his beard full of butterflies"? He seems intimate and public, both at once. Reading him is like meeting him.

# FROM NOON TO STARRY NIGHT

# 1

# The Unfinished Country

To read "Song of Myself" is to be filled with curiosity about the young, ramshackle, brutal, and half-innocent America of Whitman's day. It was a country in the making, an unfinished country. The purity singing on behalf of multitudes at the poem's heart would scarcely have been its chief characteristic. No one knew that better than Whitman.

America in the early years of the last century was a country of huge desolate landscapes, much of it still unpeopled, though beginning to fill up at a terrific rate. D. H. Lawrence, a traveler with an acute sense of the spirit of place, went from Australia, another vast emptiness, to the United States in 1922, and spoke of the two in very similar terms. They were worlds suspended, needing hundreds of years before they could wake and live. They had what he called a "fourth dimension," their people all shadowy on the surface of the land, with their unborn souls. For him they were just *too* new, and altogether too large to grasp.

Who can say what this motionless, hoary wilderness, huge and empty as the Atlantic, must have seemed like to the first settlers who cleared land to farm in New England and tried not to look westward into the unknown interior that was the continent? These were the Puritans, destined to struggle against the aboriginal wild as they had struggled before with their consciences. Then, hot on their heels, and faster and faster after the War for Independence, emerged the pioneers, moving like nomads in from the coast into a land as trackless and frightening as the ocean, bristling with hostility beyond the blue distances. These men and women who seemed unwilling or unable to settle anywhere, bitten by the travel bug, drunk on space, were in fact the founders of the new nation after the American Revolution and before the Civil War.

One wonders why a man like Whitman, typically American in so many ways, was not afflicted by this common itch to move and to keep moving, come what may. An attachment to the sea may have held him back. Born on Long Island (called Paumanake, or Paumanack, by the Indians), spending long happy hours on the beach day and night as a boy and youth, he lived as if in thrall to the marginal nature of the shoreline, a domain that was neither one thing nor another, the land lost and regained, rising out in the swing of tides fresh and sparkling from the sea, that so different, endlessly variable element. Later he would be enamored of the mouths of rivers, the shuttlelike ferries and their crews.

Europe's Nature has a humanized, benign aspect. Its mother earth comes down through myths, after long chains of pagan centuries. American soil presents a raw resistance. It is perhaps harder to love. Melville turned to the sea. So, in his own fashion, does Whitman.

For someone so obsessed with cleanliness, the corrosive, cleansing ocean would be a great lure. People who met him would remark on the spotlessness of his clothes and person, his skin looking as though newly washed, ruddy and bright, his eyes bleary, unfocused, as if from the depths. In old age he recalled feeling that the beat of the sea breaking on the shore was what made him a poet, its elemental rhythm the constant example and influence. But for the first transients—as Daniel Boorstin has called them—the ocean was something to be left behind. You turned your back on it as you shouldered tools and loaded wagons.

If we are to see Whitman as anything other than a sort of triumphant misfit we have to consider his heritage and understand what formed him, with beliefs that remained fundamentally intact to the end of his days. We need to ask the basic questions. Why, for instance, did the Pilgrim Fathers come to America in the first place? They came, after all, with a dream of liberty nourished by those movements in European history after the Renaissance, when the idea of freedom had begun to excite men's minds in every country. All immigrants are voluntary exiles. The Pilgrim Fathers were no exception.

It was around the fulcrum of Martin Luther that the most crucial changes of consciousness took place, as the medieval Age of Faith, which meant blind, unquestioning, impersonal faith, crumbled slowly, to be replaced in the eighteenth century by the Age of Reason. Books, such as Paine's *Rights of Man* and *The Age of Reason*, were now seminal influences. So were writers like Voltaire, and Rousseau with his *Social Contract*. Montesquieu's book *The Spirit of Laws* would exercise the minds of those Americans preparing to formulate their own constitution and government.

But it is Luther and the Reformation that lie behind Whitman: the Protestant conscience. *Leaves of Grass* began life with a mission, to provide a bible for the new democratic man. A man was to look to his own soul. God was there in his own heart. The real life of the senses and flesh transcended what had gone before. "Oneself I sing."

Luther and Protestantism taught a faith that was unheard of in the Middle Ages, a supremely personal doctrine which concerned individual man and his God. Magic was dispensed with, religion brought within reach of the most humble. Whitman, of course, went further. He said flatly, and went on saying, that the priests and churches had had their day. He rejoiced to see

> . . . the mechanic's wife with her babe at her nipple interceding for
> every person born,
> Three scythes at harvest whizzing in a row from three lusty
> angels with shirts bagg'd out at their waists,
> The snag-tooth'd hostler with red hair redeeming sins past and to
> come. . . .
> Dung and dirt more admirable than was dream'd,
> The supernatural of no account, myself waiting my time to be one
> of the supreme. . . .

The Reformation soon produced its reaction, and a counterreformation generated a passion of furious hatred in Spain, culminating in the reign of terror there, in the Netherlands, and eventually throughout Europe that we know as the Spanish Inquisition. France was torn by a civil war which was essentially religious, as the Calvinist protestants known as Huguenots were persecuted. Soon the drift of dissenters across the Atlantic began. Before long there was established a line of coast colonies, mainly of East Anglian village stock, stretching from Maine to the new colony of Carolina. Behind this line, the historian Trevelyan tells us, "was founded the most strange settlement of all: Charles II's government permitted William Penn, the Quaker courtier and organizer, to found Pennsylvania as a refuge for persecuted Friends in the wilderness, where they practiced with success the unwonted principle of just dealing with the redskins." Whitman, as we shall see, came into contact as a boy with the famous old Quaker Elias Hicks, who made a powerful impression on him and was still an influence in his last years. Walt's maternal grandmother was an observing Quaker.

As races and religions mingled, following the capture by England from the Dutch of the group of colonies between New England and Virginia, the English, Dutch, Swedes, Germans, French, and Scots—and this meant Anglicans and Puritans, Calvinists and Lutherans, Roman Catholics, Quakers, and Presbyterians—came together on equal terms in a remarkable example of religious toleration. Huguenot victims of Catholic persecution and people fleeing from Anglican intolerance in England were soon making their way there.

The natural barriers of the Appalachian and Allegheny mountains served to contain the early English colonists in their farm communities along the American seaboard. This had the effect of encouraging close settlement and building great political solidity and strength of numbers. When they came to burst through these barriers in the eighteenth century, they were strong enough to sweep aside their French forerunners in the Ohio Valley and on the Midwest prairies, to take advantage of richer soil there. The stage was set for something entirely new, namely the frontier spirit and the advance westward.

The point has been made that the so-called frontier was a process, not a line drawn on a map like a boundary of Europe. These boundaries were more like chimeras, dissolving into question marks in the enormity of the West. There was something bedouinlike in the American insistence on being forever on the move, as if the movement of itself would deliver up the meaning sought, the thing looked for. True, there have been transient peoples wandering over the earth since time began; but not like this. Not on this scale, equipped with such tools; hordes of explorers whose prime aim was not to hunt or conquer or trade but primarily to create communities in the wilderness, to establish themselves and their children beneath unknown skies.

So much of this spirit is in Whitman as revealed in *Leaves of Grass*, yet here was a man who basically stayed put, on the coast or within easy reach of it. Apart from one or two brief journeys, he seemed content to know only vicariously the immense continent that was, as he put it, "the poem itself." He never saw the Pacific. Yet frontiers in his book are forever being moved on, not only on land but out in space. His cry is always the cosmos. Barriers of custom and prejudice are no more sacrosanct than tradition. In this respect too he is altogether the American iconoclast. Nothing is insurmountable; not evil, not even death. The true American is a spiritual frontiersman.

He had other characteristics in common with the pioneers. The settlers who remained behind, though frontiersmen themselves a generation or so before, were conservative in habit, a vivid contrast to the type of character prepared to push on into the unknown. And this instinct to consolidate led on to new forms of human inter-change: democratic equality, comradeship, distrust of authority—spurred on by the need for mutual aid—and before long a complete indifference to far-off Europe, if not sheer ignorance of its very existence. Resourcefulness came to be valued at the expense of intellectual and political skills.

Solidarity was a necessary virtue. The lone traveler was under threat, liable to be picked off by marauding Indians, to run out of supplies, to get lost in these enormous distances. So the dangers which made men and women move together was sometimes a factor in the creation of communities that put down roots whenever exhaustion or instinct made them call a temporary halt.

They would camp and settle for a variety of reasons, and move on again for as many reasons: their little farms drought-stricken, the mines they dug a waste of effort, the threat of Indians, the failure of hopes pitched too high.

They moved quickly because of the same pressing dangers and anxieties, and because delay might mean nothing: no water, the territory you had been aiming for snatched up by others who had moved faster. And this need to move speedily shaped roads and urged forward the development of river travel and then the railways.

These hardy men were experiencing the heady freedom and exhilaration of going where only Indians had been before, without ties, with possessions stripped down to a bare minimum, and without even the burden of a destination. They were not part of an advance, they were not even heading west. If anything, they had the direction-less turning motion of vagrants, but not their innate despair. On the contrary, their supplies always included their hopes.

Just as the conditions they found themselves in forced them to band together, so it was when they struck camp, formed communities, and evolved rough-and-ready institutions that were often crude in the extreme. All that was demanded of them was function, practical and immediate. Did it work? Laws were agreed before books and lawyers arose to give substance to them. Always the prime consideration was that of mutual need. Tiny hamlets in the wilderness one day became towns the next, mushrooming rapidly into booming cities. If the railroad failed to reach them they were as rapidly abandoned and left to rot. These transplantings, generating characters who combined prudence with brash opportunism, were the essentials of survival.

Everything was contributing to a world whose destiny seemed bound up with ceaseless motion. A whole continent was changing, on the move, growing, heading down the road, often before the highways for traveling down it existed. People were moving from east to west, south and northward, from rural to urban, homestead to factory, and—as the flow of immigrants increased—from Germany, Ireland, the Netherlands; either coalescing around the bustling new centers in the East—Boston, Philadelphia, New York—or pressing on courageously to the frontier lands of Wisconsin, Minnesota. Rough justice and rough equality were two products of this chaotic flux. In this haphazard fashion the foundations of a system of majority rule were being tentatively laid down.

The new towns and cities, unlike their medieval counterparts in Europe, had no walls. The feudal priorities of defense and preservation had little relevance here. The key to their success was twofold: rapid growth and progress. To measure up to the next community along the trail it was essential to have the power to draw in immigrants. Aspirations became identified with names: towns were baptized Rome, Athens, London. Life as experienced in the Old World was being entirely reshaped as populations swelled. In the fast-growing cities a new type, the American businessman born and bred in the thick of this dynamic growth, was soon a familiar and important figure. By Whitman's time, expansion had reached a spectacular rate of growth, as had the shift westward of populations. The United States was still predominantly rural, but the magnets attracting many European immigrants now were the cities. The most thrusting of these was Chicago, practically nonexistent in 1830 and by 1860 bursting at the seams with a hundred thousand citizens. Boorstin quotes the proud words of one of its businessmen-heroes, William B. Ogden (1805–1877): "I was born close to a saw-mill, was left early an orphan, was cradled in a sugar-trough, christened in a mill-pond, graduated at a log schoolhouse, and at fourteen fancied I could do anything I turned my hand to, and that nothing was impossible, and ever since, madame, I have been trying to prove it, and with some success."

Here was understatement indeed. Ogden was dealing in real estate before he was sixteen. He grew up in the Catskills in New York State and by the time he was thirty he had been engaged to construct the New York and Erie Railroad with state aid. He came to Chicago in 1835 and was elected its first mayor two years later. The city census stood at 4,170. In the following years, as the population rocketed to 300,000 by 1870, he was responsible for the building of miles of streets, promoted the Illinois and Michigan Canal, had a hand in the development of railroads, water supplies, sewage systems, parks.

In a world where nothing stood still, and by the nineteenth century was changing with terrifying rapidity, tensions were inevitable. There was a conflict in people's minds and hearts between the rural purity of Jeffersonian America, the simple virtues of enshrined heroes such as Washington and Benjamin Franklin, and the evidence of industrial and social progress, built from the raw ambitions of businessmen and hustlers. Opinion was deeply divided. Boasts of ever-new conquests and acquisitions of vast untouched territories overlay the fears of those who welcomed one aspect of progress and felt threatened by another. Westerners in particular wanted the creations of new supply lines and better communications but wondered if they were to be shunted off and made subservient to the increasingly powerful Northeast.

Whitman began his working life as a printer and journalist, shifting restlessly from one paper to another, assuming editorships almost overnight with an ease and nonchalance we find it hard to grasp. But if one looks at the rise and proliferation of the American press from pioneering days onward it is soon clear that the New World newspaper served a very different purpose from its European counterpart. One vital difference was the readership it aimed to capture. Originally in Europe this was literate and literary, and basically static. The pioneer newspaper was more like a railhead which had virtually to create the influx of people it wanted to serve.

When migration westward from the Atlantic seaboard began, control of the press by government, still very much a fact in the Old World, became difficult if not impossible out in the great blue yonder. Communities quickly seized on the idea of the press as a valuable tool, as important to them as any other when they faced the prospect of building a world from scratch. Newspapers instilled hope and purpose, providing evidence that their community was active and beginning to thrive. In effect they were the first boosters, advertising their almost nonexistent location by the fact of a press.

From the very outset they were at the forefront, leading the course of progress, becoming part of the history of a community's settlement and success. After them, not before, came the post office, school, and church. In effect the newspaper would be the town's first teacher. Dissemination of local news was only part of its function. Right up to and including Whitman's day the newspaper saw its role as a proselytizing one. People had to be taught, encouraged to choose the right path, be enlightened and guided morally as well as politically. No doubt because of its origins, the newspaper as a community-based enterprise has remained an enduring feature in the United States.

Many topics were clamoring for attention in the mid-nineteenth century, and nowhere more so than in Whitman's New York. Editors addressed their readers as individuals with the power—if they would only tap it—to work out their own salvation. Editorial pages reverberated with the activities of reformers, news of the temperance and feminist and health movements, proposals for penal reform, and platforms for whichever political party they supported. Social problems thrown up by the sprawling nation's growing pains were discussed with mounting fervor as a religious revival swept the land.

AMERICAN WAYS of talking were seen by foreign observers to have a distinctive flavor. Statements intended to be hopeful or wildly forward-looking were misunderstood, taken for lies or swaggering nonsense instead of the rhetoric of anticipation shrewdly noted by the English traveler Morris Birkbeck in 1817. We will find many examples in *Leaves of Grass*. Birkbeck mentions being told that Pittsburgh was "the Birmingham of America." Expecting to find himself "enveloped in clouds of smoke, issuing from a thousand furnaces, and stunned with the din of ten thousand hammers," he found instead a crude Western town whose industry was only just beginning. He realized that "what *may* be is contemplated as though in actual existence."

In the West especially, what Boorstin calls the habit of innocent overstatement was now commonplace. The prevalence of slang and hyperbole was in part due, he suggests, to the scarcity of women. "Men will say more than they mean," and women were, as always, the realists. As the aspiring townsman tended to call his town a city in a confusion of present and future, so tall talk in the West mingled fact and fiction. Settlers raising a town at the fork of the Ohio and Mississippi rivers in Illinois were inspired by what they imagined as its Egyptian-like setting and by their dreams of grandeur to call it the "city" of Cairo. There were ghost towns in Kansas with imposing names from the past—Alexandria, Athens, Berlin, Calcutta, Moscow, Oxford, Paris, Rome, Sparta—which at least testified to the yearning for wealth and culture of their disappointed founders.

The demand for names for the towns and counties coming into being every day meant that a great many were backward-looking or ethnic when they were not biblical or bizarre. Nearly thirty of the state names were derived from the Indians, as well as river names in plenty, from the beautifully named Susquehanna to the Mississippi. Whitman was not alone in wanting the Indian languages to supply place names throughout America. "What is the fitness—what the strange charm of aboriginal names?" he wrote. "They all fit. Mississippi!—the word winds with chutes—it rolls a stream three thousand miles long."

The distinction between slang and "proper English" was becoming blurred, and became progressively more so as the nation established itself with increasing confidence. Americanisms were often found first of all in the colloquial speech of uneducated men. We can see this process at work in the journals of the Lewis and Clark expedition called for by Jefferson. Clark had some formal education, Lewis a little more, but most of the party were semiliterate. The most extensive day-by-day log of the whole trip was left by one of the party's sergeants. In these journals can be found more than five hundred terms borrowed from Indian languages. Some of the Americanisms failed to survive. Others soon became part of American usage. Yankee was one. About the origin of Yankee there has been much confusion. An account of the history of the Indian nations maintained that it resulted from the Indians' attempt to pronounce the word English, which came out as Yengees. Others sought to show that it was a Dutch nickname, Yankey, from Janke, or the common given name Jan, applied to buccaneers along the Spanish Main, and was then imported as a nickname for Dutchmen in the United States. How it then came to be affixed to the English of New England is anyone's guess.

Place names figured largely, as well as botanical and zoological terms, in the Lewis and Clark journals, simply because there were geographical features on all sides that were still nameless. They were christened in numerous ways: after features which impressed them (Milk River, Crooked Falls), after one of their comrades (Floyd's River, Reuben's Creek), or after a patron (Madison's River, Jefferson's River). Various shortcomings, such as inadequate maps, meant that later surveyors renamed many of them in accordance with their own wishes.

As Boorstin points out, the fantastic and lurid names acquired by Western settlements, the mining camps in particular, were the result of self-advertisement—Gold Hill, Rich Bar—or were meant to warn off unwelcome prospectors—Hungry Camp, Humbug Canyon, Poverty Hill. Or they were named simply for the hell of it: Gomorrah, Hen-Roost Camp, Slumgullion, One Eye, Quack Hill. Often they verged on the obscene.

The Indians, asked for names, sometimes played tricks on the white man as a way of mocking their oppressors. This was language as humor as well as revenge. Some of the names offered were deliberately nonsensical, meaning "Far Away," "Good Morning," "Here," "That Is the River," "Go to Hell!"

New words appearing with such rapidity gave ample evidence of a basic need for a language unique to the continent: we had better call it American English. Its inventions were taking place at the grass roots, and its flow was upward. So that before long its rude vitality was apparent everywhere. "The American language became the apotheosis of slang." And slang, of course, derived from the working classes. Whitman was one of the first to embrace this linguistic democracy, in his *November Boughs* of 1888:

> Slang, profoundly consider'd, is the lawless germinal element, below all words and sentences, and behind all poetry, and proves a certain perennial rankness and protestantism in speech. As the United States inherit by far their most precious possession—the language they talk and write—from the Old World, under and out of its feudal institutes, I will allow myself to borrow a simile even of those forms farthest removed from American democracy. Considering language then as some mightly potentate, into the majes-

tic audience-hall of the monarch ever enters a personage like one of Shakespeare's clowns, and takes position there, and plays a part even in the stateliest ceremonies. Such is Slang, or indirection, an attempt of common humanity to escape from bald literalism, and express itself illimitably, which in the highest walks produces poets and poems, and doubtless in pre-historic times gave the start to, and perfected, the whole immense tangle of the old mythologies. . . .

The science of language has large and close analogies in geological science, with its ceaseless evolution, its fossils, and its numberless submerged layers and hidden strata, the infinite go-before of the present. Or, perhaps Language is more like some vast living body, or perennial body of bodies. And slang not only brings the first feeders of it, but is afterwards the start of fancy, imagination and humor, breathing into its nostrils the breath of life.

With all the spread and movement of peoples and the steady mingling of races, it would have been extraordinary if the language itself had not reflected so expansive a period. American English borrowed a great deal from the Spanish, initially bringing in Indian words via the Spanish language. By the nineteenth century it was employing numerous Spanish words directly. After Spanish came German as the main contributor.

Along with this virtual reconstruction of the language went the dissemination of a subliterature which narrated the exploits of popular national heroes. It has to be remembered that literacy existed from the very birth of the nation's identity, and even before that in colonial times. A popular literature, spread by the democracy of print, by newspapers, almanacs, and cheap books, circulated almost before the nation had begun to produce a literature proper. Legends were hungrily devoured and were no doubt oral legends in the first place.

Davy Crockett was for some time the most celebrated of these popular heroes. "The Crockett anecdotes plunged headlong, in a decade, from the small world of fireside anecdote and barroom wheeze into the great democratic world of print. Widely circulating, inexpensive publications dispersed the Crockett legends as they fell from the lips of raconteurs. They entered at once into a thriving subliterature."

Crockett's history is real enough. Running away from home at thirteen he married at eighteen, failed as a farmer, and served as a scout in the Creek War of 1813 under Andrew Jackson. Though he had next to no education he was elected to the state legislature in 1821. He served for three terms in Congress yet remained a backwoodsman when not in Washington. News of his adventures traveled far and wide. He claimed to have killed more than a hundred bears in less than a year. Joining the war for Texas independence, he died fighting at the Alamo in 1836.

His imaginary exploits proved irresistible to his countless readers. Here is the way he describes his escape from a tornado: "Then came a roar that would have made old Niagara sound like a kitten; the trees walked out by the roots, and danced about like injins; the houses come apart; the people screamed all sorts o' frightened-to-death-ativeness, and some of them appeared to going up to heaven heels foremost. . . . Fortunately, a stray streak of lightnin' came passin' along, so jist as it come I grabbed it by the fork, and sprung on it. . . ."

Victories had to be gigantic, but heroes were frequently clowns. This again was peculiarly American. Crockett's audience lived in a far from predictable world. Addressing them directly, he wrote, "May be you'll laugh at me, and not at my book." It was an invitation to accept him as one of themselves, and at the same time to feel secure enough to stand back and laugh at their own misadventures. What his mock-heroics give us too is a foretaste of that unstoppable optimism we find in such large measure in Whitman.

This, then, is the continent, "a rich storehouse of the unexpected," which provided the raw material of Leaves of Grass, the America that Whitman lived in as a boy on Long Island and as a youth and young man in Brooklyn and New York, part of that long foreground we know so little about. How he made use of it during those "lost" years between 1849 and 1855, pondering and waiting "like a great ploughed and sown paddock soaking up the rain and sun, not to be hurried, needing its due time," has raised questions that we are still, a hundred years later, trying to answer.

# 2

# Mothers

Starting from fish-shape Paumanok where I was born,
Well-begotten, and rais'd by a perfect mother...

When we speak of our origins, we mean our birthplace and our
parents. For good or ill we feel our mother to be the one who
may have influenced us most deeply, and for life; and before her a
whole chain of mothers. Certainly Walt Whitman felt this. No one
was greater in his eyes than his mother, no one affected him more
profoundly. In effect she was his one constant love. Faults she must
have had, but in his complete idealization of her he overlooked them.

"Mothers precede all," he said grandly. He may have had Louisa
Whitman particularly in mind, or he could have been thinking of
that Magna Mater, the sea, the watery universe surrounding his
home on Long Island where he was born. An evolutionist all his life,
he revered Darwin. "Can the churches, priests, dogmatists, produce
anything to match it?" he exclaimed. "How can we forget Darwin?
Was ever a beautiful character a more simple character? He was one
of the acme men—he was at the top."

The Whitmans at West Hills and his mother's family, the Van
Velsors at Cold Springs, both lived near enough to the sea to be able
to catch glimpses of it from high points. When all was quiet you
heard the sound of the Atlantic surf. If there were storms at night,
the peculiar sound came across even more clearly. From a small boy
onward, Walt was to grow familiar with large stretches of this island

of more than a hundred miles in length, with its bays, beaches, inlets, and sand bars, and with the lighthouses on its extreme points. At the beginning of the century a few Indians were left, and on the Montauk peninsula the lad saw and goggled at the savage-looking herdsmen, living apart from everyone, who were in charge of big droves of horses and sheep owned by farmers of the eastern towns. That "fierce old mother" the sea drew him like a magnet. He would bathe on the empty beach and hear the soothing, lisping, cradling waves and inhale the salt smell, and later on clamber on a rock and let loose into the wind with lines from Homer and Shakespeare he had learned by heart. But it was not so much the sea as the sea's edge which captivated him. In his poems he came to speak of the land as his father and the sea, mysterious, translucent, fluid, as his naked mother.

He had no doubts whatsoever concerning his flesh-and-blood mother but was ambivalent about his father. In later years, he told Horace Traubel, who recorded hundreds of their conversations, that "The reality, the simplicity, the transparency of my dear mother's life was responsible for the main things in Leaves of Grass itself. How much I owe her! Leaves of Grass is the flower of her temperament active in me. My mother was illiterate in the formal sense but strangely knowing. She excelled in narrative—had great mimetic powers. Was very original in her manner, her style."

Because of her sterling character he was able to say, "The best part of every man is his mother," and to believe it. She was the peacemaker in his increasingly troubled family. When she died the family literally fell apart. After her death he spoke as if a terrible wound had been inflicted on him. A black shadow fell on his life. He talked of a permanent cloud which had descended, leaving his heart "blank and lonesome utterly."

Whitman's conviction that his "heredity stamp" was wholly from his mother's side waned as he approached middle age. Traits appeared that he admitted reminded him of his father. He did not elaborate. D. H. Lawrence is another example of a man passionately attached to his mother who softened and swung over toward his father as he grew older. Whitman, though, was indebted to his father on a number of counts. It was his father Walter who had, like his forebears, "democratic and heretical tendencies." He named three of his sons after founders of the nation, and he brought them all up as freethinkers, encouraging them to side with the small man and distrust the power of the banks. He was a reader and brought books and pamphlets by Paine, Frances Wright, and de Volney into the house. Both he and his wife were friends of Elias Hicks, the liberal Quaker preacher from Jericho, Long Island. This was the man who defended Paine when he was being slandered in his old age by the clergy of all denominations. Partly because of this, the Quaker church split in 1826, with Elias Hicks leading off the Hicksite Quakers. Walter Whitman met Thomas Paine in New York when the pamphleteer, who lived in the vicinity of Bleecker Street, was dying, poor, alone, and—so said his attackers—drunk. The poet Whitman in *his* old age remarked with contempt that "every literary, every moralistic jackanapes who comes along has to give him an additional kick...they spare him nothing." Paine had earned his enemies, laughing at a Christianity which preached that a savior had come to die in our world because "one man and one woman had eaten an apple." Now he was a pariah, as good as dead. Schoolchildren chanted:

> Poor Tom Paine! there he lies;
> Nobody laughs and nobody cries. . . .

Whitman remembered being taken by his parents at the age of ten to hear Hicks preach in the ballroom of Morrison's Hotel on Brooklyn Heights. Long afterward, though unable to recall the sermon in any detail, he had vivid memories of his father coming in at sunset from his carpentering, throwing down an armful of wood blocks for kindling on the kitchen floor, and saying, "Come, Mother, Elias preaches tonight." A young woman from next door acted as baby-sitter for the two babies, Andrew and George. At the meeting Walt listened agog to the preacher, a man over eighty with black eyes, looking more Indian than white, in plain clothes, a wide Quaker hat covering his long white hair. He would have heard that the chief end of man was to glorify God and seek and enjoy Him forever. As Hicks reached his climax, the watching boy was amazed to see him snatch off his broad hat and hurl it to the floor. He was too young to take in what would be the rudiments of his own gospel when the time came, translated into a morality of actual living: the doctrine of the untrammeled soul, steered by "the light within."

In his last years Whitman struggled to write a book or paper on Hicks. He told Horace Traubel that the preacher was "the democrat in religion as Jefferson was the democrat in politics. . . . He was in the last degree a simple character—carried no aureole or shrine about with him—liked to be taken for one of the crowd. He kept a house over his head and a little money in the bank." He could have been talking about himself.

As a young man he heard the notorious socialist Frances Wright speak. Looking back, he believed she changed the direction of his life. The impression she made on him was a tremendous one. He never forgot it. "She spoke in the Tammany Hall there every Sunday, about all sorts of reforms. Her views were very broad, touched the widest range of themes.... She published the *Free Inquirer*, which my daddy and I often read. We all loved her, fell down before her—her very appearance seemed to enthrall us.... She was more than beautiful: she was grand! It was not feature simply but soul—soul. There was a majesty about her. I have never felt so glowingly towards any other woman. She possessed herself of my body and soul."


❧   THE WHITMAN FAMILY were of farming stock on both sides. Walt's grandparents farmed good soil only two or three miles from each other. John Whitman came over with the English Puritans in the *True Love* and settled in Massachusetts. Joseph, a son of his brother, migrated to Huntington, Long Island. Walt Whitman's mother, Louisa Van Velsor, was Dutch from her father and Welsh on her mother's side. Her temperament and coloring were clearly Dutch. Amy, or Naomi Williams, Whitman's maternal grandmother, of whom he was very fond, was a sweet old woman and wore a Quaker cap. "Major" Cornelius Van Velsor—his army rank seems never to have been explained—was a good-natured man, "a hearty, solid, fat old gentleman on good terms with the world." He liked company and was a breeder of horses. His loud, sonorous voice dominated the household.

Amy Williams's father had been a sea captain, part owner of a ship engaged in the West Indies trade. Whitman heard exciting stories of sea fights from his grandmother. He would set the frigates sailing again one day, yards entangled, sailors and old salts and cabin boys manning the pumps, hulls riddled and listing, in "Song of Myself."

At the turn of the century the farmhouses of both neighboring families had similar features, with cavernous smoky kitchens and huge beams everywhere. Common to both was the patriarchal atmosphere. A swarm of people moved in and out, including black slaves who were the house and field servants. Food and furniture were of a rude simplicity: no carpets, no wall hangings. Stoked wood fires provided the warmth and also the light on long winter nights. The men drank cider, and at mealtimes it flowed. Clothes were homespun. Books were nonexistent, though the men and women were literate, falling hungrily on the annual almanac when it arrived.

Walt's paternal grandmother, Hannah Brush, was a formidable character, as was his great grandmother—a big swarthy woman who smoked tobacco, rode around on horseback like a man, and could control the most vicious horse. As a widow she took charge of the farm work, rode everywhere directing her slaves, and swore violently if she was vexed or excited. Whitman remembered from his childhood the jolly gatherings at his grandmother Amy's, overhearing tales of his mother as a girl, a daring rider herself in her young days, growing up among those fine Van Velsor bloodstock horses.

His father seems to have been of a gloomy, taciturn disposition, liable to fall sullenly silent or break out in a rage unpredictably and briefly. Usually, though, he kept his feelings hidden. His wife, and later his children, took care not to provoke him. If he had a stroke of luck—increasingly rare as he reached his thirties—the whole family breathed more easily. But even this man, floundering angrily from one emotion to another, had his sunny moments. As Walt later reflected, "My good daddy used to say, 'Oh, what a comfort it is to lie down on your own floor, a floor laid with your own hands, in a house which represents your own handiwork—cellar and wall and roof!'" On Long Island they had a phrase—"to lie on your own dunghill."

Here at any rate is an anecdote which proves—if any proof were needed—that his father was a thinking man. Beginning politically as a Democrat, he went over to the Republicans when the time came. So did all his sons. Not that he was ever consciously political. It was more an instinctive loyalty to his fellow workingman, a sympathy for the underdog and the outcast. "We were at once," Whitman said, "what the church would call deep-dyed heretics," in both religion and politics.

The hard knocks of life and the failure to succeed in the world led his father to expect the worst. "Keep good heart," he would say sardonically, "the worst is to come." His son too had a sardonic streak. The father's instinct for bottling up his passions was a characteristic of the son. He boiled inwardly, burned up, but mostly kept his mouth shut. "I don't hurry even in my tantrums," was how he put it, tongue in cheek, to his young disciple.

It took the death of his father in 1855 to release warm, if guilty, feelings in his author son. As Walt "thought the old thought of likenesses," Paumanok became joined with his dead father in his heart and he burst out in wild grieving:

> I throw myself on your breast my father,
> I cling to you so that you cannot unloose me,
> I hold you so firm till you answer me something.

It was indicative of a desire to bring the two halves of himself together, and a reconciliation of sorts. While the father lived there was no holding and little answering. We should perhaps look here for the clue to Walt's remark to a woman friend that his boyhood was in the main restless and unhappy. Reading it gives us a shock. What could he have meant? The eldest son Jesse, quarrelsome and jealous, makes Walt appear by comparison almost unnaturally quiet and angelic. With his likable nature he made friends everywhere among the grownups, and especially with strangers, the farmers and fishermen and the pilots on the ferries. Like the gregarious Van Velsor, he gave every sign of being on good terms with the world. He would always feel at home with the simple and uneducated. He stayed a boy right into manhood, liking best of all those solitary narcissistic sensations of boyhood—swimming naked in the warm sea, lying out under the sun, touched by water, by the soft summer air—pleasures he could never prolong enough. Strangely, he seems to have had no special boyhood pals, and to have felt no need of any. What gratified him most deeply, whether in contact with people or out of doors keeping his own company, was something he could not articulate, which gave him deep thrills when he was immersed in it; something that could not be revealed. He was exploring the secret pleasures of his other world, the world of his own self. These soft-skinned ecstasies, later on tormenting because so intense, so hard to contain without betrayal, would fill his being with soft light and be his solace when human love failed him. So his double life began. Adults, unobservant for the most part, continued to see an affectionate and outgoing lad, healthily at ease with others.

His FATHER had been taught carpentry as a youth by his cousin Jacob Whitman. He went off to New York to serve an apprenticeship and then worked at his trade for several years as an employee before coming back to his native West Hills in Suffolk County, New York. There he set up in business on his own account, building houses and barns on commission. An excellent tradesman and, as was usual in those days, an all-rounder, he leased some land and erected his own two-story house, laying the footings and building the wide fireplace singlehanded. Timbers were hewn by hand, joints were pegged, walls hung with cedar shingles. At the age of twenty-seven he courted and married the lively, big-boned daughter at the Van Velsor farmstead, a girl whose blood rushed hectically to the fair skin of her cheeks.

A year later came their first child, Jesse. Fourteen months later they had their second son, called Walter after his father. His birth date, May 31, 1819, made him an exact contemporary of Herman Melville, a man he never met. Mary, a daughter, arrived next. By the spring of 1823, when the family moved to Brooklyn, Louisa Whitman was expecting again.

The move to the noisy market town on the East River signaled a retreat rather than an adventure. The financial crisis of 1819 and its following depression had brought housing development in Huntington to a halt. The population dwindled, sucked away by the booming emporium of New York. The lease on Walter Whitman's house had been proving hard and then impossible to keep up. Shortage of work drove him to try his hand at farming during the summer. In the winter he hawked firewood. He had heard that carpenters were in demand in Brooklyn. The wages he could expect would have been roughly a dollar a day.

The day they chose for their move happened to be the occasion of a horse race out at Jamaica on Long Island. They would have done well to have avoided this event, reported in the New York Advertiser as "the great race between Van Randst's horse Eclipse and Colonel Johnson's Henry." Van Velsor the horse breeder would have certainly attended, but the Whitman family, struggling with the stream of traffic jamming the turnpike, must have regretted their choice of May 27. It was four days before their younger boy's fourth birthday. Walt was still "a little one in frocks."

The father, with his experience of New York, was no stranger to town life. Even Louisa was familiar with Brooklyn and New York through her father, who drove his stage and market wagon from Cold Springs to the market close to the ferry, either to sell his produce or take horses over on the ferry to the New York markets. It was a routine he kept up for forty years. If he stayed overnight he put up at Smith and Wood's tavern on the west side of the street near Fulton Ferry. "He was wonderfully regular in these weekly trips; and in those old-fashioned times, people could almost tell the time of day by his stage passing along the road—so punctual was he." His absorbed grandson Walt accompanied him when he was older, and could recall afterward the smell of lampblack and oil painted on the canvas sheeting of the wagon, an odor so powerful it made him feel sick.

Negotiating the heavy traffic, the Whitmans pulled up outside the house they had rented in Front Street, normally a quiet location, though it was close to New Ferry at the end of Main Street. Maybe they got their furniture unloaded and had a bite of lunch before the rowdy mob of racegoers began flooding back into Brooklyn on foot and by horseback and stage. There were plenty of taverns nearby, soon filling up and spilling over with revelers roaming the streets to buy grog from grocery stores. William Cobbett, a farmer on Long Island himself for twelve months while in exile from England, took note of the unusual literacy of farmers and tradesmen like Walter Whitman, but was less impressed by their consumption of alcohol. They would "tip off their drams" from the age of twelve or even younger.

According to Walt, his father was gloomily addicted for some periods during the son's boyhood. The future poet was abstemious all his life, though not averse to a drink. He wrote a best-selling temperance novel when he became a journalist in New York. His mother had grown up among these heavy country drinkers and was not the sort of woman to condemn what to her was a sad compulsion. Once when a tipsy tramp came begging, she told her son that it was a mercy to give someone in that state of dereliction what they wanted.

Walter Whitman had brought his young family to a boom town. They were close to Old Ferry Road, or Fulton Street, and the crowded ferries crossing to Manhattan, packed solid on this day out at the big race, together with the ceaseless harbor traffic, made the place feel more like a city. Lifted above the common tumult around the river frontage were the estates and farms of Clover Hill, later to be Brooklyn Heights. Down below was a chaos of tenements, grog shops, slaughterhouses, and livery stables. James Street was predominantly black, populated by freed slaves whose children played with the white urchins of poor families, the Irish navvies, oyster sellers, bargemen, and small grocers in Front and neighboring streets.

It was a throbbing slum world, out in the open and congested, full of the crude tensions of lives plastered together, subject to the coming and going of people constantly on the move between this overgrown village and the big city of a hundred thousand citizens across the water.

This was the small boy's backyard, near to the United States Navy Yard and at the east end of what eventually became Manhattan Bridge. Conditions were primitive, with streets littered with garbage left to stink and rot or be gobbled up by wild hogs. In the city across the river it was no different. Water was communal, supplied from standpipes in the unpaved streets. There was no police force worth the name, no street lighting, a fire brigade consisting of a few carts manned by volunteers. Epidemics spread rapidly. In this dangerous playground Walt ran freely and somehow escaped injury. The deck-hands and gatekeepers at the ferries soon came to know him well, waving to him cheerily as they rode out or landed. The brutal atmosphere did not so much alienate him as pass him by, while his slow, curiously detached nature nurtured the sensuous and delicate feelings he was developing and learning how to keep disguised. On the face of it he was the most amenable of children. At home they called him Walt, but he was Walter at school and at his first job, and until he created a poetic persona for himself and blossomed forth as Walt Whitman, "a kosmos."

Expansion in Brooklyn was taking place on either side of Fulton Street and to the south, as advertising campaigns got under way to sell building plots in the aristocratic district of Clover Hill. People of means from New York City were soon clutching at the chance to settle among the fine houses belonging to the Hicks, Pierrepont, and Middagh families, sited well above the riverside squalor and with glorious views from the Heights of downtown Manhattan, the harbor, and shipping, clear across to the New Jersey shore.

Brooklyn Heights was altogether beyond the means of the Whitman family. Briefly, though, in 1824, they did find a house on its outskirts with a rent low enough for them to afford. This was Cranberry Street. Then in September, presumably while still living in the rented house, Mr. and Mrs. Whitman bought land on the corner of Washington and Johnson streets, and the West Hills carpenter built a house on it.

Here was established the pattern for years to come. The Whitmans moved like gypsies from house to house, from Johnson to Van Dyke

Street, to Adams Street. Between 1827 and the end of 1831 they did manage to stay put at one address in Tillary Street. "We occupied them one after the other, but they were mortgaged and we lost them," reported Whitman later in his memoirs of the period. Children are not usually unsettled so long as the family holds together, but by the time they reached Tillary Walt must have been aware of his father's inability to earn a decent living and of his mother's growing anxiety. The shiftless style of life was scarcely the father's fault. He was unlucky, and sometimes he failed because he felt he was bound to fail. He tried hard, but nothing succeeded for long. He was gullible, a prey to smooth talkers and sharks. His family increasing, it was now that he hit the bottle for a time. Either this was caused by his troubles or it exacerbated them. Walt's detestation of Methodists no doubt derived from the purchase of the land in Johnson and Tillary streets from Methodist ministers, the contracts drawn "so cutely...so shrewdly worded, as to make it impossible when the time for settlement came, to evade here a sum, there a sum, until my poor straightforward father was nearly swindled out of his boots."

Of the four children born after Walt, three survived: Hannah Louisa, Andrew Jackson, and George Washington. In 1825, the year a Whitman baby had died before being christened, General Lafayette visited Brooklyn to lay a cornerstone of the Apprentices Library building. Walt was a boy of six. Something extraordinary was about to happen to him.

The ceremony had been arranged for the 4th of July. The day dawned fine, the sky high and clear. The Marquis de Lafayette had come back to the United States as the people's revered guest. With his son, George Washington Lafayette, the old general and hero of the Revolution had stood in silence before Washington's coffin on Mount Vernon. He had toured the country and been greeted with fervor everywhere. This was the legendary figure who had fought beside his commander-in-chief nearly fifty years before.

At the Brooklyn ferry landing stage, met by local dignitaries and a number of stooped old veterans, he rode up Fulton Street in an unguarded, open yellow coach, waving his hat with great dignity and simplicity as he acknowledged the cries of delight. A procession formed behind the carriage at Market Street and the excited crowd, many of them schoolchildren, trooped along to the junction of Henry and Cranberry streets.

Walt was among them, though he was not yet a schoolboy. At the library site there was a gaping hole made ready for the footings and the cellar, stone and dirt flung up high around it. Men in the crowd were lifting children down for a better view. Lafayette came over himself and helped. Suddenly young Walt found himself in the arms of Lafayette. This godlike man pressed the child briefly to his breast and perhaps murmured something, smiling, before putting him down safely where the lad could see. As Whitman lingered over this memory in later years he saw himself transfigured, and in one journal version added a kiss from the fabulous old companion of Washington, as if to seal this conferring of grace and significance.

Already the boy was attending Sunday school. Saint Ann's was a progressive Episcopalian church on the fringes of Brooklyn Heights and drew in a well-educated, well-heeled congregation. Certainly Walt's mother and father never attended it. For one thing the rented pews would have been more than they could have afforded. Not that the father would have approved. He didn't go to church. The mother did, shifting from one to another. She got a Baptist to conduct her husband's funeral. One would have expected the Whitmans to have joined a Quaker group, but they seemed averse—like Walt—to joining anything.

There was no doubt that Walt liked Saint Ann's. He liked its atmosphere of kindliness, its fine leafy grounds. It was a grassy and welcoming place, shaded by willows and elms. Its members were especially attentive to the needy children they enrolled for their Sunday school, believing they were helping to combat crime by reducing illiteracy. As well as Bible study their teaching included lessons in reading and spelling. This free education supplemented the instruction Walt was receiving that autumn at the district school on the corner of Adams and Concord streets.

Unlike Saint Ann's, school was an experience that Walt remembered later without nostalgia. For a boy of spirit and sensitiveness it would have been a grim awakening, with its teaching by rote in a huge class and its rigid discipline. Teaching methods were based on the Lancastrian regime, named after an English Quaker, Joseph Lancaster. A single teacher, aided by child monitors, was expected to educate at least a hundred pupils. The children sat on wooden forms at big desks, ten children to a desk, spied on by a monitor who reported any bad behavior to the teacher in charge. Silence, obedience, and unison were the enforced rules of conduct. Infants gathered in the basement. Above them were the older girls, with big boys on the top floor.

How Walt was treated isn't known, but he left at eleven with a life-long hatred of corporal punishment. One teacher's observation has come down to us: he was overlarge for his age but "a good-natured boy, clumsy and slovenly in appearance, but not otherwise remarkable." A rider pointed out that "we need never be discouraged over anyone." This was a charity school. Parents who were able paid a nominal sum.

On June 4, 1829, the day the steam frigate *Fulton* blew up in the navy yard, killing nearly fifty of the crew, Walt was sitting in school, aged ten. An explosion rocked the classroom like an earthquake. The funeral, leaving Saint Ann's a few days later, moved the watching boy deeply, "the sailors marching two by two, hand in hand, banners tied up and bound in black crepe, the muffled drums beating, the bugles wailing forth the mournful peals of a dead march. We remember it all—remember following the procession, boy-like, from beginning to end.... And then how everything changed with the dashing and merry jig played by the same bugles and drums, as they made their exit from the graveyard and wended rapidly home."

Parades and crowds attracted him powerfully from his early days. He could never tear himself away. Whatever it was, he lingered on to the very end. There is no mention in his journals of him doing anything in the company of his brothers and sisters during this time. Often he was to be found with strangers, or mooching alone on the waterfront, half lost in the labyrinth of dockyards, white-lead facto-ries, ship chandlers, glass works, distilleries, and furnaces. But for all its mushrooming industry, the Brooklyn character was still basically rural. Men of substance kept at least one horse. Even the bigger homes had barns and cowsheds attached to the house. People would feed up pigs, geese, and chickens, and keep goats. Churches were often built of wood. Fulton Street had an avenue of elms.

Away from the slummy navy yard area, Brooklyn was becoming respectable. Rows of neat artisans' dwellings on standard plots were lining the streets. There were soon few of the violent contrasts between wealth and poverty that you could see in New York. Brooklyn, as it grew steadily to the size and stature of a city, was turning into a community of the middle class.

For this footloose boy the lawless element lay at the water's edge, whether on the beach during visits to his grandparents at Cold Springs or down on the wharves and quays waiting for the next ferry to dock. A drowsiness would gather in him; the light came off the water, and its constant glitter and promise seemed to bear him off, the sound of the sea relaxing him like sleep. It was perhaps this influence which made him appear so pliable and contented to the deckhands on the ferries, and why the gatekeepers let him through free of charge and made such a pet of him. In *Specimen Days* he wrote, "I have always had a passion for ferries; to me they afford inimitable, streaming, never-failing, living poems. The river and bay scenery all about New York island, any time of a fine day—the hurrying, splashing sea-tides—the changing panorama of steamers ... the myriads of white-sail'd schooners, sloops, skiffs, and the marvelous beautiful yachts—the majestic sound boats as they rounded the Battery and came along towards 5, eastward bound... what refreshment of spirit such sights and experiences gave me years ago. . . ." On his early crossings as a child over to Manhattan he rode on boats driven by horses harnessed to a capstan in the deckhouse. By the time of his first job the ferries to New York were steam-driven, and still, to the disgust and bitterness of Brooklyn citizens, owned by the big city.

Cannon booming out over Brooklyn harbor in October marked a major triumph for east-west communications, the completion of the Erie Canal, linking the Hudson River with Lake Erie. This meant that New York was now in touch with the entire Great Lakes region. Before, goods shipped from Pittsburgh to New York had to be routed by river to New Orleans and then by sea so as to avoid the more costly overland route. The following year, soon after the Whitmans moved yet again—this time to a house in Van Dyke's Street—they heard cannon firing again in celebration of the fiftieth anniversary of the Declaration of Independence. It was a jubilee day that became a day of mourning. News arrived that two illustrious founders of the embryo Union, Thomas Jefferson and John Adams, had died within hours of each other on the 4th of July.

In February 1830 Elias Hicks died, as wave after wave of a religious revival swamped the country. Young working men and their girls and women "got religion," though in many cases only temporarily. As a youth Walt was interested enough to go to church if he felt like it, but he had heard his father's indignation over the fate of poor Thomas Paine "who was unfortunate enough to excite the theological rancor of his time. A thousand things about him, all of them slanders. Woe to the man who invokes the antagonism of priests and property!"

In the same year he went to work at his first job. He was eleven, his formal schooling at an end, his real education about to begin. His mother must have suffered a pang as she saw her son heading out into the world at such a tender age. Presenting himself at the offices of James B. Clark and his son Edward, a firm of lawyers, he would have been ignorant of the bondage of long hours that awaited him. He had lost his freedom to roam at will but gained his escape from the hated regime of an oppressive schoolroom. Already a large, serious lad, his slow smile made him lovable. If anyone rebuffed or misunderstood him he simply went quiet, his face a little heavy and stupid-looking. At the first touch of kindness or warmth his expression would brighten and transform itself. He shambled clumsily like a clown as a way of dealing with rejection. Confrontation was never to be his style.

The Clarks were both members of Saint Ann's Church, so probably they saw the boy at Sunday school there and were struck by him, roused to interest and sympathy. He spoke gratefully of them in reminiscences later. On his first day of real contact, what might have been an ordeal turned into a pleasure. They sat him at a desk to himself, and it was in a window nook. No doubt his handwriting was painfully slow and bad, but Edward helped him to improve it, and also his composition. One pictures him perched nervously on a high stool, observed or ignored by an older clerk.

One of his tasks would have been copying incoming letters into a big entry book. Every so often the lawyers sent him off on errands around Brooklyn and, even better, across the river on the steam ferry to New York. Several times he had to deliver legal documents to the famous lawyer Aaron Burr, over the Hudson in New Jersey. Burr was a dignified, solicitous old man of seventy-five, his extraordinary career in politics far behind him. He greeted the eager boy with smiling eyes and warm gestures, traits which never failed to impress Whitman. "Burr was gentle—persuasive. He had a way of giving me a bit of fruit on these visits—an apple or a pear. I can see him clearly still—his stateliness, gray hair, courtesy, consideration."

Hurrying down a New York street one freezing, bright January— either running an errand or exploring the city on his own account— he slowed and then stopped to take in the spectacle of John Jacob Astor, America's richest man, bent, stoutly built, bearded and feeble and swathed in furs, on his head a huge ermine cap, being half carried down the steps of his high front stoop by his servants. Walt lingered long enough to see the old man tucked into a magnificent sleigh, harnessed to as fine a team of horses as he had ever set eyes on. He noticed particularly the care lavished on the old gentleman as they got him seated, and remembered the mettlesome horses champing, the driver with his long whip, an extra driver seated at his side as standby.

The philanthropic younger lawyer, Edward, who had evidently taken a shine to the boy, introduced him to the pleasures of literature by giving him a subscription to a circulating library. Whitman duly acknowledged this to be "the signal event of my life up to that time." He reveled in the *Arabian Nights*, "all the volumes," and went on to read Walter Scott's novels one after the other. From that moment he was a voracious reader of novels. He read James Fenimore Cooper's *The Sky*, *The Last of the Mohicans*, and then *The Red Rover*, a tumultuous yarn which stirred him so much that he kept rereading it. This headlong plunge into the world of romance even had him dipping his toe into Scott's verse, saying later that it was the first poetry to mean anything to him.

He went from the Clarks to be an office boy in a doctor's office. It couldn't have lasted long. By the summer of 1831 he had joined the printing office of the *Long Island Patriot*. Samuel E. Clements was the four-page weekly's showy editor. As was customary with small papers at that time, he also wrote everything in it. Founded ten years before, it was a slavish organ of the Tammany Democrats. Walt's father was a *Patriot* subscriber and must have taken his son along and apprenticed him as a printer under Clements.

The setup here was very different from the stuffy doctor's and lawyers' offices. Clements stalked around in the lanes and streets of Brooklyn and back again to his headquarters in an old brick building in Fulton Street. Lanky, lean, hawk-nosed, he was a Quaker who liked to boast of his Southern blood. After only a short stay at the *Patriot* he came to grief by outraging the local politicians with his eccentricities. The most infamous of his escapades concerned the late Elias Hicks, recently buried at Jericho. Clements and two friends, wanting to make a plaster cast of Hicks's face and head, crept into the graveyard at dead of night and dug up the body. Politicians howled for the blood of this grave robber. Friends and relatives of Hicks began a legal action, and the time was ripe for Clements to depart. He resurfaced soon after on a paper in Camden, New Jersey.

The *Patriot*'s four-page edition was set up and churned out on a hand press which was housed in the basement, together with a stationery store. In this composing room young Walt began to learn his trade from the one and only printer, a deceptively frail man by the name of William Hartshorne. He had grown up in Philadelphia and had tales to tell of George Washington, Jefferson, and Franklin. Witness to an age of honor and principle, he was "rather sedate, not fast, always cheerful, benevolent, friendly." He kept his nose out of politics and was valued for his craft. He lived to a great age, eighty-four, and Whitman would see the retired printer strolling along Fulton Street swinging a cane and chewing tobacco. He was a man with a capacity for living his own life to the full. Walt admired him for his openhandedness and for the way he had gained everyone's respect, and he longed to be like him, emulating him in his heart as he stood docilely beside his master to be instructed. In imagination in "Song of Myself" the scene was relived—

> The jour printer with gray head and gaunt jaws works at his case,
> He turns his quid of tobacco, and his eyes get blurred with the manuscript.

Patiently the quiet man with his old-fashioned manners taught his overgrown apprentice "the pleasing mystery of the different letters and their divisions—the great 'e' box—the box for spaces . . . the 'a' box, 'l' box, and all the rest—the box for quads away off in the right hand corner—the slow and laborious formation, type by type, of the first line."

It was during this period that—incredibly precocious though it sounds—Walt became a boy-author and saw his writing appear in print at the age of twelve. Clements, a sympathetic individual, allowed his apprentice to contribute a few "sentimental bits" to the *Patriot*. Whatever these were, they have not been traced.

Several other apprentices were under Hartshorne's wing, lodging with Hartshorne's granddaughter. For a time Walt lived there too, even though his family lived only a dozen blocks away in Nassau Street. Sundays the youngsters accompanied their foreman to the Dutch Reformed Church at Joralemon Street, a grim, fortresslike edifice built of stone. Around them were fields and country lanes. This was the oldest church in a Brooklyn soon to be known as the city of churches. The Calvinism preached there left no mark on the outwardly submissive apprentice.

How it came about that he was able to transfer his apprenticeship from the *Patriot* is not clear, but by the summer of 1832 he had begun to work for Erastus Worthington, a jobbing printer who also ran a bookshop and circulating library. The library would have certainly been useful, yet after a short stay he transferred again, this time to the *Long Island Star*, printed and edited by Alden Spooner. Spooner was a civic leader of some prominence, solidly identified with his community and one of the driving forces behind its prosperity. He had ambitions for his paper. Already it gave prominence to science and the arts and was remarkably sympathetic to the theatre—damned by the clergy—and to the lyceum lectures of the Scottish-born socialist and reformer Frances Wright. Refusing to be a merely political mouthpiece, it made determined efforts to answer Alexis de Tocqueville's call for newspapers that would fit men for their new dangerous equality and individualism and help "maintain civilization." Traveling through the United States, de Tocqueville had observed that America had no great historians and "not a single eminent poet." As well as serving the interests of the Whigs, Spooner gave space in his liberal pages to the poetry and prose of local authors. Walt began to flourish intellectually in the *Star*'s enlightened atmosphere.

The town continued to improve and modernize itself. Already the population had doubled to more than fifteen thousand during the Whitmans' time there. Street lamps lit by oil were being installed and streets graveled and paved with sidewalks. Moves were under way to control the spread of liquor stores through licensing and get rid of the garbage-eating wild hogs.

Then in the summer a cholera epidemic spread down through the Eastern cities and reached New York and Brooklyn. Hundreds fled to the countryside, though "poverty, quite as strong a force, also compelled many to stay where they were." The Whitmans, now living in Henry Street, joined the exodus and went inland for several weeks, probably staying at Cold Springs. Jesse, the eldest, had by this time gone to sea as a merchant sailor. Their printer son was left alone in the house.

IMMIGRANTS ARRIVING in Brooklyn carried on the long process of settling and displacing one another. The Dutch farmers, merchants, and burghers who were members of the Dutch Reformed church were having their old customs eroded. They resisted stubbornly, feeling themselves to be the legitimate founders of the settlement. The name Brooklyn itself is a corruption of Breuckelen, given by the early homesick Dutch settlers when they usurped the Indians, before being usurped themselves by the Yankees. Then in the nineteenth century came the Irish in droves, driven out of their native country by terrible famines. Later, from the middle of the century onward, came Germans, Swedes, Norwegians, ending with a mass migration of Jews from eastern Europe and from Russia.

In 1833 Walt's mother fell ill. They were living now in a house in Front Street. Maybe it was his wife's sickness which persuaded Walter Whitman to give up on Brooklyn and move back with his family to West Hills. Gay Wilson Allen comments that it could not have been because of hard times. Property prices in the area were rising phenomenally and the whole nation was experiencing a boom at last. President Andrew Jackson paraded through the town two months after his inauguration, together with the vice president and former New York governor. It was a sunny summer day. Just as Lafayette had done, he rode up Fulton Street, doffing his white beaver hat to acknowledge the cheers of the crowd.

Thomas Jefferson, Louisa Whitman's eighth child, was due in July. The family settled near Oyster Bay, not many miles from the Van Velsor homestead. Van Velsor's wife had died and he had promptly married again, which may have strained relations between the two families. The new wife, Walt noted tersely in his memoirs, "was not a good investment." His father was back where he had begun, building and farming with his usual uncertain luck. "I remained in Brooklyn," Walt recorded. Independence was his.

A chubby-cheeked boy of fifteen, big as a grown man, he must have been astonished when George P. Morris's New-York Mirror, a fine-arts weekly, published "a piece or two" by him. The mere sight of his name in print in this "celebrated and fashionable" journal was nothing short of a miracle. "I remember with what half-suppressed excitement I used to watch for the big, fat, red-faced, very slow-moving old English carrier who distributed the Mirror in Brooklyn; and when I got one, opening and cutting the leaves with trembling fingers." His heart leapt, for there it would be, his piece "on the pretty white paper, in nice type."

While he was still at the Star, joining in pranks now and then with his fellow apprentices, he became an insatiable devourer of circulating library romances, joined a town debating society, and discovered a passion for the theatre awakening in him. As a newspaper employee he would have got himself on the list for complimentary tickets. He went at first with other apprentices, dressed in his round jacket and broad shirt collar, and was probably as skeptical as his companions as he waited for the curtain to go up on *School for Scandal*.

The revelation was total: he was struck dumb with wonder. The lights dimmed and he sat perfectly still in a realm of pure magic which had a potency far exceeding that of books. The human voice and its possibilities entranced him. And then the band, striking up. "O, never before did such heavenly melodies make me drunk with pleasure so utterly sweet and spiritual!" He had stumbled on something astounding. The theatre was a place in which all the senses were lulled and seduced, stimulated, exalted, and where the ear was tuned, the eye trained. On the tiny lit area of the stage the theatregoer had his most secret dreams focused and expanded. He was invited to nourish the drama in his own breast, which existed in the humblest person whether he knew it or not. He had gone to be taken out of himself, nothing more. The revelation for the young Whitman lay in realizing that the stuff of drama exists everywhere, part of the very fabric of life.

He soon found himself in such a state of soul-sympathy and emotional excitement that he couldn't bear the company of his fellows, their stupid jokes and laughter in the wrong places. "I was so absorbed in the performance, and disliked anyone to distract my attention." The only way he could enjoy these delights to the full, alive to his common and separate identity, was to go by himself. To get a good seat in the pit he would arrive early. The vulgar antics of the crowd distressed him as he waited for the motionless dark green curtain to rise "with quick and graceful leaps, like the hopping of a rabbit."

His new passion was indiscriminate. He marveled equally at melodramas like *Jonathan Bradford, or the Murder at the Roadside Inn*, *Napoleon's Old Guard*, *The Last Days of Pompeii*, *Mazeppa*, and Shakespearean productions such as *Richard III*. Tragedians like the elder Booth hit him over the heart. Fanny Kemble enslaved him. In old age he remembered her in *Fazio* and *The Wife*. "Nothing finer did ever stage exhibit... and my boyish heart and head felt it in every minute cell." She had been in London and toured through Britain and then came "to give America that young maturity and roseate power in all their noon, or forenoon, flush. It was my good luck to see her nearly every night she play'd at the old Park Theatre...."

Best of all was what these actors and actresses symbolized. Speaking in a language that was at times tumultuous and unbridled, they plucked Walt bodily from the drab world of work and responsibility and challenged him to demand something more colorful; something else. There was no need after all to submit to what was, to accept things at face value. That was wonderful. He felt approached directly, asked to collaborate in the playwright's intentions. He had known nothing like it since that night when he was ten, listening with his parents to Elias Hicks as the gaunt man reached into the hearts of his audience and held them fast. This was his second experience of the "unnameable something behind oratory," delivered in a cadenced prose "by powerful human magnetism."

The evangelical church, and the few Methodist revival meetings he had attended, left him cold. All he enjoyed was the emotional singing. Sinners falling to the ground before the altar, fighting off Satan or wrestling with angels only made him withdraw further into himself. The theatre was different. It was like hearing the silent drama in his own soul being spoken aloud. By identifying with the players he set the drama in motion in his mind. Rooted in the earth, he could feel star-bound. "Illusions of youth" he later called these raptures in the midst of an audience of total strangers, sitting quite still and alone. He was learning firsthand of the power of words, hearing in theatres and lecture halls the oratorial music he would reach for in time, combining it with biblical prophecy to forge a unique "talking style" for the gospel he wanted to preach. In the *Leaves* he would write one day:

> O what is it in me that makes me tremble so at voices?
> Surely whoever speaks to me in the right voice, him or her I
>   shall follow,
> As the water follows the moon, silently, with fluid steps,
>   anywhere around the globe.

He had discovered the beckoning, thrilling human voice. But long before, as a boy, he had discovered in himself the power to embody what he touched, and what touched him. The world of sensation he bathed in with such delight as a boy would stay with him and enter into his literary style. In his beautiful poem "There Was a Child Went Forth" he reveals how his method works and how indebted and grateful he is for this childish instinct to gratify his senses. His senses, allowed full play, keep him in a trance of wonder at a creation which looks and smells and sounds as fresh as on the first day. One has the feeling that he can never quite believe in the evidence of his eyes. "The early lilacs became part of this child," the grass, the white and red morning glories, the white and red clover, the March-born lambs, the sow's "pink-faint" litter, the fish in the pond in their curious suspended world.

As well as the myriad details of the nonhuman world accumulating in him to form "part of this child," there were the human beings to be thanked and memorialized, from anonymous old drunks staggering home at night to the poet's parents, who not only fathered and mothered him but gave him out of their largesse the very day and the night. Here is his mother with her soft words, her clean cap and gown, so wholesome that she sheds a sweet odor on him as she passes. The father, presented with remarkable honesty and no resentment, appears as "strong, self-sufficient, manly, mean, angered, unjust." Equally honest is the writer's own doubt: "Or is it all flashes and specks?" These wonders and doubts and changes, filtered through and identified with so unreservedly in a kind of everyday religious mysticism, "These became part of that child who went forth every day. . . ."

❦ HE WAS SIXTEEN. His apprenticeship completed, he was now a skilled man, a journeyman printer. In the spring of 1835 he secured work as a compositor in New York. Where he actually lived and ate and slept during these first months in the exciting and violent big city has not been determined. The times were chaotic for a variety of reasons. In the cities of the Eastern seaboard especially, living conditions were made worse by the influx of thousands of Irish immigrants, unable to find housing or any work to support themselves and their families. Politicians touted for their votes, inflaming them with false hopes, bribing them with grog. There had been any number of vicious riots as Irish groups and nationalistic Americans fearful of losing their jobs clashed murderously. In the downtown sections near City Hall you steered clear of the Five Points area if you were wise. Starved immigrants recruited by gangs of thugs terrorized the alleys, living in derelict warehouses or sleeping rough out in the open. A bloody riot erupted at the Bowery Theatre in the heat of the summer, nearly razing the building to the ground and smashing property in the vicinity of Astor Place. President Jackson, a "man of the people" backed by the working classes, was being blamed by conservatives for dishonest promises to the masses which had led, they maintained, to the growing social unrest. Abolitionists— resented bitterly in New York and Brooklyn—added fuel to the flames. The national economy was staggering along in crisis after a series of bank failures, touched off, so it was alleged, by Jacksonian mismanagement.

On August 12 a huge fire broke out in Paternoster Row and proceeded to destroy the printing and publishing quarter around City Hall Park. Thousands of workers lost their jobs when an even worse fire raged through seven hundred buildings from Wall Street to Coenties Slip in December. There was widespread looting. Marines and armed militia stood guard over the devastated blocks. To add to the general misery, a ferocious winter descended. Banks of ice reared on either side of the streets like shining walls of black marble. Ice on the Connecticut River was forty inches thick.

In spite of these calamities Walt managed to hang on in employment till the following spring. In a story he wrote later, the hero searched every part of the city for work before giving up to become a country schoolteacher. Burying himself alive, his city independence lost, "he felt as though the last float plank which buoyed him up on hope and happiness was sinking, and he with it."

Walt rejoined his family in May 1836 at Hempstead on the south side of Long Island. He was just seventeen. The previous year his mother had given birth to her last child, Eddy, who would be mentally handicapped and dependent all his days.

# 3
# Pupil-Teacher

E quable in temperament, nevertheless he doesn't seem to have made friends easily. There were acquaintances in plenty but no mention of an intimate, no sign of a soul mate. He may even have been glad of the excuse to abandon Manhattan and the loneliness of his solitary life there. Once home, however, it was a different story. Of all his brothers and sisters, only Hannah, and later his kid brother Jeff, appeared to be on his wavelength. For Walt there was no going back meekly to the bosom of his family after a spell of making his way in the great world, proud of his ability to cope in the city with its oceanlike crowds.

Unwilling to accept a subservient role as a farmhand alongside his father, he enrolled instead as a country teacher at a school at Norwich, an area he knew well. It was only a few miles from his grandfather's farm at Cold Springs. George, his brother, testified later to his familiarity with Walt's stubborn streak. "Walt would not do farm work. He had things he liked—school teaching, for instance. . . . I don't think his father ever had an idea what Walt was up to, what he meant." The gloomy, "troubled-looking," failed building contractor and his errant son rubbed along, wary of each other.

Louisa Whitman worried over her son's odd bouts of lassitude, perhaps wondering if he would end up discouraged and depressed like his father. She loved him but was a little fearful of his fate, unable to understand what she had called his "strangeness" when he was a boy.

She did see, though, that he had a fierce if negative pride which might one day be his downfall.

Walt for his part had returned from the dynamic whirl of New York to a dismaying plunge back among the crude countrymen he felt he had outgrown. If we take the character of Archie Dean in one of the family romances he wrote later to be a version of Whitman himself, it was not so much superiority as a sense of shame he experienced. The story is so autobiographical—without being auto-biography—that we feel we are being given unconscious insights into Walt's state of mind immediately after his move back home. He identifies with Archie without inhibition as the young hero leaves the city after the great fire of 1835 and goes to Long Island, where he takes up teaching. There is mention of a sickly younger brother to whom he is devoted, reminding us of Eddy. The theme of the story, like most of his romances of the 1840s, is change, its possibility, its desperate importance. It raises the vital question for Whitman at this time of whether one could change one's nature "by means of that very nature itself."

Another obsessive theme is that of parentage, as indeed were so many mid-nineteenth-century stories insisting on the sacredness of home and mother. But Whitman's melodramas were somewhat differ-ent. The ghastly happenings and lurid detail common at the time were in his fiction too, but through his runs an insistently personal thread which had to do with a hated father, and a strangely intense concern with the importance of the family circle. Again, the worship of family was commonplace. It was Whitman's obsessional version of it that was not. Later on he dismissed these tales as being "from the surface of the mind" only, and he must have writhed at their sentimentality. But lurking under their conventional surface vibrated a private, unhappy element, disturbing in a way he had not inten-ded.

In "The Shadow and Light of a Young Man's Soul" Archie Dean doesn't know what he is or in which direction he ought to move. His being is "unstable as water." If his young friends catch him looking like a workman he feels humiliated. Shortage of money is another source of shame. He is aware of being too inward-looking, dwelling morbidly "on the dark side of his life entirely too often." Brooding on these weaknesses makes him miserable.

Things begin to change for the better. His spirits are restored gradually by nature, "by his long walks over the hills, by his rides on horseback every Saturday, his morning rambles and his evening saunters; by his coarse living, even, and the untainted air and water, which seem to make better blood in his veins." He stops looking down at the locals and instead admires "their sterling sense on most practical subjects, their hospitality and their industry."

Archie's mother is widowed. Her son is devoted to her and longs to provide for her and make her home secure. He feels this should be his main purpose in life, but he is caught up in his adolescence, trapped by the "dark side" of himself, the sapping, weak, irresolute, unmanly tendencies in his nature. Now we can see what those long walks over the hills and the pure air and water of the outdoor life are for. He yearns to be rid of impurities, to be whole. He meets and befriends an old spinster. The story of her struggles to buy back the family property lost by her drunken father inspires the young man to overcome his own want of energy and resolution. "And so he did. And the weakness of the good youth's heart never entirely got the better of him afterward, but in the course of a season was put to flight utterly. . . . With an iron will he substituted action and cheerfulness for despondency and fretful tongue. He met his fortunes as they came, face to face, and shirked no conflict. Indeed, he felt it glorious to vanquish obstacles."

In short, he achieves manhood by an act of will, out of the very nature which sought to sabotage him. This would be Whitman's task in the years ahead, to create himself anew while at the same time the passions and activities of his nation filled him with the material of his poems. Paul Zweig sees in the opening passages of "Song of Myself" the symbolic marriage of the two sides of Whitman taking place, and the consummation that delivers up the poet.


How DID THE out-of-work printer of seventeen suddenly become a teacher? His qualifications were meager indeed. All the same, his self-education at home and the general knowledge he had picked up in newspaper offices meant that he was in effect better equipped in basic subjects than most rural teachers. In country districts education was supplied grudgingly. Payment and conditions for teachers were as rudimentary as the "bare and superficial curriculum" of spelling, reading, writing, arithmetic, with a little geography thrown in. The few texts available were supplemented by textbooks the pupil's parents either had in their possession or could obtain. This made any uniform pattern of study next to impossible.

The teacher's duties included the making and resharpening of the children's quills, stoking the fire in winter, and sweeping out the schoolroom at the end of the day, a day which stretched from eight in the morning till four or five in the afternoon. The schoolhouse was usually a drafty building as cheerless as a barn. At the end of the day Walt would fasten the plank door with a padlock. Some of his students were as old as himself, and he taught between forty and fifty of them at a time. Birching was the favored method of maintaining order. Given Whitman's detestation of corporal punishment, how did he manage to keep control? Those who remembered him paid tribute to his natural aptitude as a teacher. He played games of twenty questions with his charges. During break he played baseball with them. According to one ex-pupil, Charles Roe, who knew him at Little Bay Side in Jamaica, New York, all the class were deeply attached to him and sorry to see him go.

The wage for a three-month term was thirty-five to forty dollars plus lodgings. To cut down on the expense of paying for accommodations the authorities had devised a system of boarding around, with each parent providing a room and "coarse fare" in turn. Walt would find himself sleeping on a straw pallet. In the evenings the pupil's family would be his only company. Lonely as he often was, it was privacy he sometimes craved. Then he would go back to his desolate schoolroom and drink hot toddies at his teacher's desk. Once at a farm there was nowhere for him to sleep and he was reduced to lying down next to an ailing cow.

George Whitman, not one to compliment his older brother lightly, was his pupil for a year at one school and admitted that Walt made an excellent teacher. But the general impression adults had was of a person whose mind was elsewhere, rather dreamy and abstracted, not really committed to the job. Each term ended with a visit by a committee appointed by the school board to inspect progress. On this depended Walt's reengagement or dismissal. Between 1836 and 1841 he held at least eight posts, possibly because examiners were displeased by his unruly classroom. On the other hand he had no difficulty finding new appointments. Teachers in those days were frequently changing schools.

His brother remembered that "one of the greatest things about Walt was his wonderful calmness in trying times when everybody else would get excited. He was always cool, never flurried." But an incident near Babylon when his family had a farm there showed he could be far from imperturbable. He was out in a boat fishing on a big pond and a local boy angered him by heaving stones in the water and steering across his lines. Walt waited for him on shore and attacked him with his pole, seriously enough for the boy's father to bring an unsuccessful charge of assault. "We find that 'e did not 'it 'im 'ard enough," was the verdict of the court foreman, a cockney Englishman.

"He was a muscular young man at that time," said his brother, "very strong." Consciously he aimed to be like his mother, whose Quaker composure he so much admired. He cherished her peaceableness and tried to cultivate it in himself as an ideal. For the most part he succeeded. Every now and then the serenity shattered, as he boiled over and gave way to his natural self. Once he was seen losing his temper with a sidesman in church who had objected to his appearance. He beat the fellow over the head with his rolled hat. As a teacher he struggled hard to fit in, dressed carefully in a plain black suit, and took care not to offend with his language.

People knew him as a polite, kind youngster, mild-mannered, friendly enough with villagers during his free time but showing no interest in the girls, though his comparative refinement would have made him appealing as a marriage prospect. Females, he was to admit later, belonged to a "class of beings" whose nature mystified rather than attracted him.

So many of the early stories he wrote and published in the 1840s depict sons cruelly treated by fathers that we have to ask ourselves whether they reveal something about his buried feelings toward his own father. The two weren't estranged, and the mother never, so far as we know, complained about her husband to her "very good, but very strange" son. Yet in story after story we read of the unloved or hated son driven from home or plotting revenge against his unfeeling father.

One of the earliest, "Wild Frank's Return," has the son running away from home to wander the world rather than submit to his father's harshness. Homesick, longing for his family, he returns at last on horseback. Unable to approach the house, he falls asleep under a tree, the nervous horse—symbolically black—attached to his arm by its bridle. There is a violent night storm. Flashes of lightning terrify the horse, which bolts across the land and kills Frank in the process. Finally the horse finds its way to Frank's home. Father and mother stand together, joined in horror before the smashed body of their lost son. Nature, as the maddened horse and the storm, has taken its revenge on the unnatural father's denial of love. The sheltering home, if its door had not been closed against him, would have saved Frank from death.

An even more alarming story, seething with strange dark rage, is called "Bervance: or Father and Son." The son here, Luke, strongly resembles the father physically. Whether or not this in some manner threatens the father, his resentment of his son drives Luke into bitter revolt and dissipation. He attacks his father with words and finally, after a drunken argument, with his fists, knocking him down. The father's loathing for this boy is now extreme. Looking at him makes him feel he is looking into a mirror. He commits Luke to a lunatic asylum. In the awful climax the father turns one night in terror to find himself confronted by the apparition of his escaped son, "un-washed, tangly-haired, rag-covered," with his glaring madman's eyes.

Not all the stories were about a father's guilt and punishment. An unfinished story transfers guilt to the boy, and concerns his obsession with his mother. He dreams that in his absorption with worldly success in a far-off city he neglects her, till a message comes to tell him she is dying. Rushing to her bedside he bends over her loved face, desperate to hear that he is forgiven, but "the words came not." Seared by this moment of truth, "everything connected with his business, his schemes of ambition, his worldly gains, his friendships and his plans of life" is quite obliterated. Waking with a vile jolt from his nightmare he thanks God that the wrong done is only an imagined wrong. He understands now what he must do, what is really important to him. His devotion to his mother is paramount. While she lives, ambition will have to wait.

In Walt's imagination he tried to shape and subdue factors that perplexed him when he brooded on his life. In the everyday world he moved by instinct. The unacknowledged transactions of young Walt's family life had begun to result in a shift of power as his father relinquished claims to his place as head of the household. Over the years he had lost direction, dwindling in manhood, isolating himself. Walt's sisters and brothers had started looking instead to their brother for real authority. "It was as if he had us in his charge," George said. "He was like us—yet he was different from us, too." Sometimes he bore down as a guardian too heavily and strongly for their liking, as George afterward commented—a sure sign that he was assuming control, turning ever more surely into their surrogate father.

It was an obligation he never hesitated to accept. On the contrary he welcomed it. If his brothers and sisters, with the exception of Hannah, found him something of a riddle, they felt secure in his care as the father withdrew little by little from his central role. To them, and to the mother, it seemed a natural transference. How Walt regarded them can be seen in what Gay Wilson Allen has called the "thinly disguised allegory," "My Boys and Girls," written during his period as a teacher. An obligatory sentimental light falls over the characters, who are given his brothers' and sisters' actual names. Mary, by her age of fourteen, locates the time as 1835. Eddy, born in that year, does not get a mention. Hannah Louisa is rechristened Louisa and described lovingly as "the fairest and most delicate of human blossoms." An unnamed "fat, hearty, rosy-cheeked youngster" who was "an imp of mischief" is clearly Jeff. Then there is George Washington, who used to sit on his shoulders, Thomas Jefferson, cradled in his big brother's arms while he learned to spell, and little Andrew Jackson, his wrestling partner.

Thoughts and forebodings about Mary's future apparently worried the young author. He wrote of her that "Flattery comes too often to her ears. From the depths of her soul I now and then see misty revealings of thought and wish, that are not well." It is natural to speculate on these fears of "the dim phantoms of Evil standing about with nets and temptations" to cause her downfall. What was it he imagined might happen to her? Is it possible he was fearful of character weaknesses he had noticed in himself? She may have been acting stubbornly and rebelliously in outbursts against her parents, just as he had done. In fact she made a good marriage at the age of nineteen to Ansel Van Nostrand, a mechanic, and went off to live happily at Greenport.

Whitman was twenty-five when he came to publish "My Boys and Girls." References to the "youthful innocence" of this "child of light and loveliness," poised to lose her virginity and then look back with remorse at "wrongs done, and mean or wicked deeds performed," could well have been expressions of regret for his own lost innocence, or projections of experiences that had shamed him.

Another child in the story, who dies in infancy, receives a mention. In an age of frequent infant mortality the mourning over such a death would have been perfunctory. "It was not a sad thing—we wept not, nor were our hearts heavy." Throughout this tale the narrator insists that he is a kind of father—a curiously intimate, brotherly, loverlike one. "Though a bachelor, I have several boys and girls that I consider my own." He yearns to possess them, for them to become part of him, just as in his poem "There Was a Child Went Forth" "the friendly boys that passed, and the quarrelsome boys, and the tidy and fresh-cheeked girls, and the barefoot negro boy and girl" became part of him. He cannot bear to let go of a single one. When a youngster dies and is irretrievably lost, a quite voluptuous sense of love and death is evoked which lifts the prose momentarily into near poetry and breaks it free from its popular magazine setting. "Very beautiful was he—and the promise of an honorable manhood shone brightly in him—and sad was the gloom of his passing away. We buried him in early summer. The scent of the apple-blossoms was thick in the air—and all animated nature seemed overflowing with delight and motion." The dead boy is regained by an imaginary father who makes the sensual blossom and all of nature become a lover like him.

Limitations and restraints have to be acknowledged and taken into account. The narrator recognizes that he must bow to the inevitable; these boys and girls cannot all be treated as children. "Another H. has lately come among us—too large, perhaps, and too near manhood to be called one of my *children*. I know I shall love him well when we become better acquainted—as I hope we are destined to be."

Justin Kaplan in his biography makes a tellingly suggestive reference to a passage in Edgar Z. Friedenberg's *The Vanishing Adolescent*. Friedenberg leaves psychoanalytical jargon aside to make the point that young men such as Whitman "love boys as a way of loving the boy in themselves and themselves in the boy. They need have no antipathy towards women and may have warm friends among them, but are likely to be too self-centered to pay much attention to them." Caught "in the predicament of earliest adolescence" and "encapsulated within the personality of his mother," he sees his way of escape as "through his love for the young men he might have become."

There is an obscure episode which is said to have occurred in Southwold, where Whitman had a teaching post. As a result of it the teacher was obliged to leave. It may have been the same story told by Whitman many years later to his friend Nelly O'Connor. The son of the farmer with whom Whitman was staying while he taught school had begun to cling to him, he said, adding candidly that they were fond of each other. The father objected that Walt was spoiling the boy. In the story "Bervance," a subplot describes the father bitterly resenting his son's affection for a resident teacher. Another story, "The Child's Champion," echoes the farmer-and-son controversy but ends rapturously. John Lankton comes across an innocent twelve-year-old farm apprentice in some danger from a gang of tipsy sailors in a saloon and takes charge of him. They go off to spend the night in John Lankton's room, pure as angels in each other's arms.

Lankton's life before his rebirth in the embrace of his tender farm boy had been unfulfilled, empty and purposeless. Walt too had been working diligently but mechanically, lacking "energy and resolution." When he had had his fill of the privations involved in teaching he rejoined his family for a spell. In August 1836 the Whitmans moved to a region near Babylon. Walt joined them soon after. It was then that the only outright clashes took place between the waning father with his stored memories of past failures and his parvenu son. Attempts to make Walt acquiesce and knuckle down to farm work were stubbornly resisted. Hanging around to begin another teaching job, he would have been a constant irritant, reading and musing, loafing, keeping to himself.

That summer saw the start of a no-holds-barred presidential campaign. Martin Van Buren was the Democratic candidate, and the opposing Whigs were launching a series of assaults against him. The reformer Frances Wright had returned to the United States and was backing Van Buren wholeheartedly. Here at any rate Walt and his father were on common ground. The newspapers carried reports of her meetings, and it is likely they both went over to New York to hear her lecture. The Whig press set about attacking her viciously with smear campaigns. All her life she would be subjected to scandalmongering. Whitman told Horace Traubel that she was "a woman of the noblest make-up whose orbit was a great deal larger than theirs—too large to be tolerated for long by them—a most maligned, lied-about character. . . . She had a varied career here and in France—married a damn scoundrel, lost her fortune, faced the world with her usual courage. Her crowning sorrow was when that whelp who had been her husband tried in France to take her daughter from her, charging that the child needed to be protected from the danger of her mother's infidelistic teachings. Think of it!"

Walt was engaged to teach for a term at a school near Babylon, then taught briefly at a new school at Long Swamp. This took him to the spring of 1837. At some point he held down a gardening job; it could have been during this otherwise jobless summer. By the autumn he was back teaching at the school at Smithtown, ten miles from West Hills. Still essentially solitary, passively absorbed in his own sensations, he gives the impression of being aware of something folded and unready deep in his being, that he was perhaps unwilling to disturb. Yet there were signs that he did at times want to unfurl and blossom. Clinging to children and to his own memories of childhood was in some sense a delaying tactic, an attempt to forestall things, to give them their due span. What could be more satisfying in any case than a world bounded by his own skin, that drew everything into its own consummately peaceful existence? How could such delights be given up? Even as a mature male he still clung to the sensuality of this baby joy, writing in *Leaves of Grass*, "I merely stir, press, feel with my fingers, and am happy, / To touch my person to someone else's is about as much as I can stand." He was the unripe bud of that new democratic species analyzed by Tocqueville: "Not only does democracy make each man forget his ancestors, but it hides his descendants and separates his contemporaries from him; it throws him back upon himself alone and threatens in the end to confine him entirely within the solitude of his own heart."

Not long after his arrival at Smithtown he helped revive a debating society which met Wednesday evenings in his schoolhouse on the green. The society soon elected him secretary. At the age of eighteen this precocious debater was engaged in contests with the town's leading figures, including doctors, lawyers, two judges, a dentist, a congressman, and several well-to-do farmers. Debating societies were popular forms of mental gymnastics throughout the country. Discussion was all the rage. Subjects ranged from capital punishment, the need for controlling immigration, crimes against the Indians, to topics ranging further afield: Napoleon's good or evil character, slavery or abolition, health as an influence on morality. Only the year before Emerson and George Ripley had publicly discussed a topic soon to be close to Whitman's heart: "American Genius—The Causes Which Hinder Its Growth, Giving Us No First-Rate Productions." Even more important for the embryo poet Walt Whitman would have been Emerson's "American Scholar" declaration of independence delivered the following year at Cambridge. "The study of letters," he announced, "shall no longer be a name for pity, for doubt, and for sensual indulgence. . . . Our day of dependence, our long apprenticeship to the learning of other lands, draws to a close. . . . A nation of men will for the first time exist, because each believes himself inspired by the Divine Soul which also inspires all men." The new age, if not yet the new man, was now born.

When the debate on the system of slavery "as it exists in the South" came up, it was Whitman who won the argument for his side, carrying the motion that it was wrong. Not that he was then, or ever, an abolitionist, maintaining all his life that he was in everything an evolutionist. Evils, he held, would be eradicated through natural processes, in their own time.

His success as a debater against men so much older and more experienced than himself was surprising. Slow and indolent, big, muscular, he seldom excelled at thinking on his feet. His instinct if in doubt was to delay, procrastinate, stay silent. Hurrying for any reason was anathema to him. He joked to Traubel, "There may be reasons for hurrying but I can't hurry. William O'Connor said to me more than once, 'Walt, you're as fast as frozen molasses!'"

# 4

# "This Is the City"

His two terms of teaching over, he suddenly became, in the spring of 1838, a newspaper publisher, printer, and editor. His influential friends at the debating society may have helped him with the raising of funds. He rented an office with a room above for his headquarters in nearby Huntington and launched a weekly, the *Long Islander*. Out came the first number a week after Walt's nineteenth birthday. Grand though the venture sounds, it boiled down to a secondhand press, a case of type, an office above a stable. For assistant he had his brother George, who kept him company and shared the living space at night.

A paper in a country town had to justify itself by means of advertisements. Barter arrangements—subscriptions and advertising settled with bales of cordwood or sacks of potatoes—took the place of money. Local news had priority over the bits clipped from city journals. But compared with teaching it must have been a time of glorious freedom. Whitman wrote about the experience later with obvious relish. "Everything seem'd turning out well (only my own restlessness prevented me gradually establishing a permanent property there). I bought a good horse, and every week went all round the country serving my papers, devoting one day and night to it. I never had happier jaunts—going over to south side, to Babylon, down the south road, across to Smithtown and Comac, and back home. The experiences of these jaunts, the dear old-fashioned farmers and their wives, the stops by the hayfields, the hospitality, nice dinners, occasional evenings, the girls, the rides through the brush, come up in my memory to this day."

The unemphatic reference to girls in the plural seems to rule out any passionate affairs. George, questioned by an interviewer after his brother's death, said without hesitation, "I am confident I never knew Walt to fall in love with young girls or even show them marked attention." Daniel Brinton and Horace Traubel, questioning two Huntington friends of Whitman, were told by one that "He seemed to hate women," an expression the interviewers discounted as "too strong."

What he did like was being his own boss. It was the nearest he ever came to an ideal existence. At night groups of friends came over to his room and chatted. He played cards with George, and rode off on his leisurely rounds astride Nina, the white mare he had bought. Along the way he would dismount and pass the time of day with his farmer customers in their hay fields, "hospitable, upright, common-sensical" men. As often as not they would invite him to supper and maybe to stay the night. With ample time to indulge in sports and hunting, he had little use for either. He didn't go to dances, didn't drink or smoke. Always he would be clean and simple in his living habits.

Suddenly the business ended. He sold up his bits and pieces and—hardest of all—let go of Nina. Though he gives restlessness as the reason, it is clear he had no systematic approach to the paper he had only founded on a whim. The practical difficulties were perhaps too onerous. And those unfolded centers waiting darkly in him were sending out curious shoots, such as the Bryant-like poem he wrote and couldn't resist setting on his hand press in the office. "Our Future Lot" mourns

> This breast which now alternate burns
> With flashing hope, and gloomy fear,
> Where beats a heart that knows the hue
> Which aching bosoms wear;
>
> This curious frame of human mould,
> Where craving wants unceasing play—
> The troubled heart and wondrous form
> Must both alike decay.
>
> Then cold wet earth will close around

Dull, senseless limbs, and ashy face,
But where, O Nature, will be
My mind's dwelling place?


**FREE AGAIN,** he stayed temporarily with his family while pondering his next move. It is likely, of course, that his parents had more or less given up on him, baffled by his insouciance. His brief foray as an editor and journalist encouraged him to think he could find a place now in New York journalism. It was something to dream about rather than act on. He did nothing. His instinct for inactivity took over, and he settled down to enjoy an idyllic summer. Some fragments of an early story sum up his assessment of his own character. "He remained much by himself, although he had many brothers, sisters, relations and acquaintances. He did not work like the rest. By far the most of the time he remained silent." This "lethargic waitingness" was, he remarked afterward, characteristic of his brother George as well. Later he made a conscious virtue of it, calling it an ability to "lay back on reserves...to take time."

He seemed half aware that he was approaching a crossroads, vacillating, unsure of his direction. He shelved the problem and either went on solitary expeditions to the beach or joined in with the Long Island summer custom of beach parties, running about on the sand with the young men of his acquaintance, flopping in and out of the surf, digging clams and spearing the plentiful fat eels. Mainly though he loved to swim in the sea, an element which dissolved all distinctions and took away any nagging desire to think or ask. "I was never what you could call a skilful swimmer but was quite good. I always hugely enjoyed swimming. My forte was—if I can say it that way—in floating. I possessed almost unlimited capacity for floating on my back—for however long. Could almost take a nap meanwhile. That's to say I was very much at home in the water. I never could do any of the stunts of the other boys when I was young but I was a first-rate aquatic loafer." And to the same confidant he said, "I always was deliberate—I never was quick or nervous. I had, I may say, an unusual capacity for standing still, rooted on a spot, to ruminate—hours in and out sometimes."

He did rouse himself sufficiently to write poems like "Our Future Lot" as well as a number of essays. He aimed this juvenilia at James J.

Brenton, editor of the *Long Island Democrat* at Jamaica. Brenton, favorably inclined, published several items. It seemed logical, in the course of this correspondence, to apply to Brenton for employment. In August he went off to Jamaica and began working on the *Democrat*. The arrangement included board at the editor's house, which meant he was able to accept a nominal sum for his actual work of setting type and writing for the paper. He was no doubt glad of the experience. His input was it seems mainly literary. Before accepting the offer he had been job-hunting around New York without success.

Jamaica, an expanding town along the route of the Long Island Railroad, suited Walt well enough. The fleshy, large-boned youth, not yet twenty, got along fine with his editor but soon fell foul of Mrs. Brenton. Her daughter-in-law, Orvetta Hall Brenton, said that her mother took an instant dislike to Whitman. She found him lazy—a maddeningly dreamy youth who lounged around the house and was always "underfoot." Offended by his uncouth appearance, she nagged him into wearing a coat at the dinner table. This contrast to the informality of his home life would have certainly made him resentful. The feeling of antipathy was no doubt mutual. His apparent disregard of her two young boys only made matters worse. What kind of teacher must he have been? The children may have got on his nerves, or more than likely he was happier sitting around in his shirtsleeves talking to Mrs. Brenton's husband.

Brenton himself had no quarrel with Walt. He appreciated his "marked ability as a writer" and was prepared to overlook his manners. The stubborn young man could have been responding to Mrs. Brenton's strictures by exaggerating his slovenliness. Here at any rate was the situation which irritated him into writing an essay extolling the delights of loafing, with its defiant opening, "How I do love a loafer!" It went on: "What was Adam, I should like to know, but a loafer? Of all human beings, none equals your genuine, inbred, unvarying loafer."

He had begun to fashion his art of idling. Even Brenton, a remarkably considerate employer—though we might ask how much he was paying—did his best to make the youngster realize that in this world you had to make a living. The very notion of regular hours seemed foreign to the fellow. After lunch he would amble out of the print shop and find an apple tree to lie under. Brenton would send his "printer's devil" to fetch him back. Like as not he would be found studying the sky, which he could do quite contentedly for whole afternoons at a time. "I don't know what or how," he wrote in *Specimen Days*, "but it seems to me mostly owing to these skies— while I have of course seen them every day of my life, every now and then I think I never really saw the skies before—that I have had this autumn some wondrously contented hours—may I not say perfectly happy ones?"

It was enviable, this ability to experience what Rousseau, the "Wild Philosopher," once called the "sensation of existence stripped of every other feeling, which is in itself a precious sense of contentment and peace."

A character in Dostoevsky, when asked, "Are you happy?" could only burst into tears. It was typical of Whitman that the word "happiness" came spontaneously to his lips. He spoke of it in a major essay, *Democratic Vistas*, as the absolute crown of life:

> Present literature, while magnificently fulfilling certain popular demands with plenteous knowledge and verbal smartness, is profoundly sophisticated, insane, and its very joy is morbid. . . . I say the question of Nature, largely considered, involves the questions of the aesthetic, the emotional, and the religious—and involves happiness. A fitly born and bred race, growing up in the right conditions of outdoor as much as indoor harmony, activity and development, would probably, from and in those conditions, find it enough merely *to live*—and would, in their relations to the sky, air, water, trees, etc., and to the countless common shows, and in the fact of life itself, discover and achieve happiness— with Being suffused night and day by wholesome ecstasy, surpassing all the pleasures that wealth, amusement, and even gratified intellect, erudition, or the sense of art can give.

Utterances like this led Henry Miller, another Brooklyn boy, to call Whitman "thoroughly Polynesian." Whitman himself, when paralyzed and waiting for death, was not averse to the idea, convinced that "Somewhere, back, back, thousands of years ago, in my fathers, mothers, there must have been an oriental strain or element introduced—a dreamy languor, calm, content."

The job with Brenton had been temporary, never more than a stopgap. After Christmas we find him back teaching at a school at Little Bay Side. Charles Roe, who had been a boy of ten in his class there, remembered that though the teacher "did not care for women's society—seemed, indeed, to shun it," he was apparently no more closely in touch with young men of his age. His friendliness was general rather than intimate. But he wasn't "offish," and he made no enemies. What he did enjoy, Roe guessed, was the company of older people. For instance, while boarding with the Roe family he spent time discussing books with the boy's father. The mother was sad to hear that Whitman wasn't a churchgoer. Charles Roe had the impression that his teacher was "atheistic," an assumption far from the truth. Whitman kept his views on religion to himself. Quite likely at this time he took in one of the lectures of Frances Wright, always a firm advocate of religion as the bedrock of all culture.

After leaving Little Bay Side Walt taught briefly in the West Hills region. By the following summer he was still in that vicinity, teaching at Woodbury. Sandford Brown, a resident of West Hills all his life and an old man by the time he was questioned by two English "Whitmaniacs" in 1890, was of the opinion that Walt had no inclination for teaching. Whitman had been his first teacher. "He warn't in his element," said Brown. "He was always musin' and writin', 'stead of tending to his proper duties."

Gay Wilson Allen is rather dubious about this witness and his aged memory, but in one respect the man was right. Whitman had other fish to fry. In this same spring he wrote the first of a series of essays entitled "Sun-Down Papers from the Desk of a Schoolmaster" for his ex-employer to publish in the *Democrat*. Poems too, wooden and derivative though they were, continued to appear. Charles Roe still knew by heart a stanza or two of a poem of Whitman's which the teacher had set his pupils to memorize. Called "The Punishment of Pride," it carried the usual mixture of sentimentality and moralizing that contemporary taste expected.

> Oh he was pure! the fleecy snow
> Sinking through air to earth below
> Was not more undefiled!
> Sinless he was, as fleeting smile
> On lip of sleeping child.

His essays were similarly intended to instruct, dealing with vague abstracts such as the search for "Truth," warnings against the dangers of smoking and the excessive drinking of coffee, and one rumination on ambition and the dreams of youth which touched on his own fantasies of authorship and was understandably self-mocking. The essayist might put together "a wonderful and ponderous book" one day, though who knows what would be in it? However, "Who should be a better judge of a man's talents than the man himself? Yes: I would write a book! And who shall say that it might not be a very pretty book? Who knows but that I might do something very respectable?"

In the autumn of 1840, as the presidential contest between Van Buren and William Henry Harrison heated up, these misty yearnings were set aside. Brenton's *Democrat* was a main protagonist when this furious battle broke out. Jamaica's other paper, the *Long Island Farmer*, was staunchly Whig. Whitman, glad to jettison education for politics, managed to get himself appointed as Democratic electioneer for Queens County—probably on Brenton's recommendation. At the end of September Daniel Webster arrived to speak in support of the Whig candidate Harrison. Following him on the platform was Charles King. According to the *Democrat* King's speech was a pack of lies and slanders. Van Buren, so King alleged, was unfit to be a president since he was in favor of goods, wives, and children held in common in an immoral community.

A few days later came a public debate; in one corner "Walter" Whitman and in the other John Gunn. In its report the *Long Island Farmer* derided the "champion of Democracy" and leveled veiled threats against his person for calling King "a liar and a blackguard." This was the stuff of roughhouse politics. Whitman responded in a letter to the *Democrat* that was a little masterpiece of superior dignity. "From my very soul," he wrote calmly, "I look with sorrow on the pitiable and blacksouled malice which actuates such men as this young Gunn, who has lately been uttering the most reckless falsehoods, and endeavoring to stain, by mean and ungentlemanly misstatements, the standing of our most reputable citizens."

No one picked up the glove he threw down. The threat of violence against him in "Buckeye's" column never materialized. But he was on the losing side. Frances Wright had predicted a Democrat defeat. In the November elections Jamaica itself went Democrat, but the Whigs came out victorious in New York State and across the nation as a whole. Whitman was out of a job. In the winter of 1840–1841 he took up his old standby again, teaching for a couple of terms—his last—at Whitestone near Brooklyn.

Crossing over on one of the steam ferries to New York City the following May, he set his face to the future and made a vow: no turning back. It was now or never if he was to gain a foothold in the raucous world of the new independent journalism, ushered in since the mid-1830s by the rise of the penny press. Rival newspapers warred with each other for a share in the market, launching aggressive attacks on the personalities of editors and shifting the emphasis from the partisanship of politics to the struggle for readers.

Whitman's venture into local politics had been an exciting diversion: not that he was ever a truly political animal. What drew him always was the power of oratory. He had been bobbing aloft, intoxicated by speeches. Now he came down on the hard ground of raw reality with a bump, fully engaged at last in the daily business of earning a living. He had wavered back and forth for years, half-hearted about a career, often ending back home where he began. In the heaving maelstrom of Jacksonian New York the pace of his life quickened, took on a direction. Once there it was a matter of survival. There was no standing still. You either moved or sank.

He was nearly twenty-two. In this city with a population of more than three hundred thousand and rising he soon found lodgings in the boarding houses available everywhere for clerks and tradesmen and their families. Wealthier citizens occupied the large houses along Broadway. Laborers, sailors, business failures, together with the unemployed and the derelicts, congregated in basements and ruinous hovels off the Bowery. Whitman launched himself on the metropolis from the establishments he listed without comment in his notebooks: "Mrs. Chipman's at 12 Center Street," "Mrs. R. in Spring Street," "Mrs. Edgarton's in Vesey," "Mrs. Bonnard's in John Street." These were just a few. At the breakfast table in the mornings would be Jewish gentlemen, clerks, dry goods keepers, jewelers, elderly ladies, and "several others, ladies, etc., whom we feel delicate about mentioning." Keeping an eagle eye on this assortment would be the landlady herself behind the tea and coffee urns. Bleak and friendless though they often were, these boarding houses were much in demand in an age before the spread of apartment leasing. A fellow boarder at 68 Duane, Henry Saunders, a lad of seventeen employed as a junior clerk, turned out to be an embezzler who ended up in the prison at the Tombs. In his temperance novel *Franklin Evans*, composed in a terrific hurry the following year for money, Whitman speculated on the fate of some of these boarders, driven by their experience of cheap and miserable accommodation into bars and brothels for some spurious warmth.

He found work easily, sticking type in the din and confusion of the *New World*'s large pressroom in Ann Street. He was nobody but he had made a start. Park Benjamin and Rufus Griswold were the powerful personalities behind this popular weekly. At first they were joint editors of this paper and the *Daily Signal*. There was a dispute and Griswold left, leaving behind him the legacy of his strenuous Americanism. Papers in the city were multiplying at a rapid rate. Usually one editor with an assistant or two made up the editorial staff. The tremendous growth of the popular press meant that printers, setting the type laboriously by hand, were in constant demand.

Park Benjamin, lame as the result of polio in his youth, was a man of ruthless ambition, out to make the *New World* the "largest and cheapest and handsomest newspaper" by outstripping the competition with his rushed out "extras." Usually these were pirated editions of British books arriving by steamer from Liverpool or London to be set up overnight. A whole squad of typesetters would stand by to get these special editions on the streets by next morning, if possible ahead of the competition. Whitman must have been part of this frantic activity.

The young country teacher, journalist, and temporary political worker who had plunged into the print jungle of New York and who proceeded to wade around in it without the least fear or hesitation, sets us a puzzle. How did he come to accept the big-city world of mass journalism so readily unless he was—as he would repeatedly insist later—as ordinary as the next man? How did he swallow and to some extent emulate the braggadocio of Park Benjamin, Horace Greeley, Nelson Herrick, John Ropes, and the other bulldozing proprietors except by calling up in himself something of that same comic boastfulness of the American frontiersmen, the fabled Davy Crocketts and Mike Finns? The truth is that he was a man of strong digestion, comfortable with his age and at home with its contradictions and crudities. There was room in him for the bad as well as the good. He took to the new journalistic culture like the newspaperman he always was. Later, casting about for an American-bred poetic persona for the vast poem he dreamed of writing, he could see no reason why "The Poet" called for by Emerson shouldn't combine religion and news, be part of the daily round as well as providing food for the soul.

In these preliminary years he was nothing special as a journalist.

Only when he found his voice as a poet did he transform himself into a superb "reporter" of every aspect of the New World. He refused to admit to being anything other than ordinary, "average." His poem-leaves, lifting out of the ground common as grass, belonged to everybody. They had, he said, been produced by everyone. He simply came along and "edited" them. *Leaves of Grass* would celebrate, in Paul Zweig's phrase, "the mystery of ordinariness." Here was a literary man who only wanted to be seen as the spokesman for nature and for human nature. "The trouble is that writers are too literary—too damned literary," he grumbled half teasingly in his old age.

The country boy had entered a sphere in which newspapermen were expected to be evangelists for the new immediate age. "The nineteenth century," says Zweig, "transposed the religious quest for salvation into a variety of secular idioms." The idiom of the New York newspaper was a case in point. Morals were hammered home in every issue with evangelistic zeal. The nation founded on high Jeffersonian ideals was now intent on convincing itself, in the midst of urban squalor and the spread of cheap factory labor, that man and everything he touched was perfectible. In the Victorian pursuit of progress and its insistence on the moral worth of just about everything, it was the self-made man who led the field. Into the news sheets and from lecture platforms and politicians' halls poured contributions on the great debate convulsing the nation: what did democracy mean, what did culture mean, and nationalism? Nothing was left out, nothing forgotten. Utopians, feminists, penal reformers, abolitionists, health cranks, and spiritualists all had their say. So did the bigots, as politicians and editors gleefully stirred the pot. Piety, hypocrisy, and now and then genuine prophecy jostled one another, often impossible to separate. Onto the breakfast tables every morning flopped this extraordinary mixture of coarse abuse and righteousness, eager to give its readers "something piquant and something solid, and something sentimental, and something humorous—and all dished up in our own peculiar way...."

We can read what one sharp-eyed traveler, Charles Dickens—the most famous victim of the pirate publishers—made of the scene. "What are these suckers of cigars and swallowers of strong drinks, whose hats and legs we see in every possible variety of twist, doing but amusing themselves?" he asked in his *American Notes*. "What are the fifty newspapers, which those precocious urchins are bawling down the street, and which are kept filled within, what are they but

57

amusements? Not vapid waterish amusements, but good strong stuff; dealing in round abuse and blackguard names; pulling off the roofs of private houses, as the Halting Devil did in Spain, pimping and pandering for all degrees of vicious taste, and gorging with coined lies the most voracious maw; imputing to every man in public life the coarsest and the vilest motives; scaring away from the stabbed and prostrate body-politic, every Samaritan of clear conscience and good deeds; and setting on, with yell and whistle and the clapping of foul hands, the vilest vermin and the worst birds of prey."

*Martin Chuzzlewit* finds Dickens in better humor, though just as sardonic. Martin's steamer is boarded and overrun by a pack of newsboys yelling their wares:

" 'Here's this morning's New York Sewer!' cried one. 'Here's this morning's New York Stabber! Here's the New York Family Spy! Here's the New York Private Listener! Here's the New York Peeper! Here's the New York Plunderer! Here's the New York Keyhole Reporter! Here's the New York Rowdy Journal! Here's all the New York papers!'

" 'Here's the Sewer!' cried another. 'Here's the Sewer's exposure of the Wall Street Gang, and the Sewer's exposure of the Washington Gang, and the Sewer's exclusive account of a flagrant act of dishonesty committed by the Secretary of State when he was eight years old; now communicated, at a great expense, by his own nurse. Here's the Sewer's article upon the Judge that tried him, day afore yesterday for libel, and the Sewer's tribute to the independent Jury that didn't convict him, and the Sewer's account of what they might have expected if they had! Here's the Sewer, here's the Sewer!' "

" 'It is in such enlightened means,' said a voice almost in Martin's ear, 'that the bubbling passions of my country find a vent.' "

Further on in the novel Martin meets one of the self-made boosters circulating in increasing numbers in the dynamic American urban centers, his natural habitat. Preposterous as this new businessman—so different from the eighteenth-century "man of business"—seems to Martin, we have to remember that Whitman saw nothing extraordinary in him. He rubbed shoulders with him every day in the dining room at Tammany Hall, or in the Pewter Mug, hangout of politicians in Spruce Street. In the next decade Whitman would emerge as America's first urban poet, ready to include every Manhattan type in the tidal rush of his poem. These living street crowds would feed the hungry eye of a new "equable man" who, if he judges at all, "judges not as the judge judges, but as the sun falling around a helpless thing."

Martin is introduced to Major Pawkins, a Pennsylvanian whose yellow forehead is massive. So, it appears, is his sagacity. He has a "heavy eye" and is the kind of man who, "mentally speaking, requires a deal of room to turn himself in." The major is a politician and a patriot but could just as easily turn his hand to swindling, starting a bank or forming a land-jobbing company. In short he is an admirable example of a new-age businessman who "could hang about a bar-room discussing the affairs of the nation for twelve hours together; and in that time could hold forth with more intolerable dulness, chew more tobacco, drink more rum toddy, mint julep, gin-sling, and cock-tail, than any private gentleman of his acquaintance."

Whitman the young tyro, feeling around for openings, had sufficient confidence in himself to escape from behind his typecase in Benjamin's hectic pressroom and get himself known. Only two months after starting work he made use of his familiarity with editors and journalists and his knowledge of Democratic politics and how it worked, and got himself invited to make a speech at a rally in City Hall Park. No more exceptional a speaker than a journalist, he was at least visible. The Tammany paper the *New Era* and William Bryant's *Post* both ran generous reports of his speech. Not that he had anything striking or remarkable to say. All the same his address was impressively mature in sentiment. He urged his audience of Democrats to concentrate on "great principles" rather than personalities, asking them to make sure that their policies and measures were the right ones. The next Democratic presidential candidate, he believed, would arise of his own volition and achieve power "on the wings of a mighty reaction." This was high-principled stuff, and the party bosses were not interested. No one invited him to make another speech.

One can't imagine him being too disappointed. His main concern was to find a platform for his stories, essays, and poems. Park Benjamin may have been approached. That autumn the *New World* did publish two indifferent poems. Benjamin may have been influenced by Whitman's success in getting himself accepted by the *United States and Democratic Review*, to give it its full name. It was the best literary magazine around, and Whitman had set his sights on it. After only a few weeks in New York he started placing work with them. They took a number of his stories, among them "Wild Frank's Return" and a nightmarish tale, "Death in the Schoolroom," in which a brutally sadistic teacher flogs away at a pupil who is already dead.

The *Democratic Review* was a prestigious monthly. As a contributor Whitman was in the company of such names as Bryant, Hawthorne, Poe, Whittier, and Lowell. Founded in Washington in the late 1830s by John L. O'Sullivan, its editorial policy suited Whitman down to the ground. Only those diehards of patrician culture who were convinced that democracy and literature were at separate poles refused to be associated with it. In its first number O'Sullivan had flatly declared that "The vital principle of our literature must be democracy. . . . All history is to be rewritten, political science and the whole scope of moral truth have to be reconsidered in the light of the democratic principle." This ebullient Democrat, who later put into national usage the phrase "manifest destiny" and saw America as the spearhead of a world advance toward republicanism, was intoxicated by the vision of the continent's hugeness, its emptiness, and its promise of ample living space for "our yearly multiplying millions." So indeed was Whitman. At the end of his life he was as drunk on this great space as in the days of his youth. "Think of it," he exclaimed to Horace Traubel, "think of it: how little of the land of the United States is cultivated—how much of it is still utterly untilled. When you go West you sometimes travel across vast spaces where not an acre is plowed, not a tree is touched, not a sign of a house is anywhere detected. America is not for special types, castes, but for the great mass of people, immigrants—the vast, surging, hopeful army of workers."

In 1841, the year of Whitman's arrival in the city, European immigrants were pouring onto the docks in boatloads, sometimes at the rate of two thousand a day. Whitman wished they could be sent on their way to the clean open spaces of the West. Instead they were forced to seek shelter in the dirtiest and cheapest districts, the "rookeries" of Ridge and Attorney streets, the firetraps and thieves' kitchens, the more unfortunate of them soon mingling with the thugs and derelicts and drunks of the Five Points area. "This is the place," reported Dickens in his *American Notes*, "these narrow ways, diverging to the right and left, and reeking everywhere with dirt and filth. Such lives as are lived here, bear the same fruits here as elsewhere. The coarse and bloated faces at the doors have counterparts at home, and all the wide world over. Debauchery has made the very houses prematurely old. See how the rotten beams are tumbling down, and how the patched and broken windows seem to scowl dimly like eyes that have been hurt in drunken frays. . . . From every corner, as you glance about in these dark retreats, some figure crawls half awakened, as if the judgment hour were near at hand and every obscene grave were giving up its dead. Where dogs would howl to lie, women and men and boys slink off to sleep, forcing the dislodged rats to move away in quest of better lodgings."

It was a city of glaring extremes. The worst examples of filth and prostitution would give way after a few blocks to the grand boulevard of Broadway, justifying with its prosperity the most extravagant claims made for the new democratic society. Funneling its carriages and freight wagons and white-and-gold omnibuses from Union Square to the Battery, it was a broad channel lined with elegant buildings, the best stores and galleries, and with oyster cellars, ice cream parlors, barrooms, and hairdressers. Customers in their glossy hats and soft gloves flooded it during the day, and then for a brief hour in the evening came an army of clerks heading for home. Whitman in his heyday as a New York editor, a dandified peacock of a fellow, loved nothing better than to saunter along it with the best of them.

The dire poverty made him uneasy, but not unduly. He was the archetypal young man in a hurry, even if he did affect to dawdle. The feverish haste which seemed to drive rich and poor alike propelled him with it. He had yet to find his feet. He saw the congestion and chronic overcrowding and was split between concern and an instinct to convert what he saw into copy. Outbreaks of fire were frequent and inevitable. Here is Whitman reporting on one fire in Broome and Delancey streets, placing his piece in the *Aurora* in 1842 and then a few years later selling it, with an adroit change or two, as a news item to the *Brooklyn Daily Eagle*. He came on "stacks of furniture upon the sidewalks and even in the street." There were small children sobbing and clinging terrified to their mothers. The hubbub of the crowd, the fire engine trumpets, the roaring fire, all added to the din caused by "the lamentations of those who were made homeless by the conflagration." He couldn't deny his excitement and was honest enough to call the spectacle "a horrible yet magnificent sight."

In time, when he hits on his grand unifying idea of the all-identifying persona, he is able to recast these eyewitness accounts and weave them into his verse in "Song of Myself":

> Lads ahold of fire-engines and hook-and-ladder ropes no less to
>   me than the gods of the antique wars,
> Minding their voices peal through the crash of destruction,
> Their brawny limbs passing safe over charr'd laths, their white
>   foreheads whole and unhurt out of the flames.

Identifying, he is carried out, a survivor. How sweet it is, as

> I lie in the night air in my red shirt, the pervading hush is for my
>   sake,
> Painless after all I lie exhausted but not so unhappy,
> White and beautiful are the faces around me, the heads are bared
>   of their fire-caps,
> The kneeling crowd fades with the light of the torches.

Only a few years before his death a terrible fire raged through a block of New York tenements. Reading the account in his morning paper he was less sure of the magnificence than he had been as a young man, and uneasily conscious of the criticism in some quarters that he had turned a deaf ear to human misery. Admitting the possibility of a certain truth in the charge, he stuck stubbornly to his Hegelian beliefs. Disease fattens in the tenements, he said, along with every other affliction. Nevertheless, "one of the painful facts in connection with this human misery is that evil cannot be remedied by any one change, one reform, but must be accomplished by countless forces working towards the one effect."

Struggling for recognition as a young freelance in the quagmire of Manhattan journalism, he came out in support of Dickens and his sympathy for the poor. The occasion was Dickens's visit to America in 1842. Whitman was writing penny-a-liners for the *Aurora*. A speech by Dickens calling for honest dealing and an international copyright agreement to put a stop to his works being pirated enraged a large section of the press. Even the *Democrat Review* weighed in with an attack on the "atrocious exaggeration of his characters." Whitman, flush with the opportunities of his new outlet, replied in the *Aurora* with a staunch defense of one of his heroes. "Mr. Dickens never maligns the poor. He puts a searing iron to wickedness, whether among poor or rich; and yet when he describes the guilty, poor and oppressed man, we are always in some way reminded how much need there is that certain systems of law and habit which lead to this poverty and consequent crime should be remedied." He went on to argue that the wicked of the world should be portrayed with realism, exposed in their "unclothed deformity." Dickens, he declared, unlike those "feudal" authors of the Old World for whom he had little time, was a democratic writer.

PARK BENJAMIN WAS an unpredictable, aggressive newspaper boss who launched character assassinations on rival editors, quarreled with partners, and insulted employees whenever he felt like it. When Whitman was asked later what he thought of him he had nothing to say. His silence spoke volumes. If he fell foul of him personally and moved to the *Aurora* for this reason, he kept quiet about it. Evidence that he bore the man a grudge turns up in a violent attack on Benjamin's credentials, headed "Bamboozle and Benjamin," believed to be by Whitman although the piece was unsigned. Apparently Benjamin had some pretensions to literature. The article derided him for "possessing little tact at stringing together sentences, and very great tact of impudence, conceit, and brazen assumption—one of the most vain pragmatical nincompoops in creation" who "sets himself up for a poet!"

Operating as a freelance for space rates would have been more congenial to Whitman than working as an employee, whether for Benjamin or anyone else. The *Aurora* covered topics that were very much to his liking, ranging over activities of local interest, impressions laced with local color, character sketches, prizefights, lectures, art, crime trials, with political subjects taking second place. The new two-penny daily, started only six months before by Nelson Herrick and John F. Ropes, was definitely his kind of paper. Herrick and Ropes ran their business from 162 Nassau Street, near Tammany Hall, the Printing House Square district where many of the Democratic papers were located. They also produced the *Atlas*, a Sunday sheet, from the same stable, as well as two other weeklies. Whitman would have been alerted by their first issue with its bold announcement that "American writers of equal talent will always be preferred to Foreigners, simply because they understand better the genius of the people for whom they write."

Not long after Whitman began writing for the paper the *Aurora* editor was sacked. Thomas Low Nichols had printed libelous accusations of corruption involving the city authorities. Whitman, an unknown quantity, had gained notice with his *Democratic Review* contributions. With the right political credentials he was well placed to be considered for the editor's chair, and changes happened almost overnight in this highly unstable profession. On March 28, not yet twenty-three, Whitman found himself responsible for the four-page metropolitan daily, assisted by a police reporter and backed up by a roomful of printers. The paper, Democratic in sympathy, was, he stated in his first editorial, "bound to no party." He aimed to make it *the* paper of the city. Expanding his breast, he called it "the most readable journal of the republic," quite a claim for a newspaper with a circulation of about five thousand. The *Aurora*, he promised, would be "fearless, open, and frank in its tone." It was one promise he intended to keep, and he was soon alarming the owners.

New editors needed targets in order to make their mark. With his distrust of the clergy Whitman found a handy one in Bishop John Hughes, a young Catholic who had begun organizing the fast-growing Irish immigrant population into a political pressure group. Its objective was to achieve state support for parochial schools. Tammany politicians resisted. Finally they caved in, after several weeks of violent "blackguarding of the Catholics and Irish" by the *Aurora*'s hot-blooded new editor. Abusive, rabble-rousing phrases had sunk him to the level of racism endorsed by the Native American party. Intolerant railing would alternate with sanctimonious expressions of moral principle, as Whitman issued dark warnings, planting the *Aurora*'s flag on "high American ground."

But not for long. As the Tammany echelon wavered, Whitman came under editorial pressure from his bosses and was ordered to soften his tone. Out in the streets there were ugly scenes. Pitched battles between Protestants and Catholics ended in a mob hurling stones at the Bishop's residence adjacent to Saint Patrick's Cathedral. Whitman had increased circulation substantially with his anti-foreigner line but now it all turned sour. Backtracking hastily, he tried out the voice of liberty with which he would eventually be associated, pleading for "the widest extension of immunities of the people, as well as the blessings of government. Let us receive these foreigners to our shores, and to our good offices."

Too early success may have gone to his head. It had certainly altered his appearance. By a strange metamorphosis the slovenly dressed country youth who had offended Mrs. Brenton's sensibilities had become "rather stylish," as George Whitman put it. Strolling down Broadway in his self-consciously angled high hat and his frock coat adorned with a flower in its buttonhole, Whitman carried a cane and did his best to assume an air of importance. Maybe he was amusing himself, but more than likely he was reveling in his good fortune.

"We glory in being true Americans," he had written buoyantly in an editorial. That glory was real, and it lit him with bliss. And this was *his* city, Manhattan, resplendent in its aboriginal name. How brave he felt, how thrilled and satisfied! The newspaper was no more than a doorway, the city only a room—but what a room! Feeling on the threshold of something fine and wonderful and undiscovered, he would take himself up as far as Battery Park, mingling with society folk, taking in the sights and inhaling the tangy air with them, the equal of them. From the Castle Garden swimming barge he slipped into the water and indulged in a favorite pastime, floating on his back and gazing at the sky. It was a beautiful time. He loved the world and everything in it. One day he sat watching as "a tow-boat from Philadelphia with a long string of barges in her wake, and another from Albany, looking like a floating village, came along at the same moment...when suddenly there darted out from the apparently inextricable mass of floating worlds a little fairy-looking yacht, with 'Osprey' emblazoned on her stern, and with sails that sat like a new coat on a dandy."

Reclining after his swim, relaxed and satisfied with his life, alone there "or in the rush of the streets," it seemed to him that he was splashing ahead toward some goal and yet staying where he was, content to tread water and let the world go by. He watched the young men who floated on their backs with their white bellies bulging to the sun. Unconscious of him, their silent admirer, they hauled themselves out on the flat barge close by to rest. When he had gained his singing voice and was delighted with its fullness he would summon up these memories and relive these moments, as

> The beards of the young men glisten'd with wet, it ran from their
>   long hair,
> Little streams pass'd all over their bodies.

Never one to start work early, he would have missed seeing on

Broadway the sweepers and junior clerks, the cleaners and laborers arriving, rubbing the sleep from their eyes and clutching their lunch boxes. It's doubtful if he would have seen either the bundles of damp morning papers dumped at the kiosks. Once up and about, he roamed freely and got paid for doing so, supposedly hunting down copy but in reality feeding an ever-ravenous curiosity. He liked the touch of it all on his skin, the sights and sounds of a city fuming as if for him, in connection with him. Sometimes though the dissonances, the sheer rush and rage of it would be too much even for his appetite and he would lose the sense of it, nauseous suddenly in his belly. The soul in him would quail in the face of this onslaught, all this indomitable energy and enterprise. People went under, lives were smashed. What was the point of it, if it ended in a man driven mad, jumping overboard from the ferry and drowning in front of everyone's eyes? He had reported these things—he had even seen them. What could justify someone falling and being crushed to death between the dock and the ferry's prow? "Still the trips go on as before." Nothing waits, nothing is allowed to rest. "A moment's pause—the quick gathering of a curious crowd (how strange that they can look so unshudderingly on the scene!)—the paleness of the more chicken-hearted—and all subsides, and the current sweeps as it did the moment previously." Living in a city tended to make one callous, deadening something in the soul. If posterity was handed no more than this as a record, "It will be bad for us." Then his young man's stomach would recover and he would start absorbing again as tirelessly as ever the endless show and street theatre, part of the thousand-footed crowd,

> Looking in at the shop windows of Broadway the whole
>   forenoon, flattening the flesh of my nose on the thick plate
>   glass,
> Wandering the same afternoon with my face turn'd up to the
>   clouds. . . .
>
> The blab of the pave, tires of carts, sluff of boot-soles, talk of the
>   promenaders,
> The heavy omnibus, the driver with his interrogating thumb,
>   the clank of the shod horses on the granite floor . . .
> The hurrahs for popular favorites, the fury of the rous'd mobs . . .
> The excited crowd, the policeman with his star quickly working
>   his passage to the center of the crowd.

Loitering on corners, following his nose, the young editor in his guise as gentleman-spectator went trawling for material as the fancy took him. He combined a little business with a great deal of pleasure. Nevertheless he worked hard in fits and starts. In facetious chats with his readers he liked to give the impression that he did next to nothing. In fact he churned out large quantities of features as well as character sketches of New York types—firemen, omnibus drivers, butchers. He dashed down rapid impressions of waterfront and market life. He described firsthand what it was like to live in a boarding house. On his jaunts during the course of a single day he would drop in at a pistol gallery or a gymnasium, have his fortune told, visit a museum. In the evening he took in a speech or lecture before heading back to his office to catch up on neglected work.

His journalism of the time had little to distinguish it from the showy, pretentious prose of his fellow editors and reporters. Describing the butchers in Grand Street—butchers seem born entertainers—he could have been commenting on his own mannered style. "With sleeves rolled up, and one corner of their white apron tucked under the waist string—to whoever casts an enquiring glance at their stand they gesticulate with the grace, the affected bendings and twistings of a French dancing master. . . . With amusing perseverance they play off on every new passenger the same lures and the same artifice that have been tried and failed in so many previous cases."

To be an editor was to be a master of bending and twisting, as he had quickly discovered. Now and then, however, he did come out in the open and face an issue head-on. For that to happen he had to be fired up, made genuinely indignant by an injustice. The mass arrest of about fifty prostitutes on Broadway was one such event. Broadway, for all its opulence, was a thoroughfare in which hogs rooted in the gutter and were attacked by packs of ownerless dogs. Thieves preyed on the crowds, and pathetic gangs of child prostitutes hung around at intersections. Brothels were thick on the ground among the hideous tenements of Cherry, Water, and Walnut streets and around Five Points.

Whitman took on the newspaper moralists and the New York legislature at one and the same time. He struck out at police brutality and harassment and demanded to know what their orders were. Did they have warrants for herding these unfortunates into prison? He laid it on so strong that the alarmed proprietors forced him to issue a reluctant apology the following day. "The language we used in our article of yesterday," he explained stiffly, "denouncing the kidnapping of women in Broadway by the police authorities, was not intended and does not apply to them as citizens. We meant only to say that the kidnapping and imprisoning of these women on Wednesday night was a ruffianly, scoundrelly, villainous, outrageous and high-handed proceeding, unsanctioned by law, justice, humanity, virtue or religion." Not much of a climb-down, but he got away with it.

Whether or not he had ever been a client himself, he believed that nineteen of every twenty young men living unattached like him in cities made use of prostitutes. He passed the girls often enough on the nighttime pavements, and they met his glance with "your frequent and swift flash of eyes offering me love." In "Song of Myself" he calls up his most original language to honor the most wretched of them and to make his stance clear. He feels shame, and guilt by association, a neutral among leery men, as

> The prostitute draggles her shawl, her bonnet bobs on her tipsy
>   and pimpled neck,
> The crowd laugh at her blackguard oaths, the men jeer and
>   wink at each other,
> (Miserable! I do not laugh at your oaths nor jeer you). . . .

The readership of his day, shaken by this brilliant realism, were more shocked in 1860 by the outright expression of solidarity in his notorious little poem "To a Common Prostitute":

> Not till the sun excludes you do I exclude you,
> Not till the waters refuse to glisten for you and leaves to rustle
>   for you do my words refuse to glisten and rustle for you.

On April 20 he took issue again on the same subject, criticizing in a remarkably mature and balanced editorial the tabling by the New York legislature of a bill, the effect of which was to render "all practices of licentiousness penal." "You cannot," he told his readers, "legislate men into morality." And went on: "Were communities so constituted that to prune their errors, the only thing necessary should be the passage of *laws*, the task of reform would be no task at all." He endorsed wholeheartedly the motto flown by the *Democrat Review* at its masthead—"The best government is that which governs least"—and went on to amplify it with his own credo of the individualist, a faith he would cleave to for the rest of his life. He believed that "every being with a rational soul is an *independent man*, and that one is as much a man as another, and that all sovereign rights reside within himself, and that it is a dangerous thing to delegate them to legislatures." Thomas Paine, always one of his agents of liberation, had stated it with characteristic succinctness: "Society is produced by our wants, and government by our wickedness." But Whitman would never accept the corollary of this, which said that government itself was the greatest of all reflections on human nature.

A Democrat with free access to Tammany Hall, he made use of the dining room in the hotel attached to it. Either there or in the Pewter Mug nearby he met Colonel John Fellows. The old man's stately bearing, silvery hair, and his brass-buttoned blue tailcoat impressed themselves on the young editor's memory. He heard Fellows reminisce about Bunker Hill where he had fought, about his friend Thomas Paine (who hated to be called Tom), about his correspondence with Madison and Jefferson. This was living history, the best kind so far as Whitman was concerned.

William Cauldwell, a junior printer under Whitman on the *Aurora*, gives us some interesting glimpses of his editor at this time. Whitman usually wandered into the office around eleven or twelve, glanced over the excerpts or exchanges from other papers, and then set off down Broadway in the direction of the Battery. After an hour or two "amid the trees and enjoying the water view" he strolled off to his lodgings at Mrs. Chipman's for his lunch. He got down to work on the paper in earnest in the middle of the afternoon. He was on first-name terms with the printing staff and was particularly taken with Cauldwell. "Frequently, while I was engaged in sticking type, he would ask me to let him take my case for a little while, and he seemed to enjoy the recreation." Cauldwell mentioned in passing that there was friction between the editor and Herrick over interference in Whitman's hotheaded editorials.

In those days it was common for editors to jump like fleas from one paper to another, and in the early 1840s the profession had never been in a more jumpy state. By the end of April Whitman was no longer editor. Cauldwell mentions a violent quarrel that the editor had with his employers. "Write it yourself," Whitman is supposed to have said, before turning on his heels and walking out. Herrick and Ropes held to their story that they'd been forced to kick him out, citing his incorrigible laziness. As usual in the trade following a dispute, they "blackguarded" him in print. On May 3 they wrote satirically about someone supposedly still about the office that he was "so lazy that it takes two men to open his jaws when he speaks. If you kick him he's too idle to cry, for then he'd have to wipe his eyes. *What* can be done with him?" A fortnight later the *Aurora* carried an announcement: "Mr. Walter Whitman desires us to state that he has been for three or four weeks past, and now is, entirely disconnected with the editorial department."

Invective and abuse being the order of the day, Whitman wasted no time in hitting back at the "trashy, scurrilous and obscene daily" owned by two "ill-bred vagabonds." On his high horse, he explained how the two "dirty fellows" had engaged him, "a literary person," to make something of their miserable rag. Herrick and Ropes had the last word, ridiculing this "pretty pup" for his "indolence, incompetence and blackguard habits," as a result of which they were obliged to show him the door.

James Robinson Newall, another associate on the paper, recalled Whitman's affable and unassuming temperament. One day he arranged to stand in for Whitman so that the editor could disappear for a stroll on Long Island. Herrick got wind of this and called Whitman a lazy devil. Newhall couldn't agree. In his opinion Whitman was simply obeying an instinct "to indulge uninterruptedly in some train of thought, the fruit of which might soon appear in print." On the other hand, it might not. His bosses were out of patience, and in a matter of weeks Whitman began editing a small daily, *The Tattler*, at its offices in Anne Street, right opposite the premises of his first employer, the *New World*.

Whitman the public figure is visible enough throughout the 1840s, but his private thoughts are hardly ever available to us. It is as if he has inwardly disappeared. Here was an extraordinary man who managed to sound so ordinary, "so undistinguished from his colleagues that it is almost impossible to tell how many of the newspaper articles attributed to him he actually wrote." For all his gregariousness, there was a certain reserve, something aloof about him. He seemed able to make his person available without surrendering his real self. It was as if he followed the law of natural selection. There was no hurry. If nothing was happening to him on the personal level, that only meant it was not the time. What was odd to others was satisfactory for him. Like the poetry waiting in him, encounters waited somewhere outside him. Everything was all right, people felt, looking at him, though they were at a loss to say why. There was perhaps something physically reassuring about him.

When he came to write "Song of Myself" he had a new mask. He liked to tease people, intellectuals especially, with the paradox of himself. It is doubtful whether he knew, any more than the next man, how to solve the puzzle. What he did know was that while he lived in New York he *was* New York, the worst and the best.

> This is the city and I am one of the citizens,
> Whatever interests the rest interests me, politics, wars,
>     markets, newspapers, schools,
> The mayor and councils, banks, tariffs, steamships,
>     factories, stocks, stories, real estate and personal estate. . . .
>
> The little plentiful manikins skipping around in collars and tail'd
>     coats,
> I am aware who they are (they are positively not worms or fleas),
> I acknowledge the duplicates of myself, the weakest and shallowest
>     is deathless with me,
> What I do and say the same waits for them,
> Every thought that flounders in me the same flounders in them.

ONE PERSISTENTLY floundering thought circled around the enigma of death. In one of his earliest stories, "Tomb Blossoms," death and love and the soul are entwined as morbidly as anything in Poe. The conclusion though is pure Whitman. A "withered female" who lives in a workhouse visits the graveyard where her husband is buried, only to discover that no one could tell her which grave was his. The sexton "could only show two graves to the disconsolate woman, and tell her that her husband was positively one of the twain. . . . The miserable widow even attempted to obtain the consent of the proper functionaries that the graves might be opened and her anxieties put to rest. When told that this could not be done, she determined in her soul that at least the remnant of her hopes and intentions should not be given up." Every Sunday morning in the spring and summer she took flesh flowers and decorated the two graves. "So she knew that the right one was cared for, even if another shared that care."

The flowers and leaves gathered by the widow to lay on one grave or the other were "fresh, and wet, and very fragrant—those delicate soul-offerings. . . . White hairs and pale blossoms, and stone tablets of Death!" The old woman who longs for death "as a tired child for the night" is told by the author that the grave "is a kind friend. What foolish man calls it a dreadful place? . . . I do not dread the grave. There is many a time I could lay down and pass my immortal part through the valley of the shadow, as composedly as I quaff water after a tiresome walk."

Two graves, two ghosts. Whitman's work is a labyrinth fashioned right from the start from his two great obsessions, doubleness and death. In old age he tended to dismiss the validity of these youthful reflections. After all, he had embodied them in his elegies—and in a sense all his poems were elegies—without recourse to Poe's ghastly ghosts. One should get on with life when one is young, he told Horace Traubel. "I don't believe a young fellow can *think* death. . . . Thinking life is a condition of being alive." Instead of yielding to what he called black fancies, young people should, he thought, go on doing what they were required to do. "The rest will take care of itself." He repeated what he had so often said, that he was not afraid of death. "It all belongs to the same scheme."

D. H. Lawrence saw Whitman as a great poet of death, of disintegration as well as of resurrection. What were the poems in *Leaves of Grass*, he asked, but "really huge fat tomb-plants, great rank graveyard growths." Van Gogh, another connoisseur of graveyards, was a fellow Victorian whose paintings could be regarded in the same terms. A dark river of dissolution flows under all his work. Life, he said once, was "a constantly going from darkness to light." In nature he saw the evidence of dying and being born again which endlessly inspired him.

The essential message of "Song of Myself" is the reconciliation with death. Unless death can be made part of life, lived with and not feared, how can the exultant song of the open road be sung? He tackles the problem bravely, and with perfect naturalness, in the section which begins with a child's question: "What is the grass?"

> How could I answer the child? I do not know what it is any
> more than he.

> I guess it must be the flag of my disposition, out of hopeful

green stuff woven . . .
Or I guess the grass is itself a child, the produced babe of the
   vegetation.

And now it seems to me the beautiful uncut hair of graves.

Tenderly will I use you curling grass,
It may be you transpire from the breasts of young men,
It may be if I had known them I would have loved them,
I may be you are from old people, or from offspring taken
   soon out of their mothers' laps,
And here you are the mothers' laps.

This grass is very dark to be from the white heads of old
   mothers,
Darker than the colorless beards of old men,
Dark to come from under the faint red roofs of mouths.

Then come the unanswerable questions: "What do you think has
become of the young and old men? And what do you think has
become of the women and children?" The assertion of optimism that
follows—and in the homeliest of language—takes our breath away.
We have been mistaken—

They are alive and well somewhere,
The smallest sprout shows there is really no death,
And if ever there was it led forward life, and does not wait at
   the end to arrest it,
And ceas'd the moment life appear'd.

We are not to think of death as a goal, an end. It is a process. Van
Gogh, after stumbling on a clearing in a pine wood that was
overgrown with grass and heather and finding the wooden markers of
graves, inscribed with half-obliterated names, painted a picture
called *Peasant Cemetery*. He wrote to his brother to say how moved
he had been by this forgotten resting place, and by its utter
simplicity. He had tried to express in his painting the feeling he had
that death was "as simple as the falling of a leaf. . . . And now those
ruins tell me . . . how the life and death of the peasants also remain
forever the same, budding and withering regularly like the grass and
the flowers growing there in the graveyard."

If *Leaves of Grass* represents Whitman's lifelong effort to bring
about a reconciliation between death and life without the need of

dogma or clergy, in his huge, lumbering essay *Democratic Vistas* he admits that more has to be done. He calls to the future to bring forth something greater. Out of some nagging dissatisfaction he tried to say in garrulous prose what he had said time and again through the symbols and metaphors of his poems: "I feel and know that death is not the ending, as was thought, but rather the real beginning—and that nothing ever is or can be lost. . . ." He called for great poems of death which would surpass his own. "Then will man indeed confront Nature, and confront time and space . . . and take his right place. . . . And then that which was long wanted will be supplied, and the ship that had it not before in all her voyages, will have an anchor." It was a call that Lawrence, approaching death himself, would answer with his profound and beautiful poem "The Ship of Death."

❧ WHILE HE WAS still editor of the *Aurora* a news item he wrote reported the desecration by land-hungry developers of a burial ground at Delancey Street. His shame and anger were genuine even if his account was written for effect, the ghoulish details intended to thrill us with horror. A woman armed with a pistol stood guard over the threatened graves of her husband and children. An angry mob gathered. Along came the Hudson Fire Insurance Company, acting as if by divine right. Hired laborers started work "with spades and pick axes to dig down and pitch out the decayed relics of bodies buried there. Fleshless bones, and ghastly skeletons, and skulls with the hair still attached to them, and the brittle relics of young infants and the shrouded ashes of age, and forms of once beautiful maidens, now putrid in corruption . . . were struck in by the cold steel, and pitched to and fro." The anchors Whitman was to call for in *Democratic Vistas* were being grubbed up before his eyes as the city exploited every foot of land with its "pull-down-and-build-all-over-again spirit." Graveyards gave way to cemeteries. These latest dormitories for the dead had to be in suburbs, so as not to remind the living of something that was very different from its nonstop itching eagerness for change and expansion, and the rush and clang of its advance.

Whitman's new editorial position on the *Evening Tattler*, a paper sold at midday with the aim of scooping up sales not caught by the morning and evening dailies, gave him the chance to swap further punches with Herrick and Ropes, those "dirty fellows" so incapable of writing grammatically that they needed the help of someone literary like himself. During his few weeks with them, Whitman charged, "we" saw "more mean selfishness, more low deceits—more attempts at levying 'black mail'—heard more gross blasphemy and prurient conversation than ever before in our life." The *Aurora* of course dismissed this actionable stuff with contempt. Their ex-editor had plainly become vindictive, they said, because of their refusal to go on paying him for loafing about the office. And that was the end of that.

A few months later this second editor's job came to an end. Casting around for something else, he had a stroke of luck. Park Benjamin had hit on the idea of a temperance novel and for some reason he thought of Whitman. Temperance societies were flourishing in the increasingly moralistic atmosphere of Victorian America. England's temperance movement produced tracts that were attempts to curb the nation's drinking habits, and propaganda in the form of fiction, an altogether more palatable fare. *The Sons of Temperance*, with a membership of three hundred thousand, had just been founded in New York. Benjamin found himself staring at a potential money-spinner.

Later, when he would have dearly liked to disown *Franklin Evans, or the Inebriate*, "A Tale of the Times" by Walter Whitman, the embarrassed author put it about that he wrote the "damned rot" in three days flat, or twenty thousand words a day. He had rushed most of it off in the reading room of Tammany Hall, he said lamely, with "the help of a bottle of port or two." So it was a joke. In subsequent tellings the liquor varied, to include gin cocktails and whiskey. Drink of course was an occupational hazard for editors and journalists. Poe is a famous example. No one has reported seeing Whitman under the influence. As an indentured apprentice he would have had to sign the pledge, and behind him always was the taint of his unresponsive father's grim lapses, casting shadow on the mother and all her brood. During his debating days Walt argued passionately in favor of prohibition.

George Whitman remembered his brother playing down the book, uneasily laughing off any mention of it. Whitman's old-age recollections were altogether more relaxed. "It was not the business for me to be up to," he admitted. "I stopped right there. I never cut a chip of that kind of timber again."

It was lucrative timber for all that, and, as Gay Wilson Allen remarks, the only writing of his ever to reach a mass audience. He must have realized the irony later. He had been a people's writer of sorts with this torrent of "rot of the worst kind—not insincere perhaps, but rot nevertheless."

There is a comic anecdote to go with this. One evening in 1888 Horace Traubel had quite a shock when his abstemious old friend and mentor, survivor of numerous strokes and more often in bed than out of it, suggested they open a bottle of homemade wine that one of his well-wishers had left. Walt had his contrary moods, hated to be taken for granted, and liked to turn the tables on those who "catechized" him. When the devil was in him he enjoyed acting out of character. The faithful Horace was further dumbfounded when Walt dived into his capacious pocket and came up with a corkscrew. His self-appointed Boswell went home that night and recorded the following exchange:

WW: Open it, Horace.
HT (laughing): Do you carry the corkscrew about with you, Walt?
WW: Yes.
HARNED, a friend: That's bad, Walt—they'll throw you out of the temperance society.
WW: They can't—I was never in.
HT: But didn't you write a temperance novel once?
WW: Yes, so I did—for seventy-five dollars cash down. And by the way, seventy-five wasn't the end of it, for the book sold so well they sent me fifty dollars more in three weeks.

He wasn't romancing. Benjamin issued the novel as an Extra on November 23 at twelve and a half cents per copy, or ten for a dollar. He cleared the edition fairly smartly and probably reprinted, for he still had the title on sale the following August.

Whitman's boost for the novel, when he reviewed it anonymously in the *New York Sun*, would be a habit in years to come, as he attempted to push *Leaves of Grass* in its various editions on a reluctant public. Four years after the launch of *Franklin Evans*, when he was editing the *Brooklyn Eagle*, he serialized his novel under a pseudonym, "J. R. S.," renamed it "The Fortunes of a Country Boy," and boosted it on its way with moralistic zeal. In his preface to the Park Benjamin edition, aware that many readers saw fiction as frivolous, he sought to give the impression that what he had to tell was in reality a true story: "I narrate occurrences that may have had a far more substantial existence than in my fancy." But introducing the same book to his Brooklyn audience he told them grandly, in his straight-from-the-shoulder style, "We consider temperance one of the great regenerators of the age; and all who, in truth of heart, labor in its promulgation, deserve well of heaven and men."

The novel begins autobiographically, then turns progressively more and more farfetched in the melodramatic fashion of the time. The eponymous hero, a poor country boy from Long Island, friendless and innocent and a mama's boy, leaves home in a country-market wagon and stage bearing a marked resemblance to the one owned by Van Velsor. Arriving virtually penniless in the "wicked and deceitful" city, he lives in an attic and is soon being led astray by bad company. Saloons and brothels ensnare him and are soon his downfall. A drunkard, he marries a "good woman," then not only breaks her heart but is the cause of her death.

He wanders off in the direction of Virginia, falls for a Creole slave woman—whose owner inexplicably sets her free—and drunkenly marries her. Sober, he is filled with murderous hate for her. As the story departs still further from reality and from the author's meager experience of women in the real world, episodes are interspersed with dreams and the maudlin narrative bolstered with material filched from unused short stories. Evans is seduced by a blonde widow, thereby unleashing yet more destructive forces. The widow dies, the wife dies, and Evans's sorry tale ends with his drift back North, hitting the bottle again and saving a child from drowning—to be rehabilitated by temperance and a large sum of money, the Victorian reward for a return to virtue and bodiless love.

# 5

# Reunion in Brooklyn

Whitman as a young man had established himself in New York at a time when its culture was becoming polarized. A patrician elite which held to European patterns of culture had not produced its expected crop of *philosophes*, falling short of the dreams of men like John Pintard and De Witt Clinton, who saw after 1830 a split in the intellectual life of the city. The New York diarist George Templeton Strong, a man acutely aware of the growing threat of urban poverty, wondered whether it was right and proper for his class to indulge in cultural pursuits while thousands of his fellow New Yorkers were fighting for a crust.

There were those who held, for instance, that literature and politics must be kept apart, with learning and culture firmly based on the classics. In the opposite camp there was now a very different group, mainly artisans and mechanics, who wanted to use elite learning in the service of a working-class self-awareness which saw knowledge as inseparable from the city's work. For the founders of the Mechanics Institutes learning was a means of self-improvement. It ought to be possible, they thought, to acquire knowledge while continuing as mechanics and tradesmen. Culture, these founders maintained, should create a community for its members. "Common interests, and similar vocations, create ties and attachments that are interwoven with the strongest ties of the heart," said Thomas Mercian in his address on opening the Apprentices Library. Annual courses of popular lectures were set up. If these were only for the benefit of members, we can be sure that Whitman attended similar ones around the city that were open to anyone.

This shift in the direction of a democratic intellect deeply influenced Whitman, even though he belonged to no group and was to a large extent unaware of the changes taking place in the structure of intellectual life, as fears, concerns, and disappointments were translated into new aspirations. If he was more directly involved with the literary confederacy that styled itself the "Young America" movement than any other, it was a matter for him of a kind of symbiosis, sucking in those theories that appealed to him instinctively as his poetics unconsciously developed. He was too green, too much the newcomer, and socially too much the outsider ever to be intimately connected with any confederacy of well-heeled writers and critics.

Evert Duyckinck, who had his own magazine, *Arcturus*, played host to his fellow intellectuals at a town house in Clinton Place, in a library stuffed with his seventeen thousand books. If Whitman had ever gone to one of those evenings he may have met Herman Melville, but the slow-moving, large-bodied arriviste, a whiff of printer's ink about him, was not invited. He had no credentials, and he would stay that way. Writing his stories and trying to place them under the name Walter Whitman, if he submitted anything to *Arcturus* he got nowhere. He would have been put off in any case by its rarified air. Still encouraged by his success in getting into the *Democratic Review*, he sent off a manuscript entitled "The Angel of Tears" to a miscellany in Boston, naming his price, eight dollars. The editor declined politely.

*Arcturus* was a monthly. It did have a certain radiance. Aiming to represent the city as a whole, its politics, society, culture, it did so rather thinly. Reading it in the two years of its life Whitman might have been struck by the sentiments of Cornelius Mathews, one of its associate editors, who believed the American writer should direct his attention not just to nature but to "the crowded life of cities, the customs, habitudes and actions of men dwelling in contact, or falling off into peculiar and individual modes of conduct, amalgamated together into a close but motley society, with religions, trades, politics, professions and pursuits, shooting athwart the whole live mass, and forming a web infinitely diversified."

One would not have expected the literary culture of the legal gentry to have been upset by something so diffuse and precious as *Arcturus*, but one lawyer certainly was. Sent a complimentary copy,

George Templeton Strong poured vehement objections into his diary. The magazine's contents were unreal, he thought, and bound to degenerate into "puppyism and pedantry." He saw the whole thing as an example of art for art's sake. "Where such a litterateur is feeble himself," he confided, "and is dealing with and laboriously commenting on and striving to magnify the writings of people like himself, his productions are apt to be among the most pitiful specimens of human infatuation that are to be found anywhere. And Mr. Duyckinck and Mr. Mathews, criticizing and comparing and weighing with the nicest accuracy the relative merits and demerits of the small fry of authors, foreign and domestic, exhibit and illustrate in their own person the ridiculous side of humanity and with painful force and clearness."

At the opposite pole to the Young America group of free intellectuals, open—in theory at least—to men and women of every background, was Lewis Gaylord Clark's *Knickerbocker Magazine*, a journal that was more like a club for gentlemen, thriving on literary gossip and the necessity of cash as a qualification for membership. Whitman could have been referring to it when he said later, "Do you call those genteel little creatures American poets?"

Setting themselves up as a response to this urbane wit, conservatism, and emphasis on style, the writers clustered around the flag of Young America saw themselves as radical Democrats as well as democrats devoted to a new American literature. The *Democratic Review* got its backing at the outset from Democratic party money, through its ties with Van Buren and Attorney General Benjamin Butler. Its first subscriber was Andrew Jackson. When the editor John O'Sullivan's mother was awarded twenty thousand dollars by the government in compensation for the false prosecution of her husband for piracy, the review really took off, first of all in Washington. In 1840 it moved to New York. Far more vigorous and realistic than *Arcturus*, its political flavor, says the historian Thomas Bender, made the city's Whig culture sit up and take notice, retaliating with a conservative version a few years later.

It was O'Sullivan's literary circle of Young Americans that first gave the spur to Whitman's vague literary aspirations. Young progressives were excited by his periodical. Perry Miller still found it stimulating when he turned its pages a hundred years later.

O'Sullivan was a literary patriot, an Irish romantic whose expansive schemes were liable to founder even as he seduced others with their practicality. Shooting into prominence and sputtering briefly in the New York firmament, he lost control of the magazine in 1846 and disappeared in pursuit of various projects which invariably ended in disaster. His father before him was a wanderer, something of a freebooter, holding minor consular appointments, at one stage under suspicion for piracy. John, just as extraordinary a character, was actually born on the high seas during the War of 1812. Surfacing in Europe at the time of the Civil War, he dismayed his former friends, all of them—like Whitman—Free Soil Democrats and then Republicans, by coming out in support of slavery and the cause of the South.

Thomas Bender repeats the story of O'Sullivan popping up again in 1886 to speak in French at the dedication of the Statue of Liberty, though no mention of him appeared in the newspapers. Lapsing into total obscurity again, he died a year after Whitman in a small hotel on East Eleventh Street, leaving neither will nor estate. The old poet, retired in Camden, remembered the magazine but was hazy about its editor. "Sullivan I think was his name...a handsome, generous fellow." A young girl named Julia Howe who saw him as a guest at her father's house thought him tremendously romantic, and when she met W. B. Yeats in *her* old age it was O'Sullivan who rose in her memory.

Behind the figure of this larger-than-life political intellectual and the program he and his colleagues on the *Democratic Review* adopted was William Leggett, a man whose ideology had already influenced the equal-rights wing of the New York Democrats. Both Whitman and his father were ardent admirers, as they were of Fanny Wright. Walt would adhere to Leggett's assertion that "if we analyze the nature and essence of free government we shall find that they are more or less free in proportion to the absence of monopolies" for as long as he was involved in politics. As a man Leggett inspired great affection and was esteemed even by those who disagreed with his political writings. Whitman saw him as someone as fundamental to democracy as Jefferson. Leggett joined William Cullen Bryant's *Evening Post* and published a number of his seminal essays there before Bryant was obliged to get rid of him to placate his subscribers. After leaving the *Post* he set up his own magazine, the *Plaindealer*, but it failed for financial reasons, like his earlier review *The Critic*. Out of funds and ill, he died in 1839.

The *Democratic Review* believed with Leggett that democracy would redistribute wealth, giving leisure to the masses and stimulating their desire for "elevated and refined enjoyment." Eventually a democratic literature would evolve, for "the Spirit of Literature and the Spirit of Democracy are one." The magazine, which saw itself as an instrument of cultural and social change, expressed the kinds of views that we find incorporated in poetic form in *Leaves of Grass*. Only the alchemy that would transmute them was missing. True intelligence, the *Democratic Review* writers insisted, was not the monopoly of a learned class but was to be found throughout the masses, an intelligence manifesting itself best in "action," which was nothing less than "God acting through the People." This was why intellectuals should not isolate themselves but become acquainted with the masses. They had no ordained right to a privileged position in society. The uneducated, seeking the "services of educated individuals," should not necessarily put their trust in them. Before even starting his magazine O'Sullivan, the journalist in Washington, had dreamed of finding a way to "strike the hitherto silent string of the democratic genius of the country."

At its finest, in 1843, the *Democratic Review* published stories by Hawthorne, Horatio Greenough's essays on American art and architecture, contributions by Brownson, Whittier, and Park Godwin, and a translation of Balzac. An essay by a New York critic, William Alfred Jones, "Poetry for the People," issued challenges that the as yet unborn "Walt Whitman" would one day meet. Calling for a "Homer of this Mass" Jones saw poetry as the medium for these "master passions of the age." A "world-renowned" American bard would sing "the necessity and dignity of labor" and the "native nobility of an honest and brave heart," oppose the accepted "distinctions of rank and wealth," and stand up for the "brotherhood and equality of man."

O'Sullivan's creed of democracy as a vital principle of literature was more than Emerson could swallow, sympathetic though he was to radical movements. Corresponding with the highly intelligent Margaret Fuller—to the susceptible Whitman another goddess like Frances Wright—Emerson objected to O'Sullivan because of his "politico-literary" slant. The interdependence of literature and politics was to him something to be regarded with suspicion. O'Sullivan, he thought, saw "Washington" in everything.

WHITMAN, LONG BEFORE he saw himself as the one destined to be his country's first democratic poet, was reading and hearing calls for a messianic figure. The spacious art necessary for dealing with the vast subjects of Oregon and Texas, not to mention the reeling new cities, was nowhere in sight if frequently predicted. Even in the *Knickerbocker* in 1836 a piece called "Prospects of American Poetry" outlined the unknown poet's credo. "The poet who would be the literary redeemer of the land must not only dissever himself from the base associations of the day, but he must kindle new altars, at which his innermost soul may worship." Whitman was nearly twenty years away from his new altars, and when he came to kindle them he would make over those base associations for his own purposes. Otherwise how could his "innermost soul" rest easy? He would also include the "superb music" of workingmen's voices, which the *Knickerbocker* would never have allowed over its threshold. On his rambles through the streets in the direction of the East River it was a kind of spice to him to hear "the voices of the native-born and -bred workman and apprentices in the sparyards, on piers, caulkers on the ship scaffolds, workmen in iron, mechanics to or from their shops, drivers calling to their horses." After all, these were his own kind. Only a few years before he had taken to dressing for the part of editor and man about town, he had been one of them himself, as farm boy, printer's apprentice. As a child he had gone racing down Fulton Street to the waterfront and made friends with anyone who would pause from his hammering and sawing and casting off to pass the time of day with him. He was bound to scoop them up one day into a poem which was at once an elegy and an epic of labor. What Paul Zweig calls "happy work" was a nineteenth-century dream, cropping up in Victorian writing and art everywhere, in Van Gogh and Marx, in the cooperative ideals of Charles Fourier and Albert Brisbane, in William Morris and the Pre-Raphaelites.

Later, Whitman met Brisbane. Though he was never won over by the ardent Fourierist, he must certainly have read his *Social Destiny of Man*, which contained passages like this:

> Far away in the distant future I saw a globe resplendently cultivated and embellished, transformed into the grandest and most beautiful work of art by the combined influence, generation after generation, of true social institutions; a humanity worthy of that Cosmic Soul of which I instinctively felt it to be a part. I saw this

resplendent humanity as a child of God, a god itself upon its planet; and the old intuition which had led me to combat the cold atheism of my father was now becoming clearer.

In the first two weeks of March 1842 Emerson came to deliver a series of six lectures at the New York Society Library on Broadway. Under the heading "The Times" he announced an era of self-fulfillment to match and redeem the material prosperity. On March 5 his lecture on "The Poet" was reported in print by Whitman as "one of the richest and most beautiful compositions, both for its matter and style, we have heard anywhere, at any time."

He would come to regard Emerson later as too coldly detached for his liking, but at the time of his lectures he was his ideal philosopher, a living man of obvious force and beauty. He gazed admiringly at this elegant personage standing behind his lecturer's desk. The transcendental New Englander, tall and slender, mesmerized the young autodidact listening reverently in the fashionable audience. He was so bright, so "cute." Whitman heard again the call for an indigenous literary genius who would make these shining predictions come true. In Emerson's imagination he had already arrived but had yet to declare himself. "He is in the forest walks, in paths carpeted with leaves of the chestnut, oak and pine; he sits on the mosses of the mountains, he listens to the echoes of the woods; he paddles his canoe in the rivers and ponds. He visits without fear the factory, the railroad, and the wharf." Without fear? Visits? Here was a measure of the limits placed on him by his patrician circle, his New England reserve, and by his own nature. He pictured the long-awaited genius as having "nerve and dagger," able to strike poetry from "our incomparable materials," from its huge geography and staggering diversity, but never dreamed that such a figure would emerge from the people and do with the raw materials of experience what no poetry had done before.

Whitman in those days was as abstract in his sympathy and excitement as Emerson himself. He felt at one with Emerson's conviction that such a person would appear, for to doubt it "is to doubt the day and night," but going off in the crowd and making his way back to his lodgings with "Mrs. R. in Spring Street" he was more than likely unable to quite grasp the implication of Emerson's question: "Is Poetry possible in the present time?" Wasn't he writing it himself, along with Whittier, Bryant, Longfellow, and scores of lesser writers? But certain parts of Emerson's oration would have gone on resonating in him; sentences like "When he lifts his great voice, men gather to him and forget all that is past, and then his words are to the hearers, pictures of all history; and immediately the tools of their bench, and the riches of their useful arts, and the laws they live under, seem to them weapons of romance."

Weapons of romance! Emerson had already begun to speak of America as a poem. In Whitman's 1855 preface to *Leaves of Grass* he would call the United States not only a poem but the greatest poem. Paul Zweig sums up the era with fine concision. "Jacksonian rhetoric," he says, "had turned America into a Romantic idea: a secular heaven in which social justice, the healing powers of nature, and the fellowship of men appeared to be changing the conditions of history."

If the rhetoric was Jacksonian, the vision was Jefferson's. The reality could hardly have been more different. Prophets and social critics such as Carlyle and Ruskin and Dickens had been drawing attention to the wretched conditions of the poor in England for years. Wage slavery and the division of labor debased the lives of factory workers. As foreign-speaking immigrants flooded into America and large cities became ever larger, the English pattern of degradation was being repeated. Prosperous superstructures were rising on the backs of armies of low-paid workers. Sectional conflicts exploded daily and threatened to rip apart the social fabric.

After listening to Emerson on that March evening, Whitman stepped out of the lights and urbane clutter of the lecture hall into a New York bristling with danger, stoked with violence. Frontier life had always been synonymous with brutality, but in the city streets a sinister new breed was being spawned, christened "roughs." These ugly specimens were soon recruited for use by corrupt politicians. Isaiah Rynders, a Tammany boss, formed them into gangs of hoodlums and used them to manipulate voters in his notorious Sixth Ward. If they weren't stuffing ballot boxes they would be mugging passersby who had strayed into the territory of the Five Points gangsters. By organizing these gangs adroitly, Rynders, previously a gambler and knife-fighter in the South, created a powerful domain for himself based on Tammany Hall. Other men beside Rynders had seen how the underworld could be exploited politically. A system of favors and rewards got under way.

A sharkish, near criminal transgressor, blatantly on the make, "with dimes on the eyes walking," was gaining ground among the business and civic boosters at the top. Shoving the weak aside was normal. Faces intent on the manipulation of stock could be as degenerate and ugly as those seen among the whores and petty thieves of the Bowery. They flare up in their spotlighted nastiness when Whitman comes to trawl the city for his all-inclusive, Hegelian poem.

> This now is too lamentable a face for a man,
> Some abject louse asking leave to be, cringing for it,
> Some milk-nosed maggot blessing what lets it wrig to its hole.

> This face is a dog's snout sniffing for garbage,
> Snakes nest in that mouth, I hear the sibilant threat.

> This face is a haze more chill than the arctic sea,
> Its sleepy and wabbling icebergs crunch as they go.

On his visits to America Dickens affected disgust at the sight of men chewing tobacco and spattering it on floors around spittoons. Bully boys in the slums fought each other with a ferocity born of deep rage and misery. The folklore of the frontier abounded in tales of horrific battles of strength, and now the urban myths were proliferating. One of them featured Mose, a Bowery Boys leader who expanded in legend to a fearsome giant of eight feet with gorilla-like arms and great hands dangling below his knees. He fought his fights armed with anything from an iron lamppost to a butcher's cleaver. If caught unawares he would get hold of a tree with his ten men's strength and tear it out of the ground, smashing skulls right and left with this huge club.

🎋 OUR ONLY CLUES to Whitman's inwardness in a period that was so turbulent and tangled, when outwardly he seemed so gregarious and back-slapping and fast-living, lie in the stories he wrote and published then. Some of them were in fact already written although unpublished, thrown into his bag when he packed his few belongings and set off for the Fulton Street ferry and his first real baptism in the city across the river. We want to know how it was with him in his spells of quiet, when he was in a torpor sometimes, sitting apart or lying awake at night in the loneliness of a rented room. Did he ever long to go back? Were there pangs of yearning for his old irresponsible life and the warm safety of home, for a loved figure quietly placing the dishes on the supper table? One of his innumerable landladies may have spoken to him one day in a motherly fashion, or been wearing something that reminded him of his mother. What was happening inside him, in the undeclared, unshared part of him?

He loved his mother because she could touch and enlighten him without words, by her feelings alone. He distrusted and feared and at times hated his father because he seemed hard and unresponsive and lacked tenderness. Sometimes his father appeared to favor Walt's elder brother. At others he sank away into miseries of drunkenness, with terrible silences and mad outbursts, nursing God knows what grievances, living in a place where no one could reach him. But Walt saw that his mother pitied and loved the man. He, the watching and flinching son, would be torn between love for one and rejection of the other, with a secret dream he hugged of a time to come when he would console his mother and care for her, taking charge of everything like a man, the man his father was ceasing, in his invalidism, to be. In the midst of family usages which comforted, like the familiar furniture, the old routines, he was growing less sure, more disillusioned with himself and with everybody. Sometimes, in a quandary, he chafed against all restrictions, unsure of what was real and what was unreal, in "the doubts of the daytime and the doubts of nighttime." What did the street mean, the façades of houses, goods in the windows—were they just composed of "flashes and specks," and the people too? Was there anything he could call real outside his skin, beyond reach of his touch?

Often in his stories there is a hero-victim who shamefully or vengefully seeks the death or downfall of his father, or is frustrated in his destiny by a harsh, uncomprehending father, sometimes drunk and given to violent rages. Murderous scenes lead to false, treacly conclusions. Imitating the manner of such masters as Hawthorne and Scott and Poe, drawn especially to Poe's "dark nights, horrors, spectralities," and his obsession with burial, Whitman was a child of his age. The theme of descent into a darkness, there to find salvation or be destroyed horribly, cropped up in endless variations in contemporary fiction. Loss, the eating away of relationships, and the menace of growing into adulthood occur repeatedly in his tales. There is much ignominy and humiliation. Sons are ripped from the sides of parents. Nightmares light up the failure and incapacity of a youth or young man to do what is right, to be true to himself. They bemoan a cruel fate: "I have been wronged. . . . I am oppressed. . . . I hate him that oppresses me; I will either destroy him, or he shall release me."

In one story, confused by gestures that offend others and make him a wronged person, "the scholar kisses the teacher and the teacher kisses the scholar." The youth's greatest terror is to be cut off from home, sick in spirit and slipping nearer to the grave. In "Wild Frank's Return" the vital umbilical cord is a piece of rope tethering Frank to his horse, significantly a mare, "an image of beautiful terror" stampeded by a storm which shakes the world to its foundations. Black Nell drags the corpse of Frank to the door of the forsaken home. There it is, the cord, "dabbled over with gore." The mother sinks into her deathly swoon.

On the face of it Whitman had adjusted well to the brassy aspects of city life, its squalor and ruthlessness and Jacksonian drive. Yet these stories reveal another Whitman. He was having to struggle inside a manly exterior which convinced others but not himself. There was a theatricality about his actions. His maturity was not what it seemed. He had too much solitude. With no intimate friends he found himself alone with his fears. What was he, after all—what did he amount to?

It is possible to see his urge to write family romances in terms of escape and reunion. Rooted in his mother and in his brothers and sisters, the desire to be reunited with them must have been at times irresistible. As a fiction writer he was led stumbling down dark paths into bleak, frightening regions of the mind. The "happy son" others depended on fell into helplessness, vacillating and passive. He regained his mother, but more often it was the black grudging father who loomed over him, threatening him in his imagination as he had never done in reality. These meetings came accompanied by hideous deaths, sickly dreams, boys on the run. Stories betrayed his dread of what was lying in wait within himself. If he hoped for answers, he was let down. "Wherefore is there no response?" he asks of the darkness in "Eris: A Spirit Record." The passion in that tale is, as always, "unreturned and shallow." The sexuality budding in him fell back in a cold fear before women who were so unlike the only females he had known, his pure mother with her wholesome odor, his simple grandmother, his sisters.

It took till 1855, when the sluice gates opened and the first untrammeled poems poured out, for him to gain a mastery over the confused tumult of his emotions. He could now clarify them as never before. The laboring vocabulary and stilted phrasing fell away as his creative self thawed and flowed. From being at the mercy of his guilty feelings, the lustful scenes of adolescence which tormented his mind and forced him underground, he could now, wonder of wonders, plunge zestfully into the dread night itself and come up with prizes. Form became content and content form.

In his great poem in praise of the night, "The Sleepers," he speaks as someone who has been taught a profound lesson. The language hardly seems written, or as something to be read. It wells out, simple as speech. It is the thing itself. He is in a savage and beautiful country, and its ramifications fill him with awe. All his inner riches, he now sees, come from the very darkness he had feared for so long:

> Why should I be afraid to trust myself to you?
> I am not afraid . . . I have been well brought forward by you;
> I love the rich running day, but I do not desert her in whom I
>     lay so long. . . .

He has made a great discovery and is in raptures, from being in the deepest, most dangerous of waters without coming to any harm. On the contrary he is released from everything which has impeded him till this moment. Feeling enormous gratitude to this resplendent night mother—after all, he owes the very kernel of his soul-self to her—he pledges himself to her in his final lines.

> I will duly pass the day O my mother and duly return to you;
> Not you will yield forth the dawn again more surely than you
>     will yield forth me again,
> Not the womb yields the babe in its time more surely than I
>     shall be yielded from you in my time.

But before this he immerses himself and us in his old terrors and sweats, in his new role of the poet as healer. The medicine night soothes away all conflict. Paul Zweig in an inspired phrase calls the poem a dark twin of "Song of Myself." What had been until now a vile phantasmagoria is now something to be enfolded, as the night "pervades and enfolds" the sleepers. The images of sick introspection are paraded one by one, without revulsion but in their true poisonous horror,

The wretched features of ennuyees, the white features of
corpses, the livid faces of drunkards, the sick-gray faces of
onanists,
The gashed bodies on battlefields, the insane in their
strong-doored rooms, the sacred idiots,
The newborn emerging from gates and the dying emerging
from gates . . .

and the newborn onlooker and guide is humbled but not diminished.

Beginning gravely, the extraordinary processional speeds up. It turns into a wild dance and whirls us about. The wavering young man uncertain of his identity has been overtaken by this astonishingly sure being who rejoices in his power to identify with every object and person, as he did with perfect naturalness as a child. Now though, he becomes clairvoyant, a kind of shaman. "Genius," writes Baudelaire, "is childhood recaptured at will." Whitman's short story obsession with sepulture recurs now, but his whole attitude toward death has significantly changed. Intimacy with the night has made him spiritually healthy. He is even able to imagine his own body without fear as it is wrapped in a shroud and laid in the coffin. Soothing and calm, he speaks to us from the other side.

It is dark here underground . . . it is not evil or pain here, . . . it is
blank here, for reasons.

This delighted voice, confessing every weakness and yet growing stronger by the line, convinced that everything is as it should be, will either give us reasons in due time or admit to the absence of reasons—"it is blank here." Either way, the voice keeps insisting, it is glorious, perfect.

At one point, in the dark privacy of the night, the poet confides his young man's hidden shames to us with total candor:

O hotcheeked and blushing! O foolish hectic!
O for pity's sake, no one must see me now! . . . my clothes were
stolen while I was abed,
Now I am thrust forth, where shall I run?

Even here it is an entranced voice. Peacefully setting forth his gospel of peace and night, imbued with "measureless love," it pays a final tribute to the darkness from which all comes, in which all is possible. Not only the night itself and its chemistry but everything asleep in it is necessarily beautiful, it declares, whether human or animal, vegetable or mineral. "The wildest and bloodiest is over."

In a very real sense it is true. The Civil War and its ghastly slaughter lies ahead, but the internecine strife within him has been put to rest. Although nothing is ever finally ended, the music of germination, of unstoppable new growth, will hold sway over his soul from now on.


FOR THE NEXT two or three years we lose track of Whitman's journalistic activities. We pick up the trail again when he crosses back to Brooklyn. All the facts can tell us are that he shifted restlessly—or unavoidably—from one paper to another. He was on the *Sun*, the *Democratic Statesman*, and the *New York Democrat* in fairly rapid succession. Just as frequently he changed addresses. His notebook reports only that in "Spring of 1843 boarded at Mrs. Bonnard's in John Street—also at Mrs. Edgarton's in Vesey. Summer of '43 at Mary's and at Brown's in Duane St. October 1843 commenced with Winants."

What is clear is that he chose to stay close to the Printing House Square district of the city, no doubt because he was freelancing between editorial jobs. New magazines starting up provided additional outlets for stories. Publishing fiction helped to eke out a precarious living. "Eris: A Spirit Record" saw the light in the March issue of the *Columbian Magazine*. He lodged another one with them and they printed it in May. "Dumb Kate" was a tearjerker about a lovely deaf girl who died brokenhearted after being deceived by a callous boy. "The Little Sleighers" was nothing more than a rosy impression of children playing on the frozen waters of the Battery, with a moral tag for a conclusion.

Dropping in at Tammany Hall from time to time kept him in contact with the Democratic editors and politicians who gave him papers to edit. For all his nonchalance there are signs that he was losing faith in his ability to conjure appointments out of thin air. With Isaiah Rynders and his ilk in the ascendancy, his prospects were unsure. Suddenly he struck lucky again. The editor's chair at the *Democrat* fell vacant and he moved in. He set about campaigning vigorously to secure the nomination of Silas Wright for governor. Wright was a respected and loved liberal Democrat, hated by the conservative "Hunker" wing. The party, split by new schisms on a number of issues including slavery, was just as divided on local policies. The "Old Hunkers" wanted their man, Governor William Bouck, reinstated, but even they doubted whether they could win the election with him. Why the nomination of Wright—though he was reluctant to leave the Senate—and his success in strengthening the national ticket and helping James Polk to victory should have led to Whitman losing his job remains a mystery. But he was a known enemy of the Old Hunker politicians, labeled by them a Barnburner after the radical faction he favored. He would tangle with them more damagingly when he got back to Brooklyn.

A free agent again, he wrote as a penny-a-liner for the *New-York Mirror*, filling in for someone temporarily absent. He seems to have been too busy in the next few months to write fiction for the magazines. Thomas Dunn English, a newcomer on the scene, founded a magazine of reviews, politics, and light literature called the *Aristidean*, and in the spring of 1845 Whitman published two stories there. In May he had a story taken by the *American Review*, a Whig journal started to counter the influence of O'Sullivan's *Democratic Review*. Then in the summer, after a gap of two years, a long story by Whitman appeared in the *Democratic Review*. Called "Revenge and Requital," it was at once a temperance tract and yet another variation on the theme familiar to his readers: it tells of a young man cruelly treated. The hero, driven beyond endurance by an abusive guardian who insults both himself and his sister, kills their persecutor in a drunken rage.

Thomas Dunn English's career as a magazine editor was a short one: the *Aristidean* lasted only a dozen issues. In that time he managed to clash with Poe but was no match for the disdainful Southerner. When the magazine collapsed, Poe remarked witheringly that its editor had sufficient talent as a man of letters "to succeed in his father's profession—that of a ferryman on the Schuylkill."

At the end of the year Whitman submitted an essay entitled "Art-Music and Heart-Music" to Poe's *Broadway Journal*. Poe was no ordinary journalist. Meeting him for the first and only time when he went to collect his fee, Whitman was curiously taken by a man so completely different from himself. By then Whitman was back in Brooklyn. The twenty-six-year-old journalist who wrote fiction and poetry in his spare time came face to face with an author famous for "The Raven," a poem which had begun to obscure everything else

Poe had written. Whitman knew he would be meeting a poet who was highly strung, etiolated, haunted, by no stretch of the imagination the American Adam called up in Emerson's lecture on "The Poet." Yet here was an undeniable influence, one he did his best to play down. Nearly all the fiction he had published in the past four years was crudely derived from Poe, Hawthorne, and the Gothic novel. "'The Raven,'" Whitman was to say later, "did not enthuse me.... Poe was morbid, shadowy, lugubrious.... I could not originally stomach him at all."

Meeting him in the *Broadway Journal* office in Nassau Street, however, he was won over at once by Poe in the flesh, shaking hands with a quiet, cordial man who may or may not have been sober. Always swayed by courtesy and kindness, Whitman was charmed. "I have a distinct and pleasing remembrance of his looks, voice, manner and matter; very kindly and human, but subdued, perhaps a little jaded." Asked about him over forty years later by Traubel, he remembered Poe as "dark, quiet, handsome—Southern from top to toe. Languid, tired out, it's true, but altogether ingratiating," adding that he was "curiously a victim of history—like Paine."

Like them an easy target for critics and scandalmongers, Whitman was bound to have been aware by then that he ran the risk of a martyrdom as terrible as Poe's. So it is no surprise to find him turning up to pay his respects at the reburial of Poe's remains in Baltimore in 1875—the only writer of note to do so. Poe was in disgrace—like Paine before him. Whitman said informally to a reporter that though he had always "until lately" had a distaste for Poe's writings, wanting for poetry "the clear sun shining, and fresh air blowing—the strength and power of health, not of delirium," he had nevertheless come to appreciate Poe's place in literary history.

Editing the *Brooklyn Eagle* in 1846 he went to press with a poignant news item: "It is stated that Mr. Poe, the poet and author, now lies dangerously ill with brain fever, and that his wife is in the last stages of consumption. They are said to be without money and without friends, actually suffering from disease and destitution in New York."

Whitman, always conscious of health, had of course heard the rumors circulating about Poe. One would have expected him to have had more antipathy than he did for a man widely regarded as decadent, addicted to drugs and alcohol. But Whitman was deceptive, his temperament often baffling. He could be spellbound by a voice, by personal "magnetism," even by touches of luxury. Poe of course was painfully poor. All the same he gave an impression of fastidious elegance. His pale intellectual's face had a certain delicacy, with its clever, small mouth. He dressed always in black and was excessively neat. The voices of journalists were invariably brash and loud, whereas his was pitched low, hinting at disdain. Whitman would certainly have been taken by the man's evident intense seriousness. What to others was a job of work was to Poe a mission.

He had little time for the literary standards of his day. "It cannot be gainsaid that the greatest number of those who hold high places in our poetical literature are absolute nincompoops," he said contemptuously. His uncompromising views made deadly enemies, and so did his irony, which ran corrosively under everything he said and did. Poe wanted to see standards raised to the level of the best English journals yet looked forward to a literature that would be American, distinct from that written in England. Characteristic of him was his demand for a tone that was Southern, an aristocratic, romantic style. Though he had nothing but loathing for the democratic tastes of the New York writers gathered around O'Sullivan, in his own way he was just as fervent a patriot. "Our necessities have been mistaken for our propensities," he wrote sardonically. "Having been forced to make railroads, it has been deemed impossible that we should make verse." Strikingly original, he speculated in *Marginalia* on the throwing up of hypnagogic images from the unconscious when on the brink of sleep, calling these soul stirrings "a class of fancies, of exquisite delicacy, which are *not* thoughts. . . ."

D. H. Lawrence, faced with this kind of clinical analysis by Poe of his own processes, saw him as a scientist rather than an artist, "reducing his own self as a scientist reduces salt in a crucible." The double rhythm of true art, of creation as well as destruction, was, he thought, missing in Poe. In a brilliant essay he went on: "Moralists have always wondered why Poe's 'morbid' tales need have been written. They need to be written because old things need to die and disintegrate. . . . Poe had a pretty bitter doom. Doomed to seethe down his soul in a great continuous convulsion of disintegration, and doomed to register the process. And then doomed to be abused for it, when he had performed some of the bitterest tasks of human experience that can be asked of a man."

For all that, he saw Poe as obscene. We know the writers who affected Lawrence most profoundly by the ferocity of his attacks on them: Dostoevsky, Blake, Poe. All of them were what he called "obscene knowers." Whitman too was deeply ambivalent, recoiling instinctively in his nervous health from Poe but disturbed and fascinated in spite of himself by the craving for ecstasy which he recognized in his own being.

Eventually he delivered his own verdict on Poe, in his ragbag collection of jottings "all bundled up and tied by a big string" which he entitled *Specimen Days*. Deploring "the inevitable tendency of poetic culture to morbidity, abnormal beauty—the sickliness of all technical thought or refinement in itself—the abnegation of the perennial and democratic concretes at first hand, the body, the earth and sea, sex and the like—and the substitution of something for them at second or third hand," he held Poe up as a particular case. "Poe's verses illustrate an intense faculty for technical and abstract beauty...an incorrigible propensity towards nocturnal themes, a demoniac undertone behind every page—and by final judgment, probably belong among the electric lights of imaginative literature, brilliant and dazzling, but with no heat."

Needless to say, Poe was not concerned with Nature, nor with healthy bodies, healthy sex. Whitman, who knew this perfectly well, found himself in a dilemma. He dwelt on the verse but nowhere mentioned the lurid and melodramatic tales of ghastly living deaths and entombments and poisonous sensations, all the obsessional circlings of self-love which had transfixed him when he was young and guilt-ridden, unable to leave the underground passages of his own psyche. It was as if the early stories were his secret sins. He acknowledged his debt to Poe by a strangely appropriate device, the memory of a dream he once had:

> I saw a vessel on the sea, at midnight, in a storm. It was no great full-rigg'd ship, nor majestic steamer, steering firmly through the gale, but seem'd one of those superb little schooner yachts I had often seen lying anchor'd, rocking so jauntily, in the waters around New York, or up Long Island sound—now flying uncontroll'd with torn sails and broken spars through the wild sleet and winds and waves of the night. On the deck was a slender, slight, beautiful figure, a dim man, apparently enjoying all the terror, the murk and the dislocation of which he was the center and the victim. That figure of my lurid dream might stand for Edgar Poe, his spirit, his fortunes, and his poems—themselves all lurid dreams.

STEPPING ONTO THE ferry in August 1845 and floating back to Brooklyn, Whitman we can be sure had mixed feelings. He had served a second apprenticeship, this time in New York journalism, and it was over. What did it mean to leave, and how final was it?

He had proved his worth in a tough profession. Running into a bad patch and throwing in his hand, he must have felt he could return whenever things changed again in his favor, as they were surely bound to do. The raucous city with all its excitements was only a ferry ride away, and it had opened itself to him with its "shapes of doors giving many exits and entrances." Its hurrying footsteps had included his; he had slept under its roofs, had tasted success and bitter loneliness there, had been on nodding terms with hundreds and not made a single real friend. And what had he achieved by his attempts to make his mark as a serious writer? His fiction and poems had disappeared without a trace, lost in the copious flow of magazine fodder. He had contributed nothing distinctive, discovered no recognizable voice.

He had filial reasons for returning. Brooklyn, for all its restrictions, meant more to him emotionally than New York. His family had recently moved back there after a long stay—for them—of four years at Dix Hills. His father, farming and jobbing, barely scraping a living, bought a plot of land in Prince Street and decided to give Brooklyn another try. In May of the following year he moved his brood to a rented house in Gold Street while continuing to build on his own bit of land. He was back where he had arrived twenty-two years before, working as a town carpenter. That September the relative who had taught him his trade, Jacob Whitman, Walt's first cousin, died and was buried at Dix Hills.

Whitman didn't come home jobless. When he moved in with them at 71 Prince Street it was to start work with the *Long Island Evening Star*, where he had completed his apprenticeship as a printer at the age of seventeen. Alden Spooner had been the owner then but had since handed over the Whig paper to his son Edwin. The paper, which had made a joke of its former apprentice's presumption in climbing onto a political platform before "those big children of Tammany Hall," was now keen to make use of whatever expertise Whitman had gained on the metropolitan dailies he had edited. Though he was in fact more experienced than Edwin Spooner himself, he worked on the *Star* as a columnist, doubtless because they saw him as politically suspect. The pay, said to be only four or five dollars a week, could have been a sort of retainer. He got by on it by joining his family at Prince Street instead of boarding.

Still at home were Hannah, his favorite sister, now twenty-two, and his brothers George, Jeff, and Eddy. The older boys, Jesse and Andrew, lived away. Jeff was a schoolboy, and George, a youth of sixteen, worked in Brooklyn. Walt's other sister, Mary, out at the whaling village of Greenport with her shipwright husband, had a young family of her own.

Happy to be home again, Walt spent most of his leisure time with Jeff. Conscious of his place as the experienced supportive son, he adored his brother's so different nature, a boy who was all quickness and fun, such a contrast to his slow, thoughtful self as he rolled along with his sailor's gait on their trips to the eastern end of Long Island. After Jeff's death in 1890 he wrote a few words as a kind of obituary: "As he grew a big boy he liked outdoor and water sports, especially boating. We would often go down summers to Peconic Bay . . . and over to Shelter Island. I loved long rambles, and he carried his fowling-piece." Walt would wander across and make himself known to the bluefishers and sea-bass takers there. The brothers were inseparable, searching along the sand for seagulls' eggs to bring home, picking them up warm from being left to hatch in the sun. They were half the size or more of hens' eggs.

Eddy, mentally retarded, needed looking after and would always be at home while his mother lived. Walt took over responsibility for him in due course, and would leave the bulk of what there was of his estate to him. In Brooklyn he was cast again in the character of manly sternness he had accepted willingly on Long Island, as protector and family adviser. His father had paid a first installment of twenty-five dollars on the mortgaged land at Prince Street, and in May 1845 he paid another hundred dollars.

The documents and receipts of these transactions bore Walt's name as well as that of his father. It was concrete proof of the son's growing importance. Two years later he transferred the title deeds to his own name and made himself responsible for the mortgage and the city taxes.

By then he was as prosperous materially as he would ever be. He had come into his own as an established and respected citizen of Brooklyn without undue effort. His bulky figure gave an impression of someone much older, down-to-earth and yet somehow not to be fathomed, with his veiled, half-dimmed eyes and a subtle softness to his speech. Moving unobtrusively from being his father's deputy to an unopposed role as his surrogate, it was as if his assumption as virtual head of the household had been decreed from the beginning. The years of living alone in New York had only strengthened his links with them. He had been back often on visits; he had kept in touch with dutiful letters and sent money home to help out. Involved now up to the hilt and shouldering his new financial burden, he made clear his commitment by treating himself to a silver watch costing ten dollars and a gold ring and gold pencil. He splurged on a formal suit with a frock coat and paid the hefty sum of thirty-two dollars for it. He bought a carnelian pin for his mother, thimbles and a purse for his sister. Nor did he neglect his brothers, buying them all new boots and getting their down-at-heel ones mended. He put in hand improvements to the house, bought furniture and gilt picture frames, a nameplate for the front door, and planted a garden with trees and shrubs. He seemed every inch a man in his natural element, confident of his permanence, looking round appraisingly with the detachment of a guardian.

The pieces he wrote for the *Star* are for the most part what we would expect of a dutiful son and citizen, a Brooklyn journalist eager to participate in the affairs of his town and county. Mostly they were moral injunctions of one sort or another. He stopped writing fiction and poetry. It was as if some instinct told him that what he dreamt of producing one day, whatever that was, would be thwarted by his limitations. People like Duyckinck and Cornelius Mathews, as well as O'Sullivan and his contributors to the *Democratic Review*, were college graduates to a man. Where did that leave him? By comparison his education was nonexistent. As though to overcome this handicap he began snipping articles from magazines and newspapers on subjects which aroused his curiosity. They could be about anything: soon his collection bulged with excerpts, samples from art and literature, music, but also zoology, geology, history, law, and miscellaneous reflections fitting no particular category. His only method was the eclectic one of choosing what pleased him. Gradually he would come to realize, after a decade of this random ransacking, that he had a mind which loved to play with contraries, to combine and contain them.

Most of his articles in the *Star* were concerned with moral improvement. He delivered his thoughts on a favorite topic, education, giving advice to apprentices under such headings as "Hints to the Young" and "Some Hints to Apprentices and Youth." Loafing, he warned in one, could be a pernicious habit—here he was speaking from experience. So was the chewing of tobacco, foul language, and, curiously, when we think of his recent spell of dandyism, dressing fancily. He talked down to his Brooklyn readers from the superior heights of his knowledge of New York society, such as it was. "The coming season," he wrote airily, "promises to be one of considerable stir in the fashionable world. . . . Parties, concerts, balls and lectures are announced at a great rate. The Polka increases in popularity. As for manners, we are assimilating the Parisian more and more—and I must confess I like it so. . . . We are now speaking of the *true* fashion—the heart of hearts—of New York society." So spoke the strutting gay dog who made it sound as if doors in these circles flew open everywhere at his approach.

He kept well clear of politics, either by request or by exercising unusual discretion. Patriotic issues were different. He felt free to add his voice to his fellow editors on the issue of England and the Oregon boundary dispute. Whitman took his stand with Bryant and the *New York Post* in opposing those spoiling for a war. No one believed more passionately than he in the republic's "high and glorious destiny," but if it meant spilled blood "and the groans of dying men" then he could "almost say, let us never be a great nation!"

The noble rhetoric would suddenly give way to skittish humor, in facetious reviews of amateur dramatic productions. Playing the smart New Yorker he waded into some unfortunate players and their performance of *Hamlet* like a veteran theatre critic. Never able to be discourteous to females he concentrated on the men, especially Hamlet, "a long-necked, shambling fellow, with a walk such as never before was seen in Christian, Jew or Pagan. . . . Then such monstrous spasms as passed over his face at times—the token whereof was certainly never seen except in a cholera hospital!" And so on. Behind the condescension and ridicule may well have been, suggests

Gay Wilson Allen, some enmity between the young columnist and the Brooklyn teachers in charge of the production.

More seriously, he fulminated from time to time against the contemporary stage for its unhealthy tendencies. It had to be "made fresher, more natural, more fitted to modern tastes—and above all, it must be Americanized." There should be no more of the nauseating rubbish which disgraced the Chatham and Bowery stages nightly. Nor was the Park Theatre exempt, importing the "castings-off of London and Liverpool" and parading "anti-republican incident and feeling."

Beyond the tedious finger-wagging disapproval of Brooklyn schools and teachers one can detect the throes of something genuine, a personal concern which drove him to condemn again and again the use of corporal punishment. He attacked outright the common practice of flogging, seeing it as an admission of failure on the part of teachers. Protest letters came in. He attended a lecture by the educator Horace Mann in Brooklyn and afterward quoted him as saying that "They who expel wrongdoing by means of physical chastisement cast out devils through Beelzebub, the prince of devils." Weren't some of Brooklyn's teachers and protesters "a little too profuse of this satanic power?" he asked. Continuing to hammer at the cause of a reformed educational system he chivvied the school board repeatedly to provide night and technical schools in the town.

Not yet a convert to opera, he took time off from the *Star* to write the essay on "Art-Music and Heart-Music" which Poe bought for the *Broadway Journal* and published at the end of November. Whitman had made a point of praising local teachers who taught singing in Brooklyn schools. Later he would experience transports and ecstasies, his soul reeling and swooning before the sound of a singing voice. The song of a mockingbird would move him as deeply. Nothing was greater in this world than a singer. It was what he would want more than anything for himself. But what had delighted him at Niblo's Saloon in New York was hardly grand. All he had listened to was a quartet, three brothers and a sister from Vermont calling themselves the Cheyneys. They sang in country style, like another family singing group he heard around the same time, the Hutchinsons. This to him was the real thing, not artificial, and such a contrast to "the stale, second hand foreign method...with its trills, the agonized squalls, the lackadaisical drawlings, the sharp ear-piercing shrieks, the gurgling death-rattles, the painful leaps from the fearfullest eminences to a depth so profound that we for a while hardly expect the tongue to scramble up again." No, give him the simple fare, "Heart-Music," American to the core.

He had tried opera and been intoxicated by the occasion, but somehow he could not get beyond the spectacle. The singers were such a pain, dressed absurdly and going on interminably. This outlandish foreign stuff did nothing for him. He sat in the midst of the strange noise and joined in the applause, caught up by the wild excitement of the audience, but the performance left him cold. He didn't have the clue to it. The rich colors, the touches of luxury among the audience, the soft fall and dying of lights, these were what stirred him inside the theatre:

What costly and fashionable dresses! What jewelry! What a novel sight to you—those white-gloved hands, lifting or holding the large opera glasses! What an odor of the different perfumes—the whole combined and floating in one faint, not unpleasant stream, into one's nostrils. What an air of polished, high-bred, deliberate, heartless, bland, superb, chilling, smiling, repelling fashion! How the copious yet softened gas-light streams down from hundreds and hundreds of burners! What a rim of fire up overhead encircling the base of the dome! What a rich and gay aspect from the profusion of gilt ornaments on the iron pillars, and on the white ground! What a magnificent spectacle to see so many human beings—such elegant and beautiful women—such evidences of wealth and refinement in costume and behavior!

Yet in the end it was music that affected him most, in the secret depths of himself where he liked to sink and lie hidden. Confiding these religious sensations to his readers after hearing *The Oratio of Saint Paul* sung in the New York Tabernacle, he wasn't simply out to prove that he could appreciate higher things. From the beginning his response to vocal music was mystical. America, he declared, ought to heed this refining balm, so feminine and restorative, affecting both manners and outlook. "In musical Italy and musical France," he went on, blithely ignorant of both countries, "the commonest man, the most ordinary grisette has an ease, grace and elegance which are not too often found in what we call good society here." This was why the teaching of singing in schools was so essential.

IN FEBRUARY 1846 the editor of the *Brooklyn Eagle* died sud-
denly. William B. Marsh was a well-loved man who had been, like
Whitman, a printer in New York. He had counted Horace Greeley,
the evangelistic editor of the *Tribune*, as a friend. Under Marsh's
editorship the *Daily Eagle* had been making a name for itself in both
Brooklyn and New York. A week after his death, which had left his
wife and children in dire straits, Whitman launched an appeal in the
*Star* to assist the late editor's family. Soon afterward he was ap-
pointed editor in Marsh's place.

He was back in the Democratic fold. The *Eagle* was partisan, its
proprietor a leading figure in the party. Exerting a strong influence
on the paper's policy behind the scenes was Henry C. Murphy, a
local politician Whitman had seen coming and going at the *Patriot*
when he was an apprentice there.

The *Star*, a smaller paper overshadowed by the more robust and
influential *Eagle*, signaled its disgust at Whitman's defection with
a squirt of bitter invective. Who did he think he was, this "coun-
try schoolmaster" and "hectoring scrivener" who reduced his fellow
Democrats to "convulsions" of helpless laughter with his ill-informed
opinions? Edwin Spooner's attack was unjust and unkind, Whit-
man retorted, when he had done nothing to deserve it. On the
contrary he had put some backbone into their rather tepid, re-
spectable, but old-fashioned sheet. Readers enjoyed contemplating
the furious quarrels of battling editors, and Whitman gave them
full measure. Writing with evident relish he countered the charge
of his alleged weakness by describing the *Star* as "the incarna-
tion of nervelessness, the mere dry bones of a paper, with all
the marrow long withered up," reduced now to "sere and yellow
leaf." How dare they call him weak when their paper was so feeble
that it needed someone's assistance "before it could even lean
against the wall and die." He took care, however, in this exchange of
insults, to exempt the old man, Colonel Spooner, for whom he had a
soft spot.

In the same *Eagle* editorial he found space to hit back at another
editor, the Whig in charge of the *Brooklyn Advertiser*. The man had
written satirically to complain of Whitman's faulty grammar. This
was a sore point. The fellow was an English cockney, Whitman
answered, stung by the implication of general ignorance: what could
the man know about American usage? But the gibe hurt. It could
only have served to drive him farther along the path of self-education

he was now bent on following. He went on clipping and salvaging. In effect, he was using the *Eagle* to create a personal reference library for himself. He had enrolled in a college, even if no one knew it but himself. An editorial that December noted that "Some of the wisest and most celebrated men, whose names adorn the pages of history, educated themselves after they had lost the season of youth."

Afterward he would describe his time on the *Eagle* as "one of the pleasantest sits of my life," though he must have worked hard, getting the paper out more or less singlehandedly. Probably he preferred it that way. The owner, Isaac Van Anden, gave him carte blanche, provided of course he hoed the party line. He had already mastered the art and went about it skillfully. If he had an ideal editor in mind it was Horace Greeley, who saw a newspaper as an open university for the masses, aiming specifically "to advance the interests of the people, and to promote their Moral, Political and Social well-being."

At the end of April the young editor of the *Eagle* went across to New York to interview the great showman P. T. Barnum, who had arrived on the *Great Western* from Europe. Barnum had brought with him two additions to his American Museum at City Hall Park, the twenty-five-inch-high dwarf Tom Thumb, and an orangutan, Mlle. Jane. On asking whether Barnum's experience of Europe had detracted from his love for "Yankeedom," Whitman got the answer he desired. "My God, no!" Barnum cried, "not a bit of it! Why, sir, you can't imagine the difference. There everything is frozen—kings and things—formal, but absolutely *frozen*. Here it is *life*."

As an editor he endorsed Greeley's progressive stance and shared his vision of a paper reaching into households on every level, combining human interest stories, current events, and a strong editorial lead. When it came to tone, his preferred approach was the intimate and fatherly. On the *Eagle*, writing about modern marvels, civic outings, and the kind of Brooklyn he could see developing, he seized the chance to draw close to his audience in the way he liked. By turns reproachful, stern, confiding, he sought to embrace them at times like a friend, inviting them in to share some new excitement. In the early summer, proudly announcing the installation of a steam-driven Napier cylinder press, "about as pretty and clean-working a piece of machinery as a man might wish to look on," he went on to define the relationship he saw as existing between him and his readers. "There is a curious kind of sympathy (haven't you ever thought of it before?) that arises in the mind of a newspaper conductor with the public he serves. He gets to *love* them. Daily communion creates a sort of brotherhood and sisterhood between the two parties. As for us, we like this. We like it better than the more 'dignified' part of editorial labors—the grave political disquisitions, the contests of factions, and so on."

How straightforward a declaration of his innermost desire! He wants nothing less than to make these workingmen and farmers part of his family in some unspecified, large context that he cannot, as yet, quite visualize. By substituting "conductor" for "editor" he manages to swing the location of his vision to a stage, a theatre. The emphasis is revealing. As an editor he seeks that collusion between performer and audience which had affected him so intensely on his theatre visits. The power to stir emotional natures such as his own in a communion, so that the actor-conductor-editor "gets to love them" and they to love him—this was what he wanted to happen. As an old man he recalled spending much of his time in theatres, "say from nineteen on to twenty-six or seven . . . going everywhere, seeing everything, high, low, middling—absorbing theatres at every pore." As he got to know theatre people in later life he admitted feeling close to them, very close—"almost like one of their own kind." But most intoxicating in those early days, more so indeed than the plays and operas themselves, were the audiences, those "alert well-dress'd full-blooded young and middle-aged men, the best average of American-born mechanics—the emotional nature of the whole mass arous'd by the power and magnetism of as mighty mimes as ever trod the stage—the whole crowded auditorium, and what seethed in it, and flushed from its faces and eyes, to me as much a part of the show as any—bursting forth in one of those long-kept-up tempests of handclapping peculiar to the Bowery—no dainty kid-glove business, but the electric force and muscle from perhaps 2000 full-sinewed men."

WALT'S IDEA of himself as a poet-singer, if it had ever yet really existed, was certainly lost to sight now. It would be another five years before it began to coalesce recognizably in his mind and notebooks. Even then it would be vague, fluid, changing only slowly to something more or less solid, coagulating by a process of trial and error, false trails, unlikely aspirations. "Way back, in the Brooklyn days," he was to tell Traubel, "and even behind Brooklyn, I was to be an orator—to go about the country spouting my pieces, proclaiming my faith. I trained for all that—spouted in the woods, down by the shore, in the noise of Broadway where nobody could hear me. . . . I thought I had something to say—I was afraid I would get no chance to say it through books: so I was to lecture and get myself delivered that way."

This dream of a rebirth through oratory had ceased to have any reality by 1846. If he had thought seriously of being an orator, his trial runs at Tammany Hall and elsewhere had made him think again. The "genius of poetry" Emerson had seen out there somewhere, "Yankee born," about to lift his "great voice," was surely not this man, the rising young citizen and respected local editor deeply embedded in the fortunes of his town. Whenever there were parades through the streets he took his place in the forefront, shoulder to shoulder with civic leaders. He stood among them on reviewing stands at public celebrations, obligated and glad to be so. It was a year when the Independence Day festivities were held at Fort Greene, a hallowed site under threat from land-hungry developers and the subject of a long campaign by Whitman to have it made into a park. It is one now. He composed an ode—"O God of Columbia! O, shield of the Free!"—intended to be sung to the tune of "The Star-Spangled Banner," and got it in the *Eagle* in good time for the crowd to have it handy.

Since boyhood he had been enmeshed in the patriotic fervor of these days, and he shared it absolutely. In a column specially written for his fellow patriots went his re-creation of the highly emotional tableau depicting Washington's farewell to his Sacred Army:

When the last of the officers embraced him, Washington left the room followed by his comrades, and passed through the lines of light infantry. His step was slow and measured—his head uncovered, his large breast heaving, and tears flowing thick and fast as he looked from side to side at the veterans to whom he then made adieu forever. Shortly an event occurred more touching than all the rest. A gigantic soldier, who had stood at his side at Trenton, stepped forth from the ranks and extended his hand, crying, "Farewell, my beloved General, farewell." Washington grasped his hand in convulsive emotion, in both his. All discipline was now at an end! the officers could not restrain the men, as they rushed forward to take the Beloved One by the hand, and the convulsive sobs and tears of the soldiers told how deeply engraven upon their affections was the love of their commander.

When Whitman came to write "The Sleepers" the revered hero of the republic rose again, muted this time, but in the same sorrowing image.

Now of the old war-days...the defeat at Brooklyn;
Washington stands inside the lines...he stands on the
   entrenched hills amid a crowd of officers,
His face is cold and damp...he cannot repress the weeping
   drops...he lifts the glass perpetually to his eyes...the color is
   blanched from his cheeks,
He sees the slaughter of the southern braves confided to him by
   their parents.

Uncorrupted, beautiful old men, fiercely proud and wise, would continue to appear on the *Eagle*'s pages during his editorship, and through all the editions of *Leaves of Grass*. So many of his contemporaries were hero-worshipers like him. The Founding Fathers were saints to him, as they were to millions. His adoration of old men, rooted here, was transferred in his work to anonymous old farmers, firm honest souls of every description, and to Abraham Lincoln, whose education had been as rudimentary as his own. As his ambition to be America's first poet slowly crystallized he came to see Washington as the legendary father who had freed the body of the nation. Now another great individual must free the American soul. By middle age he was already his own patriarch, a transformation he had long anticipated. Some even saw it as a willed thing. "My mother and sister would say to me: You're an odd one, Walt. Whereas everybody else seems to try all they can to keep young, you seem to glory in the fact that you're already beginning to look venerable."

🌿 IN ONE OF those editorials of his where he leads his readers off on a walk, hitting a note as he goes which veers awkwardly between the personal and the preachy, Fort Greene crops up in passing. A man of two cities now, he moves freely as an accredited native of both places in his ramble, reporting on "Matters Which Were Seen and Done." He points out in an aside that the large number of houses being built in East and South Brooklyn will create a need for churches for the new residents. At present all he can see is a new Methodist church under construction in Bridge Street. Crossing over the river he positions himself in Battery Park. What a fine thing it would be, he muses, if Fort Greene were a park like this, enjoying a similar panoramic view. Off on a leisurely saunter uptown he pauses at galleries and museums and takes in a production of *King John* at the Park Theatre.

Mindful of his duties as a spokesman for his community, eager to open his public's eyes to wider issues and educating them at the same time as himself, he doesn't forget to have fun along the way whenever possible. Now that he's more or less his own master he likes nothing better than to sketch freely and impressionalistically something he has just experienced firsthand.

Opportunities come up, plenty of them. Sponsored outings to Concy Island jostle in his pieces with reports of various official visits. In an omnibus pulled by six magnificent white horses he rolls out to Greenwood Cemetery "where affection seems to have selected the prettiest burial spots" on an excursion with a group of children from the local orphanage. He wanders contentedly through the groves and sits on the knolls and plays with them, eating strawberries and cake and sampling the lemonade. The Long Island Railroad, aiming to publicize its marvelous new facilities and the wonders of high-speed travel, invites him one day as a guest on a hundred-mile trip out of Greenport where his sister lives. He manages to fit in a call, then climbs back aboard to savor the pleasures of the dining car on the return journey. It was "filled with first-rate refreshments; and the obliging waiters served the passengers—no small portion being ladies—just as the latter might have been served in an ordinary public dining or ice-cream room."

Installed in his upstairs sanctum at the *Eagle* offices he seems to have created a satisfactory routine for himself. What was his working day like? Henry Sutton, a fifteen-year-old apprentice at the time, has recorded a few memories. Already working there when Whitman took over, he remembered his new boss as a "nice, kind man" with a clipped beard, neatly and quietly dressed, his presence a dignified one. Whitman was soon making a pet of the lad, calling him "Hen" and sending him off on errands, the sorts of things he would have recalled doing himself when he was an apprentice. Surprisingly, he lived now as a boarder at Adams Street and not with his folks, possibly for some privacy and quiet. Some of his newspaper work he did back at his digs. Now and then Henry was dispatched there to hunt up manuscripts his forgetful editor had left behind.

It was natural and it was also part of the game with him to appear lazy. It fooled others, even his brother George, who noticed that Walt took himself off to the New York libraries whenever he could but thought nothing of it. If one moved slowly, determined not to be hurried, arriving in one's own time even if it meant coming in last, was that stupidity or stubbornness? Whitman's innate resistance to the will of others was part of his sly, undeclared disobedience, a refusal to go along with the world. If his mother said worriedly, "What will people think?" her strange son with his contradictory moods, his changeable, restless nature, would answer quietly, "Never mind what they think."

And it was true that he could be terribly obstinate. All Sutton saw of it was his editor's insistence on a routine that suited him. His way of floating through life was deceptive. Really he was busier now than he had ever been, giving all his time and energy to the paper. Toward the boy, though affectionate, he maintained a distance. Sutton had the impression of someone inwardly absorbed.

He came in early to the office, a new thing and an indication of the heaviness of his work load. Climbing upstairs, he set about composing his editorials. During the morning he would perhaps receive a few visitors, mostly politicians, Sutton thought. Van Anden the proprietor stayed in the business office below. Down the editorials went to the composing room, and their author took himself off for a stroll, unless, that is, Sutton was being allowed to try his hand at the setting. Then he'd find Whitman at his side, checking the spelling and punctuation and ensuring that his copy was being followed to the letter.

Back from his walk, Whitman proofread. Finishing this task was the signal for him to take a break. He made for Gray's Swimming Bath at the bottom of Fulton Street and swam for half an hour, then stood under the shower while young Sutton pumped water for him. Unless pressed for time he went from there over on the ferry to New York. Passersby would catch sight of him on one of the Broadway stages, up aloft with the driver.

What did those drivers make of him as they swayed along on the teeming sea of the city like mariners, free animal natures who lived for the moment? What was this carefully dressed young man after, more a listener than a talker, happy to cross a border line that was invisible to them? They accepted him without question, or he would never have been able to picture them so rapturously in his reminiscences, the Yellowbirds and Redbirds they drove, and their way-out names: Broadway Jack, Dressmaker, Balky Bill, George Storms, Old Elephant, his brother Young Elephant, Tippy, Pop Rice, Big Frank, Yellow Joe, Pete Callahan, Patsy Dee, "and dozens more; for there were hundreds."

They released him into another age as he listened to their yarns, telling himself they were a race apart. They belonged, he thought, in the pages of Rabelais and Cervantes, Homer, Shakespeare. In the thick of the "immediate age" he had the delicious sensation, riding alongside these men and becoming acquainted with their preoccupations, eating, drinking, women, of being somewhere else, ages back. Just for the hell of it he might yell out at the top of his voice some passage he had learned by heart from *Julius Caesar* or *Richard III*—"you could roar as loudly as you chose in that heavy, dense, uninterrupted street-bass." In them he felt he had found the unquestioning comradeship he had been looking for, and an affection which made no demands. They were rough, ignorant, but openhanded, generous-hearted for the most part, "perhaps a few slouches here and there, but I would have trusted the general run of them, in their simple goodwill and honor, under all circumstances." Here was the trust which activated the long gestation of *Leaves of Grass*. These human studies at close hand would serve as models for comrades. Each time he clambered up beside one of these weather-beaten drivers and began to laugh, exhilarated, glad to be alive, he re-entered paradise.

IN HIS NEW situation, nothing pleased him so much as being able to make over the *Eagle* into something nearer his ideal of what a newspaper should be. He couldn't hope to emulate Greeley's *Tribune* with its great resources, but he did find room, in two columns among the advertisements on the front page, for poems, stories, and reviews. The editorial second page carried news items condensed from other papers. First of all, after writing his editorials and reviews, he read the incoming exchanges and took clippings from them, and made summaries or quoted extracts. Then he was off down to the composing room, reading proof, and out on the town reporting. He gave his novel *Franklin Evans* another title and used it as a filler, and did the same with several of his already published short stories.

Settling himself in with a will, busily occupied with the most congenial newspaper work he would ever have, he read of the departure for Europe of the transcendentalist Margaret Fuller. He had already reviewed her collection *Papers on Literature and Art* in the *Eagle*, as well as the work of George Sand, a pioneer of feminism who would influence him deeply. "The people of the United States are a newspaper-ruled people," he had declared in his paper, echoing his mentor Greeley. Margaret Fuller had put it less crudely. Writers should understand, she warned, that the life of the intellect was going to be found more and more in the weekly and daily papers. In them she saw increasing opportunities for the "condensed essay, narrative, criticism." She was only too aware of the reluctance of intellectuals to turn to this medium, but she believed it to be increasingly indispensable as a means of "diffusing knowledge and sowing the seeds of thought."

Margaret Fuller was a New Englander of considerable distinction who entered New York journalism in 1844, the same year as Poe. Horace Greeley had persuaded her to write for his *New York Tribune*. Accepting, she became the first full-time book reviewer in American journalism. Friends of hers on *The Dial* looked down their fine noses, telling her this was a coarse, man's world she was entering, altogether beneath someone of her subtle mind. She disagreed. She was in fact keen to join the paper of a man of the people and to get her hands dirty. Wanting to immerse herself in the social problems bedeviling the city, she went off at once to investigate conditions at the women's asylum on Blackwells Island. Her experiences on New York's biggest newspaper would, she hoped, give her writing relevance and broaden her range generally.

Reading her *Papers* for review, Whitman knew he had stumbled on another agent of spiritual liberation, a midwife for his frail embryoself. This woman was one of the big generous spirits. She saw literature as "a medium for viewing all humanity, a core around which all knowledge, all experience, all science, all the ideal as well as the practical in our nature could gather." These advanced women, situating themselves in the world as it is, would always inspire him. They were a great antidote to those "who regard literature as an exercise, a plaything, a joke, a display—they are the small of the small." He was not yet capable of saying, as Fuller did, that "Literature may be regarded as the great mutual system of interpretation between all kinds and classes of people. It is an epistolary correspondence between brethren of one family, subject to many and wide separations, and anxious to remain in spiritual presence of one another." She was a cosmopolitan, eager for the mingling of cultures without which a truly American literature could not, she said, begin. For "It does not follow, because the United States print and read more books, magazines and newspapers than all the rest of the world, that they really have, therefore, a literature." This was the kind of challenge Whitman would take to heart and act on eventually, though he was far from meeting it at present, or even grasping it fully. But he was stirred when he read these things, feeling the rosy glow of them, thrilled without knowing why. He tore out the chapter on American literature from Margaret Fuller's book and it joined his ever-growing collection of bits and pieces.

"What suits Great Britain," he read, "with her insular position and consequent need to concentrate and intensify her life, her limited monarchy and spirit of trade, does not suit a mixed race, continually enriched with new blood from other stocks and most unlike that of our first descent, with ample field and verge enough to range in and leave every impulse free, and abundant opportunity to develop a genius, wide and full as our rivers, flowery, luxuriant and impassioned as our vast prairies, rooted in strength as the rocks on which the Puritans landed. . . . That such a genius is to rise and work in this hemisphere we are confident; equally so that scarce the first faint streaks of that day's dawn are yet visible."

Though unable yet to fully comprehend Margaret Fuller's call for the forging of a national identity, in time he would plant it deep in prepared ground and grow his *Leaves* from it. Meanwhile he sucked in nourishment like a savage. The crudities of the press, loud, angry, seething with contradictions, fed into his mind the raw American scene. In its voices he heard reproduced through megaphones the speech of the streets. Lying fallow, he let seeds fall into him, mixed with whatever ephemera that came to hand—the slogans of politicians and reformers, of cranks and utopians and faddists, and all the blowy rhetoric of journalists on the national stage. He soaked everything up. Who was to tell him what to concentrate on and what to discard? The whole epoch excited him, rushed the river of its life through him. At one with his fellow Americans, he exulted in his country's "manifest destiny," contemplating with them the vast territories opening up, bounded only by the Pacific. He was joyfully in motion, active, feeling that a fine, tumultuous future awaited him somewhere. The gloomy claustrophobia of his family situation with its quarrelsomeness and discontent acted on him like a goad. With no father figure to turn to, he let his sympathies guide him.


THEY LED HIM to books, to philosophy, religions, general knowledge of every description, the sciences; but long before all that it was the theatre. Theatres were still paramount. First of all it was drama, and then within a year it would be the grand passion of opera.

The pieces he wrote on the theatre for the *Eagle* have an intensity lacking in his other reviews. Having digested so much already, most of the great actors of the time, Kean, Kemble, Cushman, Ellen Tree, he wrote with authority, almost with a swagger. He even put aside his gibes at feudalism and priest-ridden regimes abroad, "the old and moth-eaten systems of Europe" and the iniquities of tyrants. The truth was that if he had to choose between acting styles he would go for the British. He admitted that the great American actor Edwin Forrest could excite him madly, but he would object later to the man's posturing, his method of conveying emotion by a series of loud tirades and "by all kinds of unnatural and violent jerks, swings, screwing of the nerves of the face, rolling of the eyes."

He saw Mr. and Mrs. Charles Kean in a stunning performance of *King John* at the Park. He never forgot it, stirred almost beyond words, so impressed that it became one of his two favorite Shakespeare plays. The other was *Richard III*. Strangely, he was unaffected by *Lear*, *Hamlet*, *Macbeth*. Histrionics a la Forrest were one thing, but the electrifying portrayal of the "widowed and crownless Queen" by Mrs. Kean stayed with him for the rest of his life.

By the end of the third act half the audience, men and women alike, were weeping. Mothers in such harrowing circumstances, grieving over murdered children, were bound to arouse his compassion. Women in trouble caused him to suffer in the yielding, maternal part of himself. His luxuriating, easeful body, tending to voluptuousness, was encouraging him to develop a reverence for mothers which had always been latent. Rooted in his childhood, it was a tendency wrapped around with fantasies of comfort and safety. Gradually there was taking hold in his mind a dream of womanhood which would lead on to a worship of the great mother of all things. In this "bath of birth" the fruitful earth and the sea were mothers, the dark night a mother. Death itself was the mother of mothers, gathering young and old into its grassy lap. Everything was a door, a threshold, a hymn to maternity. The very cosmos itself copulated and gave birth to "orchards of spheres," stars ripening and growing in endless space on an unimaginable pasture of heavenly germination. The language of creation spoke in all things, great and small.

In due time he would make these sacred mothers central, visions of plenitude and goodness, enshrined like his own mother in a remembered grove of little ones. In "Song of Myself" he blurs the distinction between them and him, a man who is "maternal as well as paternal." So that there can be no mistaking his position he stops in full flight to say, in deliberate ringing tones,

> I am the poet of the woman the same as the man,
> And I say it is as great to be a woman as to be a man,
> And I say there is nothing greater than the mother of men.

Out to provoke as well as praise, to shock with his physiology as well as to shame with his honesty, he invites his reader to accept the holiness of

> ... the mechanic's wife with her babe at her nipple interceding for every person born...
> The sprawl and fulness of babes, the bosoms and heads of women, the folds of their dress, their style as we pass in the street, the contour of their shape downwards...
> The female soothing a child, the farmer's daughter in the garden or cow-yard...
>
> This is the nucleus—after the child is born of woman, man is born of woman,
> This is the bath of birth, this the merge of small and large, and the outlet again...

Be not ashamed women, your privilege encloses the rest, and is the
   exit of the rest,
You are the gates of the body, and you are the gates of the soul.

The feminist movement was gaining ground steadily in the 1840s
and 1850s, but only Whitman was to insist on placing the female
principle and its benefits at the very center of his appeal for love and
the continual marriage of opposites, in his outrageous "nondescript
monster of a book":

> The female contains all qualities and tempers them,
> She is in her place and moves with perfect balance,
> She is all things duly veil'd, she is both passive and active,
> She is to conceive daughters as well as sons, and sons as
>    well as daughters.

A FELLOW CRITIC, one just as devastated that evening by Mrs.
Kean's Queen, thought that "the intensity of maternal grief poured
forth in tones that actually harrow up the soul... the vehemence of
woe, the shriek of despair, the impassioned action... could not be
paralleled on the modern stage." Equally unforgettable for Whitman
was the sight of Charles Macready as Richard III. For him this was
an entirely different "mental" style of acting, altogether more subtle,
seemingly artless, and wonderfully intimate and magnetic. Declaim-
ing from his own stage in a review in the *Eagle* he confided that
"Though we never acted... we know well enough, from the analogy
of things, that the best way in the world to represent grief, remorse,
love, or any given passion, is to feel them at the time, and throw the
feeling as far as possible into word and act. This is a rare art, we
admit; but no man or woman can be really great on the stage who
has it not. The strange and subtle sympathy which runs like an
electric charge through human hearts collected together, responds
only to the touch of the true fire."

Whitman was drawing nearer here to his watchword, sympathy,
the great doctrine he would evolve in his effort to break new ground
beyond Christianity and the other world religions bogged down in
panaceas and messiahs. To have compassion was to start a flow of
sympathy in recognition and acceptance of all the other "human
hearts collected together." Only then would a true democracy be

ushered in, the republic of loving comrades along an open road he had not yet envisaged. He had begun to want, however, a freedom for himself, and to seek a means of liberating his audience so that they could meet intimately with him. It was a relationship he had begun to imagine in dramatic terms because of his experiences in the theatre. He strove to project himself in editorials, even if only through a restricted, public voice. The voice he heard in theatres over the footlights was something else. It made him tremble, it raced his heart. It was the voice he yearned to unloose from his own throat, the trapped songbird within him. Surely if others heard it they would recognize a heart like theirs, burning in isolation and longing to hear the sound of another "right voice." His real poetry when it came bore no resemblance to a manufactured art work. Instead it reached out for his readers in heightened conversations and monologues and asked them to follow him, "As the water follows the moon, silently, with fluid steps, anywhere around the globe." It was a one-man show, his own production, from a stage.

Long before his *Eagle* days he had seen benefit performances of *Richard III* starring Junius Brutus Booth, father of Edwin and John Wilkes Booth, at the Bowery Theatre. In the 1880s he drew on his memories of this evening of "fire, energy, *abandon*":

> I can, from my good seat in the pit, pretty well front, see again Booth's quiet entrance from the side as, with head bent, he slowly and in silence (amid the tempest of boisterous hand-clapping) walks down the stage to the footlights with that peculiar abstracted gesture, musingly kicking his sword, which he holds off from him by its sash. Though fifty years have pass'd since then, I can hear the clank, and feel the perfect following hush of perhaps three thousand people waiting. (I never saw an actor who could make more of the said hush or wait, and hold the audience in an indescribable, half delicious, half irritating suspense.) And so throughout the entire play, all parts, voice, atmosphere, magnetism, from "Now is the winter of our discontent" to the closing death fight with Richmond, were of the finest and grandest.

The curtain descended like nemesis in a flood of green crepe and the young Whitman went out into the night with the glittering crowd, convinced that he had had "one of the grandest revelations of his life." He fastened on the medium of Booth, his "electric personal idiosyncrasy," as the vital factor in this conversion. The individual was all-conquering, or rather it was that something subtle and powerful and "special" in the actor which had worked its conquering magic.

He told a friend that the first time he felt moved to write something from his heart and soul was when he saw a ship under full sail off Long Island. He might have said it was when he heard a Shakespearean actor in full sail. Soon it would be a prima donna.

He was greatly disappointed when he saw, much later, John Wilkes Booth in his father's role of Richard III. What was missing was everything he had experienced in the secret compact between him and the old man as he gave his performance, "when his best electricity was flashing alive in him and out of him."

Whitman's musical passion, he tells us in *Specimen Days*, "follow'd my theatrical one." His conversion to opera was by no means a lightning-flash affair. He took some time to overcome his loyalty to the homely tunes of groups like the Cheyneys, children of a Vermont preacher. They were, he thought, truer to the plain country heart of his native land than the dubious foreign stuff with its pointless complexities. Their simplicity and smiling ease and the words of their sentimental ballads took him back to the pure, clean living of his childhood in West Hills. And he liked the look of them for the same reasons, the innocent, fresh girls and their husky brothers. Songs with titles like "My Mother's Bible," "Lament of the Irish Emigrant," "The Mariner Loves O'er the Water to Roam," and "The Soldier's Farewell" belonged to an idyll he would never finally forsake.

It would be interesting to know which came first, his seduction by opera or his reading of a novel by George Sand which had once belonged to his mother, a book read so many times that it was in danger of disintegrating. *Consuelo* combined for him the virtues of country living with the sophisticated pleasures of opera, blessed of course by his pious old mother who had passed the tale on to him. "The pure contralto sings in the organ loft," he wrote in "Song of Myself." Consuelo in the novel sang in the organ loft of Saint Mark's in Venice, and then in her country church after her return as a village heroine, when "A sort of dizziness seized upon her, and as it happened to the pythonesses in the paroxism of their divine crises . . . she was led to manifest the emotion with which she overflowed, by the expression that was natural to her. She began to sing in a brilliant voice."

Louisa Whitman would not have been aware that she was reading one of the most popular and prolific writers of the nineteenth century. George Sand's influence extended over a whole generation of writers, in France and elsewhere. Balzac, Musset, Chopin, Delacroix, Liszt, Turgenev, and Flaubert were among the artists she counted as friends. Georges Lupin dubbed her "the Trojan horse in which liberal ideas traveled for the first time into Tzarist Russia." In an era of enormous turbulence when all aspects of morality were being questioned and challenged she was one of the pioneers of feminism—a term coined by Fourier, one of the leaders of radical reform. Widely regarded as androgynous, she bore children but dressed in men's clothes if she felt like it, and smoked cigars. Her father was an aristocrat, her mother proletarian. She befriended political prisoners and peasant-poets and involved herself in the new schools of thought. "George Sand's appearance on the literary scene," wrote Dostoevsky in A Writer's Notebook, "coincided with the first years of my youth. . . . The great mass of readers in the 1840s, in our part of the world at least, knew that George Sand was one of the most brilliant, the most indomitable, and the most perfect champions."

⁂ ONE WAY or another, if only in his editorials and reading, Whitman was making forays into the realm of women. Sensitive to the emerging feminist movement, he vacillated between calls for more realism and an end to the hypocrisy which forbade any discussion of women's bodies—as in a review of a book by Dr. Edward Dixon, *Women and Her Diseases*—and the coy ogling he indulged in unconvincingly, noticing the "bevies of our Brooklyn belles on their way to the ferry." Usually he was able to accept without blinking the awful sentimentality of the typical women's novel, finding in popular authors like Frederika Bremer the sanction for his ideals concerning mothers and families. Given his unlettered background and his devotion to his own mother it is perhaps not so surprising. Contemporary writers such as Melville and Hawthorne found these home-sweet-home-with-Mama novels loathsome. Not Whitman. Women to him were refining influences, representing salvation for men in a brutal age, literally the route to the godhead. In his article in the *Eagle* he recommended Miss Bremer's sticky sentiments unreservedly.

"If goodness, charity, faith and love reside not in the breasts of females, they reside not on earth. . . . In their souls is preserved the ark of the covenant of purity. To them is given the mission of infusing some portion of those good things in the minds of all young children; and thus it is that amid the continuous surging of the waves of vice, each generation is leavened with the good withal."

As a freethinker he couldn't abide the doctrine of Original Sin, insisting on the right to bear full responsibility for himself. He saw women, purified by motherhood, as the saviors of men, but really it was his wholesome mother with her Quaker background who was fixed in his mind's eye. In another part of himself he was fascinated by a very different kind of woman. This was the type, darkly and voluptuously clever, epitomized by Fanny Wright, Margaret Fuller, and George Sand. Hawthorne was said to have seen an "evil nature" in Margaret Fuller, and supposedly modeled his dark seductress Zenobia on her in *The Blithedale Romance*. Whitman, receiving currents of sympathy from afar, saw her, as he did Frances Wright, as lustrous, someone who "possessed herself" of his body and soul. She was awesome. He kept his distance, satisfied to remain unknown, to feel "glowingly" toward her, preferring to worship anonymously from the depths of a crowd, "listening to orators and oratresses in public halls."

Instead he gave himself up in sensual excitement to the voluptuous orientalism of music and opera. From opera he would learn how to make his poems sing by using arias and recitatives, saying later that but for opera he could never have seen how to write *Leaves of Grass*. More vaguely, he thought he should acknowledge his debt to "actors, singers, public speakers, conventions, and the Stage in New York, and to plays and operas generally." He would have liked to perform himself, and in the 1850s he did join an amateur dramatic group. He had tried public speaking, at one point imagined himself as a lecturer on the circuit, and in his teaching days had been an enthusiastic debater. He sang from the top of New York omnibuses against the thunderous bass of the traffic, he sang and recited on beaches, clambering on a rock and declaiming to the waves. Music, drama, and the human voice fed his growing ambition to reach and move the hearts and minds of men and women across the land:

> With music strong I come, with my cornets and my drums,
> I play not marches for accepted victors only, I play marches for
> conquered and slain persons. . . .

His first surrender proper was probably on August 5, 1847, when he heard Anna Bishop, the lead soprano in Donizetti's *Linda de Chamounix*. Afterward he wrote exultantly, "Her voice is the purest soprano—and as of a silvery clearness as ever came from the human throat—rich but not massive—and of such flexibility that one is almost appalled by the way the most difficult passages are not only gone over with ease, but actually dallied with, and their difficulty redoubled. They put one in mind of the gyrations of a bird in the air."

They put him in mind, too, of the swooning gyrations of his own soul. Describing them in "Song of Myself" he overcame the near impossibility of the task by inventing a wonderfully original language—the weird and brilliant orchestrations reeling with his new drunkenness:

I hear the violoncello ('tis the young man's heart's complaint),
I hear the key'd cornet, it glides quickly through my ears,
It shakes mad-sweet pangs through my belly and breast.
I hear the chorus, it is a grand opera,
Ah this indeed is music—this suits me.

A tenor large and fresh as the creation fills me,
The orbic flex of his mouth is pouring and filling me full.

I hear the train'd soprano (what work with hers is this?)
The orchestra whirls me wider than Uranus flies,
It wrenches such ardors from me I did not know I possess'd them,
It sails me, I dab with my bare feet, they are lick'd by the
     indolent waves,
I am cut by bitter and angry hail, I lose my breath,
Steep'd amid honey'd morphine, my windpipe throttled in fakes
     of death,
At length let up again to feel the puzzle of puzzles, that we call
     Being.


❧  SUDDENLY THE ordinary journalist, steeped in the journalistic culture of his time and pounding away with his clichés and moral lessons, had begun to sound like a writer, to deal in subtleties, ambiguities—using words like "dallied" and phrases like "their difficulty redoubled." Under the spell of that "honey'd morphine" he had broken through to something else. But not for long. The windy rhetoric came blowing back. We are misled into thinking that a "fine writer" is about to emerge. Whitman would never be one. He often insisted that he abhorred fine writing. A man of letters was to him an absurdity. He stayed a newspaperman for the whole of his life.

"A new world—a liquid world—rushes like a torrent through you," he wrote after his first exposure. Washed over by this gorgeous sound he saw no difference basically between it and his experience of great oratory. The man grappling with his audience, like the poet with his text, was engaged in a struggle toward mutual understanding which wasn't about winning people over but drawing closer to them, breast to breast, clinched into oneness, transfigured by the gladiatorial effort. Voice, gesture, tone, music, it was all combative. Its aim was to become entwined and then given up to something greater, godlike. In a notebook he tried to clarify it for himself. "The place of the orator and his hearers is truly an agnostic arena. There he wrestles and contends with them—he suffers, sweats, and undergoes his great toil and ecstasy.... From the opening of the oration and on through, the great thing is to be inspired as one divinely possessed, blind to all subordinate affairs and given up entirely to the surgings and utterances of the mighty tempestuous demon."

The soprano voice ran into him and convulsed him almost sexually, "like the lovegrips of her in whose arms I lay last night" he confided in the secrecy of a notebook. It was what he had always sought and dreamed of achieving, an abandonment capable of "dilating me beyond time and air—startling me with the overture of some unnameable horror—calmly sailing me all day on a bright river with lazy slapping waves... the chanted Hymn whose tremendous sentiment shall uncage in my breath a thousand wide-winged strengths and unknown ardors and terrible ecstasies."

He heard the incomparable Bettini, a large, robust, expansively generous young man, singing in Donizetti's *La Favorita* at Castle Garden, and on another occasion stunning New York operagoers in Verdi's *Ernani*. It was Bettini who brought home to him "what an indescribable volume of delight the recesses of the soul can bear from the sound of the honied perfection of the human voice... all words are mean before the language of true music."

And then the Italian prima donna Marietta Alboni: he heard her singing in a dozen operas as well as concerts, and in Rossini's *Stabat Mater*. According to Whitman she was the finest of them all. It was to her that he attributed "the foundation, the start, thirty years ago, to all my poetic literary efforts since." Listening to Alboni he began to understand how it would be possible to go beyond the metrical, rhymed forms that had always condemned him to artificial responses, cramped his rhythms, and restricted his breathing. When he came to compose his great poem "Out of the Cradle Endlessly Rocking" he would follow quite deliberately "the method of Italian opera." Music— and especially the musical human voice—was to be above all else the godlike combiner of contraries, sensuous, spiritual, mourning, delighting, "a god, yet completely human."

He used an editorial to urge young people to study music if they possibly could, observing significantly if obscurely that "music, in the legitimate sense of that term, exists independently of rhyme." He bought a musical instrument or two but apparently never learned to play one. To encourage his brother Jeff to take lessons he purchased a rosewood piano in 1852, paying $180 for it.

New York in the mid-nineteenth century was hearing a tremendous amount of opera, more in fact than at any time since. Whitman feasted on it, not only at theatres but attending concerts at Palmo's in Chambers Street, Niblo's Gardens, and elsewhere. He recalled his favorite, Alboni, in the title role of *Norma*, plotting the death of her children "with real tears, like rain, coursing down her cheeks," and felt impelled to acknowledge his debt to her yet again. "My younger life was so saturated with the emotions, raptures, up-lifts, of such musical experiences that it would be surprising indeed if all my future work had not been colored by them."

This was explicit enough. Characteristics of the Italian operas he most admired, by Donizetti, Verdi, Bellini, Rossini, were an extensive use of the flowing melody—introduced by Rossini—so that solo flourishes were subordinated to the whole, with even the most coloratura passages given significance. Whitman, unable to understand Italian, was bewitched by the music of the human voice alone, falling as if wordlessly on his ear. When he came to attempt his own art of flowing passages, this was the miracle he strove to perform, in his sweet fantasy of a rhapsodic book which would sweep all peoples together in its anarchistic embrace. Listening to the opera music which so moved him, he believed he heard the very voice of wisdom itself. Trying to convey its mystery, and the parallels and correspondences with his own work, he told Horace Traubel, "The words of my book nothing, the drift of it everything."

His inspiratrice, Alboni, would be memorialized one day in a major poem, when

> The teeming lady comes,
> The lustrous orb, Venus contralto, the blooming mother,
> Sister of loftiest Gods, Alboni's self I hear. . . .

> Across the stage with pallor on her face, yet lurid passion
> Stalks Norma brandishing the dagger in her hand.

There was no one afterward to take the place of his goddess, who in *Lucia* "used to sweep me away as with whirlwinds." He was immune to the Swedish coloratura Jenny Lind when she arrived under the auspices of Barnum and the city went wild, cunningly manipulated in advance by the showman's publicity. A crowd of twenty thousand swarmed up Broadway to see her drive to the Irving House. George Templeton Strong wrote a week later in his diary that the Jenny Lind mania "continues violent and uncontrolled."

As an editor Whitman felt constrained to go and sample the marvel for his readers if not himself. The man who had been moved to tears by Bettini sat as a coldly sarcastic observer to hear Lind's Castle Garden concert. "The Swedish Swan," he reported, "never touched my heart in the least." And it was clear he found her vulgar in the extreme. She offended most unforgivably against his ideal of simplicity, the path for him to all that was grand, true, and beautiful in art. He admitted her virtuosity was remarkable and "curious to hear," but such technical brilliance meant no more to him than the writhings of a contortionist. If she had an India-rubber voice, what was that to him? "There is something in song that goes deeper—isn't there?" And did she have to look and sound so absurdly showy? His distaste mounted as he wrote. "She was dressed in pink satin, with black lace flounces and cape—great, green cockades in her hair— white kid gloves, fan, handkerchief, and the ordinary fashionable et ceteras. Her cheeks were well rouged, and her walk bad. The expression on her face is a sort of moral milk and honey." He did concede that her voice had an extraordinary fluency—one was reminded of rich plate glass. To sum up, he thought Barnum had conned the public with this meretricious songbird.

Though he usually went to operas by himself, now and then he took Jeff along, no doubt in the hope of converting his malleable young brother. Jeff showed sporadic interest and would eventually learn to play the piano. George, too, was approached. He said only, "There was nothing in opera for me." We can picture him scratching his head and laughing, baffled as usual by the brother he had long ago stopped trying to understand.

During whitman's two years on the *Eagle* it is possible to notice the strange duality of his nature emerging. It was a trait that would reveal itself more dramatically in the years to come. Here he was, steadily engaged, whereas his attention worked as a rule by fits and starts, falling into abeyance when he could no longer see his way forward. His editorials on national affairs, for instance, show a man who seemed to bear no resemblance to the rapt worshiper of Alboni. Nor can we recognize the future dreamer of a new society, one born from the nucleus of a wordless union, that went beyond democracy. If the two parts of him were related, how conscious was he of the relationship? Often there seemed to be no common ground, no contact at all. Nor, apparently, did the split put any obvious strain on him. In one of his later notebooks he recorded the paradox, only to give up on it. "I cannot understand the mystery: but I am always conscious of myself as two (my soul and I)." He would go on to exploit this twoness brilliantly in "Song of Myself" in a running series of linked duets, but in terms of development this was still a very long way off.

The outbreak of the Mexican War of 1846–1848 plunged him back into his political allegiances with a vengeance. While on the *Star* he had advised caution over the disputed Oregon lands, pointing out that a war with Britain could not be justified if it entailed the sacrifice of young American men. Now, in a *volte-face*, he waded in with loud cries of support for President Polk. "Mexico must be thoroughly chastised... with prompt and *effectual* hostilities.... Let our arms now be carried with a spirit which shall teach the world that, while we are not forward for a quarrel, America knows how to crush as well as how to expand." He was secretary of the local branch of the Democratic party, and at an open-air meeting he proposed and recorded a resolution which gave the gist of his truculent editorials, but expressed more soberly.

Over both the Oregon issue and the Mexican crisis hung the slogan of "manifest destiny," a potent one for Whitman. Surely the powerfully expanding nation had a right to expand its free institutions over the vast continent, argued Polk and his supporters. Whitman was with him up to the hilt. But his patriotic clamor for annexation was in reality one of the first signals we have of his longing for an expanded inner being, a craving to push out beyond the boundaries of his own self, to be large, to "contain multitudes." The cause was just, its logic inexorable, he insisted, as the brutal land grab got under way. "The daring, burrowing energies of the Nation will never rest," he declared excitedly, "till the whole of this northern section of the great West World is circled in the mighty Republic—there's no use denying that fact!"

Fantastic prizes were being dangled before the new nation. First of all, Texas, a republic in its own right after breaking away from Mexico, asked to be joined to the Union. Mexican incursions were the flash point giving Polk the pretext he had been waiting for. "The cup of forbearance has been exhausted," he told Congress. General Zachary Taylor was dispatched to the Rio Grande with a hastily mustered raggle-taggle army of young rustics and old codgers.

Enormous territories, long coveted, were opened up for the taking by the time the war ended. New Mexico, Utah, Arizona, Nevada, and large areas of Wyoming and Colorado were gained as well as the state now known as California. In addition to these unsettled lands there was now talk of Cuba, Canada, Nicaragua, and Mexico itself. If America had hung back, England, France, or even Russia might have moved in on these riches—so the justification went.

Emerson, James Russell Lowell, Thoreau, and others disagreed. Watching the hostilities with a sick heart, Emerson wrote bitterly,

> Go, blindworm, go,
> Behold the famous States
> Harrying Mexico
> With rifle and knife.

Lowell saw only a sinister outcome to the establishment of a young giant in the West. It would, he feared, contribute to the extension of the life and territory of slavery. He imagined the West becoming the arena in which the terrible conflict brewing between North and South would be fought out, and indicted the expansionists in his Hosea Biglow voice because

> They just want this Californy

So's to lug new slave-States in
To abuse ye, an' to scorn ye,
An' to plunder ye like sin. . . .

Whitman, meanwhile, was too busy hero-worshiping "Old Rough and Ready" General Taylor to pay much attention to the New England dissenters. Other opposition came from Northern Whigs who suspected the war was a plot engineered to reinforce the Southern slave society. Joshua Giddings of Ohio opposed the war, as did John Quincy Adams and his fellow "conscience Whigs" of Massachusetts.

In the middle of these attacks and counterattacks David Wilmot of Pennsylvania introduced an amendment to Polk's appropriation bill which sought to forbid the extension of slavery into any of the new territories. First approved and then suspended, it became the momentous Wilmot Proviso. Its effect would be to sunder the Democratic party from top to bottom and begin the Free Soil movement.

All his life Whitman would be a free-soiler. President Polk, baffled by the new issue, failed completely to understand its significance as a factor that was soon to divide the American people. "What connection slavery had with making peace in Mexico is difficult to conceive," he said, dismissing the amendment as "foolish and mischievous." Wilmot for his part hastened to stress that he was no abolitionist, had "no morbid sympathy for the slave," but aimed to protect the virgin lands for free white labor, or as he put it, for "the sons of toil of my own race and color."

Whitman had been reading newspaper accounts of Taylor's exploits, the man historians have since seen as lacking in intelligence. Whitman simply admired him for his wild appearance and disregard of protocol, and loved him for his bravery. Outnumbered three to one at Buena Vista, Taylor told the opposing general to "go to hell!" and won a victory that inspired the *Eagle's* editor for days. He went to print with panegyrics of his own and compared the newsworthy soldier—already being wooed by the Whigs as their candidate for the presidency next time—with Washington and Julius Caesar.

Taylor was a general who dressed as roughly as the men in his backwoodsman army and shared their common manners and speech. Nevertheless he was hardly the man of the people Whitman imagined. He was in fact a crusty Southerner who owned a hundred slaves and was military in spirit to his backbone. His undisciplined men adored him as a leader who seemed to be one of them and fought unquestioningly under his command—that is, when they were not fighting each other. On the day another general, the West Pointer Winfield Scott, was given command over Taylor's head, Whitman reacted with angry rhetoric in the *Eagle*. Polk himself was no happier: he now had a second potential presidential candidate about to turn himself into a Whig national hero. But he had little choice; his advisers in Washington saw Scott as the man who would win him the war.

It was Whig strategy on the floor of Congress to brand Polk as a warmonger. An unknown "lone Whig from Illinois," a Congressman by the name of Lincoln, attracted attention for the first time by his forthright stand against the Mexican War. He demanded to know the exact spot where American blood had been spilled. In his view Polk had ordered soldiers into a peaceful Mexican community, thereby creating a war where there was none before. To listen to Polk's attempts to shift the guilt onto Mexico was to listen to "the half-insane mumblings of a fever-dream," the meandering of a "bewildered, confounded and miserably perplexed man" whose intelligence had been "taxed beyond its powers."

Others taking an antiwar stand included the famous radical clergyman Theodore Parker, who condemned the action from a platform in Boston's Melodeon Hall: "Aggressive war is a sin...a denial of Christianity and of God." Whitman, at odds with this pacifism, and now—as he often was—an angry journalist, raged at the antiwar faction in his own party. What disgusted him in particular was the attitude of some of his fellow editors, notably Horace Greeley, whom he saw as acting treasonably in their attempts to smear "our officers and men." Whitman's fury was as unreasoned here as was his highly emotional response to Taylor, who embodied for him the frontier spirit.

Nor did his feelings have much to do with politics in the sectarian sense. "The best Americans," writes D. H. Lawrence, "are mystics by instinct." Whitman's floundering overview had a mystical basis. His confused and overheated patriotic blusterings would be transmuted splendidly in his first piece of major prose, the famous 1855 preface to *Leaves of Grass*. For the present he could only blunder into print with a dreamlike mixture of optimism and baulked power, which one feels could swing him into something entirely personal at any moment. Instead we get more of the "public opinion" that shackled him. "The scope of our government," he wrote, "is such that it can readily fit itself, and extend itself, to almost any extent, and to interests and circumstances the most widely different." California and New Mexico he saw as two new stars about to shine in "our mighty firmament." All of this was only one part of a visionary design yet to be unveiled, and "the mere physical grandeur of this Republic... is only desirable as an aid to reach the truer good, the good of the whole body of the people."

And not only the people of his own country. "We look on that increase of territory and power... with the faith which the Christian has in God's mystery." This was the vision he held to in his imagination, the big swerve back to the Founding Fathers with their shining ideals, and to all those early Americans who placed democracy in the vanguard of the struggle against oppression throughout the world. He never doubted that the New World symbolized freedom for the downtrodden everywhere. Others besides England were looking askance at the American experiment, wondering if they should intervene. "What has miserable, inefficient Mexico," he asked in his editorial, "with her actual tyranny by the few over the many—what has she to do with the great mission of peopling the New World with a noble race?" The dawning of a new day and the end of darkness and subjection everywhere were being heralded by these acquisitions. So far as the struggle for human freedom went, America was already "ages ahead" of the rest of the world.

Whenever Whitman was carried away into deeper water in his journalism we hear echoes of the old-fashioned protestant he would always be, faithful to the vocal minority of his father's Workingman party meetings. It is to his credit that in the end he could belong to no party but his own. Happiest as a loner, it is this that redeems him. Finally the Natty Bumppo in him triumphed, the unlived frontier life within him ever beckoning. His innermost wish was to be a Pathfinder, side by side with his Chingachgook, the "friendly flowing savage" he imagined endlessly, evaded, recoiled from, could not quite bear to have close. Better the dream, the wish, than the bitter ash in the mouth of one's disillusionment. But he did hold steadfast to his conviction that America's greatest role was as a rescuer, helping into its boundless tracts the wretched of the earth. The "Native America" faction would find no comfort in any newspaper of his. How could any man with a heart in his breast, he asked, "begrudge the coming of Europe's needy ones to the plentiful storehouse of the New World?"

William Cullen Bryant endorsed these sentiments almost to the letter in his poem "Oh Mother of a Mighty Race":

> Oh mother of a mighty race,
> Yet lovely in thy youthful grace!
> The elder dames, thy haughty peers,
> Admire and hate thy blooming years. . . .
>
> There's freedom at thy gates and rest
> For Earth's downtrodden and opprest,
> A shelter for the hunted head,
> For the starved laborer toil and bread.
>     Power, at thy bounds,
> Stops and calls back his baffled hounds.

While he was based in Brooklyn Whitman made a friend of Bryant: the New England lawyer came over on the ferry to join him a number of times. They were both enthusiastic walkers. "We took rambles, miles long, till dark, out towards Bedford or Flatbush, in company. On these occasions he gave me clear accounts of scenes in Europe—the cities, looks, architecture, art, especially Italy—where he had travelled a good deal."

After *Leaves of Grass* came out, this well-connected friend and crusading editor turned somewhat chilly and withdrew his friendship to a safe distance. The irony was not lost on Whitman, but when Bryant died he still felt a desire to speak well of the poet who had once been so "markedly kind" to him. In a combined tribute to four poets, Emerson, Longfellow, Bryant, and Whittier, he praised Bryant as a "bard of the river and wood, ever conveying a taste of the open air, the scents as from hayfields, grapes, birch-borders—always lurkingly fond of threnodies—beginning and ending his long career with chants of death" and with "morals as grim and eternal, if not as stormy and fateful, as anything in Eschylus."

He happened to be in New York when he heard of Bryant's death, and was there at the funeral of this "stainless citizen." Sifting through a chaotic pile of old photographs one day with Traubel he unearthed a grubby one of himself and laid it beside a formal portrait of Bryant which he had fished out of the same heap. "Do you think this could ever be tinkered into that?" he wanted to know. "That this loafer, this lubber, could ever be transmuted into that gentle-man?"

⚜ IN HIS *Eagle* articles and editorials we can see him jumping in and out of Democratic party policy but at the same time digging away at it, delving under it. He had begun searching beneath the social turbulence of his age for some pattern, a way of interpretation that would show things to be more meaningful, even beneficial in the long run, than had hitherto been supposed; and this in spite of their apparent destructiveness. He called for strong nerves, for vision. He seemed to be implying that there was a necessary destructive passion at work. Violence shouldn't, he thought, be condemned out of hand or feared, not if it broke down the old dead consciousness and cleared the ground for new vigorous growth. "It is the fashion of a certain set to despise 'politics' and the 'corruption of the parties,' and the unmanageableness of the masses . . . their weak nerves retreat dismayed from the neighborhood of such scenes of convulsion. But to our view, the spectacle is always a grand one. . . . The great winds that purify the air, and without which nature would flag into ruin—are they to be condemned because a tree is prostrated here and there in their course?"

Nothing if not consistent, he was making virtually the same assertion near the very end of his life. Out of curiosity Traubel had asked the old man what place, if any, he could find in his scheme of things for corruption in politics. Whitman's answer was trenchant. "I don't need to find a place for it—it has found a place for itself. But there's more, much more to the story than that. . . . Science tells us about excretions—the throwings off of the body—that the chief results are secured in the form of invisible exhalations—the whole flesh casting it forth. That strange, inarticulate force is not less operative in the institutions of society—in politics, literature, music, science, art—than in the physical realm. We mustn't forget such forces—not one of them. The spiritual influence back of everything else—subtle, unseen, mainly discredited—they finally arbitrate the social order. Society throws off some of its ephemera, its corruption, through politics—the process is offensive—we shudder over it—but it may be true, it is still true, that the interior system throwing off its excreta this way is sound, wholly sound, prepared for the proper work of its own purification."

This startling theorist in favor of upheaval, who sounded sometimes like the abolitionists and evangelists of his day (Wendell Phillips, for instance, likened an emergent republic to a constant overflow of lava), was by temperament a man who liked to go slowly, to tread warily. On his paper his tone moderated as he aligned himself cautiously with the potentially explosive Wilmot Proviso. Only too aware that the *Eagle*'s owner was a conservative Hunker Democrat, he trod a fine line with considerable agility. Strident, soothing, fatherly, boiling over angrily, he tried to educate and enlarge and in the same breath to speak as the voice of the people.

When we ask what it was he really wanted to do with his audience we see a man frequently at cross-purposes with himself. Principles were his main concern now, rather than the tossed-up bones dragged into view daily by politicians and fought over. He told his readers that the social scene interested him primarily as a philosopher. He was intent on feeling out the direction democracy should take, and if this meant a return to Jeffersonian principles then so be it. Why look to "mere politicians, sweating and fuming with their complicated statutes"? He intended his words—like the truest laws of democracy themselves—to fall direct into "the hearts of men."

How could one have both apocalypse and caution? He would have to wait for his immersion in poetry before he could begin to make his meaning clear. From a Union "always swarming with blatherers" he would insist on the primacy of the spirit. His rallying call for poets to join him in liberating the soul of a nation was remarkably like Emerson's, but with one essential difference. He did not mean alone inwardly, from the refuge of a study, but out in the open, journeying down a road, on foot. Not till his own astonishing bolt for freedom in 1855 would he feel able to declare his faith in the individual, integral soul as it travels and meets the souls of others, men and women, fellow voyagers taking life forward in lovely currents of sympathy on the long journey, in new compacts of love:

> I heard the voice arising demanding bards,
> By them all native and grand, by them alone can these
> States be fused into the compact organism of a Nation.
>
> Soul of love and tongue of fire!
> Eye to pierce the deeps and sweep the world!

I swear I begin to see the meaning of these things,
It is not the earth, it is not America which is so great,
It is I who am great, or to be great, it is You up there, or any
    one,
It is to walk rapidly through civilizations, governments,
    theories,
Through poems, pageants, shows, to form individuals.
Underneath all, individuals,
I swear nothing is good to me now that ignores individuals. . . .

O I see flashing that this America is only you and me,
Its power, weapons, testimony, are you and me,
Its crimes, lies, thefts, defections, are you and me,
Its Congress is you and me, the officers, capitols, armies,
    ships, are you and me,
Its endless gestations of new States are you and me. . . .

"It is I who am great." How bombastic this would sound if it were
not for that qualifying clause, "or to be great." How preposterous, if
we failed to recognize behind the spiritual frontiersman the person
not properly born, half in and half out of the womb, enmeshed in
the desperate process of remaking himself. We have to remind
ourselves that this passionately involved advocate of unfettered love
was more often than not the delighted spectator, the outsider looking
on. He practiced something he called "prudence" and did his best to
emulate the example of his calm mother, the simple woman who had
forbearance and stood back wisely from the fray, who exemplified for
him the "mild virtues" of the feminine.

Yet there were difficulties he had still not resolved, things he
couldn't obtain and others he didn't want from his fellow man. He
had seen firsthand in his own torn family that "indulgence in stormy
passions leads inevitably to sorrow." If only he could avoid such a
fate! It was true that he wanted the presence of other people,
connection with the multitude. But he craved also to be alone,
immune, "a kingdom of happiness to himself," loved, like his
mother, for his serene inner peace.

*Leaves of Grass* is his book of many marriages. It shows him
experimenting with different solutions, trying on the clothes of his
various aspirations. How was he to combine the various strands of his
contradictoriness and at the end deliver his wayfarer, an individual in
happy proximity to others but separate, living a life that was

unadorned, "simple as grass"? Putting his book together it seemed that every trial-and-error solution was a poem in its own right, part of a shape that was no shape, until finally, in a snap action, the diary scraps and secret jottings and memoranda to himself, all the impromptu bits and pieces had to be allowed to stand just as they were. They made sense only if they were not tampered with but left as "nature without check." Confusedly or not, these disparate fragments belonged together. When the time came he summoned up his courage and in an act of great recklessness threw it all, slag and diamonds, into the melting pot at once. The multivoiced story would be allowed to tell itself in the sea-rhythm of its own motion, with nothing smoothed away. The crude and exquisite, the farouche, rowdy, and naive would have to coexist somehow in the live movements of the sentences running out from him like nightlines, into the unknown. Typically, when he had no answer to a problem, he let it be.

WHITMAN'S READING and self-educating, gathering pace slowly in the 1840s, was indiscriminate during his time on the *Eagle* and would remain so. But now literature had begun to preoccupy him, and sometimes it ousted politics altogether. His reading, though unfocused and without recognizable pattern, was never more plentiful and varied. Books and magazines came into him for notice on his innovative literary page, and many of them were British: reviews such as the *Edinburgh Review*, the *Westminster*, the *North British Review*.

It was in the *North British Review* that he came across an essay on a life of Keats by R. M. Milne. He had got into the habit of underlining and annotating before he scissored something out for his collection. In this one he took exception to Keats's view of the poet he found quoted in it. "A poet," he read, "is the most unpoetical of anything in existence, because he has no identity; he is continually in and for and filling some other body." Not realizing how completely he would one day illustrate the truth of Keats's definition, he preferred an amended version which he expressed as follows: "The great poet absorbs the identity of others, and the experience of others, and they are definitely in him or from him; but he perceives them all through the powerful press of himself." This was much better, nearer to the ideal he had begun to set for himself. Evidently he found the Keatsian poet altogether too self-effacing for his taste.

In another article, where a critic emphasized the need for concrete imagery in poetry, obviously Whitman could not agree more. "Materialism as the foundation of poetry," he scrawled in the margin, anticipating one of the main planks of his future poetics.

He would object to Keats on these same grounds, complaining of irrelevance and ghostliness. "Of life in the nineteenth century it has none, any more than statues have," he wrote of Keats's poetry in a notebook. "It does not come home at all to the direct wants of the bodies and souls of the century."

Though he hadn't quite reached the stage where he would claim the entire material universe for inclusion in poetry, he was drawing closer. How it could be included was of course another matter. At the bottom of the same article he gave his own idea of the perfect poem, what it should and should not contain. Essentially it had to be "simple, natural, healthy—no griffins, angels, centaurs—no hysterics or blue fire—no dyspepsia, no suicidal intentions." Never too impressed by the romantic poets, he was in two minds about Tennyson, whom he would admire later as a man. He applauded with much underlining and arrowing the opinion of a critic that "the soul of art is gone, when religion has finally taken her departure."

The list of authors covered in the *Eagle* is an extensive one, and includes Emerson, Carlyle, Margaret Fuller, Schiller, Ruskin, Coleridge, George Sand, Michelet, and Goethe. Many of them were to be seminal influences later. The comments he made in his reviews were usually perfunctory, often moralistic. It was in his articles and editorials that he expressed something of himself, especially if he touched on a subject of importance to him personally. The power of words was one topic which certainly exercised his mind.

"Where," asked an editorial, "is, at this moment, the great medium or exponent of power through which the civilized world is governed?" And he commenced to wade into his answer with a gusto fueled by the force of an untapped ambition. "Neither in the tactics or at the desk of statesmen, or in those engines of physical terror and force wherewith the game of war is now played. The *pen* is that medium of power—a little crispy goose quill, which, though its point can hardly pierce the sleeve of your broadcloth, is able to make gaping wounds in mighty empires—to put the power of kings in jeopardy, or even chop off their heads—to sway the energy and will of congregated masses of men, as the huge winds roll the waves of the sea, lashing them to fury and hurling destruction on every side!"

Lecturing his readers earlier on the benefits of turbulence, he had called his country "a young giant, getting his maturer strength," its body politic "expanded to the sun and air." His was a newly literate age, unconstrained by monarchs and tyrants and free to express ideas without fear and to channel opinions, ideas, and all manner of information. What was it but the power of the word, in newspapers, books, on platforms, issuing from the tongues of orators and the soliloquies of actors, which could be seen and heard flowing over the giant's skin in a life-giving bath? Entranced by the romance and power of his own pen, Whitman got into his stride. "At this hour in some part of the earth, it may be that the delicate scraping of a pen over paper, like the nibbling of little mice, is at work which will show its results sooner or later in the convulsions of the social or political world. Amid penury, and destitution, unknown and unnoticed, a man may be toiling at the completion of a book destined to gain acclamations, reiterated again and again, from admiring America and astonished Europe! Such is the way, and such is the magic of the pen."

Now and then a book came his way that his mind would fasten on. The Whitman who "saw connections everywhere" was not yet awake, and it is too early yet to speak of models. But his words would quicken to reveal a personal interest and show that he was challenged, stirred, fascinated, so that we begin to anticipate his coming metamorphosis. One day Goethe's *Autobiography* in Parke Goodwin's translation landed on his desk. In it he read, "What a man wishes for in his youth, he obtains abundantly in his old age." He had been dreaming idly for years of a book of his own, whether of prose or poetry he had no idea. In his review we can see him toying with the thought of such a book and the shape it might assume. "What a gain it would be if we could forego some of the heavy tomes, the fruit of an age of toil and scientific study, for the simple easy truthful narrative of the existence and experience of a man of genius—how his mind unfolded in his earliest years—the impressions things made upon him—how and where and when the religious sentiment dawned in him—what he thought of God before he was inoculated with books' ideas—the development of his soul—when he first loved—the way circumstances imbued his nature, and did him good, or worked him ill—when all the long train of occurrences, adventures, mental processes, exercises within and trials without, which go to make the man—for *character* is the man, after all."

Who knows, perhaps the transparently told story of a psychic life could be the way forward for him, a man of his scrappy education who had no connections worth mentioning, and no money. Didn't he feel a "simple easy truthful narrative" welling up in him too, if he could only transcend his mundane circumstances—and yet embody them, represent them—by a powerful wish, an act of sheer will?

꙳ IF THERE WAS one author more than any other who stirred the will to power in him it was Thomas Carlyle. In 1846 and 1847 he reviewed six books by Carlyle. The man stayed with him throughout his life. In the late 1880s he was as fascinated by the tormented Scot's "dyspeptic Presbyterian temperament" as he had been during his time on the *Eagle*. *On Heroes, Hero Worship and the Heroic in History*, with its rapt oratory and its extravagant praise of natural leaders, rushed through him like a great wind and left him gasping. It was so eccentric, original, exalted, and it was written in a gnarled prose that lurched along uncouthly, insisting on truth before civility— like a farmer marching grimly over his muddy acres, reluctant to speak but burningly sincere, as if driven to using language as a last resort: a man driven to go stamping on and on until he had hunted down the Truth. A man no one was going to stop. Above all, a prophet shaking with "the old Hebraic anger and prophecy," a rasping, questioning, uncompromising voice which caused dislocation and agitation "in our comfortable reading circles."

Whitman loved the coarse rasp of it, the plain dress and hardiness. In *Specimen Days* he took pains to open out the meaning of the word "prophecy." If we call someone a prophet, he said, we mean someone "whose mind bubbles up and pours forth as a fountain from inner, divine spontaneities revealing God. Prediction is a very minor part of prophecy. The great matter is to reveal and outpour the God-like suggestions pressing for birth in the soul." In fact he was describing the doctrine of the Friends or Quakers.

He adored Carlyle's extravagance, his wild claims, his passion. His reservations about Carlyle's obsession with heroes and power would come later, when he would puzzle over the hold this man had over his mind, with his black pessimism about the human race and his contempt for democracy. Trying to answer one of Horace Traubel's leading questions he admitted that Carlyle was "satisfied with nobody, nothing. No god existed for him." On all the evidence this "gloomy pabulum, full of growl, darkness, venom," was an unpleasant creature. What redeemed him in Whitman's eyes was his integrity. He was "honest from top to toe, with every hair of his head." He was a man who couldn't help himself. Which made him irresistible, gave him his lasting appeal. Whitman could accept most things from such a man.

There was a reactionary lurking in Whitman, getting stronger as he aged. He had no real difficulty taking on board a man for whom "reform was a sham, democracy a humbug, civilization a lie. Everything was turned helter-skelter, everything was wrong-ended—everything meant despair—dead death. But the question returns: wasn't Carlyle more than that? The honest reflex of some incontrovertible fact? And there I stick."

Whitman grew up in an age of exaggerated claims; not only those of America's boosters, pioneers, and frontiersmen, but rising out of the poetic extravagance, as Paul Zweig puts it, of the nineteenth century itself. Wordsworth claimed for the poet the role of priest of nature. Shelley called him one of the unacknowledged legislators of the world. Byron used poetry as an audacious advertisement for himself. Emerson saw the poet as the only man of wholeness in a world of half-finished men. Now here was Carlyle, who celebrated the poet so emphatically as a "hero" of humanity.

The Young America group had a high regard for him. Before that, Margaret Fuller wrote in the *Dial* as far back as 1841, "Where shall we find another who appeals so forcibly, so variously to the common heart of his contemporaries? No living writer exercises a greater influence than he in these United States."

Whitman, always the slow starter, was merely catching up with the others in 1846–1847. And not only with this author. Carlyle's essays were his introduction to German culture, to Goethe, Schiller, Jean Paul Richter.

Then he came on a book he must have been surprised by—and it would go on intriguing him for years to come. Carlyle's *Sartor Resartus* can be seen now as an early model for Whitman's own composite book. When he came to review it in the *Eagle* he was stumped for a description. What kind of fowl was this? How to sum up this weird, wacky creation, a great bag spilling out its mixture of strange wild phrases, ridiculous words, orations, exhibitions, ejaculations, monologues, at once maniacal and inspired, dominated by a monstrous egotism and punctuated with self-parody, launching without warning into catalogues, fantasy, pedantry? At its center was a ridiculous hero, Diogenes Teufelsdröchh, Professor of Things in General and author of "Clothes, Their Origin and Influence." Alone with him and the firmament in his attic we are presented with the prospectus for a "new Bible," one as difficult to penetrate as Blake's *Prophetic Books*.

Instead of an autobiography Carlyle's crazy hero has accumulated "Six considerable Paper-bags containing miscellaneous masses of Sheets, and oftener Shreds and Snips. . . . Anecdotes, oftenest without date or place or time, fly loosely on separate strips, like Sybylline leaves. Interspersed also are long purely Autobiographical delineations; yet without connection, without recognizable coherence. . . . Selection, order, appears to be unknown to the Professor. . . . Close by a rather eloquent Oration . . . lie washbills marked *bezahlt* (settled). His travels are indicated by the Street-Advertisements of the cities he has visited."

It was bewildering, enigmatic, grotesque, Whitman warned his readers, and went on to explain its supposed aim as the creation of "a quite new human Individuality, an almost unexampled personal character." But how could a book putting itself forward as a secular gospel be taken seriously when it was jammed full of pranks? Whitman didn't care. He could smell rebellion. Here was the artist as innovator, tantalizing him with an invitation to prosodic freedom that he would take up one day. *Ossian* was another taste, "though I can't say I ever read it with any great fervor." But he kept a copy by him, even though Macpherson was "a sort of rascal—had scamp qualities." He found in *Ossian* what he found in the King James version of the Bible, affected powerfully by the Bible's different voices, chantings, rhythmic effects. Carlyle's rhythmical prose, and Ruskin's, was, he sensed, part of a reaction against "chained cadences" which had already been voiced in Blake's credo, prefacing his *Prophetic Books*:

> When this verse was first dictated to me I considered a Monotonous Cadence like that used by Milton and Shakespeare, and writers of English Blank Verse, derived from the modern bondage

of Rhyming to be a necessary and indispensable part of the verse. But I soon found that in the mouth of a true Orator, such monotony was not only awkward, but as much a bondage as rhyme itself. I therefore have produced a variety in every line, both of cadences and number of syllables. Every word and every letter is studied and put into its fit place: the terrific numbers are reserved for the terrific parts, the mild and gentle for the mild and gentle parts, and the prosaic for inferior parts: all are necessary to each other. Poetry Fetter'd Fetters the Human Race.

By Whitman's day a kind of diffuse choric prose, influenced by the strong rolling music of the Bible's prose poetry with its intense feeling, was being given trial runs in the journals of Thoreau and Emerson, although none of it had appeared in print. In Europe a need for something that deserted culture and went back to "the naked source—life of us all—to the breast of the great silent savage all-acceptive Mother," was making poets like Baudelaire crave for a lawless new medium that would be as untamed as nature but include the urban: "Who among us has not dreamt, in moments of ambition, of the miracle of a poetic prose, musical without rhythm and without rhyme, supple and staccato enough to adapt to the undulations of dreams, and the sudden leaps of consciousness." Such a work would be a "child of the experience of giant cities, of the intersections of their myriad relations."

Whitman had already heard the original of that music as he tramped the shoreline of Long Island. As a youth he had dreamt moonily of one day writing something to express that "liquid, mystic theme." Gradually he realized that it was "too big for formal handling." Instead of trying to do something with it directly, he let it sink into him as "an invisible influence." In *Specimen Days*, musing on the sea, he broke off to give a hint to writers coming after him. "I am not sure but I have unwittingly follow'd out the same rule with other powers beside sea and shores—avoiding them, in the way of any dead set at poetizing them...." All the same, how the sea and shore spoke to him! "How one dwells on their simplicity, even vacuity! What is it in us, arous'd by those indirections and directions? That spread of waves and gray-white beach, salt, monotonous, senseless—such an entire absence of art, books, talk, elegance—so indescribably comforting, even this winter day—grim, yet so delicate-looking, so spiritual—striking emotional, impalpable depths, subtler than all the poems, paintings, music I have ever read, seen heard." Then he was compelled by his honesty to add that "perhaps it is because I have read those poems and heard that music."

As HE KEPT faith with Carlyle, so he did throughout his life with George Sand. *Consuelo* went back a long way, linking him to his mother's girlhood, so it was natural that he should have gone on to *The Countess of Rudolstadt*, its sequel. He once said that he preferred Sand's Consuelo to any of Shakespeare's women. In the sequel he discovered the same vital connection between religion and spontaneous art.

Two young visitors hear a journeyman carpenter playing a violin in a ruined country church. The musician looks older than his years—as did Whitman, another carpenter's son. His "thick grey hair waving around his face increased the brilliancy of his large black eyes. His mouth had an indefinable expression of strength and simplicity." Music, strength, simplicity, humble work—these were key words denoting potent ingredients for Whitman. And there was more, much more. The joiner by trade—dressed like Whitman's father, and like Walt himself in a few years' time, in denims and workshirt—was in fact a worker-poet. The poem the young men heard, reciting his rhapsody as if it was music, was all-embracing and took in the whole of the human condition, both history and future. To Whitman this was no surprise. As he wrote in an early notebook, "the great translator and joiner of the whole is a poet." Here in George Sand's novel the joiner-poet

interpreted all the religions of the past, all the mysteries of the temples. . . . all the efforts, all the tendencies, all the labors of anterior humanity. In those things which had always seemed to us dead or condemned he discovered the elements of life, and from the darkness of the very fables he made to shine the lightnings of truth. He explained the ancient myths; he established in his lucid and ingenious demonstration all the bonds, all the points of contact of the religions. . . . He showed us the true requirements of humanity, more or less understood by the legislators, more or less realized by the people. He reconstituted before our eyes the unity of life in humanity, the unity of doctrine in religion; and from all the materials scattered in the old and new world, he formed the bases of his future world. . . . He filled up the abysses of history which had so terrified us. He unrolled in a single infinite spiral the myriads of consecrated bandages which enveloped the mummy of science. . . .

Whitman was an omnivorous reader. Quick to grasp this, Emerson called him "a copious book man." Afterward, though he made light of his reading, he went on with the habit of plundering as he read. There was plenty to pillage in *The Countess of Rudolstadt*. The book abounds in Whitmanesque assertions such as "No one lives in vain; nothing is lost," "And we also, we are on the road, we walk forward!" We know too that he reviewed Michelet and may well have come across his book *The People* and digested passages like this:

> This book is more than a book, it is myself. . . . Son of the people, I have lived with them, I know them, they are myself. . . . I unite them in my own person.
> The rise of the people, its progress, is often nowadays compared to the invasion of the Barbarians . . . straining to give everything at once—leaves fruit and flowers—till it breaks or distorts the branches. But those who start up with the sap of the people in them do not the less introduce into art a new burst of life and principle of youth; or at least leave on it the impress of a great result.

When Whitman read in *Sartor Resartus* that life was nothing but an "immeasurable steam-engine, rolling on, in its indifference, to grind me limb from limb," he may well have been reminded of his years in New York, and of how a big city could crush the sympathy out of you. Reading the description of the Professor's apartment, full of books and dog-eared papers and shreds of "all conceivable substances, united in a common element of dust," must have been like looking into one of his own attic rooms that were always ankle-deep in paper: except that he didn't possess many books. But he was turning them over in great numbers in the Astor Library in New York, taking the ferry on those regular visits his brother George casually noticed and puzzled over.

What was he searching for? America's ideal of the self-made man was his, too. It was encouraging to read examples of men as ordinary as himself who had reached the heights, men of the laboring class who became bards, orators, composers; men like Shakespeare, son of a father who dressed sheep and kidskins, or like the Quaker George Fox.

The Corn-Law rhymester of Carlyle's uplifting essay was the kind of worker-poet Whitman's imagination seized on. This was stirring stuff, and he was always grateful for it. When Carlyle died his old admirer summed up his value to him. "It is time the English-speaking peoples had some true idea about the verteber of genius, namely power. As if they must always have it cut and bias'd to the fashion, like a lady's cloak!" Did it matter that Carlyle didn't at all admire the United States and its democracy? "I doubt if he ever thought or said half as bad words about us as we deserve."

"Two conflicting agnostic elements seem to have contended in the man," he went on, "sometimes pulling him different ways like wild horses. He was a cautious, conservative Scotsman, fully aware what a foetid gasbag much of modern radicalism is; but then his great heart demanded reform, demanded change—often terribly at odds with his scornful brain. No author ever put so much wailing and despair into his books.... He reminds me of that passage in [Edward] Young's poem where as death presses closer and closer for his prey the soul rushes hither and thither, appealing, shrieking, berating, to escape the general doom."

You could say it was Carlyle's *sound* which inspired Whitman. At odds with his views he went on liking him, being heartened, impressed, grateful. Carlyle upset people. Best of all, he put heart into you, braced you up. Isolated as Whitman increasingly was, that counted for a great deal. Carlyle was a passionate hater, a naked sliding force, loose and dangerous. He exerted power by the human voice alone, commanding the kind of attention Whitman wanted for himself. And like Whitman he was contradictory, exalting men of humble origin and despising the herd, a loveless prophet roaring for love. Whitman heard that thunder-roll of the sea in his voice which meant so much to him. Even the black humor appealed to him.

Trying to convey the flavor of this humor to the solemn Traubel, he told him an anecdote. "Charles Dana the editor said to me: 'See here, Walt—have you spent all these years in the world and not learned what a sorry mean lot mankind is anyhow?'" That was it, Whitman laughed: the Carlylean humor. "Things all wrong, a bad smell in the car, bed bugs at home, the cocks noisy next door, a huckster crying his wares in the street, a little bit put out at the stomach, a cold in the head, somebody's unruly children. . . . Carlyle was chronically victimized by this defect of temper."


IF HE WAS restive now when it came to politics and elections, the only signs were a tendency toward general principles and a certain reluctance to deal in personalities. By the end of 1846 he was embroiled in political debate again, ostensibly over the suitability of Silas Wright as governor. He had campaigned previously for Governor Wright. Possibly he was the only kind of politician Whitman could wholeheartedly believe in. He admired the man's integrity, his reluctance to put himself forward for reelection at all. Wright's refusal to grant political favors in New York was another reason for idealists like Whitman to back him. Ironically it was this very incorruptibility of Wright's which allowed the opposing Hunker section in. Acting through President Polk, they filled all available vacancies with their recommendations.

As the breach in the Democratic party widened, Whitman seemed unaware of its seriousness. Even when the New York election that year was lost he was casting about for causes other than the schism. By the following spring he was busy developing his theory of turbulence as a good, seeing in the apparent destructiveness of elections a sign that people, like nature, erupted from time to time. If the party line was breached, didn't that make for greater fluidity, vitality? In the long run the people were not fooled. Not for the first time he was anticipating Lincoln.

The paper's owner, Van Anden, never a Wright man, was having to put up with an editor whose policies were an embarrassment. It says much for his personal regard for Whitman that he held his peace. The crisis in the city came after the sudden death of Wright. Seizing their chance the Hunkers, one of whom was Van Anden, gained control of the party machine. Whitman saw the radical wing as most truly representative of the Democratic principles of free trade and territorial expansion, and went on blithely supporting it. His one proviso—the Wilmot Proviso—was that new lands should be kept free of slavery.

It was his first open declaration in favor of Free Soil. Urging it on his readers he made clear his position regarding slavery. It was remarkably like the stand Lincoln would take. Whitman's main concern was not the moral issue of slavery but the threat posed to the Union, and to white labor. He had a deep-seated objection to extremists, saw great danger in them, in particular the rantings of the abolitionists. Nevertheless he stood for the prohibition of slavery in the annexed lands and was under the illusion that his fellow Democrats were of the same mind. The truth was that the party dissidents—called Barnburners after the farmer who set his barn burning to get rid of the rats—were in retreat. By August 1848 they were in an unholy alliance with antislavery Whigs and abolitionists, flying their flag of "free soil, free speech, free labor, and free men." The Democratic party lay shattered.

One doesn't need to be charitable toward Whitman's stance vis à vis the plight of slaves. The prospect of contemporary America was his context, and we have to place him within it. He had never been in the South; had a fortune-teller predicted he would soon be in Louisiana it would have astounded him. What did he know of the reality of black slavery? In principle he opposed all forms of involuntary servitude, holding with Emerson that the oppressed spirit shamed and tainted "the republic of Man." He had once heard the great man end a lecture by asking the rhetorical question, "What right have I to speak of slavery? Are we not *all* slaves?"

Whitman thought like Fourier that man's duty was to keep the Sacred Flame, and he wanted liberation for all. No one was going to shunt him into a corner. For him the chief issue was not "our colored brethren" but the principle of prohibition itself. Slavery in the slave states was part of the social fabric of the South and he could find no grounds for objecting to it, repugnant though it might be to him personally. Tussling with himself, he came out with his statement of intent in an *Eagle* piece entitled "Set Down Your Feet, Democrats!"

"If there are to be States to be formed out of territory lately annexed or to be annexed by any means to the United States," he wrote grandiloquently, "let the Democratic members of Congress (and Whigs too, if they like) plant themselves quietly, without bluster, but fixedly and without compromise, on the requirement that *Slavery be prohibited* in them forever."

He was at least out in the open. He had in fact served notice on himself. With Van Anden breathing down his neck, he claimed for the *Eagle* the proud distinction of being the first Democratic paper to come out unequivocally under the banner of Free Soil. What appeared to Whitman a unanimity of conscience in the party, at any rate in the North, soon buckled under the strain. Various dubious allies were joining the supposed coalition. One was the arch-Whig Daniel Webster. Whitman suspected him of being corrupt as well as addicted to the brandy bottle.

It would surely have been extraordinary if Whitman had revealed himself to us as a lover of blacks and Indians. He had no time for the smug half-lies of the abolitionists, afire like holy rollers with their own righteousness, willing to bring down the whole of society on everyone's heads for the sake of their consciences. Whitman blamed them and their "abominable fanaticism" for turning American against American. He detested even more the English of the species. Back in his *Aurora* days he had drawn attention to a widely circulated lithograph which compared "Slavery as It Exists in America" with "Slavery as It Exists in England." Contented slaves were shown on cotton plantations, side by side with a picture of starving English farm laborers shivering in their wretched hovels or cowering in the workhouse. How dare the British, Whitman fulminated, preach to us about the Southern slaves? Yet English reformers were backing their American counterparts with money and with tracts calling for universal brotherhood.

Pictures. We can find other pictures in *Leaves of Grass*, lovely narratives and word-scenes instinct with a very different kind of awareness. Whitman seemed particularly fascinated by dispossessed Indians, the aboriginal ghosts and demons haunting his America. Usually they were red girls and squaws, rather than the males appraised by Lawrence in New Mexico "with their curious female quality, their archaic figures, with high shoulders and deep archaic waists, like a sort of woman."

At the start of the century both the Whitmans and the Van Velsors owned slaves. At sundown in the Whitman farmstead a swarm of young blacks "squatted in a circle on the kitchen floor"—it was a vast interior—"eating their supper of Indian pudding and milk." One of Walt's grandmothers, Sara White, would heave split wood at her house servants, "a whole troop of 'em," Whitman said. His paternal grandmother remembered seeing at least a dozen slave children eating supper in her kitchen in the old days.

Once his mother told him of her encounter with an itinerant red Indian woman "when she was nearly a grown girl living at home with her parents on the old homestead." The woman appeared at the door like a gypsy. His mother's account moved him strangely and it stayed with him. When he came to retell the story in his poem "The Sleepers" it glowed in its parts like a benediction.

> On her back she carried a bundle of rushes for rushbottoming
>     chairs;
> Her hair straight shiny coarse black and profuse halfenveloped
>     her face,
> Her step was free and elastic . . . her voice sounded exquisitely
>     as she spoke.
>
> My mother looked in delight and amazement at the stranger,
> She looked at the beauty of her tallborne face and full and
>     pliant limbs,
> The more she looked upon her she loved her,
> Never before had she seen such wonderful beauty and purity;
> She made her sit on a bench by the jamb of the fireplace . . .
>     she cooked food for her,
> She had no work to give her but she gave her remembrance
>     and fondness.
>
> O my mother was loath to have her go away,
> All the week she thought of her, she watched for her many a
>     month,
> She remembered her many a winter and many a summer
> But the red squaw never came nor was heard of there again.

In "Song of Myself" he noticed a squaw reduced to peddling her wares in the new buying-and-selling world of white America, "wrapt in her yellow-hemmed cloth" as she stood "offering moccasins and bead-bags for sale." Earlier comes the dreamlike wedding of two Rousseauesque children of nature, where the joining of white and red is accomplished with biblical simplicity in the open-air Eden of the West.

> I saw the marriage of the trapper in the open air in the far west,
>     the bride was a red girl,
> Her father and his friends sat near cross-legged and dumbly
>     smoking, they had moccasins to their feet and large thick
>     blankets hanging from their shoulders,
> On a bank lounged the trapper, he was drest mostly in skins,
>     his luxuriant beard and curls protected his neck, he held his
>     bride by the hand.
> She had long eyelashes, her head was bare, her coarse straight

locks descended upon her voluptuous limbs and reach'd to her feet.

A far cry this from the opinionated journalist, product of his age and indistinguishable from other white Northerners, who saw nothing to disagree with in the sentiments of William H. Seward, soon to be Lincoln's Secretary of State. "The African race here is a foreign and feeble element," Seward said, "and like the Indians incapable of assimilation. . . . A pitiful exotic unnecessarily transplanted into our fields."

Whitman had grown up in a Brooklyn where manumitted blacks holed up in slums along James Street sloping up from the waterfront. They were bone-poor and shiftless. They let their children run wild. Either they were odd-job men or they begged cravenly from passersby. As a boy and youth he would have absorbed all the bigotry and rumor concerning them. They were said to degenerate into insanity and drunkenness as soon as they were freed, unable to grasp the concept of freedom. Turning in the 1850s to a poetry which changed his blood as it was meant to change ours, Whitman opened channels of sympathy in himself toward flesh other than his own. Sympathy and identity were the watchwords of his approach to worlds that had been walled off from him till then. Suddenly, dark company was being kept. In his book of weddings he wrote of strange meetings taking place: this in an America calling itself free, a democracy hemmed in with all the old fears and denials.

> The runaway slave came to my house and stopt outside,
> I heard his motions crackling the twigs of the woodpile,
> Through the swung half-door of the kitchen I saw him limpsy and
>    weak,
> And went where he sat on a log and led him in and assured him,
> And brought water and fill'd a tub for his sweated body and bruis'd
>    feet,
> And gave him a room that enter'd from my own, and gave him
>    some coarse clean clothes,
> And remember perfectly well his revolving eyes and his
>    awkwardness. . . .

As a frontiersman in his cabin, firelock leaning in the corner unattended, he draws near to the heart's brother whose color we do not even notice. There and then, by a little miracle of humility, he achieves peace and trust. It is the gospel according to Saint Walt. If we can't quite go all the way with his gentle picture of heaven, we have no trouble with the hell that follows.

> I am the hounded slave, I wince at the bite of the dogs,
> Hell and despair are upon me, crack and again crack the
>     marksmen,
> I clutch the rails of the fence, my gore drips, thinn'd with the ooze
>     of my skin,
> I fall on the weeds and stones,
> The riders spur their unwilling horses, haul close,
> Taunt my dizzy ears and beat me violently over the head with
>     whip-stocks.

But before this we find ourselves confronted by a black giant in all his physical luxuriance and then invited to love him by this "caresser of life," simply because he is so splendidly *there*. It is Chateaubriand's Noble Savage, but with a difference. Whitman loved the health of the body, loved the ancient Greeks and was always ready to be pagan, given half a chance. His realism nearly but not quite vanquishes the Ideal. But we get a real man for all that, one he asks us to accept, sweat and all, be enamored of him, and then go on, "do not stop there":

> The negro that drives the long dray of the stone-yard, steady and
>     tall he stands pois'd on one leg on the string-piece,
> His blue shirt exposes his ample neck and breast and loosens over
>     his hip-band,
> His glance is calm and commanding, he tosses the slouch of his
>     hat away from his forehead,
> The sun falls on his crispy hair and mustache, falls on the black
>     of his polish'd and perfect limbs.

Yes: perfect. Only no one knew better than Whitman that nothing is ever perfect in this world. Melville, roaming over the high seas and coming to the paradisal South Seas, thought he had found the Golden Age in the huge blue dream of the Pacific. His gentle laughing islanders seduced his soul before he fled back to those ugly beasts of his own tribe, the white man. The whaling ship was one hell, New York the other. Gauguin, another escapee, painting his childlike, inscrutable models, was never more French. Tahiti was like Samoa, a mirage. Whitman too dreamed of his "friendly flowing savage" who could confer the blessing of life on him by touching him, liking him; who had "behavior lawless as snow-flakes, words simple as grass, uncombed head, laughter, and naiveté." Was this enchanting creature lost, or waiting there beyond, for the disease of civilization to be worked through? Or was he all the time inside him? Was it nothing more or less than the "all" feeling Melville experienced sometimes, despite himself, wriggling free from the straitjacket of his wretched separateness? "You must often have felt it," he wrote to Hawthorne in a letter, "lying on the grass on a warm summer's day. Your legs seem to send out shoots into the earth. Your hair feels like leaves upon your head."

Whitman would have known exactly what Melville meant. It was the sensation he had bathed in from an early age, delighting him so much that

> I think I could turn and live with animals, they are so placid and
>     self-contained,
> I stand and look at them long and long.
>
> They do not sweat and whine about their condition,
> They do not lie awake in the dark and weep for their sins,
> They do not make me sick discussing their duty to God,
> Not one is dissatisfied, not one is demented with the mania of
>     owning things. . . .

But he knew there was no going back, no being a savage again. All the same, when it came to being civilized he was profoundly ambivalent and did his best to circumvent it by various means: by the casualness of his dress, by his loafing, his sea and sun bathing. Always he was having to find new outlets for the savage in him who kept clamoring to be let out. The most important of course would be *Leaves of Grass.*

It was the savage in Melville who urged Ishmael in *Moby-Dick* to reflect that "long exile from Christendom and civilization inevitably restores a man to that condition in which God placed him, i.e. what is called savagery." But Melville was aristocratic, far removed from Whitman's laboring ancestors, although both came from the same stock, English and Dutch. What he did share with his unknown contemporary was a sense of the absurdity of a literary career. It was just unreal. He was the "helpful giant"—Whitman was the other—expected by Emerson to come "out of unhandselled savage nature."

While the self-educated editor of the *Eagle* was having intuitions of his own about the explosive nature of the age, Emerson was writing in his journal of 1847: "In history, the great moment is when the savage is just ceasing to be a savage . . . that moment of transition— the foam hangs but a moment on the wave. . . ."


✵ His time at the *Eagle* was drawing to an end. In a round-about fashion it was the Wilmot Proviso that finally unseated him from the editor's chair. But in reality it was sheer intransigence. He simply refused to compromise. The actual issue was in the end less crucial than some heaven-and-earth absolute he steered by in his heart, represented by the image of Silas Wright.

Whether he ever saw his situation as invidious is unclear, but when Senator Lewis Cass of Michigan, nominated for president in 1848, entered the fray, time began to run out for Whitman.

Cass was the Democrat who by his previous efforts had managed to undermine support for the Wilmot Proviso in the House of Representatives. Supporters and foes had been batting it to and fro so many times before it was quashed that members of the House— Lincoln was one—remembered voting for it again and again in the years leading up to the Civil War.

When Cass wrote to a friend in Tennessee outlining his objections to the proviso, the letter was leaked to the Democratic press. Whitman devoted an editorial to countering Cass's arguments in detail. The senator's main assertion was that the slave debate was not the business of Congress but should be settled by those who actually lived in the new territories. Only they had the right to do so.

Two days after Whitman's rebuttal a column of extracts from the Cass letter appeared without editorial comment in the *Eagle*. Either Whitman had been relieved of his editorship by then or the owner had gone over his head and intervened. A story of his, "The Boy Lover," which he was reprinting in installments, came out on the same day. Possibly this was already set up. In his *Specimen Days* piece, "Starting Newspapers," Whitman merely records the bald facts. "The troubles in the Democratic party broke forth about these times (1848–1849) and I split off with the radicals, which led to rows with the boss and the party, and I lost my place."

By the end of January a new editor had replaced him. The

Brooklyn and New York papers soon got wind of Whitman's dismissal and were happy to get mileage out of the affair. The *Brooklyn Advertiser* reported with glee that a "great disturbance" caused havoc at the *Eagle* office—some fracas involving the editor and one of his visitors. More explicitly, "When personally insulted by a certain prominent politician, Mr. Whitman kicked the individual down the editorial stairs." The *New York Globe* joined in the fun.

Goaded by the satire the *Eagle* under its new editor felt impelled to issue a statement. "The publisher, in the course of his business arrangements, has found it necessary to dispense with one of its editors"—they only employed one—"and although he did not see fit to consult the *Globe* in regard to the matter, yet he claims that it has no right to misrepresent his motives, or in any way meddle in his affairs."

Both the *Tribune* and Bryant's *Evening Post* had, it seems, been aware for some time of the long-running dispute inside the *Eagle*. They knew as well that Whitman's radical friends were aiming to start a new daily of their own with Whitman in charge. The *Eagle*, they said, had looped the loop and gone back to its Old Hunkerism again.

Political disagreements aside, Van Anden and Whitman had respect and even liking for each other. After the ex-editor's departure at least seventeen contributions by him went into the paper. But gossip about the rupture and the reasons for Whitman's sacking continued to rankle. Eighteen months after the event Van Anden went public, his style the usual mixture of derision and huff used in the trade to explain an action. "Mr. W. came here from the *Star* office where he was getting four or five dollars a week; he was connected with the *Eagle* for about two years and we think we had a pretty fair opportunity to understand him. Slow, indolent, heavy, discourteous, and without steady principles, he was a clog upon our success, and reluctant as we were to make changes we still found it absolutely necessary to do so. . . . Mr. W. has no political principles, nor, for that matter, principles of any sort. . . . Whoever knows him will laugh at the idea of his *kicking any body*, much less a prominent politician. He is too indolent to kick a musketo."

Whitman, unemployed again and not overconcerned about it, never sorry to be off the leash and wondering about his next move, was probably a fair way from being broke. He was a thrifty man and had had a good long run, enjoying as prosperous a time as he would ever have. Something would turn up. A man of the pen now, though never a man of letters—he would mutilate a book without a qualm, tearing out a chapter to take off to the beach with him—he was working class still in his loyalties but seen as middle class by society and increasingly by himself. He had his name on title deeds. He had money in the bank. He had done plenty but been nowhere. His enormous country, sprawling emptily to the west and south, was as unknown to him as Asia.

Something did turn up. One evening, it was a Thursday in February 1848, he was lounging in the lobby of the Broadway Theatre near Pearl Street. It was intermission. Friends took him across for drinks with a Southern newspaperman, Sam McClure, who was about to launch a new daily in his home town with a partner, A. H. Hayes. They wanted an editor for it. The town in question was New Orleans. "After fifteen minutes' talk (and a drink) we made a formal bargain, and he paid me two hundred dollars down to bind the contract and bear my expenses." Two days later he was packed and on his way. He was twenty-nine. His brother, Jeff, fourteen, an apprentice printer now, went with him.

It was an extraordinarily rapid decision for a man like Whitman who was so cautious and liked to weigh and ponder things. The job was offered "impromptu" and accepted in the same spirit, "between acts" in a theatre. He must have felt the time was ripe—and how fitting that it should have happened in such a context. For years he had been expounding the doctrine of "manifest destiny" and dwelling rapturously on the great challenge presented by the republic's vastness. Now he could experience it for himself, on the very stage he had so far only dreamed momentously about. The future poet of democratic vistas could gaze on those vistas and wildernesses first-hand, see those gigantic, generous new sunrises flooding up as if for him.

# 6

# South

He set out on February 11, 1848, happy to shake off the dust of local politics for a while. The Mexican War had ended but New Orleans he knew was still a fulcrum, swarming with troops and with a contingent of newspaper correspondents based there. The two Whitmans boarded a train on Friday, on the first leg of a journey estimated to take a fortnight if they were lucky. They had a deadline to meet: the first issue of the new paper was supposed to come out on March 5.

They must have felt like pioneers and imagined their train carriages to be wagons rolling them into the unknown, toward the rude frontiers they had only heard about. They spent Friday night in Baltimore, then at seven in the morning climbed aboard a train that took them forward as far as Cumberland, Maryland, for the transfer to a stage and the exhausting ride across the Alleghenies to Wheeling. Probably they hardly noticed their fellow passengers' compulsive habit of spitting, described by Dickens on his first visit to America when he was astonished by "the flashes of saliva" flying "so perpetually and incessantly out of the windows all the way that it looked as though they were ripping open feather-beds inside, and letting the wind dispose the feathers!"

At Cumberland they stared out in a dying sunset at hundreds of loaded wagons and at strapping drovers lit heroically by their heaped soft-coal fires, chafing themselves to keep warm. These were the famous huge-wheeled Conestoga wagons with their hooped canvas hoods, the prairie schooners. Cumberland was a railhead, raying goods out across the West aboard the "Tartar-looking groups" camped and ready to go. Whitman was keeping notes of the trip for a series of articles he hoped to print in his new paper, the *Crescent*.

That evening in Cumberland he sat down somewhere quiet and described the "night now falling down around us like a very large cloak of black broadcloth," adding self-consciously, "I fancy *that* figure at least hasn't been used up by the poets." Startlingly close, the Alleghenies reared up " 'some pumpkins' (as they say here) right before our nasal members...." He would jettison the distancing quotation marks in due course, along with irony and his New York smartness and superiority.

Queuing at the stage station they saw their baggage dumped on a weighing machine and their names located on the passenger list. Jammed in a low compartment with seven other passengers and assorted luggage they raced for the rearing mountains, courtesy of the National Road and Good Intent Stage Company, heads thumping on the ceiling at every pothole.

It was a cold night, snow on the ground as they climbed higher. "Up we toiled and down we clattered... over these mighty warts on the great breast of nature." Every ten miles entailed a halt for fresh horses. At one of these mountain relay stations, in the small hours, the brothers got down to stretch their legs and thaw out in the waiting room, a great bare flickering hole, the crude beams blackened and dried. They joined a gang of "ten or twelve great strapping drovers, reclining about the room on benches, and as many more before the huge fire.... We had just descended a large and very steep hill, and just off on one side of us was a precipice of apparently hundreds of feet. The silence of the grave spread over this solemn scene; the mountains were covered in their white shrouds of snow...."

They were far from home, embedded in a weird, dislocating night that must have struck them as almost gruesome. Mountains pressed close on all sides around the precipitous tracks they banged along and clung to, past large leafless trees looming out; then to be tipped into a room "half filled with men curiously enwrapped in garments of a fashion till then never seen—and the flickering light from the mighty fire putting a red glow upon most objects, and casting others into a strong shadow." He was painting down his impressions, using a newly discovered visual language more or less for the first time.

It awed him, all of it, the biting cold of the wild slopes, a moon half buried in ragged clouds, large icy stars glittering. And these hard-faced drinking men sitting over ashy fires on the lumpy earthen floors of cavelike mountainside taverns. The freezing air numbed him, made him feel he had crossed a border and was out of the known world, beyond reach, in this desolate steepness under the flash of stars. But it was somehow wonderful, on the coiling road among this astonishment of raw elements. It moved awe in his soul: moved him to exclaim, "Faith! if I had an infidel to convert I would take him on the mountains, of a clear and beautiful night, when the stars are shining."

They took twenty-eight hours to reach Wheeling on the Ohio River. Their bones jarred, bodies aching as if they had been in a fight, they left the coach and found the *Saint Cloud,* a steam packet which would take them all the way to New Orleans, calling at Cincinnati, Louisville, Cairo, Natchez—not to mention endless stopping places, some of them not even boasting a landing stage.

The river steamer, a side-wheeler, must have struck them as an amazing vessel. To Dickens, also sampling one for the first time, it was more like a gimcrack floating hotel than anything you would expect to see in motion on a river. Ungainly, topheavy, the steamboat boarded by Dickens had "a long, black, ugly roof, covered with burnt-out feathery sparks; above which tower two iron chimneys, and a hoarse escape valve, and a glass steerage house. Then, in order as the eye descends toward the water, are the sides and doors and windows of the staterooms, jumbled as oddly together as though they formed a small street, built by the varying tastes of a dozen men: the whole is supported on beams and pillars resting on a dirty barge, but a few inches above the water's edge: and in the narrow space between this upper structure and the barge's deck are the furnace fires and machinery, open at the sides to every wind that blows, and every storm of rain that drives along its path."

If he was wise the traveler put the glaring furnace fires out of his mind as he ate and slept and wandered to and fro in this "frail pile of painted wood." Jeff, though, was too young to feel nervous. He was in a wonderland, a floating palace where you promenaded to and fro and felt thoroughly pampered and feasted on amazing meals. They had reached Wheeling on Sunday night. It was past ten. They found their steamboat and their comfortable stateroom and stumbled into bed, passing out at once. The first thing Walt heard next morning was the breakfast bell. They were under way. A river voyage lasting twelve days lay before them.

Jeff wrote home ecstatically, "Mother you have no idea of the splendor and comfort of these western river steamboats. The cabin is on the deck, and staterooms on either side of it, there are two beds in each room. The greatest of these splendors is the eating (you know I always did love eating) department. Every thing you would find in the Astor House in New York, you find on these boats. I will give you a little description of the way we live on board. For breakfast we have: coffee, tea, ham and eggs, beef steak, sausages, hot cakes, with plenty of good bread, sugar etc etc. For dinner: roast beef, ditto mutton, ditto veal, boiled ham, roast turkey, ditto goose, with pie and puddings, and for supper every thing that is good to eat."

The yellow-brown river seemed sometimes to be nothing more than a porridge of mud. Whitman, keyed up to rhapsodize over an America unlike anything he had yet seen, admitted that the shores of the Ohio as he gazed at them were "barren of interest." The uncultivated river bank had nothing on it to lift the spirit; the occasional settler's cabin with its windows stuffed with old hats, old clothes to keep out the wind; burned and devastated forest clearings jagged with trunks, stinking with decayed vegetation in swamp-holes. Cairo, when they reached it, only reinforced this impression. Sunk in the mud on a delta where the Ohio and Mississippi joined, it was "good for the ague" and that was all.

Every five minutes a bell rang to warn the captain that floating logs had been sighted. The journey was tortuous; only the meals were attacked with a rush. At dozens of grey towns, or at places where the landscape seemed empty of life, the *Saint Cloud* weighed anchor and unloaded barrels of pork, lard, and flour, bags of coffee, crates of live fowls, geese, turkeys, chickens, hardware, dry goods. There was even a horse on board, tethered and waiting to be delivered. Watching in astonishment as the Westerners on board fell on every meal like hogs, Whitman wondered why they were in such a tearing hurry, since there was absolutely nothing to enjoy in the way of scenery. At some halts they picked up more passengers, pausing in mid-river while the newcomers were rowed out to them. Others were landed at the base of steep banks with their possessions. These goodbyes had been bleak, despairing separations for Dickens as he stood at the rail watching the strange scenes:

"The men get out of the boat first; help the women; take out the bag, the chest, the chair; bid the rowers goodbye and shove the boat off for them. At the first plash of the oars in the water, the oldest woman in the party sits down in the old chair, close to the water's edge, without speaking a word. . . . They all stand where landed as if stricken into stone; and look after the boat. . . ."

Coming to towns around the bends was a relief after those endless miles of muddy banks, but often a letdown when you landed for a look around. Whitman found the streets of Cincinnati dirty while acknowledging it to be a "Queen City" in commerce. He liked Louisville better. Dickens on the other hand admired Cincinnati and thought it beautiful, cheerful, thriving, and animated. From his hotel window he looked down to see a black man chopping wood on the pavement "and another black man is talking (confidentially) to a pig."

THE ROMANTIC in Whitman was suffering some hard knocks. To begin with, his fellow passengers on the stage had been either surly and mute or crashing bores. A garrulous old Ohio farmer dominated what little conversation there was. Then the Ohio and Mississippi, sludgy, slow-moving waterways, were a big disappointment. "In poetry and romance," he reported, "these rivers are talked of as though they were cleanly streams; but it is astonishing what a difference is made by the simple fact that they are always and altogether excessively muddy—mud, indeed, being the prevailing character both afloat and ashore."

But for all that it was a joyful thing to be traveling south. There was a certain exaltation, glamour even, in the thought of that southern drift. To a Northerner like Whitman the South symbolized escape from the frantic change and mechanization of the North. People there were believed to have a natural equanimity, to be insouciant, with more time for pleasantries, as the Southerners he had met confirmed it. One only had to look at them, hear their mannered, slow speech, notice their Old World courtesy. Cultured New Yorkers saw the South as aristocratic, as a kind of Europe. Working people too were drawn to the glamour and mystery of the imagined South. It had forbidden pleasures, tropical nights, luxuriance. Whitman's attraction to this dream shows in his novel *Franklin Evans*. The slave woman whom Evans marries is a fantasy spun out of

Northern wishes: burning with corrupt passion, sexual to her finger-tips, all wickedness and corrosive magnetism. This fascination and sympathy for the South made New York a Copperhead city during the Civil War. A Lincoln biographer describes a Copperhead as a Southern sympathizer, so named "because of their practice of cutting the head of the Goddess of Liberty from a copper penny to wear in their coat lapels, and from the venomous snake of that name."

Somewhere below Louisville they had a fright. Suddenly the sluggish water turned devilish, rushing them over rapids and drop-ping twenty feet in less than three miles as the *Saint Cloud* pilot chose the faster route rather than the roundabout loop by canal on the Kentucky side. Passengers went pale and bit their lips. The boat gave a series of sickening lurches, rocked and slid, timbers creaking a protest as they accelerated into the "boiling place," grating here and there on the bottom and missing half-submerged rocks by inches. Jeff, writing to his mother, told her that "some of the passengers went to bed looking so gloomy as if they were about to be hung. Altho I was frightened a good deal, it was not so much as some of the men were. If the boat had sunk we were a few feet of the shore, but I don't think we could have got there, the current was so swift."

Perhaps as a result of being shaken by this ugly stretch of river, or else driven into doubt and puzzlement by the muffled night and the strangeness, listening to the river rustling, peering into the black shadows of a shoreless world, Whitman wrote his first poem in years. It is a poem of slippage, phantom-haunted. Full of apprehension, it attempts to exorcise the moonless dark with its clutching "river fiends." He thought well enough of it to publish it later in the *Crescent*.

> How solemn! sweeping this dense black tide!
>    No friendly lights i' the heaven o'er us;
> A murky darkness on either side,
>    And kindred darkness all before us!
>
> Now, drawn near the shelving rim
>    Weird-like shadows suddenly rise;
> Shapes of mist and phantoms dim
>    Baffle the gazer's straining eyes.
>
> River friends, with malignant faces!
>    Wild and wide their arms are thrown,
> As if to clutch in fatal embraces

Him who sails their realms upon.

Then, by the trick of our swift motion,
  Straight, tall giants, an army vast,
Rank by rank, like the waves of ocean,
  On the shore march stilly past.

How solemn! the river a trailing pall,
  Which takes, but never again gives back;
And moonless and starless the heaven's arch'd wall,
  Responding an equal black!

Oh, tireless waters! like Life's quick dream,
  Onward and onward ever hurrying—
Like Death in this midnight hour you seem,
  Life in your chill drops greedily burying!

Here, as Paul Zweig points out, was a poem wrenched out of a real experience at last, even if it does glance over its shoulder at Poe in every verse. It was still Walter Whitman, not yet Walt, but written out of need: an urgent poem.

On Friday morning, February 25, two weeks and twenty-four hundred miles after starting out, they were within reach of New Orleans. On the previous afternoon they had joined crowds of passengers at the rails to stare at the levees, manmade bulwarks of earth to prevent the low-lying land from flooding. Then the floating dome of the Saint Charles Hotel was sighted. There were excited shouts but still they churned on with no city in view. Finally they were inching through a cluttered river and past river steamers, ferries, ocean vessels, and then the wharves themselves stretching for three miles, with enormous warehouses behind and office buildings in rising tiers. And what wharves: heaped with hogsheads of sugar and flour, with sacked ice, pork barrels, cotton bales. Color was splashed everywhere; enormous bunches of bananas, huge crates of lemons, scenting the air and mingling with the pungent aroma of coffee. Wharfside restaurants were selling oyster stew, crawling with fish smells, lobster and shrimp. The scene was sensual and extravagant, exposed to the sky with an amazing boldness.

They docked at last on Friday night and slept the night on board the *Saint Cloud*. Next morning they went looking for a room in a boarding house. They found one in Tojdrass Street, corner of Saint Charles. It was squalid and uncomfortable. Poor Jeff, homesick already for his mother's cleanliness and love, moaned to her in a letter about the dirt and confessed how much he missed her. "You could not only see the dirt but you could taste it, and you had to too if you ate anything at all."

Soon they moved out, tried a few other establishments, and finally discovered a decent billet at the Tremont House just around the corner, where for nine dollars a week Walt could rent good clean beds and buy decent food for them both. The street noise was deafening but Walt slept through it, even if Jeff didn't. They were next door to a theatre and close to a fine park in Lafayette Square. Directly opposite their rooms were the *Crescent* offices at 93 Saint Charles Street. They soon worked out the reason for the tremendous din and activity: this street was the Broadway of New Orleans.

❧ WHITMAN'S DAY at the *Crescent* was a long one, usually from nine in the morning till eleven at night, when the paper was put to bed. How much of that time he actually spent in the office is anyone's guess. The owners were in effect joint editors, and Whitman had a staff of three under him, a large complement for a paper at that time. Leading editorials were written by a Mr. Larue. Then there was a young fellow by the name of Reeder, good-natured but often inebriated. He was the "city news" man. Another youngster, Da Ponte—grandson of one of Mozart's librettists, Lorenzo Da Ponte—translated foreign items from Mexico and abroad, and was also a general factotum.

Whitman's job seems to have been to coordinate these activities and also take charge of the papers arriving every day by mail, dozens of them. From these he "made up the news," using the scissors-and-paste technique common in his day. In the period before teletype and news agencies, this mutual exchanging between newspapers would have been the normal cannibalistic procedure. Clipping and condensing was something Walt did almost with his eyes closed.

He also wrote features, though these dwindled in number during the three months he was there. He got extra pay for these. Jeff, hired as office boy and printer's devil, earned five dollars a week. Mainly Jeff occupied himself with the exchanges which accumulated in such large quantities, bundling them up for sale at twenty-five cents a hundred. Outgoing mailbags were his other responsibility, a job too heavy for him, Walt thought. He went down a number of times with dysentery, a debilitating sickness which must have lowered his spirits badly. He wrote frequent letters home, begging for news and contact, a lonely boy experiencing his first time away from home. It took weeks for his mother to reply.

Walt had good friends still on the *Eagle* who took copies of the *Crescent* round to the Whitmans and conveyed to him what news there was, reporting on his family's health. Louisa Whitman's first letter—out of date by the time it arrived—told of the severe weather in Brooklyn. It had been too cold for the father to work. They were hard up as usual, so Walt gave instruction for thirty-one dollars to be taken from his account before the mortgage interest fell due. In this letter he asked how the saplings he had planted around the property were doing. Jeff wrote to say that his brother took care of his wages for him. When they had saved a thousand dollars they would come home, he added wistfully.

Jeff may not have been enjoying himself, but his brother undoubtedly was. "I frequently thought," he confided to his notebook, "that I felt better than ever before in my life." New Orleans was a city like no other; it issued calls to throw off Northern restraint at every street corner. And Whitman lived in the streets. The open street had been his element in Brooklyn and New York, and so it was here. The "immorality," though, was of a different order. Somehow its very laziness redeemed it.

Now and then he got up at dawn and walked down to the steamboat wharves. A haze of mist lifted off the water. It was like paddling in warm sun. A dozen bare-legged German sailors scrubbed the deck of their ship. He saw a Negro shy a large stone at the head of his mule. In his paper, in this slave-owning state, he mused aloud that if he owned that Negro he would treat him better than the man treated his mule, would give him a cowhide, he said facetiously, and get him to whip himself.

He went past a bench where a longshoreman was drunkenly snoring. The fellow wore a red shirt and blue working pants and had lost his socks. Shopkeepers were opening for business as he sauntered back. In Saint Mary's market he spotted a prominent lawyer sucking at a stick of sugar cane. In the market stalls hung "rounds of beef, haunches of venison and legs of mutton . . . that would have made a disciple of Graham forswear his hermit-like appetite." Sylvester Graham was a famous vegetarian crusader of the day.

Downtown, he admired the newsboys; they were "cute as foxes." Then he was being enveloped in the "savory smell of fried ham, broiled beef-steak with onions" seeping under the doors of restaurants, and felt hungry enough for some breakfast. At the Tremont House he sat down to "tea, a radish, a piece of toast and an egg" and opened one of the morning papers.

On these excursions he could always tell himself, strolling through the park at Lafayette Square or exploring the miles of levees, that he was collecting material for articles. True or not, he would have done it anyway. He was in a tropical, strongly foreign place which gave a spice to everything he was most accustomed to—the busy port life of a city that, like New York, opened its gates wide to immigrants. Ceaselessly busy streets led to dense copses of masts and moored boats of all sizes with their noses angled at the river. In a fanciful bit of verse he compared himself with a bewitched craft, swung by "a voluptuous languor/Soft the sunshine, silent the air," and told himself to beware of dangers lurking for a "young pilot of life."

If you're a puritan, playing with the idea of wickedness can be fun. He was always good, it seems, at skirting temptations. Not that we are told anything about his private life. Did he really have a black mistress as he later hinted, or was it a ploy to throw off the unwelcome insinuations of an effete English writer, out to embrace his example for the wrong reasons? Was he sworn to chastity like those heroes he had met in Plutarch? He loved manly grace, but only if it was unaware of itself. That was why he sought beauty where no one else was looking, in the common people. Van Gogh read his poems in Arles and knew he had found a kindred spirit.

All we are allowed to see in New Orleans is a picture of someone enjoying his sensations, and apart from that living entirely among crowds, without personal encounters of any kind. This of course was his secretiveness. As always we have to look for signs, decipher marks left in the sand, and be willing to wait.

New York, with its lurid contrasts, moral as well as visual, would have prepared him for this city. But the soft warm amorality of the air, heavy with sweet odors, was full of the relaxation of a glamorous world outside his experience. Frederick Law Olmsted, architect, visiting New Orleans a few years after Whitman, wrote: "I doubt if there is a city in the world where the resident population has been so divided in its origin, or where there is such a variety in the tastes, habits, manners and moral codes of the citizen...so that nowhere are the higher qualities of man—as displayed in generosity, hospitality, benevolence and courage—better developed, or the lower qualities, likening him to a beast, less interfered with. . . ."

If we wait till 1858 we can have a poem which has misled earlier biographers.

> Once I passed through a populous city imprinting my brain
>     for future use with its shows, architecture, customs, traditions,
> Yet now of all that city I remember only a woman I casually met
>     there who detain'd me for love of me,
> Day by day and night by night we were together, all else has
>     long been forgotten by me,
> I remember I say only that woman who passionately clung to me,
> Again we wander, we love, we separate again,
> Again she holds me by the hand, I must not go,
> I see her close beside me with silent lips sad and tremulous.

New Orleans, strangely distinct with its different "architecture, customs, traditions," was the only "populous" city Whitman had known in 1858 apart from New York. So here, surely, was a romance to contemplate. Until, that is, along came Emory Holloway in 1920, having unearthed the original manuscript of the poem. It read,

> But now of all that city I remember only the man who wandered
>     with me there, for love of me.

The "she" in the published version was in fact a "he," a

> Rude and ignorant man who, when I departed, long and long
>     held me by the hand, with silent lips, sad and tremulous. . . .

The poems in the "Calamus" section of *Leaves of Grass* are unabashed songs of male love, which makes one wonder if his rather thin heterosexual "Children of Adam" group simply had this sex-changed poem transferred to it by way of reinforcement. And still we are in the dark. Was it grounded in reality? What did happen there in the Deep South? His reference to his six illegitimate children, "one living Southern grandchild—fine boy," and the mystery he kept promising to clear up for Horace Traubel, has had scholars on the wrong scent ever since. It seems likely now that the only babies he produced with his "father-stuff" were poems. Before that his seed went into the making of a poet, "Walt Whitman." But we shall never be sure. "They used to say," he told Traubel sweetly, "some of my friends—that all the babies of the land were Walt Whitman's babies. . . . They are like the first snow, the first blade of grass, the first anything—unstudied, unelaborated, untouched by rules." And that was how he left it, for others to unravel if they could. He was a sly old man.

TIME AND AGAIN, to explain and justify the method of his mature poetry, Whitman would use the word "indirect." He meant that truth itself comes at us indirect. This is the method of art, which tells lies and deals in ambiguity as a way of revealing the truth. Fiction, lying, concealment, doubleness—that was the approach he favored. Then he was free to be as bold and "open" as he wished. His beautiful poem, "I Saw in Louisiana a Live Oak Growing" tells us nothing about the life he led in New Orleans, except by inference. For it was probably while there, separated from his friends, that he understood once and for all the difficulties of his own nature. He had thought until then that he was self-sufficient, and he was not. He wanted love, and to be loved for what he was, if he was ever to come into leaf joyously like a tree.

> Without any companion it grew there uttering joyous
>     leaves of dark green,
> And its look, rude, unbending, lusty, made me think of myself,
> But I wonder'd how it could utter joyous leaves standing alone
>     there without its friends near, for I knew I could not,
> And I broke off a twig with a certain number of leaves
>     upon it, and twined around it a little moss,
> And brought it away, and I have placed it in sight
>     in my room,
> It is not needed to remind me of my own dear friends
> (For I believe lately I think of little else than of them),
> Yet it remains to me a curious token, it makes me think of manly
>     love;
> For all that, and though the live-oak glistens there in
>     Louisiana solitary in a wide flat space,
> Uttering joyous leaves all its life without a friend or a lover near,
> I know very well I could not.

For all that, by and large "New Orleans was a great place and no mistake." One discovery he made was that the "magnet South," "glistening, perfumed," which gave such pangs of nostalgia for a vanished age of "rich blood, impulse and love" and fascinated him so strangely, could only be lived in fully if you were a kind of renegade, willing to decompose in this soft flowery heat. And he was never that. Always the abiding characteristic of Whitman in both his life and work is its forward movement. Like his great admirer Lawrence he struggled forward along some road that his soul could accept, a road with swerves and detours but leading on. But how good to pause and brush against this other existence which seemed miraculously devoid of struggle. In the wisteria-scented air it was as if the season was turned on its head. His family sat shivering in Prince Street and here the peach trees were already in blossom and he could gaze at "dark Creole beauties" going into communion in the candle-lit cathedral "with an air that seemed to say that beauty was part of their religion."

When he introduced Margaret, a tropical fruit spilling with juice in his *Franklin Evans*, he had had to imagine this scarlet womanhood. "She was of that luscious and fascinating appearance often seen in the south, where a slight tinge of the deep color, large, soft, voluptuous eyes and beautifully cut lips...combined with a complexion just sufficiently removed from clear white to make the spectator doubtful whether he is gazing on a brunette or one who has indeed some hue of African blood in her veins."

In Saint Charles Street he could see these lurid beauties parading in their glory as they went past the gaslit entrances of the hotels and theatre. Their dresses swept insolently against the flowers of street vendors who were also Creoles, smiling and winking at passersby and maybe with another occupation in the daytime. Writing coyly in the *Crescent* Whitman remarked that "it would be in bad taste to attempt to find out."

In 1888 he was altogether less reticent, living up to his reputation as a "shocking" author. "The octoroon was not a whore," he said, "as we call a certain class of women here—and yet *was*, too. A hard class to comprehend: women with splendid bodies—no bustles, no corsets. Large, luminous eyes. Face a rich olive. Habits indolent, yet not lazy as we define laziness North...always more than pretty—'pretty' is too weak a word to apply to them. Fascinating, magnetic, sexual, ignorant, illiterate...." In his woman-smothering era and with New Orleans behind him he would object in a letter to

Emerson to "writers fraudulently assuming as always dead what every one knows to be always alive," namely sex.

He felt in the thick of life for many reasons. New Orleans had been a hub of the war effort during the Mexican War. Though the war was over, steamers full of soldiers still sailed regularly for Vera Cruz and came back loaded with wounded men. Outside the city there were army camps; there were even tents in Lafayette Square. The endless movement of soldiers and officers through the streets gave him a sense of being at the center of national events.

JOURNALISTS WERE used to sitting in murkily lit barrooms, and in the flashy Saint Charles Hotel he sat sipping "cobblers," brandy, champagne, as he got acquainted with planters and cotton traders, making on-the-spot notes for character sketches he contributed to the *Crescent*. These hastily knocked-off pen portraits were invariably satirical. Even though they were heavily indebted to Dickens he was finding a light touch he had not managed before. Saturated in the grace and ease of New Orleans he forgot to moralize, lost some of his inhibitions, and acted the ironist and epicurean, a rascal observing his fellow rascals who took life as it came. Out from his pen pranced Peter Funk, confidence trickster, a Creole flower vendor, Miss Dusky Grisette—who could have been a "*jolie-grisette*" too—and Daggerdraw Bowieknife, Esq., a swaggering Southern type, elegant, well-bred, and probably a killer. A lovelorn young man, Samuel Sensitive, moons over visions of "darting eyes and tresses like the morn" until he is reduced to a "qualmish" creature who recites Burns to a bale of cotton. Later in his gallery of portraits comes John Jinglebrain, a city dandy dressed in the latest fashion, his hair thickly greased.

While employed on the *Crescent* Whitman kept discreetly quiet on the subject of racial policy and his Free Soil convictions. The magnolia was in full blossom, great laden trees of it along the streets as the brothers promenaded in the evenings and enjoyed the night air. On Sundays Whitman loved the French market, where he could eavesdrop on a dozen languages and get his large cup of coffee from "the immense shining kettle" of a massive Creole mulatto woman weighing 230 pounds.

In one of the hotel lounges he made the acquaintance of an old grey-haired farmer who, he thought, must have a soul as firm and honest as a hickory stick. The old man's son happened to be a senator. There the farmer was, gripping his cane in a clawlike hand and reading in the paper about a speech made by his son, speaking of it with tears of pride in his voice. He was a living Whitman patriarch, one of those sturdy cultivators of a soil in which the strongest and best kind of sympathy had been planted. He had spent a lifetime following natural rhythms and belonged to that fecund darkness in which a lost innocence sheltered, that Whitman depended on for the pastoral vision he intended to sow. It would knit his book together and it was under threat.

These beloved rich-mannered elders came down in a long line from the legendary Fathers themselves. As bearers of the only democracy he could believe in, he would reserve his most reverential language for them, out of awe and love. Before he came to raise Lincoln to the permanence of myth in his great elegy, he would sing of the simple farmer-god, introduced almost casually in "I Sing the Body Electric." Anonymous at the start, by the end of the passage he represents the wise human face of an epic America in mortal danger from itself, liable to come asunder in violence and lunacy. None of those dangers is mentioned, though they are everywhere present. Touch this man, the poem is saying, and all will be well. The perils facing us will fall away. Go back and start again. Once growth was from the soil, direct. Start with this man's splendid calm, his stature, the scarlet blood showing through the health of his face. Start with his common wisdom, greater than any we now know.

> This man was of wonderful vigor, calmness, beauty of person,
> The shape of his head, the pale yellow and the white of his hair
>     and beard, the immeasurable meaning of his black eyes, the
>     richness and breadth of his manners,
> There I used to go and visit him to see, he was wise also,
> He was six feet tall, he was over eighty years old, his sons were
>     massive, clean, bearded, tan-faced, handsome,
> They and his daughters loved him, all who saw him loved him,
> They did not love him by allowance, they loved him with personal
>     love,
> He drank water only, the blood show'd like scarlet through the
>     clear brown skin of his face. . . .
> When he went with his five sons and many grandsons to hunt or
>     fish, you would pick him out as the most beautiful and vigorous
>     of the gang. . . .

166

You would wish long and long to be with him, you would wish to
sit by him in the boat that you and he might touch each other.

One evening he caught sight of another hero, this time one he
had only read about. General Zachary Taylor of Mexican War fame
was expected by many to be the next president of the United States.
At the Saint Charles Theatre he had come to see a rather daring
show, Dr. Colyer's troupe of Model Artists, straight from "the Royal
Academies of London and Paris." Their seminude, absolutely station-
ary tableaux depicting famous sculptures such as the Medici Venus,
the Temptation, and Adam's first sight of Eve had been defended and
attacked in a number of American cities. Whitman was there to
write up the performance for the *Crescent*. The house lights went up
to show a man in the dress circle in civilian clothes, flanked by
uniformed aides. The audience clambered to their feet to pay homage
to the doughty hero of Buena Vista as the orchestra played "Hail
Columbia." Somehow this "jovial, old, rather stout plain man," his
face wrinkled and yellowish, laughing coarsely at everything comical,
dwindled in importance as Whitman looked at him. Should such a
man be president, he wondered, merely because of his skill and
courage on the field of battle?

Whitman was determined to stay clear of trouble and avoid
controversy during his stay on the *Crescent*. He was in a slave state,
able to witness slave auctions any day of the week, and well aware
that any opinions he might have leaked into the paper would have
cost him his job. But he was a free-soiler and the owners must have
known it. Colyer's models provided him with a safe topic. Replying
to the prudery of the *Mobile Herald* he wrote that their adverse
criticism "arises from an assumption of coarseness and grossness
intended. Take away this, and there is no need (in the cases under
discussion) of any opposition at all. Eve in Paradise—or Adam
either—would not be supposed to shock the mind." He was still left
with anger at the *Herald* and some other out-of-town newspapers,
with their "sickly prudishness that bars all appreciation of the divine
beauty evidenced in Nature's cunningest work—the human frame,
form and face."

Fuss or not, it was less controversial than the slave trade. Horace
Traubel, delving into the silt of paper in the detritus at Whitman's
feet in his Camden sick room, came up with an item clipped from
the *Natchez Free Trader* of May 11, 1848.

I have just arrived from Missouri with ten Negroes, which I will sell at a bargain for cash. I have several boys about 21 years of age that are very likely, strictly No. 1. One fine seamstress and house servant, very likely. Those who wish to purchase and will buy the lot I will most certainly give a great bargain.

Asa L. Thomson.

Forks Road, Natchez, May 2, 1848.

Whitman exclaimed, "I remember it. Such a thing means enough to make you laugh or cry. And all in the *Free Trader* too! What a lot of nonsense has got current in the world with that word [*free*]. It's been made to stand for the most devilish and the most divine of human instincts. . . . Horace, a thousand years of history have been lived in the forty since Mr. Thomson advertised his bargains in human souls. Tragedy and comedy—both have been lived. We still suffer slaveries of one sort or another—particularly industrial slaveries—but nothing quite so raw as his could be quoted in America today. It's a good thing to keep around as a reminder—a warning."

If his young interlocutor thought he had the shrewd, cautious old boy in a corner at last he was mistaken. Whitman had never been an abolitionist: no one was going to label him one now. Persisting, Traubel was back the following day to ask how Whitman had felt at the time of John Brown's execution, after his famous antislavery raid at Harpers Ferry, Virginia. The "Good Gray Poet" would only answer, "Not enough to take away my appetite—to spoil my supper. My brother George, he thought it a martyrdom. I am never convinced by the formal martyrdoms alone. I see martyrdoms wherever I go: it is an average factor in life. Why should I go off emotionally half cocked only about the ostentatious cases?"

Whitman was doing his best to scandalize. But idealists never give up; never quite take in or believe what they hear. Traubel had one last try, facing Whitman with a loaded question. The Negro problem had not been solved by the Civil War—it tormented the American psyche as much now as it had before. Which party did he think likely to give the Negro his due? Whitman shook his head and mumbled, "The negro will get his due from the negro—from no one else."

He has been accused by critics of evasion. As time went on he fell silent before slavery as a blot on the national escutcheon. If pressed he would point to the efficacy of natural processes. Only by evolution would such dark stains be subsumed, wiped out finally in the fullness of time. All men were created equal, *black as well as white*. This was the stumbling block that would divide Republicans and Democrats in the last analysis.

Whitman would take his stand alongside Lincoln. If we read his lines in "I Sing the Body Electric" literally he was there as a silent observer in slave auctions in the New Orleans crowds. And why not? It would have been perfectly in character.

> A man's body at auction,
> (For before the war I often go to the slave-mart and watch the sale),
> I help the auctioneer, the sloven does not half know his business.

Did he find the scene repugnant? We have no way of telling. He is out to jolt us by implicating himself, even to the extent of getting his hands dirty: "I help the auctioneer." If this offends our sensibilities, so be it. The auctioneer too is human, to be taken into account. No euphemisms, no apologies. The artist in Whitman, willing to take note of everything, can't help it if he appalls us with his detachment.

He is after something else, working around to include us in his grand design. What we are involved in next turns rapidly into an object lesson.

> Gentlemen, look on this wonder!
> Whatever the bids of the bidders they cannot be high enough for it,
> For it the globe lay preparing quintillions of years without one animal or plant,
> For it the revolving cycles truly and steadily roll'd.

Lincoln himself would one day proclaim that "the Negro is a man," the words branding him in some quarters as a "black Republican." Then the politician he was must rush to qualify it with: I am not saying he is my equal, only that he has equal *rights*. This of course was inflammatory enough.

Whitman has a clearer view. He is not in the business of winning votes. Nor is he concerned, like his master Emerson, with intellectually transcending what can't be stomached. He set the human body in a perspective stretching back "quintillions of years," so that we are no longer looking shamefacedly at a wretched slave on the block but examining the wonder that is man. "Red, black or white," his limbs are "cunning in tendon and nerve" and they run with blood: "The same old blood! the same red-running blood!" We are celebrants of a religious mystery, for "if anything is sacred the human body is sacred." The glory and sweet of the human physical world is unlocked by

> The curious sympathy one feels when feeling with the hand the
>     naked meat of the body,
> The circling rivers of the breath, and breathing it in and out,
> The beauty of the waist, and thence of the hips, and thence
>     downward toward the knees,
> The thin red jellies within you or within me, the bones and the
>     marrow in the bones,
> The exquisite realization of health. . . .

What do these miraculous parts, hinges and links and circlings amount to, if not a rite of the soul? And if we are looking at the soul when we gaze at a slave being auctioned, how can such slavery continue to exist? What can it be but a terrible mistake, a bad dream? So the unwritten concluding lines run on in our minds, suggested by this most "indirect" of poets.

But of course slavery was not a dream. It was a bomb, ticking away.

The blend of simple virtues and high ideals in the shrine of the constitution had been undermined in the mid-nineteenth century by a host of forces, social, industrial, and political, all racing the nation along full blast in the name of progress. Under the onslaught of this dynamism the very foundations of society had begun to quake. Some inner malaise whipped the American spirit into a frenzy of restlessness. A minority of thinkers raised warning voices, those no longer prepared to embrace unreservedly the ideal of the self-made man. Sectional conflict could soon, it was feared now, rip the democratic dream to shreds.

Leaving New York and coming to New Orleans had given Whitman a chance to stand back and ponder the danger signals for himself. Temporarily at least he was a man without a party. His slow withdrawal from politics probably began here, in 1848. Though he would swing back again in a few months, it would never be so unquestioningly. In New Orleans he was to some extent a muzzled journalist, excluded from editorial conferences because of the unreliability of his opinions and to that extent free to cast around for more satisfactory answers. Neutral, he edged nearer a new role for himself, as an amanuensis, concerned only to transmit the truth, swinging needlelike in a search for his true bearings.

Just as he would be both the slave and the auctioneer in his poem, the onlooker and the singer, so he would aim eventually to root himself in midstream. The Whitman of *Leaves of Grass* is passionate but also prudent, taking up the arguments of both sides, a stance he would later call Hegelian. Instead of seeing with the eyes of a newspaperman he would start to cultivate that eye-of-the-world overview spoken of by Nietzsche. "Do you wish to become a universal eye?" Nietzsche asked. "For that you will have to pass through many individualities, with the last using the others as functions."

Headlines everywhere caught fire in the spring when Europe erupted in turmoil. A wave of connected revolutions dubbed the "springtime of peoples" convulsed whole nations. In Paris people were at the barricades. There had been any number of unheeded predictions. Early in the year de Tocqueville had warned the Chamber of Deputies, "We are sleeping on a volcano... the storm is on the horizon." No sooner had this delirious springtime come than it was over. Insurrections petered out ignominiously. But in America there was still mad excitement, with mass rallies and banquets in support. New York succumbed to a revolutionary fever, and so did New Orleans. European refugees there danced in the streets, and the *Crescent* rushed out an edition with the text of the *Marsellaise* printed in bold type. Excited as anyone, Whitman declared, "One's blood races and grows hot within him the more he learns or thinks of this news from the continent of Europe!"

Two years later his memories of that momentous spring inspired a bad poem, "Resurgemus," which Horace Greeley printed in the *Tribune*. Whitman thought well enough of it to include it later in the first edition of *Leaves of Grass*.

> Suddenly out of its pale and drowsy lair, the lair of slaves,
> Like lightning Europe le'pt forth... half startled at itself,
> Its feet upon the ashes and the rags... Its hand tight to the throats
>   of kings....
>
> Yet behind all, lo, a Shape,
> Vague as the night, draped interminably, head front and form in
>   scarlet folds,

Whose face and eyes none may see,
Out of its robes only this . . . the red robe, lifted by the arm,
One finger pointed high over the top, like the head of a snake
appears.

BY APRIL Whitman's relations with his bosses had begun to deteriorate. It was the usual pattern. The situation didn't perturb him. Newspapers were an expanding field and he was always confident of picking up another job somewhere or other. In any case, he had never seen this one as anything other than an opportunity for a pleasant sojourn in the South. There was also Jeff to consider, increasingly miserable, fretting for home and falling sick. "Mother, just think what you would think of us," he wrote tearfully, "if we had written you only one letter since we came away. . . . If you do not write to us pretty soon we will do something but I don't know what."

Before he and his brother acted, the *Crescent*'s owners did, though how exactly is not really clear. It was most likely a shift in their attitude toward Whitman. The coming presidential elections and the likelihood of him becoming an embarrassment to their proslavery policy may have been a factor. Or they could have simply found him too individualistic and difficult an employee. Jeff had been taking time off because of illness, and their irritability toward him was making itself felt.

From Whitman's point of view, they were moving into an unpleasant season. The temperature was climbing steeply, prices were high, and in the full heat of a New Orleans summer things tended to grind to a halt, or so he understood. It was time to go. However, Whitman had his pride. He failed to see what he had done to deserve the lack of cordiality, and smarted at the manner in which, "through some unaccountable means . . . both Hayes and McClure after a while exhibited a singular sort of coldness towards me. . . ." The memorandum to himself went on: "But when the coldness above alluded to broke out, H. seemed to be studiously silent upon all these matters.—My own pride was touched—and I met their conduct with equal haughtiness on my part.—On Wednesday May 24th I sent down a note requesting a small sum of money.—M'C returned me a bill of what money I had already drawn, and stated that they could not make 'advances.' I answered by reminding them of certain points which appeared to have been forgotten, making me *not* their debtor, and told them in my reply that I thought it would be better to dissolve the connection. . . ."

Now they were ready to leave. On Saturday, May 27, the brothers were aboard the *Pride of the West* bound for St. Louis, Chicago, and the Great Lakes. Jeff went down with a fever but shook it off overnight. A week later they reached St. Louis, wandered around the city for the afternoon, and then transferred to another boat, the *Prairie Bird*. This took them on the Illinois River to La Salle. That Monday they had to transfer again. The canal boat which went the rest of the way to Chicago turned out to be the most uncomfortable part of the whole trip. It was packed with passengers and cargo. On Tuesday at ten in the morning they were in Chicago. They spent the next two days as tourists, taking in the sights and staying at the American Temperance Hotel, then boarded the *Griffith*, headed for Milwaukee.

Whitman liked this town so much after they had walked around inspecting it that he thought it would be a good place to settle, if they should ever leave Long Island. Sailing again, they passed Detroit but were unable to land, reached Cleveland and then Buffalo, docking on June 12, a Monday. A train took them to Niagara. They did some brief sightseeing and then went on to Albany, and back on the water for the final leg, a journey down the Hudson to New York which lasted all day.

Nothing was amiss at Prince Street. Whitman had come back with a sense of space, invaluable to him when he came to expand the voice of his poetry and the whole surface of his sun-and-air-bathed poem, filling it with the mobility of travel and the cunning of the navigator. But not yet: not till he had "come to himself" would that conviction of his specialness be born and the mesmeric ancient mariner in him hold sway. His editor friend Henry Lees reported in the *Brooklyn Advertiser* that the wanderer had returned "large as life, but quite as vain . . . his brown face smiling like a wicker basket filled with wooden particles cleft from timber."


His FORTUNES took an interesting turn. Being dismissed by the *Eagle* for his radicalism had made him a local hero in certain circles. Even before he was fired, before McClure and the trip south, there had been talk among his friends and supporters of providing him with a paper which would be a platform for the local radical wing of the Democratic party. The *New York Tribune*, getting wind of the rumor, ran an item informing their readers that "the Barnburners of Brooklyn are about to start a new daily paper, as, it is said, the *Eagle* has returned to Old Hunkerism again. Mr. Walter Whitman, late of the *Eagle*, is to have charge of the new enterprise."

The Free Soil issue had moved out from party politics into the national domain. Its ramifications were becoming nightmarish. At the party conventions in May and June neither party had been able to do anything other than fend off the Free Soil question. John Calhoun, the gaunt, formidable senator from South Carolina, a Southerner respected for his intellect both North and South, prophesied terrible destruction ahead for the South he loved. In his defense of slavery he pointed to the exploited workingman in the North at the mercy of his capitalist master, often enduring worse conditions than slaves in the South. Lincoln in 1860, maligned in one smear campaign after another, would be called a lunatic, a scourge, a chimpanzee, and was even rumored to be a bastard whose real father was Calhoun. Whitman may have found Calhoun's argument perverse but he admired and esteemed the man for his patriarchal integrity, seeing him as someone aloof from the grubby compromises of politics.

It was early summer. Whitman, at a loose end, took himself off to Coney Island, in those days "a long, bare, unfrequented shore." If he had worries of his own he shed them along with his clothes to wade in the surf and pound up and down on the superb firm sand, adding his prints to those of the birds. There at the margin where he was most at home he may have reflected on the nation's ills, or been aware of obscure changes occurring inside himself. Inside or out, his instinct was to let them ferment. As if prompted by them he had begun to carry a small notebook around with him everywhere. It was bound in leather, with loops to hold a pencil. He used it as a commonplace book, and to draft out poems, prose experiments. Anything at all went into it, even building accounts and new addresses.

One entry ran: "Be simple and clear.—Be not occult. . . . True noble expanded American character is raised on a far more lasting and universal basis than that of any of the 'gentlemen' of aristocratic life, or of novels, or under the European or Asian forms of society or government.—It is to be illimitably proud, self-possessed, generous and gentle. It is to accept nothing except what is equally free and eligible to any body else. It is to be poor rather than rich—but to prefer death sooner than any mean dependence.—Prudence is part of it, because prudence is the right arm of independence."

Emerson on "prudence" meant a stance of sympathetic detachment. Taking his cue from this, Whitman extended it to include both sides of any question, believing that "All that a person does or thinks is of consequence." The prototype of an ideal democrat of the future sketched in his notebook could have been the embryo of a newspaper article or notes for a lecture. He still dreamed now and then of being a wanderer-lecturer, an orator rather than a poet. It hadn't yet hit him with full force that he could let loose any fantasy he pleased within the fiction of a great poem without even moving from the spot. He could assert himself in the grand manner, like an opera singer, like God—like the most powerful of newspaper magnates. He could lead his country to a new spiritual vantage point. Meanwhile, he loafed and invited his soul, loped along the sand and scared the gulls by hurling gobbets of Shakespeare into the wind and waves. He lay on his back and studied the clouds and listened to the sound of the sea, a rhythm that he could feel swinging him in proud gathering oscillations, like an enormous heart. He never tired of hearing it. If he closed his eyes it came to him like a secret, whispering for him alone. The voice of the sea was to him the soft thunderous music of a magnificent new order, timeless and free.

When he went back to the ordinary world the wonder was lost. On the beach, lying rapt in that power, he had really thought the old order of things was finished, dead and done for. What he had done was to shed it like his clothes, and when he got dressed he took it up again, and forgot all he had heard. But not quite. In his notebook he jotted down reminders of such moments, when the dead rind of the old world broke open and the elemental smashed through.

An old friend in Brooklyn, Judge Samuel Johnson, roused him up out of his idyll with a proposal for a Free Soil newspaper to oppose the conservative *Eagle*. Johnson, a long-standing campaigner for the rights of blacks, saw Whitman as a fellow abolitionist, or as near to one as made no difference. And it was true, as he afterward admitted, that for the first and only time he came to the point of flirting with abolitionism. Johnson drew up a list of subscribers for a paper to be called the *Banner of Freedom*, its policy being to "oppose the extension of slavery and support for elective offices persons who will advocate the same."

Lewis Cass, sworn enemy of the Wilmot Proviso, had already been nominated by the Democratic majority for their national ticket. Someone had to create a channel for the radicals to express their outrage. Judge Johnson handed over his list to Whitman as the new paper's editor.

When its first issue appeared on September 9 it had been renamed the *Freeman*, a weekly intended to promote the election of Martin Van Buren, nominated by the newly formed Free Soil party. In his first editorial Whitman cited Jefferson, one of his fabled heroes, who "hated slavery—hated it in all its forms—over the mind as well as the body of man." It didn't seem to matter that Jefferson had himself owned a hundred slaves. Justin Kaplan puts it well when he says that *Leaves of Grass* began to take root in the concept of "Free Soil."

At a meeting in Washington Hall, Brooklyn, on August 5 Whitman was one of the fifteen delegates elected to represent Kings County at the new party's convention in Buffalo on the 9th and 10th, in a huge marquee on the shore of Lake Erie. It was part fair, part jamboree, and part gospel meeting. Famous orators such as the black abolitionist Frederick Douglass held forth. The heat was intense, and so was the fervor of the thirty thousand delegates assembled from far and wide. The Hutchinson family group of singers were there to provide entertainment. Apart from the sessions devoted to the agenda there was maneuvering behind the scenes of groups only partially aligned. Whitman loved best the "ensemble" crusading spirit, which always exhilarated him beyond words.

He got back from Buffalo inspired and refreshed, eager to light a fire with his new paper that no one—certainly not the *Eagle*—could put out. He rented a basement office in Orange Street and fitted it up with the best press he could afford. As usual it was a one-man show: he wrote the whole little edition himself, set it up in print, and made ready to distribute it on the first Saturday morning at two cents a copy. In his head swirled the great moving masses of the Buffalo meeting; in his imagination he sank again into that crowd-immersion which never failed to recharge him, making him feel more tinglingly alive, more real, more a radical force than when he was alone. Crowds had the same effect on him as that surging unstoppable ocean out at Coney Island. In a multitude as on a beach, he felt that something greater than himself, mystical, immense, was gathering him into itself.

In the opening editorial we see him winding up for a fight. He attacked the *Eagle* as a contaminating influence he intended to counter in a cleansing struggle. Taking the moral high ground he announced proudly: "Hardly any one who takes the trouble to look two minutes at our paper will need being told, at any length, what objects we have in view... our doctrine is the doctrine laid down in the Buffalo Convention, and expounded in the letters of Van Buren and Adams.... We shall oppose, under all circumstances, the addition to the Union in the future of a single inch of *slave land*, whether in the form of state or territory."

On the very first day of the brave new venture, disaster struck. A fire broke out in a shop selling crockery in Fulton Street. It spread rapidly, helped by the windy night. Brooklyn's wooden houses caught fire one after the other. Soon twenty downtown acres had been engulfed. That was the end of the *Freeman* on Orange Street. Fire appliances from several different fire companies tore over from New York and elsewhere and spent half their time fighting one another instead of the flames. Buildings were looted, the City Guard called out.

Whitman had lost everything in the blaze since he had no insurance. Fortunately that was not much. Not a man to give in easily, he was back in business again two months later, in a shop at the corner of Middagh and Fulton streets, supplementing his meager income with any work he could find as a jobbing printer. The local authority gave him some of its government forms to print. The *Long Island Democrat* complimented the editor on his "remarkably handsome paper" when his first edition came out on November 1. Meanwhile, the election of 1848 had come and gone and the Democrats were defeated—the Whigs and President Zachary Taylor helped into office by a third party splitting the Democratic vote.

Hard up, he stirred himself to exploit the current Brooklyn property boom by speculating modestly on a series of houses. He was following here the haphazard pattern established by his father, building one house and then moving to another. As a businessman he was marginally more successful than his father had been, even if his heart was not in it. Also the times were right. He used contractors, with whom his credit was good. His brothers George and Andrew, both carpenters, helped to fit out the interiors, frames, floors, partitions, stoves, and so did their father.

All in all, he must have been busy. There was always more to him than the loafer some people saw. As well as getting out the *Freeman* he watched over the construction of a house in Myrtle Avenue which would be his headquarters for the next few years. The corner frame structure had three stories and a shopfront window below. The family moved in during April. By then his father's health was seriously deteriorating. Whitman's forays into business were in fact brought about by the pressure of this family crisis. Long before this, though, he had made clear his willingness to take responsibility for his mother and his growing brothers and sisters. On the Prince Street house he cleared a profit of six hundred dollars, investing it in the land on which the Myrtle Avenue house stood.

Eventually the ground floor of the property became a shop and printer's. In the shop he sold assorted goods such as stationery, toys, playing cards, and books. The books were children's stories and phrenology publications mostly. After a couple of years he produced a line of his own and tried it out, a weekly sheet giving details of accommodations, routes, and transport schedules that he hoped to sell to salesmen and travelers. It lasted just a month.

Altogether more lucrative was his buying and selling of houses. In addition to the Myrtle Avenue house he owned three places in Cumberland Street by 1853. When he had sold two, he converted the third to a carpenter's and builder's workshop, presumably for his brothers to operate. At some point he tried his hand at construction work himself, enjoying the company of the workingmen, bringing his own lunch box to the site. But the monotony of physical tasks soon bored him, just as farming had done. Later his naturalist friend John Burroughs would take note of Whitman's soft hands and wonder whether he had ever done much manual work. Work of any kind was a matter of fits and starts with him. The impression that many acquaintances took away with them, seeing him as an idler "but not in a bad sense," was no surprise to his friends. They knew how hard he worked when the spirit moved him. Otherwise he carried on at his own sweet pace, regardless of protests.

The appeal of manual labor was not just the attraction of a robust, manly activity, but the opportunity it offered for real contact, for overcoming the frustrations of mere words. It had to do with the "unfinished business" separated lovers know, the growing hunger for intimacy.

> This is unfinished business with me...how is it with you?
> I was chilled with the cold types and cylinder and wet paper
>     between us.

> I pass so poorly with paper and types...I must pass with the
>     contact of bodies and souls.

In APRIL 1849 he managed to get the *Freeman* funded by his backers as a daily. His Free Soil party was looking to the future and sponsoring Thomas Hart Benton, the Missouri senator, as its candidate for ultimate election. Then suddenly the radical Democrats reneged and made a pact with their old Hunker foes. With this unholy alliance the support for Whitman's paper collapsed. Only a few issues earlier he had confided his fantasies to his readers, telling them the *Freeman* would go from strength to strength and earn its editor four thousand dollars a year.

Withdrawing from the fray with dignity, he paid back his friends' betrayal the following year in a free-verse poem in the *New York Tribune*, evoking Zechariah and the Old Testament text, "I was wounded in the house of my friends." Borrowing freely as he often did, he began calmly and then let go. His stored-up anger took over, and he struck out like a near incoherent prophet at the

> Doughfaces, Crawlers, Lice of Humanity—
> Terrific screamers of Freedom,
> Who roar and bawl, and get hot i' the face,
> But, were they not incapable of august crime,
> Would quench the hopes of ages for a drink—
> Muck-worms, creeping flat to the ground,
> A dollar dearer to them than Christ's blessing;
> All loves, all hopes, less than the thought of gain;
> In life walking in that as in a shroud.

One of his Whig enemies in Brooklyn called it a "queer little poem." It is lurid and melodramatic but true, Blakean in its angry disgust. A raging Whitman gives us a shock, like an aberration. With the passage of time this aspect of him went underground.

There was anger behind his editorial rhetoric, though much of it was staged. Now and then a personal fury showed through. More than once he had lost his temper and reacted violently: hitting the church usher over the head, attacking the boy who had fouled his fishing lines, and—if it was true—kicking the politician out of his *Eagle* sanctuary. He fought against this tendency to give way to rage under stress. As he set about consciously inventing himself as the serene comrade and lover, calm as a Buddha, sweet and loving as his patient mother, these outbursts of righteous rage were forced back down. Violence was a betrayal of his democratic ideal: he hoped it would go away. Failing that, he cast about for ways of dealing with it.

In his "Poem of the Proposition of Nakedness" (later called "Respondez!" and then dropped from subsequent editions of *Leaves of Grass*) he tried out a combination of irony and sarcastic indictment. The attack on social and political jobbery sizzles on the page with an anger that has been stood on its head—

> Let murderers, bigots, fools, unclean persons, offer new
> propositions!
> Let men and women be mock'd with bodies and mock'd
> with souls!
> Let the love that waits in them, wait! let it die, or pass
> still-born to other spheres!
> Let the sun and moon go! let scenery take the applause of the
> audience! let there be apathy under the stars!
> Let the worst men beget children out of the worst women!
> Let the priest still play at immortality!
> Let marriage slip down among fools, and be for none but fools!
> Let men among themselves talk and think forever obscenely of
> women! and let women among themselves talk and think
> obscenely of men!
> Let shadows be furnish'd with genitals! let substances be deprived
> of genitals!
> Let the infidels of these States laugh all faith away!
> Let books take the place of trees, animals, rivers, clouds!
> Let the limited years of life do nothing for the limitless years of
> death! (What do you suppose death will do, then?)

On it floods in a torrent, raving, yet at one remove, its control a matter of touch and go. There is something splendid about its passionate outcry. Injunctions are laid on with the bite of vitriol. This kind of harsh condemnation would only happen once more, when he came to write his prose pamphlet "The Eighteenth Presidency." After that it would be held back in the name of prudence, and we would hear only caustic lines now and then from the "tygers of wrath"—apart, that is, from the volcanic rumblings of *Democratic Vistas*, reminding us of fires still smoldering beneath the consciousness.

Spontaneous anger crops up and is dealt with throughout his work by an effort of reconciliation. No one understood better than he the distortions brought about by repressed desires. Anger was a passion he struggled to contain by his method of the reconciliation of contraries, and by the mystery of death, what he called the "word over all."

When Horace Traubel once teased the old man with "I don't believe it's in you to be irritable. I couldn't connect you with irritability," he was perhaps being naive as well as provocative. Whitman answered with a warning. "Don't be so sure about that— don't let that notion run away with you. You don't know what depths of devilishness I may not descend to if I get going."

"Yes, but you don't get going," prodded the indefatigable Horace.

"Maybe I don't," Whitman muttered. "Maybe I'm slow to get going, but it's not impossible."


His FINAL *Freeman* editorial was all dignity and restraint. "After the present date," he wrote, "I withdraw entirely from the Brooklyn Daily Freeman. To those who have been my friends I take occasion to proffer the warmest thanks of a grateful heart. My enemies—and old hunkers generally—I disdain and defy just the same as ever."

What next? He landed a commission to contribute a kind of travel diary to the *New York Sunday Dispatch* and went off to Greenport for a well-earned break, staying as usual with his sister Mary. Watching the crews of the fishing fleet off Montauk Point casting out their lines and hauling in the bluefish, his intense hero-worship must have made him seem a dark blind thing, an unknown force burning to itself. He was like someone absorbed in the praise of something Mary could not see. This brother of hers had always been the strange one. If it had been possible to speak he would have confessed a wish to sit in the boats with those fishermen, great unshaved fellows, their eyes bright and keen as hawks. They were largehearted and they lived like ancient heroes, feeding on salt pork and potatoes and drinking rum, sleeping at night as soundly as babes on mattresses of hay and piled sails. He joined them in the only way he could, by one glad leap of identification, and imagined the joy of his mere proximity, rocking clear in a wordless simplicity where just to act was to be virtuous and fine,

> . . . trailing for bluefish off Paumanok I stand with braced body,
> My left foot is on the gunwhale, my right arm throws far out the coils of slender rope,
> In sight round me the quick veering and darting of fifty skiffs, my companions.

SOON NOW the aroused singer he would become, full of this gleaming jubilation and teetering on the edge of the unsayable, would cry "O adhesiveness! O pulse of life!" to convey his ecstasy, pressing into use one of the phrenological jargon words he had picked up along the way. Phrenology, a pseudoscience that strikes us now as ludicrous, interested Whitman first of all in 1846 when books on the subject landed on his desk at the *Eagle* for review. He told his readers approvingly that phrenology had "gained the victory" over its denigrators and was gaining credence widely "among the sciences." Soon this latest craze was being taken very seriously by the famous. Emerson, Bryant, Henry Ward Beecher, and Daniel Webster went along dutifully and had their bumps examined for "Alimentiveness" (relish for food), "Amativeness" (sexual love), "Philiprogenitiveness" (love of humanity), "Adhesiveness" (male friendship), and so on. Its attraction for many of the best minds of the day may have been the opportunity it seemed to offer an individual to *know* himself. It followed that if one scientifically knew oneself, one could therefore improve oneself—even make oneself into a new person. The teachings of Jung in our time have made the same claims. Self-improvement for nineteenth-century Americans was part and parcel of the ideal of the self-made man.

We are inclined to see phrenology now as astrology in scientific disguise, or as the primitive forerunner of psychoanalysis. Edison's testimonial ran: "I never knew I had inventive talent until phrenology told me so. I was a stranger to myself until then."

Not to be a stranger to yourself—it was irresistible. Some saw it as a superior form of fortune-telling, others as the long-awaited science of mankind. What made it an intriguing game for many was the "scientific" basis it provided for character reading.

Whitman, eager to extend the boundaries of the possible, was inclined to accept the claims of the phrenologists themselves. Reviewing health reformer George Moore's *The Use of the Body in Relation to the Mind*, he commented: "Few persons realize how intimate is the relation of mental causes and processes towards the body and its well and ill being." He himself could hardly have realized how this line of reasoning would revolutionize his poetry and irradiate every corner of *Leaves of Grass*. In an early notebook we find him beginning to map out the outlines of his new missionary purpose. "The effusion or corporation of the soul is always under the beautiful laws of physiology—I guess the soul itself can never be anything but great and pure and immortal; but it makes itself visible only through matter—a perfect head, and bowels and bones to match is the easy gate through which it comes from its embowered garden, and pleasantly appears to the sight of the world."

Here was revelation indeed; so far-reaching yet so blindingly simple. If he had turned to William Blake, the poet he so closely resembles, he would have found a mind moving in the same direction as his. His self-education was full of holes, and he would take years to get around to Blake. He was an American materialist, immersed in the wonders of modern science. It was essential to fashion a faith that would stand up, rooted in his era. Terms like "mental faculties" and "brain" and "mind" and even "mental philosophy" were still not translated into soul and spirit.

> I accept Reality and dare not question it,
> Materialism first and last imbuing. . . .
> Hurray for positive science! Long live exact demonstration!

But he was drawing nearer to the boldness of Blake's aphorisms in *The Marriage of Heaven and Hell*. He could have read there that

1. Man has no body distinct from his Soul; for that call'd Body is a portion of Soul discern'd by the five Senses, the chief inlets of Soul in this age.
2. Energy is the only life, and is from the Body; and Reason is the bound or outward circumference of Energy.

183

3. Energy is Eternal Delight.

The union of body and spirit gave Whitman his most fruitful theme, one which he would find truly inexhaustible. In his major poems we can see him making over the axioms of phrenology and expanding them imaginatively. In a book written to commemorate the centenary of phrenology in Britain, an English phrenologist, J. Milliott Severn, writes that "Phrenologists at the present time recognize the existence of forty-two distinctive faculties of the mind, each having its special organ located in the brain; and each faculty thus far discovered is indispensable to man's happiness and well-being. There are no faculties bad in themselves; the folly and crime which disgrace human society, spring not from their legitimate use, but from their abuse and perversion."

By the time Whitman came to "I Sing the Body Electric" he was master of his own language, able to declare with the conviction of his "greater religion":

> Was it doubted that those who corrupt their own bodies conceal
> themselves?
> And if those who defile the living are as bad as they who defile the
> dead,
> And if the body does not do fully as much as the soul,
> And if the body were not the soul, what is the soul?

He can string moments of illumination into triumphant lyrics, his soul sweet within him. Whatever lies outside, nonhuman, animal, the "plutonic rocks," must be equally sweet.

> Clear and sweet is my soul, and clear and sweet is all that is not
> my soul.
> Lack one lacks both, and the unseen is proved by the seen,
> Till that becomes unseen and receives proof in its turn.

Once he has the key to creation, all else follows. He knows the biblical peace beyond understanding. There is no limit to his audacity and nothing more disarming than his knowledge, couched in such mystical and yet homely, innocent-seeming words.

> And I know that the spirit of God is the brother of my own,
> And that all the men ever born are my brothers, and the women
> my sisters and lovers,
> And that a kelson of the creation is love,

And limitless are leaves stiff or drooping in the fields,
And brown ants in the little wells beneath them,
And mossy scabs of the worm fence, heap'd stones, elder,
mullein and poke-weed.

On all sides lie confirmations, once the doors of perception are cleansed; once you become as a child and cease to struggle. Now he sees it is true, "what I guessed at,"

What I guessed when I loaf'd on the grass,
What I guess'd when I lay alone in my bed,
And again as I walk'd the beach under the paling stars of the
morning.

Even in the eyes of oxen he finds answers. Explanations come in the signatures of all things, in the "nearest gnat," in the drop or motion of waves. "The maul, the oar, the hand-saw, second my words."

Objections are cunningly anticipated and then nullified. The poet is naked, he hides nothing.

Through me forbidden voices...
Voices of sexes and lusts, voices veil'd and I remove the veil,
Voices indecent by me clarified and transfigur'd. . . .

I am not the poet of goodness only, I do not decline to be the poet
of wickedness also.
What blurt is this about virtue and vice?
Evil propels me and reform of evil propels me, I stand
indifferent. . . .


PHRENOLOGY WAS FOUNDED by two Austrians, the anatomist Johann Kaspar Spurzheim and his coworker Franz Gall, a physician. Spurzheim settled in London in 1814, then was invited to America and arrived in 1832. His lectures created a sensation, believers multiplied, and in New York two brothers, Orson and Lorenzo Fowler, who were to be phrenology's main American promoters, opened the "Phrenological Cabinet" of Fowler and Wells in Nassau Street. Orson Fowler's manuals sought to give phrenology a philosophy and to bracket it with the "physiological school" he also

conducted, providing linkages with hydropathy and "animal magne-
tism," two of the current fads.

After Whitman got back from New Orleans he described his visits
to the Fowler and Wells emporium. "Here were all the busts,
examples, curios and books of that study available. I went there
often, and once for myself had a very elaborate and leisurely
examination and 'chart of bumps' written out (I have it yet)." Not
only did he have it, he liked it so much that he included it in early
editions of *Leaves of Grass*, like a credential. By the time he reached
old age, phrenology was under attack from the satirists, notably
Oliver Wendell Holmes and Mark Twain. Whitman was too stubborn
to disown it. "I know what Holmes said," he told Traubel, "that you
might as easily tell how much money is in a safe feeling the knobs
on the door as tell how much brain a man has by feeling the bumps
on his head; and I guess most of my friends distrust it—but then you
see I am very old-fashioned—I probably have not got by the phrenol-
ogy stage yet." His reading by Fowler had given him a 6 for caution:
practically cowardice, he would say humorously. The maximum for
any trait was 7.

The invention of electricity and the magnetic telegraph had
spawned wild theories such as animal magnetism. The entire uni-
verse, these enthusiasts said, transmitted an invisible nervous fluid
which went everywhere, winding in countless circuits. Human beings
were wired into this enormous circuit. Even the dead were included:
"All substances living or dead are either in a positive or negative
condition of electricity." Whitman, never a joiner, accumulated ideas
which appealed to him and added them to his magpie collection of
borrowings. If it was claimed that every mortal thing was connected,
pulsing and filtering its messages, what a potent metaphor that made
for his poet anchored in the flux.

> Mine is no callous shell,
> I have instant conductors all over me whether I pass or stop,
> They seize every object and lead it harmlessly through me.

When in *Leaves of Grass* he started the long advance on the road
of his "perpetual journey," his goal was spiritual but his ballast
material. Out spilled the images in marvelous profusion: of the
seasons, of occupations, adventures, sensations, graves, wombs,
"threads that connect the stars," the sea's "amorous wet." But there

came the problem of how to deal with reason, logic. How did he gain acceptance for his new free-form poetry from a society gearing itself to ever faster industrialization? There is no sign anywhere of him wanting to jettison one iota of his age's materialism. It suited him; he was comfortably at home in his century. He wanted nothing left out or left behind on the road. Neither, though, did he want limits imposed by reason on his cosmic voyaging.

Blake stated baldly, uncompromisingly that "The Specter is the Reasoning Power in Man, and when separated from Imagination... it thence frames Laws and Moralities to destroy Imagination, the Divine Body, by Martyrdoms and Wars." He was not spurning reason, but "Man by his reasoning power can only compare and judge what he has already perceived."

Whitman, on a different tack, a wily customer with tricks up his sleeve, tried to circumvent the problem by beguilement.

> This is the lexicographer, this the chemist, this made a grammar of
> the old cartouches,
> These mariners put the ship through dangerous unknown seas,
> This is the geologist, this works with the scalpel, and this is a
> mathematician.
> Gentlemen, to you the first honors always!
> Your facts are useful, and yet they are not my dwelling,
> I but enter by them to an area of my dwelling.

Finally, however, like Blake, he made a clean breast of it. Logic stood in the way of his vision, which even went beyond democracy. "Logic and sermons never convince"; there was more truth in "the damp of the night." What was this truth, this greater reality? New men and women, not yet arrived but prepared for, envisaged, would create the nucleus of a new society. Inessentials would be swept away: health, sympathy, generosity the passwords. From this new beginning would arise stripped relationships, brave skies, new morals, a new heaven and earth. All that was necessary was for someone, "a kosmos," to stand up and speak the truth.

"Truth can never be told so as to be understood, and not believ'd," wrote Blake. It could have been Whitman speaking. Here then was the task and great challenge: how to speak so simply and completely that it would be a voice instantly recognizable, the call of truth out of the crowd; multivoiced and speaking for those who have been long dumb; calling for "the rights of them that others are down upon," for the "deform'd, trivial, flat, foolish, despised," for the "fog in the air, beetles rolling balls of dung." Everything was ready and in its place, affirming this resurrection in the name of truth.

The moth and the fish-eggs are in their place,
The bright suns I see and the dark suns I cannot see are in their
  place,
The palpable is in its place and the impalpable is in its place. . . .

I believe in the flesh and the appetites,
Seeing, hearing, feeling, are miracles, and each part and tag of me
  is a miracle. . . .

All truths wait in all things,
They neither hasten their own delivery nor resist it,
They do not need the obstetric forceps of the surgeon,
The insignificant is as big to me as any,
(What is less or more than a touch?).

LEAVES OF GRASS WAS by now a mere six years ahead. What an immense step it seems! In the autumn of 1849 his literary ambitions, kept fairly private up to then, were suddenly made public in a manner he would hardly have relished. He had made fun of editors, politicians, and reformers as a matter of course in the *Eagle*, but this anonymous pen portrait at his expense in the *Brooklyn Advertiser* which hailed him mockingly as a "literary genius" slid in under his guard. It was good-humored for the most part, and no more than he could expect from a Whig paper. Some of it he might even have enjoyed reading: after all it was about himself, editor Walter Whitman, temporarily unemployed, "that transcendentally fast politician . . . at whose coat tails time and events keep pulling." Whoever the author of the article might have been, he knew his subject well, describing him as a good-looking fellow, indolent in expression, sometimes bearded and at others clean shaven, as if he was still trying to decide what he wanted to do. These were shrewd touches. Whitman had tried dandyism and would soon fancy himself in the coarse garb of a carpenter's mate. Byronic around the neck, he dressed like a student and looked "civilized but not polished." This specimen of "native raw material," distinguished though he might think himself, was again "on the town"—a euphemism for out of work.

Just before this, Lorenzo Fowler had been making a survey of the exterior of Whitman's head, for which he charged him three dollars. On a scale of 1 to 7 he awarded him 6 for Amativeness, 6 to 7 for Philoprogentiveness, 6 to 7 for Self-Esteem, 6 for Intuition, 5 or 6 for Destructiveness, 6 for Adhesiveness, and 6 for Cautiousness. Other flattering scores were: Conscientiousness 6 and Benevolence 6 to 7.

The Fowler and Wells Cabinet had been a New York tourist attraction for years. People came to gawk at the skulls of "murderers, thieves... lions, tigers, hyenas, dangerous lunatics, savage tribesmen." Whitman could have been there before. At the start of the decade he had worked just around the corner from their establishment. Lorenzo's character analysis may well have been influenced by the fact that he knew Whitman was a journalist and perhaps hoped for some favorable publicity. The summary deduced from his chart and his general observations made no mention of that contradictory high score for "Destructiveness":

"This man has a grand physical construction, and power to live to a good old age. He is undoubtedly descended from the soundest and hardiest stock. Size of head large. Leading traits of character appear to be Friendship, Sympathy, Sublimity and Self-Esteem, and markedly among his combinations the dangerous faults of Indolence, a tendency to the pleasure of Voluptuousness and Alimentiveness, and a certain reckless swing of animal will, too unmindful, probably, of the convictions of others."

The reference to Whitman's physical prowess would have pleased him no end. He had a passion for health that was almost obsessive. Like the Fowlers he was antimedicine. He saw water as a cure-all, drinking it in large quantities, plunging in it at Coney Island beach and at the public baths, currying himself each morning with cold-water scrubbings. Toward the end of the 1840s he began to collect articles on health and physiology in a special file.

In one of his publications Orson Fowler wrote, "The qualities of mind correspond with the build of the body. If the latter is beautifully formed, well-proportioned, handsome, etc., not only will its motions be easy and graceful, but the feelings will be exquisite, the mind well balanced, and a beauty, perfection, taste, refinement, elegance and good taste will characterize everything he says and does." This would be absorbed, translated, and in due course assigned to "Song of Myself" and "I Sing the Body Electric."

> ... The expression of a well-made man appears not only in his face,
> It is in his limbs and joints also, it is curiously in the joints of his hips and wrists,
> It is in his walk, the carriage of his neck, the flex of his waist and knees, dress does not hide him,
> The strong sweet quality he has strikes through the cotton and broadcloth....
> You linger to see his back, and the back of his neck and shoulder-side.

The Whitmans were living and working together now, and Walt was back with them, taking responsibility for them as if he were already head of the family. He served them cheerfully. Long ago he had made himself responsible for his beloved mother in his heart, as his father lost ground and was more shadowy and ailing. Walt was his mother's man. It was self-evident, not questioned by any of them.

He made a scratch living by fits and starts, wrote cheap journalism as a freelance, kept the accounts of the various house transactions, kept an eye on the construction work, and perhaps felt the satisfaction of a certain spiritual superiority and control. Other than that, he wrote what his mother called "barrels of lectures" in preparation for a teaching or lecturing career which never took off. He even rented a shop-front at Granada Hall in Fulton Street, maybe intending to emulate the evangelistic Fowlers by disseminating the word of phrenology. This too came to nothing.

He had a way of staying cool which some found distinctly off-putting. Suddenly he was not there: he would withdraw to some place where he was unreachable, his face darkly vacant, looking insufferably entrenched. The word "indifferent" crops up repeatedly and curiously in his poetry. As he gained more knowledge of himself he cultivated this trait as an asset, later still as a strategy:

> Apart from the pulling and hauling stands what I am,
> Stands amused, complacent, compassionating, idle, unitary....
> Both in and out of the game and watching and wondering at it.

But he had always been able to do it—darken into abstraction, glimmering and intent somewhere underneath, not all that human. He would cease to fret about his circumstances, let everything go. It was an instinct with him at certain times, certain stages of his life. He relaxed his will, let it all go hang. What did it matter in the end? The globe swung around, bathed in common air, come what may. He had always been a delayer, a slow mover, sluggish in his thoughts. There was always something in him prepared to wait.

He was in one of these periods now. Exerting his will had only brought him round once more in a circle, back in Brooklyn, "on the town." Why not cease trying for a while? In truth he was happy enough. He had a presentiment of life stirring in him, in his darkness. It was buried deep, a secret, like a seed. He hugged the sense of this secret to himself. He could not have said what it was, but it excited him with its nearness.

Phrenology fascinated him for a number of reasons. The maxim on the temple of Delphos, inscribed in golden capitals, was "Know Thyself." The Fowler and Wells slogan "Self-made or never made" incorporated this, in a crude version of Emerson's "self-reliance." Whitman was delighted to hear the phrenologists say that there was no royal road to learning, and would have been intrigued to read— possibly he did—that "One of the real benefits . . . was that it inspired courage and hope in those who were depressed by the consciousness of some inability. . . . Phrenology shows us how, as Goethe says, our virtues and vices grew out of the same roots; how every good tendency has its danger, and every dangerous power may be so restrained and guided as to be a source of good."

The implications for Whitman were profound. Out of it flowed the triumphant lyric of a poet able to sing of "the foolish as much as the wise," the traitorous as well as the faithful, shame and pride, evil and good, death and life, the wasted and the well-formed, murderers and children, and claim value and meaning for them all.

His alarmingly high score for Destructiveness was a case in point. In phrenological parlance it indicated "a disposition to break, crush, tear down things, to subjugate, destroy and exterminate." In excess it could lead to "excessive severity, anger and rage, to revengefulness, malice, cruelty" and the desire to torment, punish, or annihilate. But in its positive aspect it was the "push-right-through" spirit essential for nearly all great undertakings. If lacking, there was inefficiency, passivity, lack of energy and force.

Whitman was always, he insisted, conscious of himself as two.

Born a Gemini, he scarcely needed telling that there were two sides to everything. His divided and paradoxical nature, casting about for the means to knit itself together, drew intuitively on anything that promised to bring him peace and harmony. The perfect surge of the ocean was one source, his mother's native patience another. Somewhere in him he was always waiting to respond. Phrenology came at the right time for him.

Its emphasis on health and wholeness was reinforced by the evidence of his own eyes. The supremely healthy man was his constant model for the new type of poet he wanted himself to be. He parted company with the Fowlers' idea of the poet as having a nervous temperament, large liquid eyes, and deathly pallor, a type as cadaverous as Poe. And he lived in a household plagued with ill health. His father would soon be chronically ill. Walt shared a bed with his poor handicapped brother Eddy. Jesse was already disturbed, his psychotic rages bringing him close to breakdown at times. Andrew had a sickly constitution and was tubercular. He would die young of a tubercular throat. The females of the family fared better, although Hannah would become hopelessly neurotic later on, driven into hypochondria by an unhappy marriage.

Whitman, close to his mother in numerous ways, was far from being his father's enemy. He could never have called his father a friend, as he did his mother, but he was haunted by him. In the early stories the fathers turn into ogres, huge and black. As Walt made himself the practical savior of his family, gradually his feelings for his father increased in complexity. Again and again we come across passages in *Leaves of Grass* which convince us that his father is being described, remembered, resented, reinvented even. It is as if the son was being forced to acknowledge the presence of his father in himself. He recognized his stubbornness and anger as owing something to his father. He had repeated, in a different fashion, his father's pattern of disruption in the world of work. He had changed his address restlessly, just as his home moved from place to place during his unsettled childhood and youth. When he came to construct his book he made it a solid, workmanlike structure, as if he were his father building his frame houses.

Yet there was always something about his father that seemed insubstantial and defeated by doubt, unable to get a foothold in the world through no fault of his own. Knee-deep in a succession of past failures, he came to believe he would fail at whatever he attempted.

The same feeling of unreality gnawed at his son and to some extent afflicted the whole family. Faltering to a halt in meaningless confusion at moments of crisis, only a lover or friend "holding me by the hand" would save Whitman and lead him to the safety of his "indifference":

> Of the terrible doubt of appearances,
> Of the uncertainty after all, that we may be deluded,
> That may-be reliance and hope are but speculations after all. . . .
> May-be the things I perceive, the animals, plants, men, hills,
>     shining and flowing waters,
> The skies of day and night, colors, densities, forms, may-be these
>     are (as doubtless they are) only apparitions, and the real
>     something has yet to be known,
> (How often they dart out of themselves as if to confound me and
>     mock me!).

IN A SUDDEN FLURRY of action he obtained a job as chief editor on the new *Daily News* in Nassau Street, only a stone's throw from the Fowler and Wells establishment. After two months the paper was on the rocks. He earned something from hack journalism for the *Daily Advertiser*, sketches of churches, sketches of Brooklynites, and tried to sell the idea of a twenty-two-part adaptation of a Danish historical novel to the *New York Sun*.

He spent another summer lazing around Greenport and living with his sister and brother-in-law. That autumn he took a train to Woodbury with his father, who had expressed a wish to visit West Hills again. They arrived unannounced on the doorstep of his father's sister Sarah, who lived with her widowed daughter Hannah in a house Walt's father had once built. Evidently the visit staggered Aunt Sarah, but she recovered quickly and made the Whitmans welcome. Walt found Hannah "a little vaporish" and put her vague manner down to hard work, the loss of her husband, and difficulties with her children. Her health was poor. As for Aunt Sarah, "she is indeed an original. She has very little regard for dress, but is craving for money and property. She has always shown a masculine, determined mind. Soon after her marriage [to one Walters], her husband took to drink. She separated from him, and would never live with him afterward."

Three years later they were there again—only two years before his father's death. They climbed the upland and came to the old Whitman homestead, now a carriage house and granary. It was a vantage point. Looking east they could see the "broad and beautiful farm lands" of his father's father, and the house his father had been forced to relinquish in 1810. They could even inspect the ruins of Walt's great-grandfather's dwelling "with its mighty timbers and low ceilings."

Thirty years on, he sat on an old grave on the family burial hill and was moved to jot down his reflections. Graveyards always affected him deeply. *Leaves of Grass* would be, as much as anything, an attempt at a great poem of death. Sitting there alone he could trace the remains of fifty or more graves. There was an equal number in various states of decay, "depressed mounds, crumbled and broken stones, cover'd with moss," the inscriptions obliterated by weather and time. It all affected him inexpressibly, "the gray and sterile hill, the clumps of chestnuts outside, the silence, just varied by the soughing wind." Three centuries were concentrated on this "sterile acre." If he could only read it, here was his whole family history link by link, from the first settlement onward.

In October 1850 he made one last, not exactly determined effort to get back into office journalism and secure a salary. He had heard through the grapevine that Carlos Stuart, an editor in New York who had married a girl from West Hills, was about to launch a paper of his own. His diffident letter inquiring about a possible vacancy makes one wonder if he really wanted to succeed:

"I take the liberty of writing, to ask whether you have any sort of opening in your new enterprise for services that I could render? I am out of regular employment, and fond of the press—and, if you would be disposed to 'try it on' I should like to have an interview with you, for the purpose of seeing whether we could agree to something. My ideas of salary are *very* moderate."

Moderate or not, there was nothing doing.

# 7

# Life as an Art

The years of the early 1850s baffle and intrigue us even today, a hundred years after Whitman's death. Everything suddenly changes, yet "no one has seen it happen, and nothing has happened": nothing, that is, except the moment of drama itself. In 1855, out stepped onto the stage a fully equipped poet-genius, displaying for the world's approval his extraordinary muscle-flexing new persona. How had it come about? Who was this Rip Van Winkle? How could this crude trade apprentice and run-of-the-mill journalist from across the river have so transformed himself?

Outwardly his life was as uneventful as ever. Brooklyn, like the rest of America, was experiencing another boom. Commerce with Europe and the Far East was overloading the port of New York and of Brooklyn, which was crying out for more docks. Williamsburg, Bushwick, Greenpoint, and Brooklyn itself were coalescing to form a city of more than a hundred thousand within four years. Property values in South Brooklyn were rocketing, new factories were going up. The building trade had never been so busy.

Whitman did gain some profit from all this, but not to any great extent. Phrenology had given him a low score for "Acquisitiveness." It could be that as a speculator he was no luckier or more adept than his father. Unlike his father, however, the failure to prosper did not seem to bother him. He had other irons in the fire and felt reasonably secure. He owned the house the family lived in and he paid for food and helped with running costs whenever he could. Said

George, "He had an idea that money was of no consequence." There was no condemnation in his remark. If the others did not understand him, he was more at one with them than they thought. And they knew this much about him: if he was not interested, nothing would make him stir. As George put it, he "worked now and then," wrote now and then at literary work (George's word for journalism), and loafed the summers away.

They may not have realized, but he had taken to hanging around the studios of Brooklyn artists. A few of them were his friends anyhow. Evidently they appreciated his approval and valued his support. As for him, he found their style of living attractive. The Art Union they had founded, mainly to promote and sell their work, had the effect of forming them into a brotherhood. This appealed to Whitman enormously. He liked the slant of their talk, the improvised manner in which they related to one another, freely and without malice. He sat for them as a model if they asked him, and tried his hand with a crayon a time or two. A few sketches and caricatures survive in his notebooks.

Although he was disillusioned with party politics, the oratory of national politics could still set him alight. Internationally the prospect for a new order looked grim. The short-lived glories of the "springtime of peoples" in 1848 had been crushed by ferocious reaction and repression. Marx had burrowed out of sight to write *Das Kapital* in the British Museum. Garibaldi lived in poverty on Staten Island. Mazzini was a refugee in London. One day Whitman caught sight of the Hungarian hero Louis Kossuth on his way up Broadway.

Antislavery meetings in the "turtle-shaped" New York Tabernacle drew him over the ferry. He heard the abolitionist Cassius Marcellus Clay and Senator John Parker Hale there. He admired their handling of the heavies and hecklers organized by Isaiah Rynders to break up their speeches, and their natural oratory thrilled him.

Earlier he had been enraged by Daniel Webster's action in the Senate. Webster threw his weight behind Henry Clay's compromise motion which upheld the constitutional rights of slaveholders. Until then Whitman had been, like Whittier and Emerson, a great admirer of Webster. "The word *liberty* in the mouth of Mr. Webster sounds like the word *love* in the mouth of a courtesan," wrote Emerson in stiff disdain. Yet the position taken up by Webster, arguing that disunion was an even greater evil than slavery, was close to the view held later by Whitman and identical with that of Lincoln. "I would rather hear of natural blasts and mildews, war, pestilence and famine," argued Webster, "than to hear gentlemen talk of secession. To break up this great government! to dismember this glorious country! to astonish Europe with an act of folly such as Europe for two centuries has never beheld in any government or any people!"

This brought a fire-eating speech from Senator William Seward, the substance of which was that, although the Constitution did not explicitly forbid slavery, there was a "higher law" to be considered. "The territory of the United States is a part of the common heritage of mankind, bestowed upon them by the Creator of the universe."

Now the nation was boiling. So was the emotional journalist in Whitman. Far better than any journalism, however, was his poem "Blood Money" in Bryant's *Evening Post*, a foretaste of the poetry he would soon be writing. The big rolling lines of his achieved work were not yet quite here, but this angry and passionate free verse was getting close.

Of olden times, when it came to pass
That the beautiful god, Jesus, should finish his work on earth,
Then went Judas, and sold the divine youth,
And took pay for his body.

Curs'd was the deed, even before the sweat of the clutching hand
    grew dry;
And darkness frown'd upon the seller of the like of God,
Where, as though earth lifted her breast to throw him from her
    and heaven refused him,
He hung in the air, self-slaughter'd.

The cycles, with their long shadows, have stalk'd silently forward
Since those ancient days—many a pouch enwrapping meanwhile
Its fee, like that paid for the son of Mary.
And still goes one, saying,
"What will ye give me, and I will deliver this man unto you?"
And they make the covenant, and pay the pieces of silver.

Like Lawrence in our time, he flirted with the image of Jesus all his life. When he spoke of Christ it was always tenderly. For Whitman the greatest example of love we could call up from history was that of Jesus. He reserved his hostility for the church, for the clergy and dogma. He toyed briefly with the notion of a priesthood of the future, ushering in a new moral order, but soon substituted

"Every man shall be his own priest." Mesmerized for a time by the "power and magnetism" of great men, leaders, he glorified the sacred heroes of the Revolution and then drew back from leadership fantasies. Washing his hands of reformers, extremists, panaceas, messiahs, he dreamt instead of a new evolved democratic being who would stand as an equal among others, get back in touch with nature, emulate the grace of animals, realize his own soul and take full responsibility for himself at last. The only doctrine he could fully endorse was one which included and joined everything in one Hegelian whole.

He was no *revolutionaire*. "I don't expect an upset—I expect a growth: evolution." The only valid revolution for him was the one destined to take place, he insisted, in the human heart. Meanwhile nothing could be dismissed, he said, adding mischievously, "not Catholic, Quaker, Mormon, Freethinker—not even the Unitarian!" Of course he was speaking of individuals. For the religious institutions "I have the profoundest contempt." He did not believe we would ever see the "true Jesus" except as a beautiful fable, asking Horace Traubel one evening if he knew who it was—"some cute fellow—who spoke of Jesus as 'that divine tramp.'"

One of the most enigmatic and beautiful photographs of Whitman—and there are dozens, perhaps hundreds—was taken in 1854. His friend Dr. Bucke called it "the Christ likeness," and for a while, until it made him uncomfortable, Whitman went along with the suggestiveness of this, especially the notion of himself as a prophet from nowhere, son of a carpenter. In the picture a face of negligent beauty smiles faintly, insinuatingly at us, the neck rising from a spotless white shirt open at the neck, the eyes curiously hooded, lips sensual in a short animal beard. He was easily flattered by such comparisons but knew himself too well to be really convinced. Of a photograph taken around 1860, a full-length portrait of a lounging workingman-philosopher, one hand dangling a hat, the other thrust into the pocket of his rumpled denims, he commented: "What bothers me most of all, piques me, tantalizes me, is the expression of benignity. Such benignity, such sweetness, such satisfiedness. . . ."

When he had dispensed once and for all with exceptional men he made clear a faith and a position which had long been established at the very core of his poetry. "In masses of men . . . the trend seems to me to be towards the light—towards life, growth. . . . I am not a witness for saviors—no. I am a witness for the average man, the whole." In his poetry, he explained, he was "contending for the average good heart of the people, the sterling common soil of the race. Mr. [Matthew] Arnold always gives you the notion that he hates to touch the dirt—the dirty is so dirty! But everything comes out of the dirty-everything. Everything comes out of the people, the everyday people, the people as you find them and leave them."

☙ WHITMAN SPENT so much time in the studios of his artist friends, men like William Sydney Mount and Henry Kirke Brown, that they must have seen him as a fixture. They came to depend on him before long as a propagandist for their work. At Brown's he sat for hours watching the sculptor modeling someone, always working. While there as a passive spectator, educating his eye, he made the acquaintance of Brown's visitors, passing through on their way to—or back from—Europe. "They would tell us of students, studios, the teachers they had just left in Paris, Rome, Florence." There was one vivacious fellow who either knew—or knew a great deal about—the venerable French poet of the people, Beranger, a sort of French Burns. Whitman, his hair already turning gray at thirty, was sometimes playfully called Beranger by this artist crowd.

Soon he was stimulated enough aesthetically to try his hand as a cultural commentator, as his way of seeing prodded him to articulate the reasons for his own likes and dislikes. His articles now, even those in journals like the abolitionist New Era, were about art and music. He was particularly taken with the new art of photography—studios were opening all along Broadway—and argued in favor of its immediate "drama of the eye," its ability to seize "the form and spirit of the face to a degree that defies criticism."

"One realm we have never conquered: the pure present," writes Lawrence. Motion, American action, was what Whitman and artists like Thomas Eakins and Eadweard Muybridge had in common. Eakins was a painter who, like Whitman, fell afoul of the genteel traditions of his age. He was sacked by the Pennsylvania Academy for his realism and for such statements as "a naked woman is the most beautiful thing there is—except a naked man," just as Whitman later lost his clerkship in the Department of the Interior in Washington for being the author of "an indecent book." Eakins experimented with photography, took pictures of a horse to capture its movements, and painted naked men in the act of slipping into the water in his picture "The Swimming Hole." Muybridge's folio of photographs, *Zoopraxia: Men and Animals in Motion*, astonished Degas and Messonier and would inspire Francis Bacon. Here was the way nineteenth-century people actually moved. Eakins and Muybridge were shelved, thought offensive in some undefined sense. By then Whitman had given more outright offense, but he kept publishing.

"Any reading of Whitman," says Guy Davenport in his essay on the poet, "is vastly enriched by a knowledge of Eakins and Muybridge; their arts can be seen as complementary." In the 1880s the three men were within a few miles of each other. Eakins, painting surgeons, baseball players, musicians, boxers, wrestlers, and Philadelphians, used to come over from Philadelphia to see the house-bound poet. We can see how akin he is to Whitman when he says that "nature is just as varied and just as beautiful in our day as she was in the time of Phidias." His magnificent portrait and his series of photographs of Whitman had Traubel worried; he thought the 1888 canvas too fleshy. "It made me think of a rubicund sailor with his hands folded across his belly about to tell a story." But Whitman liked Eakins's picture the best of all the portraits made of him. "I never knew but one artist, and that's Tom Eakins," he said, "who could resist the temptation to see what they thought ought to be rather than what is." Eakins, twenty-five years Whitman's junior, shared the same kind of stock as the poet, with Dutch Quakers on his mother's side.

✺ IN PAINTINGS Whitman objected to the static realism of the then popular Dusseldorf school: it was too literal, too labored, realism that might enrapture "an upholsterer's or dry-goods man's wife" but killed the subject dead. It is no surprise to find him complaining of "too little soul," but the subtlety of his responses reminds us that he was even then looking for a different kind of realism, greater, more profound, one that did not thrust itself forward out of the frame but belonged as part of a natural movement in a whole ensemble of effects, as in nature. "Too many of our young fellows, among those who ought to know better, are carried away with the false principle of working up the details of a picture to the minutest specification. This is the business of the modelist, not the artist.... Aim to produce that beautiful resemblance which will excite the motion that the real object might produce—the rest is the mere drippings, the shavings and sawdust."

He was really calling, ahead of his time, for something like the new revolutionary Impressionism that would startle France with its experiments in light and motion. There was a word around, "luminist," which went some way toward expressing the quality he had in mind. What he admired, for instance, in his friend Walter Libbey's painting of a boy playing the flute was its "delicious melting in, so to speak, of object with object; an effect that is frequently enough in nature, though painters seem to disdain following it. . . ."

Abroad, a subject like this would be constrained by "the stamp of class" and presented as a delightful young savage, essentially boorish. Libbey's boy, on the other hand, could go on to become president, or even, Whitman said with tongue in cheek, editor of a leading newspaper. "I don't know where to look for a picture more *naive* or with more spirit or grace. The young musician has stopped by the wayside, and putting down his basket, seats himself on a bank. He has a brown wool hat, ornamented with a feather, rolled-up shirt-sleeves, a flowing red cravat on his neck and a narrow leather belt buckled around his waist—a handsome, healthy country boy.... There is a richness of coloring, tamed to that hue of purplish gray, which we see in the summer in the open air. There is no hardness, and the eye is not pained by the sharpness of outline which mars many otherwise fine pictures. . . ."

In the summer of 1851 Whitman wrote a series of open letters for Bryant's *Evening Post* and signed them "Paumanok," setting down his thoughts as he wandered around Brooklyn and its environs. In one he described standing on Brooklyn Heights overlooking downtown New York and feeling that sudden hunger of the eye for as much color as it could bear. It was sunset, yet the fierce "voracity of the soul" demanded even more than that flood of molten light. "Have you not, too, at such a time, known this thirst of the eye?" Whenever he visited his friends' studios he gorged himself on as much "intense glowing color" as he could, always going back for more because it was never enough. It was as though he was inciting his feelings to ever higher peaks, urging up waves of ecstasy that might break him out of his mean tethered self, as the ocean did. But why couldn't he do it for himself?

With another piece in the *Post* he declared himself a partner in his young Brooklyn friends' efforts to establish what Paul Zweig calls a counterdemocracy of the arts, and which he hailed as "a close phalanx, ardent, radical, progressive." He had adopted these young artists now as almost a second family. Their lives might look unimpressive, he wrote, but how preferable they were as a group to the American locomotive which society had now become, "a nation of whom the steam engine is no bad symbol," clanking on its fixed course and fired by the profit motive in its belly. But he had not got clear of the mechanical society he deplored, shunting down rusty old moral tracks like everyone else. Whitman's "do-it-yourself" book, as bizarre as *Moby-Dick* and more original than anything since Blake, would be announced to the American public in only four years' time, yet the future author of it had yet to see the locomotive as beautiful in its own right, concentrated as he still was on the ideal of classical beauty.

Behind his gassy rhetoric, though, lay something else: a hankering not for art but after a different kind of human being. He would try out these ideas shortly in his notebooks. As a spokesman for the "young artist race" he wrote about the need for them to break out of their isolation and neglect and make contact with their kindred spirits across America. He recommended their characters to his readers like a fatherly well-wisher in whose pastoral care they were. "With warm, impulsive souls, instinctively generous and genial, boon companions, wild and thoughtless often, but mean and sneaking never . . . unlike the orthodox sons and daughters of the world in many things," why should they be undervalued? He went on to plead that "it need not argue an absolute miracle, if a man differ from the present dead uniformity of society in appearance and opinion, and still retain his grace and morals." In a sense he was anticipating his own future reception.

With these forthright claims being made on their behalf it was inevitable that he should be the one invited to lecture at the first awards ceremony of the Art Union in Fulton Street. The speech, virtually an anthology of quotes from favorite writers, shows Whitman striving self-consciously to present himself as the man of letters he would later despise, diving freely in and out of history and the classics for his references and examples.

Emerson, Carlyle, and Ruskin were his mainstays. He was especially mindful of Emerson's drawing together of nature and art in his essay "Nature." The artist did not, according to Emerson, see nature as rooted and fast, but as fluid, "and impresses his being thereon. ... The remotest spaces of nature are visited and the farthest sundered things are brought together."

Whitman was not yet ready or able to say in so many words that it was man's task to make of himself a work of art, and life too, or that his creations had no other purpose than to awaken and vivify. In "Song of Myself" he would announce unequivocally and with entrancing simplicity that once man is thoroughly awake a truly unique modern life will begin on earth, before which he will stand and marvel, rejoice and worship. There will be no more struggle, only joy and light and play. Beginning his speech he touched on this exploratory concept by saying that when God called his creation "good" he meant by this a fragrant new beginning. The artist's task was to demonstrate God's fresh start for the benefit of others.

He took as one text Emerson's "Why should we not also enjoy an original relation to the universe?" and moved rapidly from this to what vitally interested him, the idea that all men are artists if they did but realize it. That is, we are all capable, like God, of experiencing the exhilarating springtime of the creation. The universe we inhabit is not dying, it is dew-fresh, in its infancy. Its inexhaustible reality stands empty, an age of plenitude so marvelous that "the courts of the most sumptuous kings are but a frivolous patch, and though it is always waiting for them, not one in thousands of its owners ever enters there with any genuine sense of its grandeur and glory."

Great art, he told them, was a vestibule in which we come to terms with our fears and overcome them, seeing them as rites of passage to the greater realm which creation is. The Greeks understood, for instance, that death was not a gruesome enemy but as essential to us as life itself, as night is to day: to be loved, not feared. He touched here on a theme which had haunted his short stories and would form the central myth of his major poetry, singing in a strange poem in praise of the "tomb-leaves, body-leaves" which sprang up from the dark concealed heart of what he was; the "scented herbage of my breast." Even here, in front of his puzzled Art Union audience, the face of Death in his description of the Greek temple had his own drowsy gaze, the lid halfway down over the pupil of his cloudy light blue eyes:

". . . Death and his brother Sleep were depicted as beautiful youths reposing in the arms of Night. At other times Death was represented as a graceful form, with calm but drooping eyes, his feet crossed and his arms leaning on an inverted torch. Such were the soothing and solemnly placed influences which true art, identical with the perception of the beauty that there is in all the ordinations as well as all the works of Nature, cast over the last fearful thrill of those olden days. Was it not better so? Or is it better to have before us the idea of our dissolution typified by the spectral horror upon the pale horse, by a grinning skeleton or a moldering skull?"

He wound up his speech with an assertion that was looming ever larger in his mind. Opening out the theme of art still further he took his cue from the Carlyle of *Sartor Resartus* and ridiculed the "orthodox specimen of a man of the present time," trussed up and effete like a tailor's dummy and topped by the idiocy of a fashionable hat. If we believed with Emerson that the artist was the complete man, it followed that we should look for examples of the artistic spirit in all walks of life—the behavior of the great rebels and innovators. He cited Washington, Kossuth, Mazzini, Socrates, and linked the artistic impulse with heroic actions. "He who does great deeds, does them from his sensitiveness to moral beauty. Such men are not merely artists, they are artistic material. . . . A sublime moral beauty . . . may almost be said to emanate from them." So, he concluded, "Talk not so much, then, young artist, of the great old masters, who but painted and chiseled. Study not only their productions. There is a still better, higher school for him who would kindle his fire from the altar of the loftiest and purest art. It is the school of all grand actions. . . ."

He had got there, if only for a moment, sounding a note intended purely for his own ears. The poet of his dreams would make himself "perfect" by the very act of making his poetry. His art would be simultaneously an art of self-creation. After thus remaking himself from head to foot he would then, like the saints, merely have to *be*. Affirmation would emanate from him. Confidence would be visible in his every aspect. As a figure he would be strikingly human and accessible, at the service of all.

Privately, enveloped in a commonplace life which seemed at times a rehearsal for the anonymity he would soon glorify, Whitman did not appear to be involved with anyone, or to want to be with anyone other than himself. The fact of his own being was, almost complacently, enough. He made no attempt to prove or explain himself.

There was a fatality about him which either irritated or fascinated. Otherwise he struck others as a quiet, thoughtful man, cool in his responses. More than ever now he had a strange invisibility about him that people just came to accept. That was Walt being Walt, they said.

Women were completely outside him. In these years before his staged public appearance he is harder than ever to see. In a sense his personality was always determinedly public. His editorials show him as young and inflammable, yet in himself he had a languor, as if waiting there on his own fate, his gaze lingering voluptuously on whatever interested him. There was nothing ironical in his nature. He was a steady, uncritical watcher of people and things, all the time staying apart, not implicated. No one had power over him, unless it was his mother, a woman of pathos and maternity, like him content to wait, never pressing demands on him. Even she could get little out of him. Everyone let him be, taking their cue from her. Walt was different.

Yet he was about to become one of them again, more thoroughly than he had ever been, not just as a provider but as someone happy to share their ordinariness. The laziness of his grey-blue, half-clouded eyes created a false impression which he seemed to encourage and behind which he lived, as behind a mask. George Whitman, uninterested in depths, spoke of this in his recollections as reticence.

"Do you ask if he was shiftless? No: he was not shiftless—yet he was very curiously deliberate . . . he would refuse to do anything except at his own notion—most likely when advised would say: 'we won't talk about that. . . . ' He would lie abed late, and after getting up would write a few hours if he took the notion—perhaps go off for the rest of the day. . . . I do not think he took a word of advice from anyone. . . . It was in him not to do it—in his head, in his heart. . . . If we had dinner at one, like as not he would come in at three: always late. Just as we were fixing things on the table, he would get up and go around the block."

This maddening retreat into himself when it suited him was like a silence descending. From it, in his poetry, came his method of proceeding by intuition, indirection, suggestion. He felt music to be the subtlest language, infinitely superior to words. He edged in his poems toward wordless song, insisting on a silence that left him and his reader free to engage in something other than themselves. In "Song of Myself" he breaks off to warn,

Encompass worlds but never try to encompass me,
I crowd your noisiest talk by looking towards you.

Writing and talk do not prove me,
I carry the plenum of proof and every thing else in my face,
With the hush of my lips I confound the topmost skeptic.

The Whitman who suddenly wrote to Senator John Parker Hale during the 1852 election campaign was a man in transition, no longer talking as a politician or editor but with a sense of new independence, speaking up for "the tens of thousands of young men, the mechanics, the writers, etc" among whom he counted himself. Hale, hesitating over whether to accept the Free Soil party's nomination for the presidency, opened a letter from someone whose name probably meant nothing to him, urging him to "look to the young men." If he was reluctant to accept the nomination it was no doubt because to be a candidate for a third party that had been dying on its feet for the past two years was no cheering prospect.

The obscure Brooklynite who wanted Hale to go forth "in the old heroic Roman fashion" addressed a tough politician who was hardly the stuff from which heroes were made. And radicalism was at a low ebb. Whitman, unconcerned with temporary setbacks and infused with a belief in the eventual triumph of the ordinary, did his best to transfer his certainties to Hale. "I have never been at Washington," he wrote innocently, "and know none of the great men. But I know the people. I know well (for I am practically in New York), the real heart of this mighty city. . . . In all these young men, and behind the bosh of the regular politicians, there burns, almost with fierceness, the divine fire which . . . during all ages, had only waited a chance to leap forth and confound the calculations of tryants, hunkers and all their tribe. At this moment New York is the most radical city in America. It would be the most anti-slavery city, if that cause hadn't been made ridiculous by the freaks of the local leaders here."

AT HOME IN Brooklyn now there was a marked change of emphasis. Walt as head of his family handled the business of his carpenter-contractor brothers and ran his shop. He was doing better than his father, even if he disappointed with his evident lack of interest in the accumulation of money. Puzzling too was his sudden desire to dress like a workingman and get his hands dirty now and then. The truth was that he enjoyed the company of the framers and joiners. It refreshed him to be in contact with the ordinary and concrete, away from brash political arenas and editorial tub-thumping. He had soul-surges which carried him off, when he wanted to fling himself into the dazzling brightness the air and sea offered; but those were wild moments, frightening in their extremity. He hungered for roots again. He had come round in a circle: the rebellious youth of West Hills who had gone off to teach rather than labor in the fields with his bitter father, a man spreading a deadness around him, was now a working-class socialist, weaned like his father on Paine and Hicks. He mixed with artists in studios that were as congenial to him as carpenters' workshops.

The house-shifting went on as before. Frame houses could be erected in a month. The Whitmans moved out of Cumberland Street to a house Walt had engaged contractors to build for him in Skillman Street.

They were there a year, then bought another house—in Louisa Whitman's name—in Ryerson Street, at the other end of Myrtle Avenue. They were now affluent enough to pay $1,840 for it outright, clear of mortgage. The father was now seriously disabled; he had suffered a stroke. As a family they had achieved at last the stability of a home on which they owed nothing, even if the district was working class.

Walt's magpie-picking over books and articles went on apace. Annotated extracts jostled in his notebooks with lists of building receipts, payments, orders for materials, changes of address, mortgage details. He was collecting too, with as much technical terminology as possible, the jagged, sharp-edged vocabulary of tools and trades he would before long pack into the seams of poems in celebration of the manual worker, those unsung heroes of the sagas being enacted under everyone's noses; the ordinary acts of men earning their livelihoods. And not only men,

The wife—and she is not one jot less than the husband,
The daughter—and she is just as good as the son,
The mother—and she is every bit as much as the father.

Though the world of trades in all its diversity was undeniably a man's world—

Pasturelife, foddering, milking and herding, and all the personnel
and usages . . .
Grains and manures . . . marl, clay, loam . . . the subsoil plow,
the shovel and pick and rake and hoe, irrigation and
draining . . .

The cylinder press, the handpress . . . the frisket and
tympan . . . the compositor's stick and rule,
The implements for daguerreotyping . . . the tools of the rigger or
grappler or sailmaker or blockmaker,
Goods of guttapercha or papiermache . . . colors and brushes . . .
glaziers' implements . . .

The walking beam of the steam-engine . . . the throttle and
governors, and the up and down rods . . .
The etu of surgical instruments, and the etu of oculist's or
aurist's instruments, of dentist's instruments . . .
The anvil and tongs and hammer . . . the axe and wedge . . . the
square and mitre and jointer and smoothingplane,
The plumbob and trowel and level . . . the wall-scaffold . . .

Leatherdressing, coachmaking, boilermaking, ropetwisting,
distilling, signpainting, limeburning, coopering,
cottonpicking . . .
Shipcarpentering, flagging of sidewalks by flaggers . . . dock-
building . . .
The pump, the piledriver, the great derrick . . . the coalkiln and
brickkiln. . . .

He was two: coarse and delicate, solitary and democratic, radical
and conservative, fleshy and mystical, buffalo and hermit thrush,
man and woman. If he combined and integrated his twoness,
wouldn't he then be self-contained, complete in himself, free at last
of derivation? Did he need anything outside himself?

Yet he did. Somehow not deeply affected or aroused by women, he
was drawn to the working world as to a great easeful bath of
comradeship that was instinct with manly love, ever-laughing and
grave and physical.

The young fellow drives the express wagon (I love him, although I
do not know him) . . .
The driver thinking of me does not mind the jolt of his wagon. . . .

He had always been touched by mate-love, moved by the solidarity and trust and mutual dependence of mates, the glances and silences and shy laughs hinting at the unsayable. Workingmen did not cling. They could be aloof, leaving each other free out of trust, their love springing from one root, without the confusion of the female. Sitting with Broadway drivers, mixing easily with the joiners and framers, laughing with ferrymen, he had felt anonymous and yet included, knowing a bond which didn't seek to muddy everything in speech. Or he could pass to and fro and be a society of one, brushed around with the delights of possibilities.

Working people were easily sucked in, dragged down, distorted, used. He felt too that they were capable of other things. In them was a generous love that had not yet been tapped; more unselfish than family love, man-and-woman love. There was a deeper man, and no one had called him up. There ought to be a religion where soul met soul in a sympathy as natural as the sympathy of one body for another. "God is Man," wrote Blake, "and exists in us and we in him. All deities reside in the human breast." The love of man for his mate, his comrade, ought to be seen as sacred, a new originating power.

When he came to compose his 1855 preface to *Leaves of Grass* he began with the bedrock of the common people. He was of them, in daily intimacy with them. Wasn't he the one to speak up for them? In this astonishing monologue, at once grandiose and humble, he is beside himself with the desire to exalt the nobodies. He loves their uneducated intelligence, their instinct for what is right or wrong, their simple curiosity about the world. They live in a place of mystery and fear and vividness. No one should rule them. They are intrinsically fine, the very stuff of democracy and poetry. They move heroically in the vastness of a raw, loose country, released from the feudal grip of ages past. America, the open door they have walked through. He will be their first authentic voice. They are tongueless: he will give them tongues. The everlasting faith they have in their hearts he will have. In the finest prose he would ever write he announces,

> Faith is the antiseptic of the soul . . . it pervades the common people and preserves them . . . they never give up believing and expecting and trusting. . . . There is that indescribable freshness and unself-consciousness about an illiterate person that humbles and mocks the power of the noblest expressive genius. The poet

sees for a certainty how one not a great artist may be just as sacred and perfect as the greatest artist.

Nothing must detract from the people and the nation. They were the poems, first and foremost. Soon he was at full throttle, inspiring himself. What were his friends, when he reflected on them, but walking poems? "Their manners speech dress friendships—the freshness and candor of their physiognomy—the picturesque looseness of their carriage . . . their deathless attachment to freedom—their aversion to anything indecorous or soft or mean—the practical acknowledgement of the citizens of one state by the citizens of all other states—the fierceness of their roused resentment—their curiosity and welcome of novelty—their self-esteem and wonderful sympathy—their susceptibility to a slight—the air they have of persons who never knew how it felt to stand in the presence of superiors—their good temper and openhandedness—the President's taking off his hat to them not they to him—these too are unrhymed poetry. It awaits the gigantic and generous treatment worthy of it."

So the credo at its center was nothing less than a call for a new religion founded on these living people, overlooked and conspired against and betrayed but still with believing hearts.

> This is what you shall do: Love the earth and sun and the animals, despise riches, give alms to everyone that asks, stand up for the stupid and crazy, devote your income and labor to others, hate tyrants, argue not concerning God, have patience and indulgence towards the people, take off your hat to nothing known or unknown, or to any man or number of men—go freely with powerful uneducated persons, and with the young, and with the mothers of families—re-examine all you have been told in school or church on in any book, and dismiss whatever insults your own soul; and your very flesh shall be a great poem, and have the richest fluency, not only in its words but in the silent lines of its lips and face, and between the lashes of your eyes, and in every motion and joint of your body.

A year after this splendid utterance he lost his balance, disgusted by the squalor and turmoil of national politics. President Franklin Pierce filled him with contempt. What was this Northern "doughface" but a proslavery plotter who "eats dirt and excrement for his daily meals, likes it and tries to force it on the States"? He boiled over in a vituperative pamphlet which he called "The Eighteenth Presidency," setting it up in type himself. Then he was stumped for an audience. How could he distribute it? He wanted to reach the people direct, without intermediaries. Poetry would have to wait: it was necessary to make haste. He was even driven by the violent seizure of urgency to hope for a redeemer. "I would be much pleased to see some heroic, shrewd, fully-informed, healthy-bodied, middle-aged, beard-faced American blacksmith or boatman come down from the West across the Alleghenies and walk into the Presidency, dressed in a clean suit of working attire and with the tan all over his face, breast and arms; I would certainly vote for that sort of man, possessing the due requirements, before any other candidate."

He subtitled his broadsheet "Voice of Walt Whitman to Each Young Man in the Nation, North, South, East and West," addressing himself more specifically to "Butchers, Sailors, Stevedores, Drivers of Horses—to Ploughmen, Woodcutters, Marketmen, Carpenters, Masons and Laborers—and to all in these States Who Live by Their Daily Toil."

He sent proof sheets to editors of the independent press and to "rich persons" and appealed to them to "Circulate and reprint this Voice of mine for the workingmen's sake. I hereby permit and invite any rich person anywhere to stereotype it, or reproduce it in any form, to deluge the cities of the States with it. It is those millions of mechanics you want; the writers, thinkers, learned and benevolent persons, merchants, are already secured about to a man. But the great masses of the mechanics, and a large portion of the farmers, are unsettled, hardly know whom to vote for, or whom to believe. I am not afraid to say that among them I seek to initiate my name, Walt Whitman, and that I shall in future have much to say to them. . . ."

Only by electing a different class of men into government, he believed, would there be any hope of a change for the better. Over the heads of politicians he condemned the administration as a bunch of "limber-tongued lawyers, very fluent but empty, feeble old men, professional politicians, dandies, dyspeptics and so forth. . . . I expect to see the day when they . . . will be looked on with derision, and when qualified mechanics and young men will reach Congress, sent in their working costumes, fresh from their benches and tools, and returning to them again with dignity."

ONE OF Whitman's dropping-in places happened to be the studio of a landscape painter, Charles Heyde. Meeting Heyde was an encounter he would regret bitterly for the rest of his life. At the time, though, he was impressed enough by Heyde's work to bring his friend Bryant around to see it. A little later Walt took his new friend Charley home to meet his family.

"I wish to God we had been in hell before we ever saw him," Jeff said, looking back later with as much bitterness as his brother. Initially they all seemed to take to him, especially Hannah, who saw in the painter a promise of escape from the house plagued with sicknesses that she was trapped in. In the spring of 1852 she married him. He took her off to Vermont, hoping to succeed as a landscape artist in a period when only portraits really sold.

Heyde was impractical, proud, irritable, and as stubborn as Whitman. The unhappy letters from Hannah to her mother soon started to trickle and then flood in. She accused Charley of everything from abuse to infidelity. He told her, she said, that she was an idiot like her afflicted brother Eddy, a slut who was a hopeless cook, reacting to fair criticism with hysteria; in short "a mean stinking selfish wretch." They spent childless years of misery locked together in bitter warfare, complaining about each other to anyone who would listen. Charley sponged on Whitman as if by right, and in fact seemed to blame him for his misfortunes. Hannah, he moaned, "makes a half-barbarous life for herself, and almost baffles all my efforts to humanize her."

Finally he collapsed into chronic dementia and was carried off. Hannah shut herself away in a room with the curtains permanently drawn and concentrated on her endless ailments. Whitman, never a vindictive man, called Charley a leech, a snake, "the bed-buggiest man on earth" and very nearly "the only man alive who can make me mad."

All that lay ahead of him as his piecemeal education gathered him up in a final momentum. Astronomy was the branch of science he knew most accurately—he heard O. M. Mitchel lecture at the Broadway Temple and afterward studied *A Course of Six Lectures*. In the *Eagle* he had reviewed Olmstead's *Letters on Astronomy*. Earlier he could well have read Rafinesque's *Celestial Wonders of Philosophy*. He may even have taken a peep through one of the "space annihilating" telescopes described by Mitchel. Throughout his life he made a habit of studying the night skies. Apart from astronomy, the crucial discoveries of science came to him through the nineteenth-century popularizers—books and magazines and newspapers dramatizing their own rediscoveries. In the main he got his science from outlines, wonder and knowledge mixed.

Geology was another fascination. On its reversed scroll he read of the vast age of the earth. The cosmic evolution he believed in, cobbled together from several hypotheses, saw the universe and us with it as cyclical creations, disintegrating and resurrecting in an endless recurrence.

Much of his omnivorous gorging took place in the libraries of New York and Brooklyn. Spending hours there being awed by these immensities, he stepped clear of clock time. Indentifying, he was a mote, a speck, a grain of sand, or he grew gigantic like a molten sun and whirled off to the edges of space. He flew with the birds, crawled with serpents, stood stock still with a horse in a field. The Crockett-like sequence in "Song of Myself" in which he narrates his own vast unfolding to the moment when he arrives in the present "with my robust soul" to tell all, is unintentionally comic yet has a swaggering magnificence. And if "the clock indicates the moment... what does eternity indicate?"

> My feet strike an apex of the apices of the stairs,
> On every step bunches of ages, and larger bunches between
> the steps,
> All below duly travel'd, and still I mount and mount.
>
> Rise after rise bow the phantoms behind me,
> Afar down I see the huge first Nothing, I know I was even there,
> I waited unseen and always, and slept through the lethargic mist,
> And took my time, and took no hurt from the fetid carbon....
>
> Immense have been the preparations for me,
> Faithful and friendly the arms that have help'd me.
>
> Cycles ferried my cradle, rowing and rowing like cheerful
> boatmen,
> For room to me stars kept aside in their own rings,
> They sent influences to look after what was to hold me.
>
> Before I was born out of my mother generations guided me,
> My embryo has never been torpid, nothing could overlay it....

Vast vegetables gave it sustenance,
Monstrous sauroids transported it in their mouths and deposited
    it with care. . . .

If his maw refused to digest more books there was always the
Egyptian Museum at 659 Broadway to visit. Frequently in the 1850s
he climbed the stairs to the suite of three big rooms on the second
floor that was shrouded and dim, "dreamy, silent, eloquent." Its
owner, Dr. Henry Abbot, a portly, exhausted-looking Englishman
with a drooping Oriental mustache, was an eccentric in financial
difficulties. He had spent three decades in Cairo practicing medicine
and collecting antiques. Now he was anxious to sell his museum to
the local authority and clear his debts, and at some point enlisted
Whitman's help. His regular visitor obliged gladly with an article in
*Life Illustrated* boosting the collection.

Abbot, disillusioned by the public's indifference and grateful for
Whitman's eager questions, took his new friend on numerous con-
ducted tours around the exhibits in his gloomy rooms. Whitman used
his article to record what Abbot said. Often he was "a solitary gazer
among these wonderful relics" that most New Yorkers chose to
ignore. There were "sandals, boots, knives, spoons, needles, lamps,
combs . . . hollow reeds containing powder and ointments, toilet-
boxes, ornaments shaped like lotus flowers, headrests, bronze mirrors,
gold insects, bugs and beetles, strips of papyrus containing whole
narratives . . . the lives of persons and their funeral ceremonies."
Towering in a niche was a "colossal limestone head" with carved
almond eyes exuding immense calm, evidently the face of "some
great ruling person."

The weaving of human and nonhuman worlds in symbols, the
juxtaposition of human and animal in a single image—a bird-headed
man, a lion with the face of a woman—and the stylized language of
hieroglyphics encouraged Whitman to believe that the earth itself
and everything on it was a text recited by the "uttering tongues" of
grass, "a uniform hieroglyphic" waiting to be deciphered by its poet.
Dr. Abbot, delighted to recommend books on ancient Egypt, had
brought home to Whitman the physical reality of a civilization as
organized in its way as America. It was uncanny. "In the country
parts were agriculture, roads, canals, conveyances, barns, imple-
ments, cattle, machines. . . . In their cities were officers, streets,
aqueducts, manufactures, public institutions, quays, markets, amuse-

ments. . . . They not only had books, but these books were plentiful. Epics were common. They had novels, poems, histories, essays, and all those varieties of narratives forever dear to the people." They had their Christ, Osiris, a dying god like Jesus who was resurrected in the spears of growth each spring. An unidentified wit would refer to Walt sauntering along Broadway as like a self-styled Christ-Osiris, his red shirt unbuttoned to show the "scented herbage of his breast."

Legendary Egypt had been obliterated, swallowed up by time; but was anything really lost? Nature perpetually renewed itself. This was the force he was to marvel at in his poem "This Compost." Miracles of renewal lay everywhere around us; all was made clean "forever and forever."

> Where have you disposed of their carcasses,
> Those drunkards and gluttons of so many generations?
> Where have you drawn off all the foul liquid and meat?
> I do not see any of it upon you today, perhaps I am deceiv'd,
> I will run a furrow with my plough, I will pass my spade through
>     the sod and turn it up underneath,
> I am sure I shall expose some of the foul meat. . . .
>
> What chemistry!
> That the winds are really not infectious,
> That this is no cheat, this transparent green-wash of the seas
>     which is so amorous after me,
> That it is safe to allow it to lick my naked body all over with its
>     tongues,
> That it will not endanger me with the fevers that have deposited
>     themselves in it. . . .
>
> Now I am terrified at the Earth, it is that calm and patient,
> It grows such sweet things out of such corruptions. . . .
> It gives such divine materials to men, and accepts such leavings
>     from them at last.

❧   GRADUALLY OVER the past year or two his reading for pleasure had begun to invade his thoughts and become deliberate, impatient, more than just intoxication. He was about to discover his goal, his star. The zest for knowledge had a new meaning, burning up like a beacon in his mind.

He waded among the Greek and Roman classics in translation, and it was like being cast up on a glowing, virgin shore, reading in Lucretius that nature resolved everything into its component atoms and "never reduces anything to nothing." He read in unscientific language what he had already sucked in from astronomy, that "the universe is not bounded in any direction." He found confirmed what he already knew in his blood, listening to his own twoness—nature was twofold and consisted of two totally different things, "matter and the space in which things happen"; finding in words as shining and clear as spring water what he had long suspected, that the mind— and if the mind, why not the spirit?—shared in the body's experiences and sympathized with it. There was no natural enmity, no bitter wrestling or overcoming of the flesh, or disgust for the sensual appetites.

He absorbed instructions on how to avoid the pitfalls of love and they chimed with his instinctive caution and prudence. It was wise, then, to stay uninvolved. If you clung to love "you assure yourself the certainty of heart-sickness and pain." You loved better, taught Lucretius, if you were healthy than if love-sick. Distraught lovers clasped the object of their longing overtightly—kissed so fiercely that "teeth were driven into lips." And how it made his heart pound to read that "as feathers, fur and bristles are generated at the outset from the bodies of winged and four-footed creatures, so then the new-born earth first flung up herbs and shrubs."

Earth was the great mother. Out of it came everything. Streams of matter flowed from every object, rippling out in all directions. Sounds of every sort surged through the air. The earth was a living breathing animal. And the sea, the sea! It was a bitter teeming fluid gnawing at the shore in great exhalations, silkily breathing and then storming in a chaos.

He read in triumphant gulps, full of the delight of his recognitions and identifications. He had always hated the fear embedded in religion. Here was Lucretius saying that "the conscience-ridden mind in terrified anticipation torments itself with its own goals and whips."

His reading of Epictetus went back to when he was sixteen. He had cherished him and the Stoics ever since. "He's a universe in himself," he recalled in old age. "On the day I found an Epictetus, it was like being born again. He sets me free in a flood of light." Epictetus was part of the foundation of his *Leaves* as well as the source of his peace.

A four-volume anthology edited by Charles Knight, *Half-Hours with the Best Authors*, took him in a rapid swirl through English literature. *Memoria Technica* was a volume out of which he clipped details of historical events for a homemade encyclopedia he was compiling. He made up scrapbooks. A reference by one author led him to track down the works of another.

He lived in a seethe of conflicting influences, but there was really nothing to fear. Things came together when one submitted. And ultimately, when he gave in, it was out-of-doors nineteenth-century America that triumphed over the books, just as it was nineteenth-century popular science that swept him away and unlocked him with its revelations. The antique world shrank, and so did "the aimless sleepwalking of the middle ages." Change and progress were the engines driving the streets of his city. Whitman had grown up familiar with turbulence and unrest. He was as impressed as anyone with the new technology. Scientific knowledge was to him a romance of numbers, an expansion of vital laws. What was there to fear? The poetry he heralded would be married to science.

"Exact science and its practical movements," he wrote in his 1855 preface, "are no checks on the greatest poet but always his encouragement and support." Scientists were not poets "but they are the lawgivers of poets and their construction underlies the structure of every perfect poem. . . . In the beauty of poems are the tuft and final applause of science." All this prodigious advancement could be utilized by "one full-sized man, unconquerable and simple." Which was where he came in. America, cauldron of rebirth, contained old and new, ancient and modern. So should the American poet.

Science gave him the final spur. One evening in 1888 he broke out rapturously in praise of science and its significance. It had been in the air, part of his formative years. Materialism was the very breath of life to him. How timely it was, coming after all the religions. People everywhere were being released and leavened by science: in fact it was the spirit of religion itself, uncontaminated by priests, a great yea-sayer. At its best it "utters the highest truth— makes the last demonstration of faith. Looks the universe full in the face—looks its bad in the face, its good—and says yes to it." He went on: "After culture has said its last say we find that the best things remain to be said—that the heart is still listening to have heart things said to it—the brain still listening to have brain things said to it—the faith, the spirit, the soul, waiting. . . ."

The crowning glory of this "new evangel," he insisted, was its resignation. Horace Traubel must have blinked. Whitman was adamant. Science stood for an absolute surrender to the truth. "It never asks us: Do you want this thing to be true? Is it ugly, hateful? If it is true, that settles it." This primal quality, shared by poetry and science, was something that Heine had—"all the big fellows have it." More than any other agent science was furthering this spirit of truth on a massive, democratic scale through all the peoples of the world.

It was a passionate outburst. The old man was highly wrought, close to tears. "He regarded me with great love," Traubel recorded. The young man kissed his charge goodnight and Whitman called after him, "Goodnight, goodnight!"

꧁ IN JULY 1853, in a ferocious killing heat, an enormous industrial exhibition opened on what is now Bryant Park, next to the Croton Reservoir at 42nd Street. America's World Fair, like its London counterpart two years before, was housed in a specially constructed "crystal palace" of glass and iron, built on the pattern of a Greek cross. The site spread over four acres. On the north side rose New York's first skyscraper, the 280-foot-high Latting Observatory, with Latting's ice cream parlor at the base of it. Inside the Crystal Palace were steam and electric engines, masses of paintings and sculpture, guns, lighthouse lenses, lifeboats, furniture, perfumes, dies, stuffed birds, grain separators, raw materials of all kinds. President Pierce and the English geologist Charles Lyell were at the opening ceremonies.

Somewhere in the crowd was Walt Whitman. The merging of science, art, and industry drew him to this cornucopia like a magnet. For him it was nothing less than his nation's epic and ordinary age proudly displayed under an enclosing dome, a hold-all as capacious as the new kind of poem he was beginning to hatch in vague outline, that would have bays and annexes like this and be filled with cataloguelike lists of man's labor and the soaring of his festive "self."

He stood listening to the dignitaries, a burly figure of almost two hundred pounds, nearly six feet tall, who looked "rankly common." His face was reddened by the weather, his hair prematurely grizzled under a slouch hat. He stood there in his sweat as if dazed. His cheap clothes, a check shirt and baggy trousers tucked into his boots, put him in a class that was no class, half bohemian, half workingman. On most afternoons and evenings for nearly a year he trailed in and out of the exhibition, often with some young roustabout for a companion, an omnibus or express wagon driver or perhaps a fireman convalescing after an accident. He got to know these men by visiting them in hospital. Sitting at their bedsides he jotted down a few notes about them to pass the time. One of them was Bill Guess:

"Aged 22. A thoughtless, strong, generous animal nature, fond of direct pleasures, eating, drinking, women, fun etc. Taken sick with the small-pox, had the bad disorder and was furious with the delirium tremens. Was with me in the Crystal Palace, a large, broad fellow, weighed over 200. Was a thoughtless good fellow."

Two others who went into his notebook had father problems in their backgrounds.

"Peter ———, large, strong-boned young fellow, driver. Should weigh 180. Free and candid to me the very first time he saw me. Man of strong self-will, powerful coarse feelings and appetites. Had a quarrel, borrowed $300, left his father somewhere in the interior of the State, fell in with a couple of gamblers, hadn't been home or written there in seven years. . . ."

"George Fitch—Yankee boy, driver. Fine nature, amiable, sensitive feelings, a natural gentleman, of quite a reflective turn. Left his home because his father was perpetually 'down on him.' When he told me of his mother his eyes watered. . . ."


STRANGE THOUGH IT IS to contemplate, the "Walt Whitman" we know came fully armed out of a big battered trunk that was at the foot of Whitman's bed wherever he was living. Maybe he and Jeff had lugged it to New Orleans and back. When his first literary visitors came to look him up, riding over on the ferry and then entering Brooklyn, they found Ryerson Street and then were shown upstairs to a first-floor room. Bronson Alcott, a transcendentalist, couldn't help noticing the unmade bed which Walt shared with his brain-damaged and epileptic brother Eddy. Under it would be a brimming chamber pot. Prints of three pictures, "a hercules, a Bacchus and a satyr," were glued crudely to the tatty walls. Alcott was perhaps too bemused to take in the traveling trunk, or more likely he was invited to sit on it: there was next to no furniture.

When Whitman settled in Washington in 1863 for what he imagined would be a temporary stay he got his mother to send the trunk on to him.

He was in the habit of dumping anything in it which might come in handy, or be needed for reference. In there lay a chaos of half-completed or abandoned stories, manuscript fragments, letter drafts, business receipts, health files, old editorials, book lists, and notebooks made of scrap paper—some of it from used print runs—pinned together and then thrown into his portable repository. There were bound notebooks too, submerged in articles ripped out of newspapers and magazines. His leather notebook that he kept on his person at all times would be supplemented by these improvised ones.

The contents were as miscellaneous as his mind. Addresses of his artist friends Jesse Talbot and Fredrick Chapman, an account of the sinking of the ship *San Francisco*, reports on the Charge of the Light Brigade, on the opera singers Grisi and Mario, mingled in fructifying darkness with his trial line of poetry, prose waiting to be hewn into poems, a fractured stanza or a floating phrase looking for a home—"Observing the summer grass" would extend into a whole passage in "Song of Myself." Details of some masonry work for a house basement, orders for joinery—"Front windows on first floor—lights 13 × 17—Window five lights high—a sash of two lights across the top—the other eight lights made in two door-sides, hung each with hinges"—were there in the trunk along with the rough outline of a poem eventually to be the famous "Song of the Open Road": "I will take each man and woman of you to the window and open the shutters and the sash, and my left arm shall hook you around the waist, and my right shall point you to the endless and beginningless road along whose sides are crowded the rich cities of all living philosophy, and oval gates that pass you into fields of clover and landscapes clumped with sassafrass, and orchards of good apples, and every breath through your mouth shall be of a new perfumed and elastic air, which is love.—Not I—not God—can travel this road for you. . . ."

These 1850s notebooks were his language workshops, laboratories of the spirit, test beds. *Leaves of Grass* was actually forming here, in the stray scraps, odds and ends, torn bits, musings. Only the unique reeled-out line is missing. We see everything in embryo except the man. Even when we seem to be given something highly personal we have to beware. The heart laid bare for an instant is only some theatre "business" he is rehearsing, the emotional fluid meant to float and launch a poem or the scaffolding intended to raise it.

> I am not glad tonight. Gloom has gathered round me like a mantle tightly folded.
> The oppression of my heart is not fitful and has no pangs; but a torpor like that of some stagnant pool.

It is halfway to poetry. The simulated outcry which follows gives the game away: "O Mystery of Death, I pant for the time when I shall solve you!"

Delving into his chaotic trunk one comes up with loose papers which look at first like secret asides and are in fact trial worksheets. A journallike entry beats with throes of pain, yet the depression it describes has something subterranean and satisfying about it, as if it comes from a refuge he inhabits. "Everything I have done seems to me blank and suspicious.—I doubt whether my greatest thoughts, as I had supposed them, are not shallow.—and people will most likely laugh at me—My pride is important; my love gets no response—The complacency of nature is hateful—I am filled with restlessness—I am incomplete."

We see him working hard to get rid of the "stock poetical touches" which still stood between him and the uninhibited outflowing he had in mind. He tried the dynamite of his objectless sexuality in an attempt to blast his way through: after all, what was more subversive than sex?

> Bridal night
> one quivering jelly of love
> limpid transparent
> Limitless jets of love hot and enormous. . . .
> Drunken and crazy with love swimming
> in its . . . in the plummetless sea
> Loveflesh swelling and deliciously aching whiteblood of love.

But delirium was not the answer. By the time he came to write "Song of Myself" the astonishing clean lift of the lines, as if the words themselves were fresh-minted, came from a freedom he had worked for long and deliberately, in the deepest recesses of his character. In the run up to his *annus mirablis* we find stern injunctions to himself which make clear how conscious he was of what he was doing.

Make no quotations and no reference to any other writers.

Lumber the writing with nothing—let it go as lightly as a bird flies in the air, or a fish swims in the sea.

Rules for Composition—A perfectly transparent, plate-glassy style, artless, with no ornaments, or attempts at ornaments, for their own sake—they only looking well when like the beauties of the person or character by nature and intuition, and never lugged in to show off. . . .

Take no illustrations whatever from any ancients or classics. . . . Make no mention or allusion to them whatever except as they relate to the new present things. . . .

Clearness, simplicity, no twistified or foggy sentences at all—the most translucid clearness without variation.

Common idioms and phrases—Yankeeisms and vulgarisms—cant expressions when very pat only.

He had learned from the theatre and from oratory how to create the intimate approach to an audience, leaping the gap he had set himself to annihilate, so that his text leaned out from the page to embrace and lovingly hug the reader, obtaining for himself vicariously what the world of fact and mean limitation denied him.

My voice goes after what my eyes cannot reach,
With the twirl of my tongue I encompass worlds and volumes of worlds.

In poems evoking altered states of being, subtle shifts of temperament and emphasis he imagined the whole body of his poet-orator being brought into play, as he told himself in notes for lecture projects which never materialized. "From the opening of the Oration and on through, the great thing is to be inspired as one divinely possessed, blind to all subordinate affairs and given up entirely to the surgings and utterances of the mighty tempestuous demon. . . . Animation of limbs, hands, arms, neck, shoulders, waist, breast, etc. —the fullest type of live oratory—at times an expanding chest, at other times reaching forward, bending figure, raised to its fullest height, bending way over, low down. . . ."

Here is the man Paul Zweig has called "the masterful poet of personal change" preparing to go on stage. He accumulated lists of materials, equipment, clothing—one day he would incorporate them in passages he might write in praise of his driver friends: "Apron, cape, gloves, strap . . . wetweather clothes . . . whip carefully chosen

...spotter, starter and hostler...," and for him that meant living their lives for himself.

His digestion was strong, his hunger Faustian. He asked in one note, "What is it to own anything?—It is to incorporate it into yourself as the primal god swallowed in five immortal offspring of Rhea and accumulated to his life and knowledge and strength all that would have grown in them." Only by giving this carnal appetite full play, letting large and small alike "descend into that greedy Something in Man," could the world be understood. Here was the root of his identifying impulse. How else could the universe be assimilated? In the end only the soul was large and indiscriminate enough for this function, not even pausing to ask itself if one thing was worthier than another. What did such questions mean? "What is marvelous? What is unlikely? what is impossible or baseless, or vague? after you have once just opened the space of a peachpit and given audience to far and near and to the sunset and had all things enter with electric swiftness softly and duly without confusion or jostling or jam."

In an early notebook a sudden reservation jolts and surprises us: "I will not be the cart, nor the load on the cart, nor the horse that draws the cart; but I will be the little hands that guide the cart." The "eating drinking and breeding" rough is not always passively available. In him are the "little hands" that guide—as a woman, a mother guides.

What about his secret side? The nearest we come to the private man are those odd glimpses he reveals in abandoned fragments, oblique and yet curiously urgent with their hints of some secret he burns to share. An unfinished poem called "Death Song," for instance:

> Joy! Joy! O full of Joy
> Away becalmed at sea one day
> I saw a babe, laughing, kicking, etc etc.
> And as a swimmer floated in the waves he
> Called the child. Laughing it sprung and...

The prose version of this Blakean scrap is just as haunting and inconclusive:

"*Faith*. Becalmed at sea, a man refreshes himself by swimming round the ship—a deaf and dumb boy, his younger brother, is looking over...and the swimmer floating easily on his back smiles and beckons with his hand. Without waiting a moment the young child laughing and clucking springs into the sea and as he rises to the surface feels no fear but laughs and though he sink and drown he feels it not for the man is with him there."

This man who was both babe and protector, who seemed to regard the whole world as his mother, never wanting to wean himself, who swam in a kind of nonparticipatory androgynous fluid, infantile, dreamy, who invited sensual contact—"stop this day and night with me"—and yet was anxious at the last moment to return loved ones back to themselves, would make himself inaccessible as a deliberate ploy, as a test, but also as if helplessly.

> Missing me one place search another,
> I stop somewhere waiting for you. . . .
>
> Both in and out of the game and watching and wondering at it.

He comes at times tantalizingly close: now you see him, now you don't. Reach out and your hands go right through into air. "You will hardly know who I am or what I mean." He professes to be your soul, your elusive blood brother; he is both inside you and in the common dirt under your feet. "If you want me again look for me under your boot-soles." Suddenly he manifests himself, physically recognizable: a young man eager to be old and wise, shaking prematurely white locks and boasting that he is untamed, someone who hugs the shadows like a child and plays hide-and-seek in the vapor and dusk. Draw too unbearably, too threateningly near to him and he reacts like a magician, dissolving himself before your eyes. "I depart as air. . . . I effuse my flesh in eddies, and drift it in lacy jags."

Such an elegant way to depart. He is barbaric and exquisite both. And sometimes, embodied soul or not, how like our own uncertain selves he is, falling into self-doubt after forgetting—in his exuberant optimism—the humiliations, disgraces, betrayals, lies.

> That I could forget the mockers and insults!
> That I could forget the trickling tears and the blows of the bludgeons and hammers!
>
> I talk wildly, I have lost my wits, I and nobody else am the greatest traitor,
> I went myself to the headland, my own hand carried me there.

Shelley saw himself as the wind's lyre, and Whitman too had a mediumistic view of himself as poet. A power other than himself acted through him, he felt. For it to have free access one must encourage in oneself a trance state, a hovering between sleep and waking. "A trance, yet with all the senses alert—only a state of high exalted musing—the tangible and material with all its shows, the objective world suspended or surmounted for a while, and the powers in exaltation, freedom, vision—yet the *senses* not lost or counteracted."

I dream in my dream all the dreams of the other dreamers,
And I become the other dreamers.

# 8

# Birth of Rainbow

No one knows for certain how Whitman raised the money to pay for the first *Leaves of Grass*. It may have come from his various property deals. His brothers were working, and the outright purchase of the house in Ryerson Street could have been made possible, at least partly, by them.

Whitman came home one day at the end of June 1855 with an armful of copies of his book. His brothers were unresponsive. "I saw the book," George recalled—"didn't read it at all—didn't think it worth reading—fingered it a little. Mother thought as I did—did not know what to make of it." Probably though, unlike George, she made placatory noises. As for the sick father, he lay close to death. No one expected him to survive the year.

Whitman had taken his manuscript to a couple of friends, the brothers James and Thomas Rome, who had a printing shop at the corner of Fulton and Cranberry streets. Possibly the author had tried a commercial publisher first and had the book rejected. If so, he kept quiet about it. The Romes did print a few books but specialized in the printing of legal documents. Whitman, a proud and skilled printer, moved in on them to oversee the production of *Leaves*. They allowed him to set type himself whenever he felt like it. Ten pages or so were his own work. He had a routine and a special chair over in the corner.

During that spring of 1855 he would arrive every morning, read the *Tribune*, and then spend satisfying hours correcting proof. By July

6 the bound copies were on sale. Fowler and Wells had agreed to distribute the book in New York and also in Boston where they had another store. As well as this they undertook to advertise it in their "family magazine," *Life Illustrated.* Swayle, the other distributor, withdrew hastily as soon as he discovered the "disgusting" nature of the work he was handling.

The binding, done elsewhere, with elaborate title letters on a design of gilded leaves and entwined tendrils, had a distinctly feminine appeal. Inside, the fancifulness of the cover was contradicted at once by an engraved portrait facing the title page of a person who looked as if he might be the printer rather than the author. He was unnamed. Samuel Hollyer had made the engraving from a daguerreotype taken the previous summer by another friend of Whitman, Gabriel Harrison, who had deserted painting for the new craze of photography. A youngish bearded man stands in an uncaring pose, wearing rumpled work jeans, in short sleeves, right hand on his hip and the left shoved into his trouser pocket like a carpenter taking a break. The *Tribune* received a review copy and was quick to express disapproval of this loafer "in a garb half sailor's, half workingman's, with no superficial appendage of coat or waistcoat, a 'wideawake' perched jauntily on his head... with a certain air of mild defiance, and an expression of pensive insolence on his face which seems to betoken a consciousness of his mission as the 'coming man.' This view of the author is confirmed in the preface."

On the verso, if one wanted to search, was the name of the copyright owner, one "Walter Whitman," who could have been the publisher. Before a reader reached the dozen untitled poems there stood the barrier of the preface, an off-putting obstacle of ten pages of weirdly punctuated prose in close print, set in double columns. The poems themselves were in a more readable type, laid across a wide format to accommodate the strangely long and irregular lines. The manuscript of this remarkable book was left kicking around in the shop until 1858, when it was destroyed, so Whitman told a questioner, as if puzzled by the inquiry. "Rome kept it several years, but one day, by accident, it got away from us entirely—was used to kindle the fire or to feed the rag man." The preface would disappear from subsequent editions when its author judged the poems could stand "on their own two legs." The inking was spotty and must have given Whitman some qualms, but he had no money to spare for anything better. A Brooklyn binder, Charles Jenkins, made a handsome embossed job of two hundred copies. Someone else bound the remaining six hundred at a cheaper rate.

Whitman registered the copyright in Brooklyn on May 15, hurrying out his introductory prose while the book came off the press. The anonymous author revealed his indentity on page twenty-nine in a defiant fanfare as "Walt Whitman, American, one of the roughs.... Disorderly, fleshy and sensual...." He had no customary triple-barreled name, and his shortened Christian name gave his poetic persona the imprint he wanted. He was "no stander above men and women or apart from them." Anyone could approach him.

The centerpiece of his strange book, in the "rough and ragged thicket of its pages," was a sustained poem of fifty-two sections called "Song of Myself." Ruminating in later years on the character of *Leaves of Grass*, Whitman said provocatively that he thought of it as essentially a woman's book, and "every now and then a woman shows she knows it.... Its cry is the cry of the woman first of all, of the facts of creation first of all—of the feminine."

What did he mean? The self, released of its burdens in "Song of Myself," follows the soul and is caressed by it like a lover. The rainbowlike birth of the poem which so dazzles us with its simplicity is simultaneously the birth of its creator, or his rebirth. The narrator is both male and female. As well as heralding a resurrection, the poem rejoices in a wedding. And it's the female who brings the dowry of the unconscious to this marriage and so makes possible the first great American poem. Put another way, the womb of night receives the poet and he issues forth with his divided self transfigured, healed.

Nearly every work of genius confounds us because we feel it has been produced with miraculous ease. It is effortless. There is no hint of travail, no labor pain. "Unless from us the future takes place, we are death only," wrote D. H. Lawrence. Is the birth of "Song of Myself" taking place on earth or out in those vast spaces where love reigns? If there are birth pangs they are spiritual ones. Death here is not only not to be feared, it is to be welcomed. Without it how could we begin to grasp the nature of the birth we are witnessing? Thought flows without ceasing along the spilling lines of his poem, the "thinking with our feelings" thought of which T. S. Eliot speaks.

The announcing "I," so calm and yet so radiant, grows ever more sure of its powers as the poem unfolds. On page twenty-nine the poet introduces himself physically and stands before us, as if to say that he *is* the poem. Moreover, it is not literature we are reading but an antipoem: the "truth." It is the dream of himself as singer, orator, carrying "the plenum of proof" in his face and figure. For this everyday opera with all its voices fused into one he has moved from belief, with its doubts and vacillations, to the shining path of faith. There no longer seems any need for him to accomplish anything, to do anything other than show himself. To sing. Objections are anticipated and hushed, then woven into his song by this hand which can do no wrong. And somehow, in the shimmering element where the poem lives, serene as the planet itself as it swings around, bathed in common air, we are given to understand that he has become our soul, as he becomes in turn everything he sees and touches. Soon, though, this equalizer and guide will be gone, his function superfluous, since all along he has been leading us to a realization of our true selves.

Talk honestly, no one else hears you, and I stay only a minute longer.

ON JULY 6, his beautiful little book out in the world like a brave boat on a dangerous sea, Whitman felt himself reborn. Five days later his father—on the eve of his sixty-sixth birthday—was dead. Only his wife Louisa was with him when it became clear his death was a matter of hours away. Walt, George, and Jeff were sent for. George was only just in time. Mary, a long way off in Greenport, got there too late and was bitterly remorseful. Hannah, permanently on the move from one cheap rooming house to another with her out-of-luck artist husband, heard the news later in a letter from her mother which had been following her around. "i sent for jeffy and sent for laura and walter came," Louisa Whitman wrote in her illiterate scrawl—"they felt very much to blame themselves for not being home but they had no idea of any change your father had been ill so long and so many bad spells... mary took it very hard that she could not see her father... she was very sick coming from the evergreens where poor father was laid in a quiet spot...."

The funeral service at the Cemetery of the Evergreens in Brooklyn was conducted by a "babtist" minister, Louisa told her unhappy daughter. In her reply Hannah poured out her own grief for herself, as if something in her had died or been killed by Charley and was wandering about unburied and inconsolable. Without mentioning her father she made it plain that his death was one more blow for her to bear. "It is hard, very hard for me. I have more to regret than any of you...." In a way, she had. Her marriage, disastrous from the start, was essentially over. She would go on living in the ruins of it. If only she could return to Brooklyn. Charley, she said, would like nothing better than to be rid of her. Either she had no money for the journey or she was being histrionic again. Her tales of woe would gather in desperation and distress Walt considerably over the years.

While his father was still hanging to life by a thread Whitman had written jubilantly in his preface of an America that accepted the lesson of the past calmly, yet knew it had to be superseded, as he had long ago superseded his father. It perceived, he wrote, "that the corpse is slowly borne from the eating and sleeping rooms of the house... perceives that it waits a little while in the door... that it was fittest for its days... that its action had descended to the stalwart and well-shaped heir who approaches... and that he shall be fittest for his days."

America might, but Mary could not accept. She fell ill after the funeral. Walt accompanied her back to Greenport and stayed on as usual for part of the summer, loafing and dreaming of his future prospects. The famous Emerson letter must have been forwarded to him there. The great man, wondering where to send it, addressed it care of Fowler and Wells. "Rubbing his eyes" at his desk in Concord, he held between his hands the book in its green covers—sent by the distributors or by the author himself—which had him in raptures. Here was the genuine article at last—the American poem! Great power makes us happy, he told Whitman, and he was made happy reading it. "I greet you at the beginning of a great career, which yet must have had a long foreground somewhere, for such a start. I rubbed my eyes a little to see if this sunbeam were no illusion.... I did not know until I, last night, saw the book advertised in a newspaper, that I could trust the name as real and available for a Post-office. I wish to see my benefactor, and have felt much like striking my tasks and visiting New York to pay you my respects."

It was a tremendous endorsement, and Whitman must have felt he was on his way. Before his patron did visit him, however, he read the report of a friend, Moncure D. Conway, a clergyman and author who had gone off to meet Whitman on his home ground after hearing

Emerson talk of the marvelous book called *Leaves of Grass* which was still enchanting him with its "wit and wisdom." Conway gave Emerson precise instructions as to how to find Whitman's house. It was "fearfully far, out of Brooklyn nearly." The best way was to take the Fulton and Myrtle Avenue car and get off at Ryerson Street. In this row of identical small wooden houses with porches, lived in by mechanics, he located the house he wanted but not the man. Louisa sent him back to Fulton Street and the Rome brothers, where the poet was revising some proof for his second enlarged edition.

There this wonder sat, on the printer's desk, in a blue striped shirt "opening from a red throat." He had a blunt manner but was courteous enough. Conway made him laugh by telling him of a Boston Unitarian, Cyrus Bartol, who had been urged to read *Leaves of Grass* by Emerson and launched off on a reading from it in "polite company," then was too embarrassed to carry on.

Off they went together down to the ferry, and Whitman crossed over to New York with his visitor. The poet had a rolling gait, kept his hands in his pockets, and hailed characters along the way who struck Conway as more than a little dubious and "of the laboring class." Walt told him he belonged to that class himself and in fact knew thousands "of such, who love him but cannot make head or tail of his book."

Emerson did finally make the trip, in December. It was the first of several. After talking together the two men went off to New York for dinner. Then Whitman insisted on taking the man Carlyle called an angel, "a beautiful transparent soul," to a rowdy dive in Mercer Street for a beer. This was Freeman's Hall, a social club.

Was he simply rubbing in their unbridgeable differences? Emerson would remain uncomfortable with Whitman, as he was with New York. It would have been nothing short of miraculous if these two had become intimate friends. Later on their mutual admiration cooled, with Emerson referring to Whitman's book as "an auction-eer's inventory of a warehouse," "a singular blend of the Bhagavad Gita and the New York *Tribune*," its voice "half song-thrush, half alligator." As for Whitman, he knew at the outset that he was never going to be completely accepted. The gentle Emerson was on the pure side, inclined to be wishy-washy, very important in what he stood for and yet not quite in the world. "He would lay his hand on my coat sleeve when he was about to say something: touch me sort of half apologetically as if saying: if I may be permitted!" Always a spotlessly clean person himself, Whitman was struck by the almost ethereal purity of Emerson's face, "so clean," he remarked wickedly, "as if God had just washed it off."

He would never forget, though, Emerson's spontaneous generosity, and his first call at the house. "I can hear his gentle knock still ... and the slow sweet voice, as my mother stood there by the door: 'I came to see Mr. Whitman.'" It was something to wonder at, always. It is clear now that only Emerson's intervention and word-of-mouth enthusiasm saved Whitman's book from being consigned to oblivion, the work of a mad street versifier "who roots like a pig among the rotten garbage of licentious thoughts." Only Emerson's stature forced an unwilling literary world to attend to it. Even so it was nearly always to be seen as a curiosity, a joke. Later it would be a cult book, defended and cherished by a tight phalanx of evangelistic "Whitmaniacs." Whitman would gain notoriety, never fame and honor.

Emerson's love for the book apart, the reaction of the critic Charles Eliot Norton was typical of the literary establishment as a whole. In the September *Putnam's Monthly* he described *Leaves of Grass* as "preposterous yet somehow fascinating," fusing in some extraordinary fashion "Yankee transcendentalism and New York rowdyism." Probably he would not have bothered to notice the book at all had it not been for Emerson's word of recommendation. Norton confided to his friend James Russell Lowell that "one cannot leave it about for chance readers, and would be sorry to know that any woman had looked into it past the title-page." In fact a good many Victorian women would seize on it enthusiastically for nonliterary reasons, seeing a champion for their own cause behind this "motherman" poetry.

One honorable exception to the almost unanimous dismissiveness was a member of Emerson's circle who was not afraid to speak his mind, praising Whitman for his "simplicity and reality." Edward Everett Hale's words in the *North American Review* carried little weight but must have been welcome for all that. According to Whitman this was the only review which did the book anything like justice. Charles Dana, managing editor of the *Tribune*, had it in his power to do a great deal more but chose like the rest to hedge his bets. He applauded Whitman's "bold stirring thoughts" and "genuine intimacy with nature" but thought it a pity that the spirit of poetry had been disfigured by such "an uncouth and grotesque embodiment." A few paragraphs further on there sounded a threatening note which would grow increasingly intimidating in the years to come. "His language is too frequently reckless and indecent," Dana charged, "and will justly prevent his volume from free circulation in scrupulous circles." Soon Samuel Wells was raising similar objections, suggesting the removal of "certain passages" if he and the Fowlers were to continue dealing with the book.

Nothing, however, could alter or diminish the beauty of *Leaves of Grass* in Whitman's eyes. He had delivered it cleanly, under the curve of its rainbow, after backing into a corner and concentrating on his task to the exclusion of all else. His preface was not really a preface at all but a poem in its own right, the forceful prose driving toward the subtle rhythms of a new line, built to accommodate the rough-spoken, nourishing voice of someone actually speaking. From it rose his cry of victory. The preface was his arch of triumph; nothing could take his achievement from him. His joy in the knowledge shows in the buoyant, swarming swiftness of the prose's movement. He was in new territory and he was there on his own. He had even left his master, Emerson, behind.

His uncanny assurance contains an element of ruthlessness, as all creativity does. He had built a house, a body and spirit for himself. In the foundations he had buried his father. Freed now to be his own man, he spoke as though his father's lost strength had entered his blood in a great surge of transference. Water turned into wine. The force rushing through him like a wind made him speak blasphemously, as if he had not only moved into his father's vacant place but God's too. "How beautiful is candor." This, then, was his justification for the fantastic claims to follow. "The known universe has one complete lover and that is the greatest poet. . . . His brain is the ultimate brain. He is no arguer . . . he is judgment. He judges not as the judge judges but as the sun falling around a helpless thing."

America's prime symbol of growth and fulfillment, the road leading out into unknown territory, was nowhere more real than in *Leaves of Grass*. It was what the ever-wandering Lawrence so loved in Whitman—his vision of an uncluttered pathway for the soul to travel along on its life-journey: the soul as wayfarer. "The great home of the Soul is the open road," Lawrence wrote. The Conestoga wagons invoked the road. The concept of a transcontinental railroad was "road thinking raised to a higher power." The open road in the open air had no known direction, only the soul for compass. If that ecstatic tale of metamorphosis "'Song of Myself" incorporated a host of weddings, they were consummated along the open road.

My ties and ballast leave me...I travel...I sail...my elbows rest
  on the sea-gaps,
I skirt sierras...my palms cover continents....

I am he that walks with the tender and growing night.

WHITMAN DID HAVE one genuine admirer among the ordinary people he hoped—and failed—to reach, a man who had little in common with the transcendentalists and was certainly earthier. Henry B. Rankin, a law student working in the office of Lincoln and Herndon in Springfield, Illinois, remembered an argument breaking out over a just-published book which had been left on the office table by Herndon. It had the odd title of *Leaves of Grass*. At some point Lincoln came in and walked off with the book. He read it for half an hour, came back in and read pages aloud, commended it with one or two reservations, and took it home with him. Back with it next morning he told his staff how he "had barely saved it from being purified in the fire by the women."

Emerson's letter was burning a hole in Whitman's pocket. Even George noticed how it had "set him up." He carried it around with him everywhere, and then did something which many have since thought reprehensible. First of all he allowed his friend Dana to reprint the letter in the *Tribune,* and then had copies of the *Tribune* piece made and broadcast it far and wide. He wrote anonymous reviews of his own book in *Life Illustrated* and elsewhere. The following year he brought out his second edition with a sentence of Emerson's embossed on the spine: "I greet you at the beginning of a great career."

All his life he was a typical newsman, boosting himself by any means possible. If his collector's mania was journalistic, so was his continual self-advertising. One of his self-reviews appeared in 1856 in a paper he would be editing before long, the *Brooklyn Daily Times*:

First be yourself what you would show in your poems—such seems to be this man's example and inferred rebuke to the schools of poets. He makes no allusions to books or writers; their spirits do not seem to have touched him; he has not a word to say for or against them, or their theories or ways. He never offers others; what he continually offers is the man whom our Brooklynites know so well. Of pure American breed, large and lusty—age thirty-six years (1855)—never once using medicine—never dressed in black, always dressed freely and clean in strong clothes—neck open, shirt-collar flat and broad, countenance tawny transparent red, beard well-mottled with white, hair like hay after it has been mowed in the field and lies tossed and streaked—his physiology corroborating a rugged phrenology—a person singularly beloved and looked toward, especially by young men and the illiterate—one who has firm attachments there, and associates there—one who does not associate with literary people—a man never called upon to make speeches at public dinners—never on platforms amid the crowds of clergymen, or professors, or aldermen, or congressmen—rather down in the bay with pilots in their pilot-boat—or off on a cruise with fishers in a fishing-smack—or riding on a Broadway omnibus, side by side with the driver—or with a band of loungers over the open grounds of the country—fond of New York and Brooklyn—fond of the life of the great ferries—one whom, if you should meet, you need not expect to meet an extraordinary person—one in whom you will see the singularity which consists in no singularity—whose contact is no dazzle or fascination, nor requires any deference, but has the easy fascination of what is homely and accustomed—as of something you knew before, and was waiting for.

But of course not many were waiting. This was outrageous hustling, yet with Whitman there was always the contradictory underside. He hated to be lionized. If he suspected his friend Abby Price of wanting to exhibit him to strangers as a small celebrity he stayed away. Only two years after launching himself as a writer he was having second thoughts about authorship and the vanity of publishing. "What am I after all," he asked in the draft of a new poem, "but a child pleased with my own name? repeating it over and over."

He had set out deliberately to *be* his book, a living message, the embodiment of his words, antiliterary: not something made up but a fact. Here at any rate he succeeded. Moncure Conway wrote to Emerson that the man he had met was the real thing. "His eye can kindle strangely; and his words are ruddy with health."

Strangers began to gravitate toward him. He heard from Samuel

Longfellow, the famous poet's younger brother, another person alerted by Emerson. Longfellow happened to be close at hand, the pastor of the Second Unitarian Church in Brooklyn. Emerson had told him how he had been vexed and hurt by the "strange, rude thing" Whitman had done in releasing his private letter to the press. "Had I intended it for publication I should have enlarged the *but* very much—enlarged the but." All the same Longfellow's curiosity was excited. He sent a message over to Ryerson Street. Whitman, dressed in his usual rough-and-ready fashion, suddenly turned up unannounced on the doorstep at Pierrepont Street. Inside he sat properly, spoke in a pleasant manner, "not in the least boisterous," but kept his hat on his head, Quaker style. A second edition of his book was under way, he told Longfellow, and he was writing articles for *Life Illustrated*. "Such human tenderness at times," the pastor wrote in a letter to Hale after reading Hale's favorable review. "So keen to see, so vigorous to touch with right words."

Visits from literary personages were a novelty: necessary too if Whitman wanted to become better known. Commercially the book was a flop—most of the copies of the first edition were sent out to papers or given away to friends. One loyal friend, Mrs. Abby Price, had only moved to Brooklyn that year with her husband Edmund and their four children. They were an enlightened couple who lived in poor circumstances at 31 Hicks Street. Mr. Price owned a pickle factory in Front Street near the navy yard, where the Whitmans had first lived on arriving from West Hills.

Mrs. Price and Mrs. Whitman were friends, and Walt may have known of Abby beforehand as an activist in the women's movement. At their open house he came and went as he pleased, grateful for their easy acceptance of him. They even liked the way he dressed, except, that is, for the soft French beaver hat he sometimes wore. It was a hat that would have been worn by anyone else with the crown flattened. Walt rammed his fist into his before leaving, pushing it up high. Once Abby's sister patted in into a conventional shape and they thought he had failed to notice. No; in went his fist automatically as he made for the door.

An unobtrusive, soft-spoken visitor, sharing simple meals and playing with their children, he soon won their love. He could try out new poems on them if he wished without feeling a freak, and it was good to sit in this substitute home which was so free of strain. At Ryerson Street Jesse made them all suffer with his devils; inexplicable dark rages burst from him without warning. Jesse would grow progressively worse and be finally committed to Kings County Asylum. And there was Eddy, strangely helpless and lost, a grown man now but like a big pleading child. He seemed a living symbol of Walt's family's incomprehension.

The Prices had a lodger living with them, John Arnold, a retired preacher. Arnold was a Swedenborgian, though not a church member. Whitman liked to get him talking on the subject. Prompted by Arnold he attended a few Swedenborgian meetings in New York but was thwarted ultimately by something in the writings that "eludes being stated." Yet Emanuel Swedenborg had always interested him, not so much for his teaching as his example. It was such a dramatic instance of a man experiencing a total change after a sudden illumination—a burst of light that was almost comical. The circumstances were mundane: Swedenborg was finishing his dinner at a London inn and found himself enveloped in a mist. The mist cleared and he saw someone standing before him, a man composed of light. Ridiculous as this sounded to Whitman, the idea of another world surrounding us in which we live immersed and yet unaware was not.

As well as Swedenborgianism, he and Arnold argued about democracy. Whitman tried to share his faith in the ability of the masses to govern themselves with this man who had a poor opinion of the common people. Only certain individuals here and there were capable of such self-discipline, Arnold maintained. Instead of countering with his own view, Whitman listened quietly. Helen Price remembered him as someone who would rather listen than talk. When he did speak it was slowly. He searched for the right word, often fell silent, and started again, the opposite of fluent. But even when he failed to respond he attended keenly. The fact that he was not in the least glib endeared him to them.

After he had been calling on them for six months they introduced him to a friend of theirs, Eliza Farnum, a former matron of Sing Sing prison who had seen something of the West. Whitman said casually, glancing sideways at John Arnold, that her name was familiar to him because friends of his who had been prisoners in Sing Sing had mentioned her. Here, he seemed to be saying with a nod and a wink, was democracy in action. He went on to ask Mrs. Farnum about the fabulous new territory of California: did it live up to his dream of a model for the America to come? "Everything in California," he had written, "seems to be generated and grow on a *larger scale*—

fruits, vegetables for cooking, trees etc.—Humanity is also freer and grander. The children seem cast on a fuller pattern, grow better, breathe more air, make more blood, are sounder—in every way a superior type. The passions are also stronger, the soul more clarified and apparent, life seems more intense and determined—there is more individuality and character." It was a wholly imagined Eden, the wish-fulfilled shape of things to come.

🌿   ACQUAINTANCES OF HIS on the streets and down on the water-front, drivers and ferrymen and building laborers, were having to adjust to his new circumstances. One of the ferry hands, Tom Gere, had got wind of Whitman's authorship. Gere and his mates were more than a little possessive of him now when he joined them in the ferry house of an evening. In his recollections Gere swore he had seen a lad swabbing the deck with Walt's copy of Homer in his monkey-jacket pocket. Whether anyone saw him reading it is another matter. But his buddies were getting jealous of the literary types crossing over and asking to be directed to the author Mr. Whitman. After the second edition came out there were more of them. The 1856 *Leaves* contained twenty new long poems, including a masterpiece, "Crossing Brooklyn Ferry," called at first: "Sun-Down Poem." Poems were surfacing now at a tremendous rate. He sketched this one out in a hurry and left it to simmer for a while in his notebook:

> Poem of passage / the scenes on the river / as I cross the / Fulton ferry / Others will see the flow / of the river, also / Others will see on both / sides the city of / New York and the city of / Brooklyn / a hundred years hence others / will see them. . . . The continual and hurried crowd of / men and women crossing / The reflection of the sky / in the water—the blinding / dazzle in a track from / the most declined sun / The lighters . . . the nimbus of light / around the shadow of my / head in the sunset

At first glance it seems an unlikely, overfamiliar subject: a ferry jammed with passengers on the East River at sunset; weary impatient hordes of people loading and disembarking on the grimy docks, floating over a polluted river at floodtide. Then, as the changing seasons shift their light through it, the gulls fly through, the sun strikes the waves, the ships rock at anchor, the scene is internalized;

and what emerges is eternal, the voyage of life itself with its contra-dictory impermanence. The river's flow becomes the flow of time. How curious they are, these people he will never come to know, hurrying about their business and when he is no longer there to wit-ness them, still crowding over in their hundreds in the years ahead.

Others will enter the gates of the ferry and cross from shore to
shore,
Others will watch the run of the floodtide....
A hundred years hence, or ever so many hundred years hence,
others will see them...the islands large and small...
Will enjoy the sunset, the pouring in of the floodtide, the falling
back to the sea of the ebb-tide.

He loves the two cities, the "stately and rapid river" between, the men and women too because they are near, partaking of the same voyage, knowing the same seasons,

I am with you...
Just as you feel when you look on the river and sky, so I felt,
Just as any of you is one of a living crowd, I was one of a crowd,
Just as you are refresh'd by the gladness of the river and the bright
flow, I was refresh'd,
Just as you stand and lean on the rail, yet hurry with the swift
current, I stood yet was hurried....

The black gloom gathering below the sunset gathers in his heart. Dark patches of shadows falling on the heads of passengers fall on him too. He doubts himself, his heart gripped with uncertainty and a shaming anguish at the thought of his fear.

The best I had done seem'd to me blank and suspicious,
My great thoughts as I supposed them, were they not in reality
meager?

Had he in fact sacrificed love itself for them? Something inside him ached: what did he have to show? Failures of nerve returned to gnaw at him.

I...saw many I loved in the street or ferry-boat...yet never
told them a word,
Lived the same life with the rest, the same old laughing, gnawing,
sleeping,
Played the part that still looks back on the actor or actress,

The same old role, the role that is what we make it, as great
   as we like,
Or as small as we like, or both great and small.

Crossing over with those multitudes in the autumn of 1856 were
Bronson Alcott and Henry Thoreau, two neighbors of Emerson.
Thoreau had read the great "Sun-Down Poem" and been over-
whelmed by it. Alcott, the author of thrillers, was a utopian. He
claimed fulsomely that reading *Leaves of Grass* had taken twenty
years off his age. Thoreau, the author of *Walden*, spare and precise,
was more circumspect, still making up his mind. He had a temporary
job as a land surveyor at Eagleswood, a Fourierist community in New
Jersey. It was at communal farms like this that the transcendentalists
gathered to get "in tune with the Oversoul, like so many strings of a
super-celestial harp."

Both men were health freaks. So was Whitman, though he refused
to join anything and laughed at cranks and reformers. Thoreau and
Alcott stayed one night at Dr. Russell Trail's Hydropathic Medical
College, then went on the next day to join Horace Greeley on his
Chappaqua farm.

On Sunday they made their way to Brooklyn to hear a sermon by
the famous Henry Ward Beecher. When they reached the Whitman
house at Classon Avenue—the family had moved again—it was to be
told that Walt had gone out: no one seemed to know where. The
visitors talked instead to the mother, "a stately sensible matron,"
who simply extolled her son's virtues and told them how his brothers
and sisters believed in him absolutely, like her. He took care of their
affairs. Alcott, whose second call this was, had been told previously
by the poet that he was a housebuilder. No, Mrs. Whitman said, that
was his brother. Walt "had no business but going out and coming in
to eat, drink, write and sleep."

The two men were in the kitchen during this conversation. Louisa
had been baking cakes. Thoreau went over and helped himself to one
that was "warm from the oven. He was always doing things of the
plain sort, without fuss," said Whitman.

On his first visit Alcott had taken careful note of the poet's red
flannel undershirt open at the breast and exposing his brawny neck,
his striped calico jacket with its "Byroneal" collar, his cowhide boots,
and a sloppy topcoat with enormous outsize pockets and buttons to
match. He was particularly struck, as so many observers were, by

Whitman's eyes. They were "gray, unimaginative, cautious yet sagacious." And his voice too was singular, deep and yet sharp, and sometimes tender to the point of melting.

Nothing if not persistent, Alcott and Thoreau were back again on Monday morning, this time accompanied by Sarah Tyndale, a Germantown abolitionist whom they had met at dinner the night before. She was, in Alcott's words, an outspoken "walrus of a woman" who stood no nonsense from anyone. She took to Whitman at once—women often did—and he to her. Later she would be valued as a generous-hearted supporter. Alcott asked slyly which of the three prints on the wall depicted the poet. Whitman, always adept at steering round direct questions, murmured that there might well be all three, Hercules, Bacchus and a satyr, sitting down happily inside him somewhere.

All he wanted to do was to work at his writing, he told them. The poems, now that they had forced a breach in the wall, were unstoppable. Soon he would have to bring out a new edition with eight times as many poems in it as the first. Sizing up his audience he trotted out something homespun to amuse and disarm them. "My old daddy used to say it's some comfort to a man if he must be an ass anyhow to be his own kind of ass." He declined to be drawn into the subject of critics, about whom he was voluble when he had reached the sanctuary of old age. "Some don't like my long lines, some do," he said then, merry and serious at once. "Some don't like my commas, some do. Some cuss my long catalogues, some think them holy. . . . Perhaps it's the function of critics, even the dull critics, to bring the gods, the high ones, down from their great conceit. Drag them down, down into the mud, into the gutter. The whole world seems now bitten with the idea that to criticize, to pick to pieces, to expose, is the all in all of life—but is it?"

Alcott's attempt to bring Thoreau and Whitman together in conversation was unsuccessful. After one brief "hot discussion" the two sat eyeing each other warily from their respective bunkers. Yet in spite of himself Thoreau kept coming back.

Pleased to be sought out, Whitman never overcame his prejudices against the Concord school, "always a sort of ghostland" to him. The one literary New Englander he was prepared to like was Emerson, "the only sweet one among them." Thoreau he thought a cold fish, "a very aggravated case of superciliousness"; but he did see that the other's apparent lack of blood was in part nerves. A Concord woman remarked once that to take Thoreau's arm was about as satisfactory as taking the arm of an elm tree. His great fault, Whitman explained to Traubel, was disdain—"disdain for me (for Tom, Dick and Harry). It seemed to me a want of imagination—he could not put his life into any other life—realize why one man was so and another not so."

His insights into Thoreau were often canny. Admitting that he half liked the man, he said he detected a morbidity in him which made him turn to nature, not so much from "a love of woods, streams and hills... as from a morbid dislike of humanity. I remember Thoreau saying once, when walking with him in my favorite Brooklyn—'What is there in the people? What do you (a man who sees as well as anybody) see in all this cheating political corruption?'" After the diatribes in "The Eighteenth Presidency" and his blistering poem "Respondez!" one would have expected Whitman to be at least sympathetic to this view, misanthropic or not. No, he was affronted. The man had cast a slur on Whitman's family and friends by scrutinizing without feeling, from his chilly mind only. "I did not like my Brooklyn spoken of in this way."

Thoreau for his part thought Whitman "essentially strange," another species, but felt the need to propitiate him out of respect for the poetry and for the man's obvious truthfulness. He was aware of trespassing on staked-out ground when he said, with a cat's detachment, that he didn't think much of America or of politics. Whitman made no response. No doubt it confirmed his suspicion of the man's blind spot, his basic inability to appreciate the average life. Yet they touched at more than one point. Thoreau's declaration in *Walden* that "It is hard to have a Southern overseer; it is worse to have a Northern one, but worst of all when you are the slave-driver of yourself" had its insouciant counterpart in "Song of Myself," when

> The boatmen and clam-diggers arose early and stopt for me
> I tuck'd my trouser-ends in my boots and went and had a good time;
> You should have been with us that day round the chowder-kettle.

Thoreau had stumbled badly over two or three poems in *Leaves of Grass* which he found "disagreeable, to say the least: simply sensual. He does not celebrate love at all. It is as if the beasts spoke." What irritated him particularly about the book was its author's evident ability to see wonders and make his readers see them, and then to ruin everything by throwing in a ton of brick. Nevertheless, after his first meeting he was less concerned about the amount of "brag or egoism" in Whitman's book. "He may turn out the least of a braggart of all, having a better right to be confident."

It would have been a tense, circling meeting. Both men were frank and found things to esteem in the other. Thoreau didn't, it seems, find the Brooklyn man's appearance—his heavy, coarse but clean clothes more appropriate to a miner or farmhand than a poet—at all affected. Nor did he object to the fellow's clumsy, half-articulate sentences and lapses into silence. He liked the voice, vibrating curiously at times with a feminine tenderness, and the eyes which seemed without depth yet shining suddenly at moments of animation. There was no getting hold of the man, but in that very elusiveness he recognized himself.

ONE BROOKLYNITE who seemed prepared at first to back *Leaves of Grass* unreservedly was a popular American journalist who wrote in the *New York Ledger* under the name of Fanny Fern. She was Sarah Parton. Her third husband had just published a life of Horace Greeley. When *Life Illustrated* reprinted a favorable comment on *Leaves* from the London *Dispatch*, the inspired pen of Fanny Fern gushingly saluted the book. "Walt Whitman, the effeminate world needed thee. . . . It were a spectacle worth seeing, this glorious North American, who, when the daily labor of chisel and plane was over, himself, with toil-hardened fingers, handled the types to print the pages which wise and good men have since delighted to endorse and honor. . . ." The Fowlers hastened to reprint her broken-backed prose and include it with the gleanings from abroad.

Fowler and Wells took a gamble and financed Whitman's second edition. It went almost unnoticed, sinking virtually without trace. This time no one even bothered to abuse it. Undeterred, on a rising tide of new work, Whitman planned a third "proper" volume which would have "a hundred poems, and no other matter but poems—no letters to or from Emerson—no notices or anything of that sort. I know well enough that *that* must be the true Leaves of Grass—I think it (the new Vol) has an aspect of completeness, and makes its case clearer."

But where to find a publisher? He confided to Sarah Tyndale that

"Fowler and Wells are bad persons for me. They retard my book very much . . . they want the thing off their hands." Sarah, who had heard reports from elsewhere of the "malpractice" of his publishers, could not agree more. She sent him fifty dollars so that he could buy back the plates and be free of them.

By the winter of 1857 he was hard pressed for money. Suddenly he had a rescuer. His neighbors and fellow writers the Partons, "without the least request or hint from me," presented him with a loan of two hundred dollars. Though it came from the hand of James, the instigator was his wife. She had, it appears, worked up a fantasy romance around her toil-hardened discovery. Inevitably, this failed to jell. Whitman, unable to settle his short-term note when it fell due in the spring, was forced to suffer the humiliation of having his personal effects seized by lawyers. A no-longer-sweet Sarah Parton had sent them round to the house. Among other possessions he saw a painting by his friend Jesse Talbot carried out into the street.

Not even this stopped the outpouring of his poems. He could see the day coming, he told Sarah Tyndale exultantly, when he would issue an edition containing one poem for each day of the year, literally a scripture of everyday life. "The Great Construction of the New Bible," he wrote in a notebook. "Not to be diverted from the principal object—the main life work—the three hundred and sixty five.—It ought to be ready in 1859."

Paul Zweig reminds us, in his creative reexamination of Whitman, of the nineteenth century's appetite for new gospels. He lists Blake's *Prophetic Books*, Hugo's *Voix de Satan*, Carlyle's *Sartor Resartus*, and Nietzsche's *Zarathustra*. Calls for a practical religion, "not promising future bliss but bliss on earth," were sounded in Tolstoy's *My Religion* and in the letters and paintings of Van Gogh. In our own time we have those intrinsically religious testaments *The Rainbow* and *The Crown* by Lawrence, himself a nineteenth-century figure in so many ways. Van Gogh spoke of Tolstoy echoing his own hopes for "a private and secret revolution in men from which a new religion will be born . . . something altogether new which will have no name, but will have the same effect of comforting, of making life possible, which the Christian religion used to have. . . ." At the time of his visionary *Starry Night* painting Van Gogh wrote to his sister that he had been reading Whitman. "He sees in the future, and even in the present, a world of health, carnal love, strong and frank—of friendship—of work—under the great starlit vault of heaven, a something which after all one can only call God—and eternity in its place above the world. At first it makes you smile, it is all so candid and pure." Helen Price said of Whitman that he was "a born *exalté*," a man whose "religious sentiment pervades and dominates his life."

One evening he brought round the manuscript of a new poem and asked them to read it aloud for him. John Arnold and Abby recited passages in turn, then he read the whole work himself. When he asked them humbly for their criticism they were astonished. Helen spoke afterward of the little ceremony as a moment in her life she would cherish forever. Expecting to read a poem, they were led to kneel on the beach of Whitman's childhood and hear God speaking in the sea's shuttle and in the mockingbird's song, pouring forth "the meanings which I, of all men, know." "A Word Out of the Sea," renamed "A Child's Reminiscence" and finally "Out of the Cradle Endlessly Rocking," had Swinburne in raptures when he read it in the 1860 edition—"the most lovely and wonderful thing I have read for years and years . . . such beautiful skill and subtle power."

It has often been said that the poem is musical in structure, with its recitative aria and chorus. Whitman, who anticipated criticism, felt obliged to defend it along these lines. In a note to accompany its first publication in the *Saturday Press* he pointed out that "the purport of this wild and plaintive song, well-enveloped and eluding definition, is positive and unquestionable, like the effect of music."

Not that this takes us far. It has been described as Whitman's most perfect poem. Out from the magical shuttle of images wanders a man shaken by his tears into being a child again, throwing himself on the sand as he remembers the two mockingbirds, the she-bird crouched on her nest, the he-bird fluttering near, and he as a solitary boy coming every day to look—but never too close, never disturbing them, only

> Cautious, peering, translating.

Then the tragedy strikes. One afternoon the she-bird is missing, perhaps dead, to be seen no more. And each day and night that summer in the sound of the sea the he-bird from Alabama returns, solitary as the child.

> He called on his mate,
> He pour'd forth the meanings which I of all men know.

The bereaved bird is the brother to the man who remembers, who knows what it is to love unavailingly, to search and not find.

> Yes my brother I know,
> The rest might not, but I have treasur'd every note. . . .
> The white arms out in the darkness tirelessly tossing,
> I, with bare feet, a child, the wind wafting my hair,
> Listen'd long and long.
>
> Listen'd to keep, to sing, now translating the notes,
> Following you my brother.

What can be done with this love which has no object? It is not to be borne. How can he reach the missing one "fluttering out among the breakers," the mate he has never known?

> O madly the sea pushed up the land,
> With love, with love. . . .
> O throat! O trembling throat!
> Somewhere listening to catch you must be the one I want.
>
> Low hangs the moon, it rose late,
> It is lagging—O I think it is heavy with love, with love.
> O rising stars!
> Perhaps the one I want so much will rise, will rise with some of
>    you. . . .
>
> And I singing uselessly, uselessly all the night.

There has been a profound change. The supreme confidence of "Song of Myself" has given way here to something richer, deeper, a plangent and ruminative elegiac voice which speaks in cries and whispers, not public at all. We are being asked to turn away from past surety, told in low tones of some irrevocable alteration. Nothing can be the same after this.

> O solitary me listening, never more shall I cease perpetuating you,
> Never more shall I escape, never more the reverberations,
> Never more the cries of unsatisfied love absent from me,
> Never again leave me to be the peaceful child I was before what
>    there in the night,
> By the sea under the yellow and sagging moon,
> The messenger there arous'd, the fire, the sweet hell within,
> The unknown want, the destiny of me.

It is a dire prediction, like the wailing of someone prostrate, crippled in his very being. But then comes a subtle transition, a rather wonderful triumphant movement toward life and hope that has you catching your breath; the crying bird far out, a mere speck over the waves, dropping down almost into the sea.

The bereft man has ceased to struggle. Up flies the pathetic keening bird, changed to a muse, a demon.

> Demon or bird! (said the boy's soul),
> Is it indeed towards your mate you sing? or is it really to me?
> Now in a moment I know what I am for, I awake. . . .

What has awakened in him is not only love, "the love in the heart long pent, now loose, now tumultuously bursting" as the man falls to the sand in a paroxysm of weeping, but the need to sing. How, though? With the poem turning hypnotically on this fulcrum of self-discovery ("I know what I am for") the man asks for a clue, a word. Out of the rocking cradle of newborn life comes the paradoxical word "death," the word of "the sweetest song and all songs." Love and death are indivisible, life resides in death and death in life. All his life he has been drawn to the beach and the sea, as if to the telling of some great secret of renunciation, hoarsely surging and relapsing. Over the sterile sand it

> Lisp'd to me the low and delicious word death,
> And again death, death, death, death,
> Hissing melodious, neither like the bird nor like my arous'd child's
>     heart. . . .
> That strong and delicious word which, creeping to my feet, (or
>     like some old crone rocking the cradle, swathed in
>     sweet garments, bending aside),
> The sea whisper'd me.

✿✿ SOMETIME IN 1857 the money finally ran out. Still riding the crest of a powerful three-year wave which showed no sign of breaking, he was forced to forego his pledge to dedicate "the work of my life" to making poems, throttle back his creative drive, and go back to earning a living.

Only a year before, immeasurably rich in poems, filling his hands with these gifts from the sea and showering them on his pink-paper pages for a new book which would present him as America's "one complete lover," he lived day by day in a fantasy of power and creation. The words of his preface were all being fulfilled: "What balks or breaks others is fuel for his burning progress to contact and amorous joy." No matter what anyone thought or said or did, the truth was that he felt invincible. This self-sufficient demigod, a "stranger to pettiness and triviality," planned nothing less than to short-circuit the system—he had tried once before with his pamphlet "The Eighteenth Presidency"—and reach out to citizens who were as large in generosity and spirit as the nation. Providence would take care of him.

He had pinned a notice to himself on the wall of his shared room under the eaves—"Make the Works"—and brought the endless self-improvement of the autodidact to a halt at last. Jack London pegging up words on clothes lines across his garret space, Sean O'Casey nailing up a sentence in his crumbling tenement to aim an almighty kick at his slothfulness—"Get on with the bloody play!"—had reached the same high point, taken the same daring leap in the dark.

It had worked. He had nothing to fear. The fountainhead was not dammed or dried up; it overflowed and he was free. The capacious trunk, a hodgepodge of litter, was the quarry of personal reference he had always intended it to be.

His pen danced ecstatically, vivid and stabbing and irresistible now that he had stopped filling newspaper pages. His breast expanded to match "the blue breadth over the inland sea of Virginia and Maryland and the sea off Massachusetts and over Manhattan Bay and over Champlain and Erie and over Ontario and Huron and Michigan and Superior, and over the Texan and Mexican and Floridian and Cuban seas and over the seas of California and Oregon. . . ." Fertile as the land, "on him rise solid growths that offset the growths of pine and cedar and hemlock and loveoak and chestnut and locust and cyprus and hickory and limetree and cottonwood and tuliptree and cactus and wildvine and tamarind and persimmon . . . and tangles as tangled as any canebrake or swamp. . . ." He was surely capable of ever greater deeds. Teeming with the influx of half-formed ideas, a glowing force for good, "He drags the dead out of their coffins and stands them again on their feet . . . he says to the past, Rise and walk before me that I may realize you."

Clarified as never before, how simple his needs seemed. What if he just extended his hand and asked for help from the "rich givers" who were surely out there somewhere? Down went this rosiest of daydreams on pink paper and into the third edition. Material help would eventually arrive, but never enough, and not for many years. For the time being it was something to let drift through his mind and into the pages of *Leaves of Grass*.

> What you give me, I cheerfully accept,
> A little sustenance, a hut and garden, a little money—these as I rendezvous with my poems,
> A traveler's lodging and breakfast as I journey through the States—
> Why should I be ashamed to own such gifts? Why to advertise for them?
> For I myself am not one who bestows nothing upon man and woman,
> For I know that what I bestow upon any man or woman is no less than the entrance to all the gifts of the universe.

Which was one way of putting it. After all, why shouldn't poetry be an acceptable currency, circulating as freely as money, able to cross the boundaries as love, laughter, and death did?

HE HAD TAKEN OFF, circling through space gloriously in "Song of Myself," had come into his own, become truly his own man. All at once he felt conservative and began editing himself. Did his book, for all its multiplicity, really amount to a world? Was what he had accomplished no more than an intricately spun illusion? Was Homer's *Odyssey* no more than that, or the life of that lovely redeemer Jesus? In time he would learn to sink back into his soul and wait "till the gossamer thread you fling catch somewhere."

> A noiseless patient spider,
> I mark'd where on a little promontory it stood isolated,
> Mark'd how to explore the vacant vast surrounding,
> It launch'd forth filament, filament, filament, out of itself,
> Ever unreeling them, ever tirelessly speeding them.

Meanwhile he got a job as editor of another local daily, the *Brooklyn Daily Times*. Owned by George C. Bennett, it was published at Grand Street in Williamsburg. The two towns ran together, and the Whitmans in Brooklyn lived near the boundary between the two. His "The Eighteenth Presidency" may have arrived on Bennett's desk and caught his eye. As the owner of an independent paper he would have been interested, even though disinclined to publicize it. Charles Gaynor, the previous editor, was a playwright with two plays currently in production in New York, so it hardly mattered to him whether he stayed or left. He had objected to reading proof on the job-printing Bennett took in, and was duly fired.

We first hear of Whitman on March 14 in an editorial advocating the running of "Sunday Rail Cars." This emphasis on the widening gulf between clergy and people brought objections from the Reverend Dr. Porter, pastor of the Williamsburg Church. Whitman, expecting to meet one of the bigoted "old-liners," was surprised and charmed by a man who said he had not only read *Leaves* but wanted more. The pastor expressed the hope that Walt had retained the Dutch Reformed faith held by the Van Velsors. Whitman wrote to tell Sarah Tyndale that he had "perfect faith in all sects" and had told Porter as much. Not at all put off, the pastor invited him to dinner.

Bennett, a proprietor recalled later by Whitman as "a good, generous man," gave his editor free rein. More or less broke himself, Whitman was soon urging his readers not to panic as the worst financial crash since 1837 loomed on the horizon. By autumn it was on them. He drew attention to widespread business failures, calculating that twenty-five thousand people would be thrown out of work that winter in New York and Brooklyn, and that this would affect a hundred thousand of their dependents. Unrest among the poor fueled the mob violence that made New York streets unsafe, with running battles between "Native American" thugs and Irish immigrants.

In the *Times* Whitman threw up his hands. "Educate, Educate—it is the only true remedy for mobs, emeutes, wild communistic theories and red-republican ravings...." He felt he had a duty to encourage confidence in the Williamsburg Savings Bank. "As long as the grass grows and water runs" it would stand firm, he predicted lyrically, and was proved right, though numerous other banks ended up on the rocks. The diarist George Templeton Strong raised the specter of anarchy. "We are a very sick people," he wrote. "The outward and visible signs of disease, the cutaneous symptoms, are many."

The poet who was proud to call himself "one of the roughs" in "Song of Myself" had a doppelgänger who attacked "rowdyism" in editorials. Whitman identified with ferry pilots, drivers, deckhands, but drew the line at brutality. Prizefights were repugnant to him: they were already illegal and should remain so, he exhorted, since they gave a sanction to vicious behavior and incited spectators to blood-lust. He attended a reception in Canal Street, New York, given for General William Walker by his swashbuckling sympathizers. In his comments the following day he admitted to a loathing for Fernando Wood, the corrupt mayor of New York who had been helped to power by the Dead Rabbit Gangsters of the notorious Sixth Ward. During this period of "Dead Rabbit Democracy" the municipal police force had become a travesty of law enforcement. When a Metropolitan Police was created, controlled by the governor, the two rival forces fought for supremacy and turned streets around City Hall into a no-go area for two days. Finally the state troops were called in.

In June Whitman tackled what he called "A Bad Subject for a Newspaper Article." Without exactly endorsing the idea of a licens-ing and inspection system for prostitutes he asked readers to consider it as the lesser of two evils. Prostitutes, he said, were alternately tolerated and persecuted by the police, whose raids simply drove them in increasing numbers to Brooklyn.

This was a far cry from one of his favorite topics, the water supply. Here at last he had some success. The action he had been urging on this and his other Brooklyn papers finally resulted in a bill providing a clean supply from the ponds and springs of Long Island. Whitman thought it tasted even better than the Croton nectar enjoyed by New York. "The water itself has a character of its own," he reported. "It is deliciously sweet—it almost has a flavor. Many a time in passing along the line, and at Baisley's Pond, or at some of the springs, have we realized the sweet character of this water."

He was even more excited by the laying of the Atlantic cable. It broke down, joined up the continents once more to convey a message from the Queen of England to the president, then failed again after three weeks. But nothing could shake Whitman's faith in this frail electric thread connecting the New World to the Old. Before the success of this engineering feat became a fact he had written in a notebook, "the continents talk under the waves of the sea." He whooped happily that this technological miracle was just the start of a grand linking of hands which would encircle the globe. Next, he predicted, would come a railroad to the Pacific, and added a private reminder to himself in his notebook. "All poems or any other expression of literature that does not tally with their writer's actual life and knowledge, are lies."

He ranged as keenly over small issues as he did over large. Using some comments on education to hit back at Sarah Parton, whose humiliation of him still rankled, he said, "We want a race of women turned out from our schools, not of pedants and blue-stockings. One genuine woman is worth a dozen Fanny Ferns." He went on to condemn the pettiness of a policeman who arrested boys for bathing in the river.

There are no references to any friends he may have had. He shunned the company of writers. "We glimpse him in the streets with his young men," writes Paul Zweig, "or watching a baseball match or two boys wrestling in an empty lot." When it came to politics he was allowed to express views running contrary to Bennett's, who was now an active member of the Republican party. Stephen Douglas, the tough little lawyer who had won a senatorship from Illinois in the November elections, became the focus of Whitman's immediate hopes. He was the man he envisaged as able to create "a great middle conservative party" and steer a path through the perils of the slavery question. The Walt Whitman who had felt the terror of

> The hounded slave that flags in the race, leans by the fence,
> blowing, cover'd with sweat . . .

jumping inside the poor wretch's skin to suffer with him, to tell how

> I clutch the rails of the fence, my gore dribs, thinn'd with the ooze
> of my skin

was not to be confused with Walter Whitman in his editor's chair, the same average unimaginative journalist he had always been. Slavery was not all bad, he wrote in the *Daily Times*; it had its "redeeming points." Eventually it would die out, maybe in a century or so; but "who believes that the Whites and Blacks can ever amalgamate in America? Or who wishes it to happen? Nature has set an impassable seal against it."

He approached the delicate question of unmarried sex in an article entitled "Can All Marry?" No doubt aware that in the "city of churches" he risked an outcry, he wrote guardedly of the predicament of a single young woman reaching for "one glimpse of real life and nature—one taste of substantial joys and sorrows that shall wake all the pulses of womanhood; even though the experience be brief and dearly bought."

Midway through his two-year stint on the *Daily Times*, with his demon stalled, grinding away at work he had outgrown in order to clear debts and keep his head above water, he began dreaming yet again of an altogether different, footloose life as a "wander-lecturer." He got as far as printing up a circular outlining his plan to travel extensively in the United States and Canada, charging "one dime" and selling printed copies of his lectures. He was prepared, he told his imagined sponsors, to talk on any subject—geography, language, politics, personages (Hicks, Paine, Voltaire, Emerson)—and had become convinced that "live modern orations" were appropriate for America and the world at this point in history. "Washington made free the body of America," he declared. "Now comes one who will make free the American soul."

Convinced though he was by his own eloquence, he sounded a more ambivalent note in the draft of a letter to an unidentified correspondent. It was summer; he had been to Greenport again. Physical well-being restored him to himself, made him feel balanced and on good terms with the world, ready to accept whatever twists of fate life had in store for him:

"O you should see me, how I look after sea-sailing. I am swarthy and red as a Moor—I go around without any coat or vest—looking so strong, ugly and nonchalant, with my white beard—People stare, I notice, more wonderingly than ever. . . . I have thought, for some time past, of beginning the use of myself as a Public Speaker, teacher or lecturer. . . . Whether it will come to anything remains to be seen. . . . My immediate acquaintances secretly entertain the idea that I am a great fool not to 'make something' out of my 'talents' and out of the general good will with which I am regarded. . . ."

Could the lecture scheme have been merely a dream of travel, the pretext for an enormous jaunt, an excuse to cut and run? But he was already deeply embroiled in his family's fortunes. His widowed mother depended on him, and he would never let her down. Restless, he toyed with the idea of looking up his sister Hannah in Vermont and jotted down the train times to Rutland. Then there was a friend named William Place whom he thought of visiting at a spot on the Delaware River where raftsmen gathered. He did take himself off to see the Fourierist Arthur Brisbane in Irvington, New Jersey, perhaps at Thoreau's suggestion.

❧    Toward the end of the 1850s he went down in a slough, one that lasted until he took off at a moment's notice and began the search for his missing brother George. No one has come up with reasons: we can only speculate. He lost the pride in his songs, that much is certain. The "measureless ocean of love within him" that he poured forth without stint had not brought the response he had hoped. If we take him literally he had endured "sullen and suffering hours" and been flung into a sick dread "lest the one he loved might secretly be indifferent to him."

It might have been real or a cause imagined after the event. One can sink for no apparent reason or be pushed down by a specific incident, by a rebuff, by rejection, or by a dawning realization of something unalterable in oneself. Or it could be a mere touch.

> I merely stir, press, feel with my fingers, and am happy,
> To touch my person to some one else's is about as much as I can
> stand.

Long aware of his dangerous vulnerability to vibrations—from unknown people, unknown passions—he maintained an iron reserve. His name for it was prudence, and it made him appear, to many who met him later, "a little more than human." For him it was the only way to avoid disaster. Well defended, he sometimes came close to crumbling. In "Song of Myself" these defenders suddenly leave their posts.

> The sentries desert every other part of me,
> They have left me helpless to a red marauder,
> They all come to the headland to witness and assist against me.

For so long now the "great Camerado, the lover true for whom I pine" had been expected, glimpsed again and again in a crowd: the shapely body, the coarsely beautiful dumb hands, the brown eyes. Grievously mistaken, he had then been dragged down horribly to a base level by "a desire to know this man, to have him, as it were to eat him, to take the very substance of him."

> Is this then a touch? quivering me to a new identity,
> Flames and ether making a rush for my veins,
> Treacherous tip of me reaching and crowding to help them,
> My flesh and blood playing out lightning to strike what is hardly
> different from myself. . . .

On all sides prurient provokers stiffening my limbs...
Unbuttoning my clothes, holding me by the bare waist....

It was a sweet hell that yawned under him, a half-desired nightmare he fought off with a reserve strong as iron. Though Jeff could never have been aware of his significance, he was Walt's only "understander" in the family, a Camerado for years, Walt's only "real brother" and defender from himself. The "two boys together clinging" was the image of this indissoluble pair. Walt had bought a piano for him, hoping Jeff would be as passionate about music as himself. He was the one member of the family who expressed pride in his older brother's strange book. "Flocks of ideas beat their countless wings and clutch their feet upon me," Whitman wrote in a notebook, "as I sit near by where my brother is practicing at the piano."

Then came the inevitable betrayal, the long attachment broken at last. Jeff got married to Mattie and moved out of the house to set up his own home. Whitman claimed her as a loved sister but it was not the same. It was harder now for him to see man-to-man and brotherly love in the same safe light as he went on encountering "any man, a policeman who suddenly looked up at him as he inquired the way, or a soldier who sat next to him in a railway carriage."

An evolving ideology was now imperative, one with its own honorable language for the cherishing of manly love in that democracy of the heart he dubbed "the love of comrades," if he was ever to escape his burning torments. To a certain extent it did rescue him. The perilous, illicit encounters, real or not, flare up briefly on the stage of his imagination, exciting and flustering him even as they dismay, before dying down for good. But it took the semi-invalidism of the last third of his life finally to absolve him, leaving him free to incorporate "the most copious and close companionship of men" into his "Chants Democratic." Essentially theatrical, he renounced the opera of his life for the drama of nation-forming.

Rooting his doctrine in a love of comrades steered him around the intervention of woman, except in the "muscles and wombs" sense ridiculed by Lawrence. He solved the problem of woman by the simple expedient of finding her in himself. A lady in the West wrote to the naturalist John Burroughs about Whitman's "great mother-nature." Lawrence in his essay on Whitman snorted impatiently and brutally that "everything was female in him: even himself." Speaking as a man only too conscious of the woman under his own skin, Lawrence was especially touchy on the subject. He understood, however, the heroic message of Whitman's sympathy, and his insistence on getting the soul back where she belonged, inside the body. Not superior, but equal. For those willing to receive and exchange it, Whitman's passional affection was a morality that changed the blood, Lawrence said. It could even save a nation from tearing itself apart.

> Affection shall solve every one of the problems of freedom,
> Those who love each other shall be invincible,
> They shall finally make America completely victorious in my
> name.

⚜ IN THE *Daily Times* office was a young German poet by the name of Huene who worked in the composing office. Whitman made a friend of him. Afterward Frederick Huene remembered Whitman's habit of walking around the office for long stretches without uttering a word, sunk in the kind of impenetrable silence characteristic of his sullen father. He gave the young German a copy of *Leaves*, and Huene started work on a German translation. He broke off for no known reason. Had there been a misunderstanding of intention, a hasty retreat on Whitman's part?

It is likely that the young man who figures in the discussion on friendship one evening, reported by Abby Price, was Huene. Whitman, suddenly voluble, said there was a wonderful depth of meaning "in the old tales of mythology. In that of Cupid and Psyche, for instance; it meant to him that the ardent expression in words of affection often tended to destroy affection. It was like the golden fruit which turned to ashes upon being grasped, or even touched. As an illustration he mentioned the case of a young man he was in the habit of meeting every morning where he went to work. He said there had grown up between them a delightful silent friendship and sympathy. But one morning when he went as usual to the office, the young man came forward, shook him violently by the hand, and expressed in heated language the affection he had for him. Mr. Whitman said that all the subtle charm of their unspoken friendship was from that time gone."

Whitman would have been familiar with the myth of Cupid and Psyche. Nights of faceless love in the dark make Psyche eager to gaze on her lover, and she lights a lamp. Hot oil spills on Cupid when the lamp is upset. He flees from her sight. Knowledge brings an end to love's mystery. Knowing others was tantamount to knowing oneself, a painful and hazardous undertaking. Better to stay at a distance, concealed in the refuge of darkness.

As always, Whitman shrank from sudden declarations of feelings which threw him back on his own uncertainties. He couldn't bear demands he was not sure of meeting, or of even wanting. He had to take the subterranean, indirect route. Silence was more eloquent than action.

Basically his male-female nature was chaste and delicate, throwing up obstacles to intimacy out of a fear of losing hold on himself. He lived in a crude, naive age. Men shared each other's beds as a matter of course, as Walt did with his brother Eddy, sleeping chastely together with an innocence we have lost. Even John Burroughs, by no stretch of the imagination his sexual lover, once slept in a bed with Whitman and commented sweetly on the experience. "He kissed me as if I were a girl. . . . He bathed today while I was there—such a handsome body, and such delicate, rosy flesh I never saw before. I told him he looked good enough to eat." But the remote, touchy side to his friend's character was a permanent barrier. Burroughs found his blue eyes a little chilling, like looking through apertures of empty sky. Whitman once confessed to Horace Traubel that he hated to have people throw themselves at him "into my arms—insist on themselves, upon their affections. It is a feeling I can never rid myself of."

Sometimes it seemed nothing less than shameful, this shrinking and shuddering back from contact with what lay, after all, there inside himself. It presumed a superiority he knew perfectly well he could not claim. He was no better than the worst there was. In "Confession and Warning" we see him struggling to throw off what to him is the sickness of his secretiveness. It is the effort to come clean of a man facing both ways, mustering the courage to write love poems that will expose him as he really is, a lonely abandoned man with jealous eyes who has known and lost love. The kisses in Whitman's poems, a critic has said, are always kisses of parting.

First, though, he tries to make a clean breast of his "crimes," to own up. Others may express puzzlement, he tells his reader,

As if I were not puzzled at myself!
Or as if I do not secretly love strangers (O tenderly, a long time,
    and never avow it);
Or as if I did not see, perfectly well, interior in myself, the stuff of
    wrong-doing,
Or as if it could cease from transpiring from me until it must
    cease. . . .

Beneath this impassive face the hot fires of hell continually burn—
    within me the lurid smutch and the smoke;
Not a crime can be named but I have it in me waiting to break
    forth,
Lusts and wickedness are acceptable to me,
I walk with delinquents with passionate love.

He let the mask fall, but only to show what we had already
guessed. If there was a recognizable person with a name, he remains
hidden. He fell in love at least once, with the young Southerner
Peter Doyle, who took his fare on a Washington streetcar one
winter's night. If the Calamus poems he wrote after his overture
"Confession and Warning" were being addressed to an actual man,
there is no knowing who it was. It is hard to doubt the sense of a
crisis flaming up and dying, of a real lover somewhere causing these
bitter plaintive cries and beseechings by his cruel indifference,
forcing on Whitman the disgrace of having to say "it is useless—I am
what I am."

Hours continuing long, sore and heavy-hearted,
Hours of the dusk, when I withdraw to a lonesome and
    unfrequented spot, seating myself, leaning my face in my hands;
Hours sleepless, deep in the night, when I go forth, speeding
    swiftly the country roads, or through the city streets, or pacing
    miles and miles, stifling plaintive cries;
Hours distracted, discouraged—for the one I cannot content
    myself without, soon I saw him content himself without me;
Hours when I am forgotten (O weeks and months are passing,
    but I believe I am never to forget!),
Sullen and suffering hours! (I am ashamed—but it is useless—I am
    what I am);
Hours of my torment—I wonder if other men ever have the like,
    out of the like feelings?
Is there even one other like me—distracted—his friend, his lover,
    lost to him?

Is he too as I am now? Does he still rise in the morning, dejected, thinking who is lost to him? and at night, awaking, think who is lost?

Does he harbor his friendship silent and endless? Harbor his anguish and passion?

Does some stray reminder, or the casual mention of a name, bring the fit back upon him, taciturn and deprest?

Does he see himself reflected in me? In these hours, does he see the face of his hours reflected?

The joys of anticipation, the perfect bliss of entering that place sweeter than sunshine, buried in the dark with his beloved, has the same touching veracity as does the convulsed pride of the survivor. Step by step we shed everything that has seemed important: from being entirely separate we know the handclasp, the compact of flesh.

When I heard at the close of the day how I had been praised in the Capitol, still it was not a happy night for me that followed;

Nor when I caroused—Nor when my favorite plans were accomplished—was I really happy,

But that day I rose at dawn from the bed of perfect health, electric, inhaling sweet breath,

When I saw the full moon in the west grow pale and disappear in the morning light,

When I wandered alone over the beach, and undressing, bathed, laughing with the water, and saw the sun rise,

And when I thought how my friend, my lover, was coming, then O I was happy;

Each breath tasted sweeter—and all that day my food nourished me more—And the beautiful day passed well,

And the next day with equal joy—And with the next, at evening, came my friend.

And that night, while all was still, I heard the waters roll continually up the shores. . . .

The ocean whispers a benediction, the moon bathes them. Either they are in a room overlooking the sea or out in the open, on the beach at night. The waters roll in the night like a hymn. They lie, one sleeping, one happily awake, in the steadiness of love that is a core of bliss, the world and its inhabitants wheeling away in a faint roar of space and time,

In the stillness his face was inclined towards me, while the moon's
  clear beams shone,
And his arm lay lightly over my breast—And that night I was
  happy.

Was Whitman actively homosexual? A century later the scholars
are still out. Just as he eludes literary definition, so it is with sex.
"We imagine," says Paul Zweig, the most astute of his modern critics,
"a shy circling of the flame, a flirtation with saying the unsayable, a
moral passion for the forbidden zones of behavior, for the reproved
and excluded ones whom Whitman would defend as surrogates for
his own self-darkened self."

W. H. Auden didn't think Whitman actually went to bed with
boys. He saw "the business with the [Doyle] boy as perfectly chaste."
What seems clear is that Whitman tried to create a father-and-son
relation between them, and then his heart got desperately involved
and hurt. It could be argued that fidelity is more important in a
homoerotic relationship than in any other, since it is in effect the
only tie. It grieved and tormented Whitman—as it did Lawrence—
that there was no open, legitimate way to express love for a man, but
it makes no difference to our understanding of him to know whether
or not he went to bed with men. The secret shameful things that he
feared in himself were incorporated in his store of sensual delights.
Outwardly they seemed unexpressed. The blossoming of his body's
shamefulness was a terrible beauty to him, part of his revolutionary
inward life.

One love scene which did come to pass he imagined five years
before it happened, and then was able to act in it in real life opposite
its girlish other actor, Pete Doyle. After the last run of the young
conductor's shift they would meet at a saloon near the car sheds.
Pete would lay his head on his hands and fall asleep, with Whitman
fondly watching over him, able to invest the awkward affair with an
intensity it never in fact had. There he sat on guard,

A long while, amid the noises of coming and going—of drinking
  and oath and smutty jest,
There we two, content, happy in being together, speaking little,
  perhaps not a word.

Everything came out of his conflict and confusions. He built his
poems from flashes of intuitions and from his emotions, proceeding

by "inspired mistakes" and by delving into that chaotic trunk. But surely there is something odd about his growing notebook lists of young men: the fireman Billie; Ike on Fifth Avenue; Broadway Brownie and genteel Jakey, his friend; the round-faced, liquid-eyed Johnny; James Dalton, minus his front teeth; Mike Ellis, found wandering off Lexington Avenue one bitter cold night and taken home, and so on. They seem curiously indiscriminate, undifferentiated notations. Whitman had a collector's mania: he was an inveterate list-maker. He made lists of everything: occupations, tools, materials, weathers, dreams, clothing, addresses—young men. The suggestiveness here is misleading: this was scarcely the "network of intimacies" called for in his evangel-poem for a new democracy. The characters of this list are too casual and happy-go-lucky to be anything other than the raw material of his ideal of himself as the natural leader of a gang of comrades, open and trusted.

> I reckon I am their boss, and they make me a pet besides,
> And surround me, and lead me and run ahead when I walk,
> And lift their cunning covers and signify me with stretched arms,
>     and resume their way;
> Onward we move, a gay gang of blackguards with mirthshouting
>     music and wildflapping pennants of joy.

We have to leave him his darker purposes: the final victory of silence is his. Though he teased Traubel with hints of a great secret—"Not tonight, Horace, dear boy—not tonight"—he never divulged one. One must remember that in Victorian society the Judeo-Christian taboo was total—"friend" and "lover" were interchangeable terms. Poems written to friends were taken as part of a tradition stretching back to the Greeks. Hard though it is for us to imagine, admitting to yourself that you were homosexual would have been well nigh impossible. Not only could it not be said, it could not be thought. The term was not even in use until 1869, and then only in Germany. It is surely inconceivable that Whitman went through the modern agony of choosing this or that sexual direction. He did dream, though, of a perfect partner, and would, he thought, have been prepared to sacrifice everything for such a love,

> I am indifferent to my own songs—I will go with him I love,
> It is enough for us that we are together—We never separate again.

It didn't happen. If it had, there would have been stealth and an exquisite mutual recognition, coy and subtle on his part.

> Lover and perfect equal!
> I meant that you should discover me so, by my faint indirections,
> And I, when I meet you, mean to discover you by the like in you.

Failing this, he had to settle for the wistful yearning of the watcher from a distance.

> . . . The two men I saw today on the pier, parting the parting of
> dear friends.
> The one to remain hung on the other's neck and passionately
> kissed him—while the one to depart tightly prest the one to
> remain in his arms. . . .

Or he had to submit to being the one burning to declare himself, yet afraid.

> As I walk by your side or sit near, or remain in the same room with
> you,
> Little you know the subtle electric fire that for your sake is playing
> within me.

Powerless to alter his nature, he fashioned his book so that it resembled an ardent lover, as importunate as the answerer he at once backed away from and desired:

> Camerado, this is no book,
> Who touched this touches a man,
> (Is it night? are we here together alone?)
> It is I you hold and who holds you,
> I spring from the pages into your arms—

But he was two. His book was equally a woman, his soul. And in time the beautiful democracy of his poems became his *femme*, the six editions his six children. The verdict of fate in the end suited him. Marriages between men did sometimes endure, and sometimes men gave up their wives and families for such a marriage. Whitman had chosen his wife, married himself to his task. He supported a family, his mother and handicapped brother, and would never abandon them. Over the years he drew back from the precarious edge.

What it meant to be how he was, deeply ambivalent, threw him at times into an anguish of painful confusions. He lost touch then with *who* he was. Did others see through him, to the fraud beneath? Would they come to despise him? Not if they shared his twoness.

Some are baffled—But that one is not—that one knows me.

In his dirge "Bardic Symbols" (later "As I Ebb'd with the Ocean of Life") we are jolted by his fiercest effort of self-acceptance, a savage willingness to accept the verdict of fate. Wrecked by the jumble of his feelings he is reconciled at last with his dead father, another flawed nature, the one blood relation who might have understood his stubbornness and failures.

> I throw myself upon your breast my father,
> I cling to you so that you cannot unloose me,
> I hold you so firm till you answer me something.

As for others, the audience for his poems, strangers and onlookers, he stands exposed in these self-castigating moods for what he is, vacillating and unsure,

> Aware now that amid all that blab whose echoes recoil upon
>     me I have not once had the least idea who or what I am,
> But that before all my arrogant poems the real Me stands yet
>     untouch'd, untold, altogether unreach'd,
> Withdrawn far, mocking me with self-congratulatory signs
>     and bows,
> With peals of distant ironical laughter at every word I have
>     written,
> Pointing in silence to these songs, and then to the sand
>     beneath.
>
> I perceive I have not really understood any thing, not a
>     single object, and that no man ever can. . . .
> I too but signify at the utmost a little wash'd up drift,
> A few sands and dead leaves to gather. . . .
>
> . . . chaff, straw, splinters of wood, weeds, and the sea gluten,
> Scum, scales from shining rocks, leaves of salt lettuce, left by
>     the tide. . . .
>
> Because I have dared to open my mouth to sing at all.

He was in a dark period, a young-old man who had reached forty, already looking to old age as a safe haven from the repercussions of his sexuality. Then he could be wise and translated, living beyond temptation and at peace with his mission as a lone wanderer along the open road. Nothing was worthier than his ambition, which was to give to American young men—with their depths of tenacity and their "passionate fondness for friends" which few suspected—the words their balked feelings lacked. This was what he hoped *Leaves of Grass* would achieve. Only then would democracy's ultimate heart begin to beat.

Whitman, still in charge of the *Daily Times* in the spring of 1859, was out and footloose again by the end of June. Once again he had pushed his luck too far. His stubborn streak had done the rest. In early June he resurrected the issue of the prostitutes and the police in an editorial captioned "A Delicate Subject." He followed it next day with an article on "Unsound Churches" which drew unwelcome attention to nine churches listed as being in such states of neglect that they were fire hazards.

This could have been the last straw for the irate clergy Whitman had come to "hate—yes, even fear." Huene said merely that "Mr. Whitman resigned his place in consequence of articles which were very unfavorably criticized by ministers and church people, and about which he had quite a philosophical debate with Mr. Bennett." He left with warm feelings toward George Bennett.

Money and how to get some was again the problem. An entry in his notebook dated June 26 says: "It is now time to *stir* first for Money enough, to live and provide for M—. *To Stir.*—first write stories and get out of this Slough."

A month before, the Whitmans had made yet another move, to North Portland Avenue. With his brothers working away from home he was now the sole support of his mother. After leaving the *Times* he eked out a living as a "copyist" and proofreader and spent the rest of his time revising new poems for his third edition. His friends the Romes set up his new work in proof so that he could see the verse in type. It was a clarification and a spur, with no publisher yet in sight.

With plenty of time on his hands he fell back into his favorite routine, writing in the mornings or hanging around the Rome brothers' print shop. In the afternoons he made his way over on the Fulton Ferry and took in the harbor scene; gazed at masts jostling as the ships big and small rolled and tugged at their moorings to be gone. Perched high on the box of a Broadway stage he traveled uptown. He liked to help collect the fares, and once or twice took over the driving for a spell. One paper, in a romantic allusion to Robert Burns earning a living as a plowman, reported that he was a driver—either mistakenly or to liven up the story.

These days he was heading for Pfaff's, a haunt of his for the next few years. Pfaff's was a drinking club and restaurant just above Bleecker Street. Situated in the basement and extending out under the pavement, it was the choice meeting place of New York's bohemia. You descended symbolically into its gloomy cellar like stepping down into hell, though its devils were more spiteful than malign. Literary people, artists, and actors came to see and be seen, attracted by the good food and wine. Henry Clapp, the sardonic editor of the *Saturday Press*, might be there—a sworn enemy of the New England set and the leading light in a coterie of rebellious writers and freethinkers, wits, beauties, and vegetarians. Clapp liked to shock, hence his interest in Whitman, who was by now regarded in decent circles as needlessly provocative and obnoxious. Clapp's tongue could be waspish. He described Horace Greeley, whose biography was just out, as "A self-made man who worships his creator." A clergyman of his acquaintance impressed him as someone waiting for "a vacancy in the Trinity."

One of Clapp's authors was Jane McElheny. She wrote as Ada Clare, publishing startlingly frank confessional poems in the newspapers and getting herself known as the Queen of Bohemia. Henry Clapp was undisputed king. He fell into debt two years after the launch of his review, then into alcoholism. Drying out in a detoxification ward on Blackwell's Island, he headed his letters "My Cottage by the Sea." He succumbed, like his fellow bohemians Artemus Ward, George Arnold, and Ned Wilkins, to what Whitman called "a restless craving for mental excitement." These basement denizens were harmless enough. Ward denigrated them good-humoredly along with himself when he told a newcomer, "They won't hurt you. A Bohemian is an educated hoss-thief!"

Ada Clare was the new liberated woman, equal to men. She admired *Leaves of Grass*, and Whitman enjoyed talking to her. He was deeply shocked when she died horribly years later of hydrophobia. She was a Charleston beauty and revived his memories of the South, its sensuality and freedom. He paid tribute to her personality and her "gay, easy, sunny, free, loose but not *ungood* life," aware of how wicked she was in the eyes of the respectable. She had an illegitimate child and refused to hide the fact or to withhold the father's name—the pianist Louis Gottschalk. She made a point of writing Miss Clare and Son in hotel registers.

Whitman was intrigued also by another wild Southern lady, the New Orleans–born Adah Menken. Married four times, she was going through a divorce from her first husband and about to marry a heavyweight fighter, The Benica Boy, when Whitman knew her. She had a child with the Boy, who then insisted they were not legally married at all. Perhaps in compensation for this cruel treatment she became the scandalous actress in flesh-colored tights who starred in *Mazeppa*. Dante Gabriel Rossetti once gambled ten pounds on her failure to get Swinburne into bed with her. It was a safe wager.

If the curious could not see Clapp, there was Whitman at a large table over on the far wall which was reserved by Pfaff for his literary customers. He sat glowing with health, usually silent, in his blue carpenter's jacket and baggy trousers. The frothy clever talk amused him but he soon tired of it. This corrosive crowd of journalists and writers was to be observed rather than joined. A stranger in the midst, he felt at times as if he was stranded between the living and the dead,

> While on the walk immediately overhead pass the myriad feet of
>    Broadway
> As the dead in their graves are underfoot hidden
> And the living pass over them, recking not of them.
> Laugh on laughers!
> Drink on drinkers!
> Bandy and jest!
> Toss the theme from one to another!

The truth was that he preferred the company of off-duty doctors dropping in from the nearby hospital. One or two of them knew him from his hospital visiting. When he had had enough of bohemia he would drift off with a few street friends to one of the Bowery beer houses, weary of the literary chitchat. Back he went the next afternoon, gravitating there for what the place promised rather than for what it delivered. Admirers made a beeline for him, misled by his book into thinking him an outrageous character and then disappointed by his reserve. He sat on. It made a change from Abby Price's sitting room. And he had to hand it to Clapp for championing him so strongly, publishing a steady stream of items by or about Whitman in the *Press*, both before and after the publication of his third edition. "I can do a great deal for it," Clapp wrote to him enthusiastically. "I meant to do more last week." Only lack of funds stopped him, he assured the poet. He pounded away at friends and readers with news of this genius. "Emerson has said so, Clapp says so," commented one editor.

The drama critic Edward Wilkins professed himself an admirer. Whitman found him hard to take, remembering him as "noble, slim, sickish, dressy, Frenchy," a "dude." He liked even less the critic William Winter, that "dried up cadaverous schoolmaster" who objected to the bad smell given off by *Leaves of Grass*—"little Willie Winter, miserable cuss!"

He sat in a corner and listened and watched. "My own greatest pleasure at Pfaff's," he recalled, "was to look on—to see, talk little, absorb. I never was a great discusser anyway." John Winton of the *New York Times*, another habitué, went too far with his gushing appreciation of the man who sat self-effacingly, unwilling or unable to be forthcoming. Writing to tell Whitman how he had got hold of his book at a Brooklyn newsstand when it first appeared, he said, "Since then you have grown before me, grown around and grown into me." Put off, Whitman said tartly that the letter had "sugar in it."

William Dean Howells, a young journalist and poet from Ohio, proud to be published in the distinguished if impecunious *Saturday Press* and unaware of its editor's contempt for New England culture, arrived to meet Clapp and was immediately affronted. The man's ebullient cynicism repelled him. He had come via New England, having met his literary idols Lowell, Emerson, and Hawthorne there. Any mention of Concord was like a red rag to Clapp, who marched up and down in his office abusing the stuffiness of Boston. The naive Howells spoke of his encounter with Hawthorne. The editor asked what he was like. Howells said he was "very shy and I was rather shy." "Oh, a couple of shysters!" Clapp jeered. Someone else in the office explained that the very thought of Boston made Clapp "ugly as sin."

Disgusted by this encounter, Howells dropped in at Pfaff's that evening. He liked it at first sight no better than his jaundiced memory of Clapp's office. About to retreat from the glitter and hilarity he heard a whisper that Walt Whitman was there. Taken over to the poet's table to be introduced, Howells later described reverently "how he leaned back in his chair, and reached out his great hand to me, as if he was going to give it to me for good and all. He had a fine head, with a cloud of Jovian hair upon it, and a branching beard and mustache, and gentle eyes that looked most kindly into mine, and seemed to wish the liking which I instantly gave him, though we hardly passed a word, and our acquaintance was summed up in that glance and the grasp of his mighty fist upon my hand." This was how he exerted his will, by "his bulk and his silences." It was part of his personality then, and on the hospital wards he would put it to use as a kind of therapy.

Most of the friends Whitman made at Pfaff's were a good deal younger than himself. A group of these young men who clustered laughingly around his table he named the Fred Gray Association, since its liveliest member was Frederick Schiller Gray, a doctor's son who became a doctor too in the Civil War. The conflict scattered them, and when they formed up again their kingpin was stranded in Washington, writing to remind them of old carousings and looking forward to nights "better and mellower than ever." But that old carefree time was gone for good. None of them were to know it, but it had entered a final phase for all of them in December 1859 when John Brown, an old man, tall, with white hair, climbed up on the scaffold in Virginia to be hanged. A violent abolitionist, Brown had led a raid on the federal arsenal at Harpers Ferry, Virginia, seizing guns and ammunition designed to arm a slave rebellion. The South shuddered in fear.

🙟 OUT OF THE BLUE CAME a letter from Boston which rocked Whitman back on his heels. Here, dropped into his lap by a smiling Providence, a mirror image of the persona he had been constructing so assiduously for himself, was the opportunity to transfer his book onto a national stage. The letter, care of Fowler and Wells, came from a new publishing house. He could scarcely believe his eyes. Only a month earlier, given space by Clapp to respond to an attack in the *Cincinnati Daily Commercial* on "A Child's Reminiscence" —they had condemned the poem as incomprehensible, "unmixed and hopeless drivel"—he had admitted that his book "has not yet been really published at all." (He would go on saying so for most of his life.) "Walt Whitman, for his own purposes, slowly trying his hand at the edifice, the structure he has undertaken, has lazily loafed on, letting each part have time to set—evidently building not so much with reference to any part itself, considered alone, but more with reference to the ensemble. . . ." It sounded cool, almost truculent in its insistence on a leisurely pace. In fact he had ground to a halt and was stagnant, sitting night after night in the unreal cocoon of Pfaff's.

The electrifying letter was from two young men who might have jumped clean out of his poems, the new men he had been trying to reach with "The Eighteenth Presidency." Sounding wonderfully positive and unequivocal, they told him:

> We want to be the publishers of Walt Whitman's Poems—Leaves of Grass. When the book was first issued we were clerks in the establishment we now own. We read the book with profit and pleasure. It is a true poem and writ by a *true* man.
>
> When a man dares to speak his thought in this day of refinement—so called—it is difficult to find his mates to act amen to it. Now *we* want to be known as the publishers of Walt Whitman's books, and put our name as such under his, on title pages.—If you will allow it we can and will put your books into good form, and style attractive to the eye; we can and will sell a large number of copies; we have great facilities by and through numberless Agents in selling. We can dispose of more books than most publishing houses (we do not "puff" here but speak *truth*).
>
> We are young men. We "celebrate" ourselves by acts. Try us. You can do us good. We can do you good—pecuniarily. . . .
>
> Are you writing other poems? Are they ready for the press? Will you let us read them? Will you write us? Please give us your residence.
>
> Yours fraternally,<br>Thayer and Eldridge

They had just published James Redpath's partisan biography of John Brown and it had been a hit. Really they were abolitionist movement publishers—Whitman's would be their only literary title. They had commissioned a passionate young writer, William O'Connor, to write them an abolitionist novel, *Harrington*, and had brought him to Boston to do it, paying him a monthly salary.

By March 15 Whitman was in Boston to see his book through the press, with a free hand to design his own layout. His stagnation at an end, he set to work, bewildered by the change in his fortunes. His hero-worshiping young publishers took him round to a Boston stereotype foundry—"the best"—and told the foreman to follow the author's wishes. Whitman combined a variety of type faces and the printers thought it "crazy," he wrote in high spirits to his confidant Jeff. The staff subjected him to frowns and headshakings and "all sorts of supercilious squints," but the sheets went through the press as he wanted, and things calmed down. The foreman even ate his words, pronouncing it "the freshest and handsomest piece of typography that had ever passed through his mill." Whitman loved his book anew, in his very bones and blood, his stubborn spirit an upright flame again. He walked now with a lighter step and felt a great weight lifted from him, "a great obstacle that has been in my way for the last three years." So much, after all, was experimental—and now he was content. Still astonished by the swift turn of events, he said to Jeff, "It is quite curious, all this should spring up suddenly, ain't it." The big baggy lines strode over the page; the book's generous and expansive sprawl was a breakout from the study, into nature and the tidal waves of the streets. The proliferation and wantonness were part of the style, and part of him in the act of coming to *be*.

Exhilarated, he was in a mood to enjoy his days, his strolls along Washington Street, the season wheeling into a profuse spring. Boston was far more pleasant than he expected and so were the Yankees, friendly and generous to a fault. He had scraped together money for the trip by raising small loans from the "Fred Gray Association" and elsewhere.

Daily living he found expensive. His rented room, "gas, water, good American folks," cost two dollars a week and he ate at a restaurant, paying seven cents for a cup of coffee and nineteen cents for a beefsteak, he moaned lightheartedly to Jeff, "and me so fond of coffee and beefsteak." It tickled him hugely that he seemed to startle the passersby in Washington Street (Boston's Broadway) and State Street with his outlandish appearance, his rolling gait and hand-me-down working clobber, and liked to think he was creating a sensation. Abby Price heard from him that "Everybody here is so like everybody else, and I am Walt Whitman! Yankee curiosity and cuteness, for once, is thoroughly stumped, confounded, petrified, made desperate."

Walking around purposefully here was in its way as marvelous a triumph as the forthcoming launch of his new edition. This was the prestigious center of America's literary renaissance. *Representative Men*, *The Scarlet Letter*, *The House of the Seven Gables*, *Moby-Dick*, *Pierre*, and *Walden* had all appeared in the half-decade of 1850–1855. So had *Leaves of Grass*, virtually unacknowledged except for one man. Was that now about to change? In his buoyant mood Whitman was happy to rub out of himself "the deficient notions I had of New England character."

Behind Thayer and Eldridge's dramatic approach may well have been Emerson, or at any rate his recommendation. On a sharp day toward the end of March he walked with the Brooklyn poet under the big leafless elms on the Commons, doing his best to dissuade Whitman from including his "Enfans d'Adam" cluster of poems—shockers like "Spontaneous Me," "To a Common Prostitute," and "I Sing the Body Electric." There simply wasn't a public out there, he warned, able to accept lines as inflammatory as

This poem drooping shy and unseen that I always carry, and that
  all men carry...
Love-thoughts, love-juice, love-odor, love-yielding, love-climbers,
  and the climbing sap,
Arms and hands of love, lips of love, phallic thumb of love,
  breasts of love, bellies press'd and glued together with love,
Earth of chaste love, life that is only life after love....

Emerson argued from a purely pragmatic point of view, he insisted. Did Whitman want the book to sell, to be apprehended properly and achieve a degree of circulation, or not? Whitman listened quietly and respectfully, then asked a question. If he cut into the living roots of the book as Emerson urged, would he have as good a book? No, Emerson answered. "I did not say as good a book. I said a good book."

In years to come Whitman had no regrets over his "Emerson no," high as the price was that he would have to pay for his refusal to expurgate. "If I had cut sex out," he mused, "I might just as well have cut everything out." Down in his soul, he explained to Traubel, he felt bound to "disobey all" and carry on plowing his own lonely furrow. "The dirtiest book in all the world is the expurgated book."

His first legitimate publishers thought everything was just fine, not even bothering to ask what the book would contain. He intended to open with a much worked-over poem, "Protoleaf" (later "Starting from Paumanok"), and this would preface every subsequent edition. Each time, as well, he would conclude with the same closing poem, "So Long!" The edition's orange covers showed a globe wreathed in clouds on its front and along the spine a finger carrying a perched butterfly.

Emerson had got his visitor into the Boston Atheneum as a temporary member but failed to get him over the threshold of his own home or of his Concord friends Thoreau and Alcott: the womenfolk were unanimous in their objections. Whitman would never be allowed in the Victorian drawing room, and neither would his book.

On several Sundays he dropped in on morning services at the Seamen's Bethel down on the waterfront. He had heard of the sailor-preacher Edward Thompson Taylor, the model for Father Mapple in Melville's' *Moby-Dick*. Thrilled by the exhortations of the colorful old chaplain as "the *live feeling* advanced upon you and seiz'd you with a power before unknown . . . a curious remorseless firmness, as of some surgeon operating on a belov'd patient," he was equally captivated by the chapel interior. It had a look of a ship's cabin with its "low ceiling, everything strongly timber'd (polish'd and Rubb'd apparently), the dark rich colors, the gallery, all in half light. . . ."

A letter came from Henry Clapp angling for some Thayer and Eldridge advertising money as he struggled desperately to keep his ailing review afloat. At the end of April Whitman was still in Boston. His mother wrote to keep him abreast of her domestic worries and tell him about the Brown family, to whom she had let part of the house to make ends meet. She had expected him home before this, she said, "but your letter says you are not. . . . Eddy is some lame yet     he cant do much     I think its the rheumatics     Andrew has got quite well he has been here three days in succession." As for the Browns, a man and wife, a son of seventeen and a son of nine, "all but the 9 years one belongs to mr beechers church . . . they have the back basement and the next floor through and one bedroom in the attic . . . we are a little crampt in the basement."

He met a potential acolyte in John Townsend Trowbridge, a journalist and novelist who wrote under various pen names and so was unknown to Whitman. Living in Paris when the 1855 *Leaves* came out, he heard rumors of it, bought a copy as soon as he reached home, and thought it as bold as "nature itself," by a poet who was "a sort of Emerson run wild." Immediately he had an "intense curiosity as to the man." Now a friend told him that Whitman was in town and he tracked him to the foundry. There he met the person he expected to be imposing and Socratic and was instead merely "a gray-bearded, plainly dressed man, reading proof sheets at a desk in a dingy little office with a lanky unwholesome-looking lad at his elbow, listlessly watching him." The sickly boy Whitman had found at his lodgings and was trying to cheer up and "strengthen with my magnetism." The lad slouched off and Trowbridge and his friend stood waiting expectantly for the poet to hold forth. His low tone and subdued manner only depressed them. The one comment they heard which did interest them was when he said, gazing as if bewildered at his proof sheets, "I am astonished to find myself capable of feeling so much." They were listening to a recurrence of his doubt, the uncertainty as to what he really was. Maybe it was all illusory, "maybe reliance and hope are but speculations after all," maybe he would be mocked, unable to believe in himself. At moments like this he would look at his hands, his words, as if they were not his own.

But the following week they met a transformed being. Invited to meet Trowbridge's new bride and join them for dinner at his new house on Prospect Hill, Whitman talked animatedly and delighted the company. Emerson, opera, and the Bible were his influences, the common people his foundation, he told them, and especially Emerson, who had made it possible for him to find and come to himself. As he put it, "I was simmering, simmering, simmering. Emerson brought me to the boil." From the Bible he derived his desire to be "the bard and prophet of his own time and country," Trowbridge noted. This time the two men were on an easy footing from the start, the younger man free to joke and his visitor to laugh. No one wanted him to leave, and someone attempted to cover the clock. "Put *Leaves of Grass* there," Trowbridge laughed. "Nobody can see through that."

He made two other lifelong friends during this spring. Frank Sanborn, on trial in Boston for allegedly assisting John Brown's conspirators, spotted Whitman sitting in court in his distinctive dress and was heartened to see him there. Whitman said he had come to make sure justice was done. He also met the individual who would be his fiercest champion in future years. William O'Connor was, like Whitman, out of a job, having just lost his editorship of the Philadelphia *Saturday Evening Post*. He was hard at work on his propaganda novel featuring the fugitive slave laws, which he thought abominable. Charley Eldridge hoped he might have another *Uncle Tom's Cabin* on his hands and was dreaming of vast sales.

It was O'Connor's fanatical abolitionism that nearly upset the apple cart so far as Whitman was concerned. Extremists of whatever color were anathema to him. But this latest disciple was impossible to resist. O'Connor would go on to fight battles on the poet's behalf, organize, rage at his friend's enemies as if they were his own, and become in effect Whitman's campaign manager. At their first meeting Whitman was riveted by the "gallant, handsome, gay-hearted, fine-voiced, glowing-eyed man, lithe-moving on his feet, of healthy and magnetic atmosphere and presence and the most welcome company in the world." Now, with this thoroughgoing believer twelve years his junior at his side, he had a friend as unswervingly loyal as his enthusiastic young publishers.

He noticed how much better the blacks were treated here in comparison with New York. They worked harmoniously alongside whites, he said. In his notebook he recorded seeing a black compositor, a black clerk at the State House, a smart black lawyer. O'Connor saw another picture entirely. In *Harrington: A Love Story* he indicted Boston for discrimination. In his book blacks were shown excluded from the trades, from commerce and the professions. They had no right of entry on omnibuses, in theatres, schools, churches, "decent dwellings," or "decent graveyards"; they were shut out everywhere except "the gallows and the jail."

Whitman may have wondered whether these differences would derail them. Not so the headlong O'Connor. Writing to a friend, Poe's "Helen"—Sara Helen Whitman—he tried to say how grand it was to be near his idol; "he is so large and strong—so pure, proud and tender, with such an ineffable *bon-hommie* and wholesome sweetness of presence: all the young men and women are in love with him."

🎋 HOME AGAIN, he must have found it hard to adjust to the small pond of Pfaff's after his heady weeks and months in Boston. Nothing at Pfaff's had changed except that Clapp was drinking harder than ever. Back where he started, Whitman would have been broke and in need of a job but for the royalties from Thayer and Eldridge.

The book had a bad press. Parodies appeared everywhere, a sure sign of his growing notoriety. A wounding notice in his favorite British literary magazine, the London *Westminster Review*, was compounded by the *Brooklyn Eagle* which gleefully reprinted it. Undeterred, his zealous publishers invested in a second printing—the first printing of a thousand copies was gone. In the autumn they announced a second book as being in preparation, Whitman's *Banner at Daybreak*. That December they were forced to declare themselves bankrupt, writing to Whitman to hold back from cashing one of their checks.

His other ally, Clapp, was in the same parlous state. "Just now I am in a state of disrepair even in respect to getting out another issue of the S.P.," he told Whitman, "and all for the want of a paltry two or three hundred dollars." Only a few weeks before they went bust, Thayer and Eldridge, optimistic to the last, advanced Clapp a loan and even offered to take over his financial reins. Closed down, they turned over their stock and plates to a Boston publisher, Horace Wentworth, an "illiterate man" according to Thayer. Wentworth held a gun at Whitman's head: either buy back the plates or expect the pirating of *Leaves of Grass*. Whitman refused to deal with the man and got nothing from the printings that Wentworth did issue.

Some time in 1860 he received a declaration by mail from a total stranger. Susan Garnet Smith of Hartford had taken up *Leaves of Grass* and felt "a mysterious delicious thrill!" Now she dreamed of presenting its superb author with "a noble beautiful perfect man-child," hastening to add that "My womb is clean and pure. It is ready for thy child, my love. Angels guard the vestibule until thou comest to deposit our and the world's precious treasure. . . . Our boy, my love! Do you not already love him? He must be begotten on a mountain top, in the open air!"

Years later, Horace Traubel feigned shock when he dug this epistle out from the morass of paper on the floor of the poet's sickroom in Camden and saw scrawled on the grubby envelope "? insane asylum." Whitman could only dimly recall it—he had had plenty of others—and admitted his query was a hard assumption to make, even if exasperated. He had succeeded in his act of public intimacy too well. Since then he had been taken at his word more times than he could remember.

A more involved case of misunderstanding arose while Clapp was still riding high. He sent a review copy of the new edition to an admirer, Juliette Beach, of Albion, New York. She published the *Orleans County Republican* with her husband Calvin. She had been corresponding with Whitman for some time and had written "many beautiful letters" which John Burroughs tried and failed to get published after Whitman's death. Apparently in a fit of jealousy Calvin intercepted the book and proceeded to write a review of his own, a wild and virulent one. He passed it over to the *Saturday Press* unsigned. Clapp, who must have been drunk, added Juliette Beach's initials and in it went. The reviewer, urging the poet to commit suicide after perpetrating such unmitigated filth, held up a monster who with his "ridiculous egotism vaunts his prowess as a stock-breeder might that of the pick of the herd."

Clapp, who saw all publicity as good publicity, boasted of the pleasure it "always gives us to print every variety of opinion." The following week he had to print a retraction. Then came a review by Juliette signed "A Woman," which tried belatedly to repair the damage. "God bless him," she wrote. "Walt Whitman on earth is immortal as well as beyond it."

If there had ever been a tender romance with Juliette Beach, as William O'Connor's wife maintained, it was by letter and poem only. The poem "Out of the Rolling Ocean the Crowd" could have been addressed to her.

> . . . Now we have met, we have look'd, we are safe,
> Return in peace to the ocean my love,
> I too am part of that ocean my love, we are not so much
> separated,
> Behold the great roundure, the cohesion of all, how perfect!
> But as for me, for you, the irresistible sea is to separate us,
> As for an hour carrying us diverse, yet cannot carry us diverse
> forever;
> Be not impatient—a little space—know how I salute the air, the
> ocean and the land,
> Every day at sundown for your dear sake my love.

At New York Hospital at Pearl Street, where he spent more time as he withdrew gradually from the brittle chitchat of Clapp's circle at Pfaff's, he became a familiar figure. Visiting sick and injured stage-driver friends, he was allowed to wander freely through the wards and even to be present during operations. Doused with chloroform, a patient would catch a last glimpse of a large silent man standing near, his face and neck bronzed, his hair and full beard and mustache iron-grey.

He gravitated to the common room of the young physicians and liked to stop by the office of a resident physician, Dr. St. John Roosa. The doctor's colleagues would gather there as well to talk to Whitman when they had a moment to spare. Pleased to see him, they forgot how tired they were, taking solace in his restful presence. Roosa, after seeing him at least fifty times, didn't once hear him laugh aloud, or joke, or spin a funny yarn. "We always wondered why he was interested in the class of men whom he visited."

The Broadway stage-driver was usually a countryman: that was one bond. Their plain speech and simple good nature were a relief from the convoluted and barbed smart talk at Pfaff's. It was in the country that they had learned to manage horses. Like Whitman they were slow thinkers. They led hard, dangerous lives. There was no great distance between them and his brothers, his father, his grandfather Van Velsor. They were ruminative and uncritical, "a strange, quick-eyed and wondrous race." Relaxing with them was no problem, for it was a two-way exchange. If he had to choose, they were his boon companions. They soothed him in some inaccessible part of his nature that no one reached or knew about, that was nervous and distracted, unsure. Their genial natures worked on him like an ointment. He never tired of hearing about their adventures, collisions, strange passengers.

Roosa remembered Whitman as always dressed in a blue flannel coat and vest, grey baggy trousers, a woolen shirt low in the neck, a large felt hat. He would take some of the off-duty staff back with him in the afternoon to Pfaff's murky cellar for a beer, a smoke, and maybe to eat a frankfurter. He took care to keep them separate from his writer friends, although at that time of the day the place was practically deserted.

Whitman was susceptible to women, but hardly to them as potential wives or lovers. Women would invariably get their wires crossed about him, beguiled by his gentleness, seeing a sweet, rosy man, attentive to their femininity, infinitely responsive and listening. His soft, ambiguous body possessed a flickering sexuality which was curiously unfocused, wandering loose and homeless and seeming to appeal for succor, they thought wistfully. In the spring of 1862 he may have had a brief affair with a woman who sent her servant to deliver a letter to Whitman "At Pfaff's Restaurant, Broadway, New York," signing herself protectively "Ellen Eyre." He could have met her anywhere. Perhaps she was, like him, a hospital visitor. He did notice a lady ("I dare not mention her name, but she is beautiful") moving through the wards with small gifts she had brought to distribute, illustrated papers and magazines, stationery, fruit. On his own rounds the patients would show him what she had left. Stirred by their gratitude, he would store up this recollection and utilize it later, when he came to work in army hospitals in Washington.

Whatever pleasure he shared with "Ellen Eyre" on a Monday night in March, it was one she longed to repeat. "I fear," she wrote, "you took me last night for a female privateer. It is time I was sailing under my true colors.—but then today I assume you cared nothing piratical though I would joyfully have made your heart a captive." It was no passing mood but "a fancy I had long nourished for you. . . . My social position enjoins precautions and mystery, and perhaps the enjoyment of my friends' society is heightened while in yielding to its fascination I preserve my incognito, yet mystery lends an ineffable charm to love and when a woman is bent upon gratification of her inclinations—She is pardonable if she still spreads the veil of decorum over her actions. . . . I trust you will think well enough of me soon to renew the pleasure you afforded me last P.M. and I therefore write to remind you that there is a sensible head as well as a sympathetic heart, both of which would gladly evolve wit and warmth for your direction and comfort—You have already my whereabouts and my home—It shall only depend upon you to make them yours and me the happiest of women."

An entry in his pocket notebook noted an encounter with yet another stage-driver and put the mysterious relationship with "Ellen Eyre" in a parenthesis which implied it was over: "*Frank Sweeney* (July 8 '62) 5th Ave. Brown face, large features, black mustache (is the one I told the whole story to about Ellen Eyre)—talks very little." When he reached Camden and old age Whitman tacked up a photograph of someone he described as a New York actress—"an old sweetheart of mine"—over the fireplace. This was a woman he saw onstage at the Bowery Theatre in 1857. Her name was Ellen Grey.

John Burroughs, Whitman's great friend from the Civil War onward, hadn't yet made contact with his idol. Gleaning information about him, he met Clapp and heard from him that Walt was at Pfaff's most nights, lived in Brooklyn, was unmarried, and managed to live on six or seven dollars a week by writing for the papers.

Working as a freelance journalist again from necessity, he wrote a series of articles entitled "Brooklyniana" for the *Brooklyn Standard*, a mixture of local history and memoir. In the *Leader* he wrote occasional descriptive pieces, the type of journalism he did best, for a series he called "City Photographs," using the pen name Velsor Brush. It was as if he was determined now to keep the poet and journalist in separate compartments. One sketch, "The Broadway Hospital," speaks for a moment from the insistent dark river which moved him to awe in his greatest work, anticipating the protracted nightmare about to close over him: "What a volume of meaning, what a tragic poem there is in every one of those sick wards! Yes, in every individual cot with its little card-rack nailed at the head." Other *Leader* sketches shake the kaleidoscope of the downtown city streets, vivid with the jaunty vulgarity of the Bowery's stew of people; circus folk, Germans, Jews, roughs, and vagrants; an old stamping ground for him, poor and loud and bubbling with its cheap stores, beer halls, fleabag hotels.

It was winter, early in 1861, marooned on the top of a Broadway omnibus in the middle of traffic jammed around the Astor House, that Whitman saw Lincoln for the first time. The president-elect, guarded from assassination attempts, had heard on the train speeding eastward toward Albany that Jefferson Davis had been sworn in as president of the Confederacy. So the nation was split, hanging over a chasm. Fernando Wood, back in office as mayor of New York, was threatening to carry the anti-Lincoln city into secession and form a separate state to be called Tri-Insula. From his vantage point Whitman watched a man of "unusual and uncouth height," dressed entirely in black, step down from his hack and stretch his arms and legs. A crowd of more than thirty thousand had gathered, hoping for a glimpse of this well-hated man. It was a peculiar dumb-show, the sullen crowd staring in silence, Lincoln gazing back at them curiously. He turned on his heel, ascended the Astor House steps, and disappeared.

Whitman, his journalist's eye alert, had a perfect view. He took note of a man of almost insolent composure, his "dark-brown complexion, seam'd and wrinkled yet canny-looking face, black, bushy head of hair, disproportionately long neck, and his hands held behind as he stood observing the people." The poet sensed the menace, speculated on the possibility of "many an assassin's knife and pistol" in hip or breast pocket, yet was struck by something farcical about the scene "such as Shakespeare puts in his blackest tragedies." He thought cloudily that "four sorts of genius . . . will be needed to the complete limning of this man's future portrait—the eyes and brains and finger-touch of Plutarch and Aeschylus and Michelangelo, assisted by Rabelais." Hostile politicians and newspapermen took a less reverent line, mounting a smear campaign against the backwoods president-to-be and his "boorish" wife. He was ridiculed for wearing black kid gloves to the opera and "hanging his big ugly hands over the rail of his box," and for saying "inaugeration." What else could be expected of this log-cabin rail-splitter?

The two men never met, though rumor has it that there was eye contact. Riding by on horseback in Washington one day, Lincoln touched his hat to a stranger on the pavement who looked like a grizzled prospector and could have been Whitman.

On March 4, a day threatening rain, Lincoln stood on the giant inaugural platform before the Capitol's east wing. He wore a new black suit, polished black boots, and a stovepipe hat. In Suite 6 at Willard's Hotel (running tap water in every room), his freshly clipped Quaker beard had been inspected and approved by Mary his wife, as was his gold-headed cane. She told him how handsome he looked. Behind them now was the ugly anonymous letter he had found waiting for him: "If you don't Resign we are going to put a spider in your dumpling and play the Devil with you . . . you are nothing but a goddamn Black nigger."

Bodyguards stood behind him. Plainclothes detectives mingled with the crowds. Soldiers were sprinkled over the roofs of the adjacent buildings. Artillerymen manned a line of howtizers on a hill nearby.

His speech, tried out that morning on his family, was a noble utterance reminiscent of the early patriots. But there were significant differences. The "little Illinois lawyer," not a puppet as his secretary of state soon discovered but a president with executive force and vigor, was a fighter, son of a hick—and from the outset a beleaguered man. His first words were an appeal to the South for reconciliation, so that the Union could be saved:

In your hands, dissatisfied fellow countrymen, and not in *mine*, is the momentous issue of civil war. The government will not assail *you.* You can have no conflict, without being yourselves the aggressors. *You* have no oath registered in Heaven to destroy the government, while *I* shall have the most solemn one to preserve, protect and defend it. . . .

We must not be enemies. Though passion may have strained, it must not break our bonds of affection. The mystic chords of memory, stretching from every battlefield and patriot grave, to every living heart and hearthstone all over this broad land, will yet swell the chorus of the Union, when again touched, as surely they will be, by the better angels of our nature.

He took the oath as sixteenth president of the United States. Cannon blazed. The next day Southerners were damning his address as a declaration of war against them.


THE COTTON STATES were now afire with secession fever. Even before Lincoln took office rumors flew that President Buchanan intended to bow to the inevitable and surrender three Union forts in Charleston Harbor. "If that's true," Lincoln had said, "they ought to hang him." Two of the forts were unmanned. South Carolinians walked into them and threw a ring of guns around the harbor. Fort Sumter still flew the Union flag, its small garrison under siege.

On April 13 the unimaginable happened. The Confederates let fly at Sumter, pounding away at the fort with their batteries, then letting up to allow the evacuation by sea of Major Robert Anderson and his men. Lincoln mobilized a militia of seventy-five thousand. His administration fought shy of calling the conflict anything but a domestic insurrection, but everyone knew a war between the states had at last broken out. Dixie had been seized by a Confederate "government" which Washington refused to recognize. For the South there was no way back. As one historian has put it, "The South was stuck with slavery; its capital was tied up in it, its system of agriculture was based upon it, and its social system was founded on it."

Whitman got news of the attack from one of the extras rushed onto the streets as soon as the bombardment started. "I had been to the opera on Fourteenth Street that night, and after the performance was walking down Broadway toward twelve o'clock, on my way to Brooklyn, when I heard in the distance the loud cries of the newsboys, who came presently tearing and yelling up the street, rushing from side to side even more furiously than usual. I bought an extra and crossed to Niblo's, where the great lamps were still brightly blazing, and, with a crowd of others who gathered impromptu, read the news. . . . For the benefit of some who had no papers one of us read the telegram aloud, while all listened silently and attentively. No remark was made by any of the crowd, which had increas'd to thirty or forty, but all stood a minute or two, I remember, before they dispers'd."

Deeply affected, his reaction was curious. It was as if he wanted to wash the awful news out of his blood and yet prepare himself for unknown challenges; as though he fell back in the flesh and then recovered, his heart heavy but intact. In his notebook three days later he wrote, "I have this day, this hour, resolved to inaugurate for myself a pure, perfect, sweet, clean-blooded robust body, by ignoring all drinks but water and pure milk, and all fat meats, late suppers—a great body, a purged, cleansed, spiritualized, invigorated body."

The North, reeling with shock, turned quickly angry and contemptuous. No one could see the rebellion lasting. It would blow over in sixty days, a senator predicted. The mayor of Brooklyn, discussing matters with Whitman on a Fulton ferry, said he "hoped the Southern fire-eaters would commit some overt action of resistance, as they would then be at once effectually squelch'd forever." Whitman shared this confidence, as did the men of the Thirteenth Regiment, among whom was his enlisted brother George. The volunteers marched out of the Brooklyn armory "all provided with pieces of rope, conspicuously tied to their musket barrels, with which to bring back each man a prisoner from the audacious South, to be led on a noose, on our men's early and triumphant return."

Then came the calamitous battle of Bull Run. The phony war of the past months was at an end. What had begun on July 21 as a spectacle to be enjoyed by the gathering of spectators and correspondents, some with picnic baskets and opera glasses, ended in a shameful rout. Puffs of artillery smoke hung prettily over the woods as the Grand Army under McDowell marched against the rebels near Manassas Junction. All at once the troops broke ranks and ran for it, streaming back in full retreat, littering the ground with canteens, knapsacks, and muskets as they came. Spectators scattered on the road behind them.

Enraged senators pulled out revolvers, standing in their carriages to scream orders at the men. A stampede of raw volunteers poured back into Washington in a steady stream, spattered with mud, many of them without their weapons. Lincoln watched the debacle from a White House window. Soldiers dropped to the pavement along Pennsylvania Avenue in the fog and ran and slept there, too exhausted to stir. Some were barefoot, others wounded, being tended by nurses wrapping blankets around their shoulders. People set up stoves and heated kettles of hot soup and coffee in the roadway. The whole city lay wide open to attack and could have been taken without a struggle if the Confederates had not been as disorganized in victory as the Union troops in retreat.

Whitman, an admirer now of Lincoln as he regrouped his demoralized men, paid tribute to the "ring of clearest bugles" from the New York papers, rallying the North with a fortnight of nonstop patriotic editorials. He dashed off his own contribution, "Beat! Beat Drums!"—a poem filled with the commotion of a city mobilizing and with his own excitement.

Make no parley—stop for no expostulation;
Mind not the timid—mind not the weeper or prayer;
Mind not the old man beseeching the young man;
Let not the child's voice be heard nor the mother's entreaties. . . .

which *Harper's Weekly* and the *Leader* published simultaneously.

Why he didn't volunteer himself is not hard to understand. He was forty-two and looked fifty. With George gone he was the mainstay of his mother and his handicapped brother. Jesse, a stevedore at the navy yard, was often emotionally disturbed and unreliable. Jeff, back now with his mother, had a wife and baby to support. Andrew was in poor health. That autumn a homesick George, writing from Antietam after being promoted to first lieutenant for his bravery, tried to console himself by recalling pictures of his lost family life. "I often think that I can imagine just what you are all doing at home and ile bet now, that Mother is making pies. I think Mat is putting up shirt bosoms like the deuce so as to get through before dinner. I guess Sis is downstairs helping Mother mix the dough, Walt is upstairs writing, Jeff is down town at the office, Jess is pealing Potatoes for dinner, and Edward has gone down cellar for a scuttle of coal. Bunkum [Andrew] is around somewhere looking for a good chance to go sogering [soldiering]."

A second poem by Whitman in the *Leader*, "Little Bells Last

Night," opened with "war-suggesting trumpets" but then moved delicately toward a music that was for his ear only. In love with its faint whisperings, his flesh and blood vibrated to it.

Wings of Autumn!—as I walk'd the woods at dusk, I heard your
long-stretched sighs up above, so mournful. . . .
Lady! you, too, I heard, as with white arms in your parlor, you
play'd for me delicious music on the harp;
Heart of my love!—you, too, I heard, murmuring low, through one
of the wrists around my head—
Heard the pulse of you, when all was still, ringing little bells last
night under my ear.

Reports of the defeat of Burnside at Fredericksburg in December threw his mother and Jeff into hysterics. The family knew that George was camped nearby. It had been a crazed, suicidal attack across the Rappahannock by division after division against entrenched rebel positions. Cannon and muskets mowed down the huge army from behind the fortified stone walls. Burnside, faced with twelve thousand casualties, the screams of the dying in his ears, broke down and wept. It was another hideous blunder. "Never," wrote one critic, "was such a shambling, half and half set of incapables collected in one government before or since this world began."

The Whitmans, anxiously scouring the wounded list in the *New York Herald*, came on the name of a "First Lieutenant G. W. Whitmore, Company D." Walt had spotted the name first and gone straight home with the paper. Somehow they knew this was their George: perhaps he had told them in letters the names of the other officers in his company.

Martha was all for heading for the door at once to find and nurse her brother-in-law. Walt talked her out of it. An hour later he left himself for the front, carrying a few belongings and a purse containing fifty dollars.

A year before, he had written down the trial lines of a poem,

Quicksand years that whirl me I know not whither. . . .

His search for George was the first stage in a journey which would change the direction of his life irrevocably. In the slaughter ahead and its aftermath he would see with his own eyes the transitions and manglings that lie under so many of his poems, the rotting compost out of which his leaves spring so cleanly. Terrible deaths and disintegrations awaited him, terrible as the loss of integrity itself. The darkest of dark lovers would reach out. Malevolence would give way to strange fulfillments, blossoms of blood. He would suffer lasting damage to his own body, hear the shrieks and the final rattle in his own throat, pronounce the "word over all" of a renunciation "beautiful as the sky,"

> ... Beautiful that war and all its deeds of carnage must in
>      time be utterly lost,
> That the hands of the sisters Death and Night incessantly
>     softly wash again, and ever again, this soil'd world.
> For my enemy is dead, a man divine as myself is dead....

He had briefly loved a wish-fulfillment blood brother, dreamed of a transforming love of comrades. The war came close to smashing that dream forever. He had to make a pact with death to save it, and to save himself too, teetering on the brink. Love and death became joined, indissoluble. He passed away somewhere inside himself as his soul shuddered at the edge of death, looking down. When he came to, he was not the same. The stretching thread of his poetry held, but only just.

# 9

# Lilac and Star and Bird

He started out; crossed the East River, crossed Manhattan, and took a second ferry over the Hudson to New Jersey. There was no direct rail link from New York to Philadelphia.

In the crush and pandemonium of Philadelphia, changing trains for Washington and preoccupied with thoughts of his mission, he had his pocket picked. Then began "about three days of the greatest suffering I ever experienced in my life." He got off the train at Washington without a cent to his name.

Trailing around the forty or so makeshift hospitals either in or outside Washington on what seemed a hopeless quest, "walking all day and night, unable to ride, trying to get information, trying to get access to big people, etc.," he failed to turn up a single lead. Then he had a stroke of luck. He bumped into two friends from his Boston days, William O'Connor and Charley Eldridge, his former publisher. O'Connor was now a clerk for the Light House Board of the Treasury and Eldridge worked in the army paymaster's office. They both staked him with loans.

His tramping took him across a half-finished city, in confusion now with its trains of army wagons, a hundred or more to a convoy. The rutted roads turned to mud in the first heavy downpour. Pigs rooted in the dirt side streets. Sewage marshes made the air foul around the White House. A filthy littered mall led out to a drainage ditch "floating with dead cats and all kinds of putridity, reeking with pestilential odors." The slave pens and auction blocks had been swept away, but a large population of rootless freed slaves lived wretchedly in shantytowns alongside white colonial mansions. It was a "beginning" place, Whitman was to tell Horace Traubel. "Go into the markets; it's there you find the busiest, most curious native life of the place. Washington has the insane political element—and then it has itself, its resident blacks and whites. You are just on the edge of the South there—you begin to penetrate Dixie."

He would be brought to a halt by immense droves of cattle passing through the streets, men on horseback leading the beasts on with "wild, pensive hoots...something between the cooing of a pigeon and the hoot of an owl." Enveloped in dust clouds he would see upward of a thousand cattle passing through in a hullabaloo of yells and hoots and cracking whips. A middle-aged Whitman looked on a city in the process of being built. A shaft of white marble marked the beginning of a monument to George Washington. The Capitol itself had its unfinished dome covered in scaffolding and hedged in by cranes. The Treasury Building, incomplete, was surrounded with heaped masonry.

Desperate now, Whitman thought George might be lying in one of the camp hospitals close to the battlefield. Eldridge got him a military pass and he boarded a government boat to Aquia Creek. From there he took an army-controlled train to Falmouth, Virginia. He arrived on Friday afternoon and spent the rest of the day combing the sprawling camp for his brother. He went past a field hospital, at its entrance a huge pile of amputated limbs, enough to fill a wagon, "cut, bloody, black and blue, swelling and sickening." Surgeons worked nonstop at this grisly task, sawing off arms and legs from dawn to midnight. You only hung on to your limbs, so the stories went, by smuggling a pistol into the operating room and threatening the surgeon.

At last he tracked down George and was overwhelmed to find him in one piece and miraculously chirpy. Flying shrapnel had pierced one of his cheeks. The wound was already clean and healing nicely. After Walt had left, George wrote tenderly to his mother, "You can't imagine how sorry I was to hear how worried you have been about me, and all the while I was as well as ever, so you see how foolish it is to frett."

Whitman felt such a bond between George and himself that he was reluctant to go. He stayed on for ten days in George's tent at Falmouth, an experience he would never forget. He tried to convey his impressions in a letter to his mother. "While I was there George still lived in Captain Francis's tent—there were five of us altogether, to eat, sleep, write etc, in a space twelve feet square, but we got along very well—and would have got along to perfection, but Captain Francis is not a man I could like much—I had very little to say to him."

It was a different story with the common soldiers. The weather was dry but overcast, rough winds scouring the blasted ground. Whitman walked about freely, a wide-eyed innocent like Pierre in *War and Peace*, filled notebooks with what he saw and felt, ate and talked with the troops in their tents or crouched in shebangs—branches twisted together and bent and staked into tunnels.

Fredericksburg across the river was half in ruins, walls burst open, chimneys collapsed. He saw horrors—a man in a camp hospital with his mouth blown away. At night he wandered around in the dark and joined the groups huddled at campfires, listening to the weird mixture of laughter, song, and ghoulish tales about death. "One would tell a story of a dead man sitting on the top rail of a fence—he had been shot there at sundown, mortally wounded, clung with desperate nerves and was found sitting there, dead, staring with fixed eyes in the morning." The firelight played on the open faces of youngsters, changed by a few months into campaign veterans.

He was rejuvenated, hauled out of the dreary inertia of his New York "slough" and set moving again, plunged into the living reality of the men's stories, stirred by their uncomplaining, amazingly cheerful natures. Sitting with them at fireplaces dug from holes in the ground he could see graves everywhere as well as unburied corpses covered in army blankets lying on stretchers, and in the midst of it this curiously normal, even jocular life going on as usual. Into his notebook went: "Death is nothing here. As you step out in the morning from your tent to wash your face you see before you on a stretcher a shapeless extended object.... No one makes an ado. There is a detail of men made to bury them; all useless ceremony is omitted."

The weather changed. In bright bitter air he watched a regimental inspection, two hundred survivors lined up out of the twelve hundred who had come originally. He admired the bearing of the men "sifted by death" and knew he would have to reach for a new, different poetry with which to speak of the dead. Only the bare truth would do, a terse language, transparent as water, a voice that would let the meanings—if there were any—rise up of their own accord. Or just the voice of a man witnessing. The scenes would speak for themselves if they were presented humbly enough. "A Sight in Camp in the Daybreak Grey and Dim" is one of these almost casual journal-poems by a poet intent on understating a realism that needed no emphasis.

A sight in camp in the daybreak gray and dim,
As from my tent I emerge so early sleepless,
As slow I walk in the cool fresh air the path near by the hospital
tent,
Three forms I see on stretchers lying, brought out there untended
lying,
Over each a blanket spread, ample brownish woolen blanket,
Gray and heavy blanket, folding, covering all.

Curious I halt and silent stand,
Then with light fingers I from the face of the nearest the first just
lift the blanket;
Who are you elderly man so gaunt and grim, with well-gray'd hair,
and flesh all sunken about the eyes?
Who are you my dear comrade?

Then to the second I step—and who are you my child and
darling?
Who are you sweet boy with cheeks yet blooming?
Then to the third—a face nor child nor old, very calm, as of
beautiful yellow-white ivory;
Young man I think I know you—I think this face is the face of the
Christ himself,
Dead and divine and brother of all, and here again he lies.

When these unstressed poems succeeded it would be because of their brevity, their quiet pictures and their modesty, the personality submerged, letting a newly realized sky shine like a jewel over the blood-darkened land.

I see before me now a traveling army halting,
Below a fertile valley spread, with barns and the orchards of
summer,
Behind, the terraced sides of a mountain, abrupt, in places rising
high,
Broken, with rocks, with clinging cedars, with tall shapes dingily
seen,

The numerous camp-fires scatter'd near and far, some away up on
    the mountain,
The shadowy forms of men and horses, looming, large-sized,
    flickering,
And over all the sky—the sky! far, far out of reach, studded,
    breaking out, the eternal stars.

While at Falmouth he went out one day under a white flag to help
direct the burial of the dead, fixing the markers made from barrel
staves in the burial field close to the Rappahannock. He spent long
hours in the camp hospital, a large brick mansion called the "Lacy
house" which had been requisitioned, looking for Brooklyn wounded
and visiting a young Confederate captain from Mississippi, a boy of
nineteen taken prisoner at Fredericksburg. One of his legs had been
amputated before Whitman's arrival. Their friendship developed into
something "tremendous." Walt was still calling to see him after the
captain was transferred to a Washington hospital, telling a friend,
one of the Pfaff crowd, that "our affection is an affair quite ro-
mantic."

On Christmas Day, with troops moving out, he was there on the
debris-strewn campground looking over the mule trains of a supply
convoy. Fences had been ripped down, trees felled for fuel and for
building. Past a hill of carcasses of horses and mules he could see
several teamsters' camps. He sat on a pine log and surveyed the
panorama, "the depression in the landscape where the Rappahan-
nock runs, and one or two sights of Fredericksburg. . . . I hear the
sounds of bugle calls—a fine large troop of cavalry is just passing, the
hoofs of the horses shaking the ground, and I hear the clatter of
sabres." This on a pleasantly warm and sunny day under a sweet sky,
as if all the carnage had never been.

Field hospitals were still operational, and he found it hard to
depart. Already he felt beseeched by the eyes and hands of legions of
sick and dying young men. He jotted down observations on their
grim conditions in these division hospitals. "They are merely tents,
and sometimes very poor ones, the wounded lying on the ground,
lucky if their blankets are spread on layers of pine or hemlock twigs,
or small leaves. No cots; seldom even a mattress. It is pretty cold.
The ground is frozen hard, and there is occasional snow. I go around
from one case to another. I cannot see that I do much good to these
wounded and dying, but I cannot leave them. Once in a while some

youngster holds me convulsively, and I do what I can for him; at any rate, stop with him and sit near him for hours, if he wishes it."

When he finally tore himself away one Sunday at the very end of December it was in charge of a consignment of wounded heading for Washington. He attended to the worst cases as they were loaded on flat-topped carriages for the ten-mile rail journey to Aquia Creek. There they were manhandled again onto a steamer on the Potomac. The numbers swelled: as many waited at the landing stage for transport as there were in his party. Fully absorbed, he went from stretcher to stretcher, copying down messages for transmission to the families. He made a discovery which was to affect all his days ahead for years: no one else was going around like this on simple errands of mercy. He saw how grateful and responsive the young men were. Already the desire was stirring in him to stay close to the war and these men, most of them naive country lads fresh from the farms and hills or recruited from workshops.

Long afterward he said, "It always struck me in the War, how honest and direct the private soldiers were—how superior they were, in the main, to their officers. They would freely unbosom to me—perhaps go into minutest details—always as if everything was a matter of fact, of no value—as if nothing was of enough significance to be bragged about. Their stories justified themselves—didn't need to be argued about." They told him their spooky yarns, spiced with backwoods humor; cried openly of lost comrades, described their forced marches—coming once to an open space in the woods and a large old church converted to a hospital, sunk in darkness, the interior lit by moving candles and lamps,

And by one great pitchy torch stationary with wild red flame and clouds of smoke . . .

Listening, it was the easiest thing in the world to be with them on their unknown road, entering the eerie space with its flung black shadows, to see a sight "beyond all the pictures and poems ever made":

At my feet more distinctly a soldier, a mere lad, in danger of bleeding to death (he is shot in the abdomen), I staunch the blood temporarily, (the youngster's face is white as a lily). . . .

☙ BACK IN WASHINGTON, he called on the O'Connors at L Street, near Fourteenth. Maybe his friend could help him in this "mad, wild, hellish city" swamped by a tide of newcomers, office seekers, profiteers, and swindlers, prostitutes, bereaved wives and families, strangers like him hunting for missing loved ones. He was fortunate, but where could he live? Accommodations were scarce, prices rocketing. Deserters and derelicts roamed the night streets. O'Connor's Irish landlord had fastened seven locks on his front door and had a bulldog inside.

The O'Connors rented rooms on the third floor. They insisted Whitman eat with them and their five-year-old daughter, at least till he was able to find his feet. On the second floor there was a "werry little bedroom" going vacant, so he moved in there. When he later changed his address—he was always a restless mover—he came back to them on countless evenings and shared their home. "William, Nelly—my understanders, my lovers; they more than any others. I am nearer to them than any others—oh! much nearer. A man's family is the people who love him—the people who comprehend him."

Nelly and William were both passionate radicals. When Whitman entered their lives they were grieving over the death of a baby son. Nelly had been active in women's rights before her marriage. William was a strangely abstract creature, somehow absent as a husband, loving his wife's mind and ideas as if they were separate and interesting in themselves, apart from her. He was fiery, fascinating, yet confusing to her, lean and concentrated and male, a zealot, unswervingly principled and brave. His purpose, honed down to a fine edge, overpowered her. She marveled at his detachment, his objectivity, which in the end left her outside him. He put himself beyond reach, fell into black silences. Sometimes he wandered the streets after work and came home at midnight, uncommunicative.

To her, Whitman was a great relief, and to William a cause he had been seeking. He lighted the room when he came in, physically warm and rosy. In time she came to regard him as essential to her sanity. If he stayed overnight she heard him singing in his room after taking a bath. Arriving one night out of a snowstorm, the snow stuck like fluff in his heavy beard, he was Christmas personified, reaching down in his deep pockets for a lemon, a flash of whisky, and some lump sugar for hot toddies. Nelly, thin, angular, looking a little bloodless beside her handsome, vividly flashing husband whose voice rang with defiance and anger, was, so Whitman thought, "rather intellectual than physical." When William died she wrote to Whitman that she had been dreaming powerfully about him and wondered whether "my astral body went to you, or yours came to me."

Charley Eldridge came to the rescue again, finding Whitman work as a copyist in the army paymaster's office for two or three hours a day. It was meager pay, but he had survived on less. More important, it gave him plenty of free time for visiting the boys in the surrounding hospitals. In this respect it was ideal. It was only when he decided to widen the scope of his visits by taking in an assortment of gifts to distribute that he began to cast around for extra funds.

The army paymaster, Major Hapgood, was a pleasant enough superior. After Whitman finished his office duties each day he could stay on if he wished, writing letters and roughing out prose drafts of poems. He was on the top floor of a massive building on the corner of F Street and Fifteenth. The windows gave on to a splendid panoramic view of Georgetown and the Potomac. Any enjoyment he might have derived from his vantage point was spoiled for him by the sight of soldiers dragging themselves upstairs from the hospitals to draw their pay. He wrote to his sister-in-law Matty abut the sad procession of "poor, sick, pale tattered soldiers" who came in exhausted to find their pay delayed, their papers incorrect, or to be told they were in the wrong place entirely—"this is the greatest place of delays and puttings off, and no finding the clue to anything."

On the day of this letter he called at Campbell Hospital to visit two Brooklyn boys he had located. One was minus a forearm, the other suffering from frostbitten feet. They were cheerful enough, but on his way out he came on a young fellow, John Holmes, lying half dead after severe bouts of diarrhea and bronchitis and receiving no attention from anyone. Whitman called a doctor, who examined the man and said he would survive once he recovered the will to live. Whitman coaxed the soldier's home address from him, sat down and wrote his family a letter, and gave the poor devil some change to buy a glass of milk. Overcome, the man began to cry.

He went in again later and the patient was reviving. Diarrhea and "camp fever," blood poisoning, tetanus, and gangrene were the main killers, he learned, rather than the battle wounds themselves. Medical science was primitive, food too coarse and badly cooked, patients inadequately clothed and left to fend for themselves out in the field. Surgeons dabbed at wounds with unclean sponges, sharpening their knives on the soles of their boots. There was much brutality and indifference. At one hospital in the city, at Judiciary Square, the dead were slung out naked on a vacant site for burial.

Whitman began to understand that he had something precious to give. John Swinton, his friend, now editor of the *New York Times*, got him some work hacking in the press and he wrote him a description of the hospitals which now totally absorbed him, called "The Great Army of the Sick." He had stumbled on a therapy and found his true vocation: as nurse, consoler, and psychic wound dresser, who wrote poems on the side. He was released by the hospitals, saved from his doubts and the uncertainty of his lonely path. Not only did he find he was a born nurse, he found it wonderful to be so wanted, to feel his love instantly returned. The wards were the open road he had until then only written about. How extraordinary that slaughter and suffering should be such a source of life. The very nearness of death seemed to energize him, and his inner divisions would be momentarily healed by the harsh epiphany of a death rattle. "To many of the wounded and sick," he told his *Times* readers, "especially the youngsters, there is something in personal love, caresses, and the magnetic flood of sympathy and friendship, that does more good than all the medicines in the world."

The long drafty sheds with whitewashed walls, the wounded lying in rows a hundred to a room, were his arena and testing ground. All he had experienced before this was overthrown. He would want to go to the front and see an actual battle, but he was at the heart of the war right here, with all its human debris, its turmoil and waste and misery. He made up his mind: he would hang on here if he could, moving every day from his cell of a room containing a bed and a coal stove to these terrible and welcoming bedsides. Worldly success was a far cry from this existence, he wrote to Jeff: "merely to *live*, and have one fair meal a day, is enough."

As the war staggered on from one disaster to another and the dreadful casualties mounted, the wounded were housed everywhere —in churches and schools and mansions. Whitman found rows of them in the Patent Office, "a curious scene, especially at night when lit up. The glass cases [of models representing dozens of inventions], the beds, the forms lying there, the gallery above, and the marble pavement under foot—the suffering and the fortitude to bear it in various degrees—occasionally, from some, the groan that could not be repress'd."

Looking further ahead, he wrote to enlist Emerson's help in landing a government job which would be more secure than the foothold he already had:

Dear Friend,
> Breaking up a few weeks since, and for good, my New York stagnation—wandering since through camp and battle scenes—I fetch up here in harsh and superb plight—wretchedly poor, excellent well (my only torment, family matters)—realizing at last that it is necessary for me to fall for the time in the wise old way, to push my fortune, to be brazen, and get employment, and have an income—determined to do it, (at any rate until I get out of horrible sloughs).

Emerson obliged with a character reference in which he drew attention to his friend's genius, scarcely a recommendation for wary politicians anxious to safeguard their positions. Neither was the observation that "If his writings are in certain points open to criticism, they yet show extraordinary powers, and are more deeply American, democratic, and in the interest of political liberty, than those of any other poet. He is indeed a child of the people, and their champion."

The word "poet" would have been worrying enough. "Champion of the people" made him sound like a firebrand.

Whether inhibited by a strange *pudeur* or simply too engrossed in his nursing to care, he did nothing with this letter for nearly a year. By then another friend made in Boston, John Townsend Trowbridge, had arrived in Washington to write a campaign biography of Secretary of the Treasury Salmon Chase, a man with ambitions to be Lincoln's successor after the next election. Wasting no time, Trowbridge passed Emerson's letter to Chase. The politician would take no risks, however, with the author of a disreputable book now applying for a clerkship. Trowbridge realized too late that he should have withheld Emerson's letter. Whitman for his part was unsurprised. Chase, he believed, was "just the meanest and biggest kind of shyster."

Everything he witnessed in the hospitals drove him to the conclusion that diarrhea was the great army disease. Instead of moving the wounded out from camp hospitals as quickly as possible, the doctors left them to linger and weaken horribly, till they came crawling "pale and faint" into Armory Square and elsewhere, near to death, maimed by neglect as much as by shot, some with their wounds alive with worms.

He was affected and haunted by the mute look in the men's eyes as they lay helpless like children, desperate to see him again. "It is wonderful." He would play games such as "Twenty Questions" with the walking wounded, just as he had with his pupils in the schools on Long Island. They loved as well to have him read to them. He read poetry, declamatory pieces usually, but never his own. He played cards and checkers with them. He "often read the Bible, read anything." Whatever they wished done, whatever pleased them—that was his only guide. He even prayed at the bedside with them and discussed points of doctrine. "I think I see my friends smiling at this confession," he wrote, "but I was never more in earnest in my life." He read the New Testament to a dying soldier who asked him in tears if he was a religious man. "I said, 'Probably not, my dear, in the way you mean.'" And then he kissed him.

There was a new book of poems germinating, "Drum-Taps," and he wanted to convert his war memoranda into a prose book which would tell the truth about his crippled America, "feeble, bandaged and bloody" like his boys, "brought to hospital in her fair youth . . . and deposited here," he told Emerson, "in this great whited sepulchure."

He made an attempt to interest a Boston acquaintance, James Redpath, author of *John Brown*, in a war book called *Memoranda of a Year*. Redpath doubted whether he would have the resources to publish but encouraged him to complete it anyway and send it on, and "if I can't publish it, I will see if some other person won't." Earlier that year Redpath had published Louisa May Alcott's *Hospital Sketches*, but Whitman had something different in mind, more in accord with his instinct for "the order of disorder." It would be a book "full enough of mosaic, but all fused into one comprehensive theory":

My idea is a book of the time, worthy of the time—something considerably beyond mere hospital sketches—a book for sale perhaps in a larger American market—the premises or skeleton memoranda of incidents, persons, places, sights, the past year (mostly jotted down either on the spot or in the spirit of seeing or hearing what is narrated). . . .

I have much to say of hospitals, the immense national hospitals—in them too most radical changes of premises are demanded—(the air, the spirit of a thing is everything, the details follow and adjust themselves). I have many hospital incidents that will take with the general reader—I ventilate my general democracy with details very largely and with reference to the future—bringing in persons, the President, Seward, Congress, the Capitol, Washington City, many of the actors in the drama—have something to say of the great trunk America, the West etc etc—do not hesitate to diffuse myself—the book is very rapid—is a book that can be read by the five or ten minutes at (being full of small parts, pieces, paragraphs with their dates, incidents etc)—I should think two or three thousand sale ought to be certainly depended on here in hospitals in Washington, among departments etc.

He wanted it to cost no more than a dollar, and to be on sale in time for the holiday season. It would wait at the bottom of his trunk for the next twelve years until he brought it out himself—as usual—entitled *Memoranda During the War.*

He soon held decided views on nurses and nursing, seeing plenty of room for improvement. Young society ladies, however noble their intentions, were no match for middle-aged healthy mothers of children. "The presence of a good middle-aged or elderly woman, the magnetic touch of hands, the expressive features of the mother, the silent soothing of her presence, her words, her knowledge and privileges, arrived at only through having had children, are precious and final qualifications. It is a natural faculty that is required; it is not merely having a genteel young woman at a table in a ward. One of the finest nurses I met was a red-faced, illiterate old Irish woman; I have seen her take the poor, wasted, naked boys so tenderly up in her arms. There are plenty of excellent, clean old black women that would make tiptop nurses."

He knew perfectly well, from the very beginning, that the giving of little gifts was by itself not sufficient. What mattered was the way in which they were given. All the same he kept jotting down in a special notebook the requests and successes he had, the new thoughts that occurred to him. "Bed 53 wants some licorice; Bed 6 (erysipelas), bring some raspberry vinegar to make a cooling drink with water; Bed 18 wants a good book—a romance; Bed 25 (a manly, friendly young fellow, independent young soul) refuses money and eatables, so I will bring him a pipe and tobacco, for I see how much he enjoys a smoke; Bed 45 (sore throat and cough) wants horehound candy; Bed 11, when I come again, don't forget to write a letter for him. . . . One poor German, dying—in the last stages of consumption—wished me to find him in Washington a German lutheran clergyman and send him to him. . . . One patient will want nothing but a toothpick, another a comb, and so on. . . ."

He changed dressings, stayed all night if he was asked, left at dawn with hideous memories, and tried to exorcise them in poems:

> From the stump of the arm, the amputated hand,
> I undo the clotted lint, remove the slough, wash off the matter and
>     blood,
> Back on his pillow the soldier bends with curv'd neck and
>     side-falling head,
> His eyes are closed, his face is pale, he dares not look on the
>     bloody stump,
> And he has not yet looked on it. . . .
>
> I dress the perforated shoulder, the foot with the bullet-wound,
> Cleanse the one with a gnawing and putrid gangrene, so
>     sickening, so offensive,
> While the attendant stands behind aside me holding the tray and
>     pail . . .
> (Many a soldier's loving arms about this neck have cross'd and
>     rested,
> Many a soldier's kiss dwells on these bearded lips).

He had heartening letters to write of good progress being made, and the letters reporting a death that sickened the heart in his chest.

> Come up from the fields father, here's a letter from our Pete,
> And come to the front door mother, here's a letter from thy dear
>     son. . . .
>
> Alas poor boy, he will never be better, (nor maybe needs to be
>     better, that brave and simple soul),
> While they stand at home at the door he is dead already,
> The only son is dead.
>
> But the mother needs to be better,
> She with thin form presently drest in black,

By day her meals untouch'd then at night fitfully sleeping, often
  waking,
In the midnight waking, weeping, longing with one deep longing,
O that she might withdraw unnoticed, silent from life escape and
  withdraw,
To follow, to seek, to be with her dear dead son.

The solicitude and succor of his letters of condolence to bereaved
parents were worked for painstakingly, often drafted out in rough
beforehand and then laboriously copied in his large headlong scrawl.
They are among his most touching writings, full of the inspiring
presence he was noted for in the wards. To Mr. and Mrs. Haskell he
wrote in mid-August 1863:

Dear Friends, I thought it would be soothing to you to have a few
lines about the last days of your son Erastus Haskell, of Company K
141st New York Volunteers—I write in haste, but I have no doubt
anything about Erastus will be welcome.

From the time he came into Armory Square Hospital until he
died there was hardly a day but I was with him a portion of the
time—if not in the day then at night—(I am merely a friend
visiting the wounded and sick soldiers). From almost the first I felt
somehow that Erastus was in danger, or at least was much worse
than they supposed in the hospital. As he made no complaint they
thought him nothing so bad. I told the doctor of the ward over
and over again he was a very sick boy, but he took it lightly and
said he would certainly recover; he said, "I know more about these
fever cases than you do—he looks very sick to you, but I shall
bring him out all right"—Probably the doctor did his best—at any
rate about a week before Erastus died he got really alarmed, and
after that he and all the doctors tried to help him but it was too
late. Very possibly it would not have made any difference. I think
he was broken down before he came to hospital here—I believe he
came here about July 11th—I took to him. He was a quiet young
man, behaved always so correct and decent, said little—I used to
sit on the side of his bed—I said once, jokingly, "You don't talk
much Erastus, you leave me to do all the talking." He only
answered quietly, "I was never much of a talker"—The doctor
wished everyone to cheer him up very lively—I was always pleasant
and cheerful with him, but never tried to be lively. Only I tried
once to tell him amusing narratives etc but after I had talked a few
minutes I saw that the effect was not good, and after that I never

tried it again—I used to sit by the side of his bed generally silent, he was opprest for breath and with the heat, and I would fan him—occasionally he would want a drink—some days he dozed a good deal—sometimes when I would come in he woke up and I would lean down and kiss him, he would reach out his hand and pat my hair and beard as I sat on the bed and leaned over him—it was painful to see the working in his throat to breathe.

. . . One thing was he could not talk very comfortably at any time, his throat and chest were bad—I have no doubt he had some complaint beside the typhoid. In my limited talks with him he told me about his brothers and sisters, and his parents, wished me to write to them and send them all his love—I think he told me about his brothers being away, living in New York city or else-where.—From what he told me I take it that he had been poorly for several months . . . he was not well—didn't do much—was in the band as a fifer—while he lay sick here he had the fife on the little stand by his cot,—he once told me that if he got well he would play me a tune on it, "but," he says "I am not much of a player yet"—

—Some nights I sat by his cot far in the night, the lights would be put out and I sat there silently hour after hour—he seemed to like to have me sit there, but he never cared much to talk—I shall never forget those nights in the dark hospital, it was a curious and solemn scene, the sick and wounded lying around and this dear young man close by me, lying on what proved to be his death-bed. I did not know his past life, but what I saw and know of he behaved like a noble boy. . . . Farewell, deary boy, it was my opportunity to be with you in your last days. I had no chance to do much for you; nothing could be done—only you did not lay there among strangers without having one near who loved you dearly, and to whom you gave your dying kiss.

Mr. and Mrs. Haskell, I have thus written rapidly whatever came up about Erastus, and must now close. Though we are strangers and shall probably never see each other, I send you all Erastus's brothers and sisters my love. I live when at home in Brooklyn, New York, in Portland Avenue, fourth floor, north of Myrtle.

There was Thomas Lindly, 1st Pennsylvania Cavalry, shot badly through the foot, dosed with morphine and in horrible pain, his face ashy, his eyes glazed. "I give him a large handsome apple; hold it in sight; tell him to have it roasted in the morning, as he generally feels easier then and can eat a little breakfast. I write two letters for him."

One day he hit on something that proved extremely popular. Often the men able to sit up liked to have a pencil and something to write in. He took in cheap pocket diaries and almanacs, interleaved with blank paper. They especially liked picture magazines, story papers, and the morning and evening newspapers. Books that were too valuable to give he circulated through the wards, making sure they were passed around fairly. And he made another simple discovery. Many of the wounded were penniless. What better way of lifting their spirits and demonstrating that someone really cared than by handing out bright new ten-cent and five-cent coins, or even twenty-five and thirty-cent denominations if they were warranted?

His haversack grew heavier with an increasing assortment of goodies: "Fruit, preserves, pickles, ice cream, candy, cookies, wine and brandy, chewing and smoking tobacco, handkerchiefs, shirts, socks, and underwear, writing materials, postage stamps and small change." To finance this expenditure he held out his hat to all and sundry. Donations trickled and then flowed in from New York and Brooklyn friends, the O'Connors, Swinton—passing his hat around at the *Times*—Emerson and his circle, even "two wealthy ladies, sisters, who sent regularly for two years quite heavy sums, enjoining that their names should be kept secret." Word got around and contributions came in from total strangers. Always needing more, he learned "one thing conclusively—that beneath all the ostensible greed and heartlessness of our times there is no end to the generous benevolence of men and women in the United States when once sure of their object."

Visiting the sumptuous rooms of the Capitol one afternoon he was simultaneously dazzled and repelled. Trying to convey the glories of these half-finished rooms to Jeff in a letter he suggested he should think of Tiffany's on Broadway or the interior of Taylor's saloon. Underfoot ran a gorgeous tesselated pavement, while overhead "the paintings of Cupids and goddesses...spread recklessly over the arched ceilings and broad panels." But what did any of it have to do with the sights he saw every day and carried around with him everywhere he went?

His APPEARANCE, always significant for him, took on a new importance. He prepared carefully each time before setting out to visit a hospital, understanding the psychology of "emanating ordinary cheer and magnetism." He took a bath, put on clean clothes, had a good meal, and arrived with "as cheerful an appearance as possible."

He bought himself a pair of army boots with magnificent black Morocco tops and stuffed his trousers in them, telling Jeff with boastful facetiousness that he was "as much of a beauty as ever. . . . Well, not only as much but more so—I believe I weigh about 200, and as to my face (so scarlet) and my beard and neck, they are terrible to behold. I fancy the reason I am able to do some good in the hospitals among the poor languishing and wounded boys is that I am so large and so well—indeed like a great wild buffalo, with much hair. Many of the soldiers are from the west, and far north—and they take to a man that has not the bleached shiny and shaved cut of the cities and the east."

Shaggy like a bluff old man, looking like a down-at-heel Southern planter in his country garb and floppy broad-brimmed felt hat, he wrote thanking his mother for a parcel with a cake in it, as welcome as a piece of home. "I was so glad—I carried a good chunk to a young man wounded I think a good deal of, and it did him so much good." He went on to tell her about his purchase of a "nice plain suit, of a dark wine color . . . single breasted sack coat with breast pockets etc and vest and pants same as what I always wear (pants pretty full)." No doubt dismayed to hear that his only clothes had been the ones he stood up in and were nearly in rags, she at once knocked up several white shirts, cut roomily as he liked them. Sallying forth now he "cut quite a swell."

He relished his body's health, its fat, its juices, except for moments when he felt almost ashamed of being so well and whole. "I cannot give up the hospitals yet," he wrote to Jeff. "I never before had my feelings so thoroughly and (so far) permanently absorbed, to the very roots, by these huge swarms of dear, wounded, sick, dying boys." He had begun to believe he could actually save lives by invigorating and cheering and loving—

O despairer, here is my neck,
By God, you shall not go down! hang your whole weight upon
me. . . .

and asked his mother if she had any idea how "these sick and dying youngsters cling to a fellow, and how fascinating it is."

He had come to terms with his body's neutrality and would even turn this to his advantage when he nursed soldiers. Its dumb acquiescence, genial and hopeful, exuding sunshine and cleanliness—he was compulsively clean always—made it a sight as comforting to the stricken men as their longed-for mothers would have been. He was never more content, carrying in his satchel filled with presents and doling them out, spooning jellies into slack mouths, writing their messages home. His bearded face gave off a smell of soap as he settled heavily beside them, patient and soft and large, for as long and often as they wished. Often he didn't speak, unless to answer some question or soothe away as well as he could a sudden gripping terror. He lowered his head time and again to the tumult of their fears. He was mother, father, a shining brother, their happy rock. They clung on, sweating and thrashing, moaning for water, for love, for pity. If he got up to leave them he always murmured he would be back, and was as good as his promise. He sat with them through their terrible moments, eyes rolling as they went under the knife, and was still there when they came around, whimpering and lost, his helpless children. "There is no time to lose, and death and anguish dissipate ceremony here between my lads and me."

He had foreseen it all. Now he had to live with his own words, suffer with his own flesh under

> The hiss of the surgeon's knife, the gnawing teeth of his saw,
> Wheeze, cluck, swash of falling blood, short wild scream, and
>    long, dull, tapering groan,
> These so, these irretrievable. . . .
>
> To anyone dying, thither I speed and twist the knob of the door,
> Turn the bed-clothes toward the foot of the bed,
> Let the physician and the priest go home.
>
> I seize the descending man and raise him with resistless will,
> O despairer, here is my neck. . . .
>
> Ever love, ever the sobbing liquid of life,
> Ever the bandage under the chin, ever the trestles of death.

On June 30 he wrote to tell his mother that he had caught sight of the president driving past Fourteenth Street toward the Soldiers Home at the edge of the city as he did every evening. His shabby barouche was drawn by horses that Walt's driver friends in New York would have called "old plugs." He wondered if it was wise for Lincoln to expose himself to danger like this out in the street—the thirty cavalrymen following behind wouldn't have saved him from a mad assassin. Shortly before, he had glimpsed Lincoln's face at the White House and been reminded of "a hoosier Michel Angelo, so awful ugly it becomes beautiful, with its strange mouth, its deep-cut criss-cross lines and its doughnut complexion." He saw him as a man going his own lonely road, refusing guides and warnings, retorting to advisers, "I want the battle fought—I want that battle won, I don't care how or when, but fought and won!" He had noticed him talking to a friend, one hand on his friend's shoulder, the other holding his hand. The thought struck him, "I love the President personally." Now he wrote to his mother of Lincoln's careworn, grey look, his deep sadness. He had said to Nelly O'Connor, watching with her from the window, "Who can see that man without losing all wish to be sharp upon him personally? Who can say he has not a good soul?"

The O'Connors had to find fresh accommodations when their house was suddenly sold from under them. Whitman found himself a room nearby for seven dollars a week. His landlord, "a mixture of booby, miser and hog" named Gwynne, was hard to take, though his wife compensated to some extent with her kindness. By October he had moved again, close to Pennsylvania Avenue and a short distance from the Capitol. It was a fair-sized room, up under the eaves, facing south and with low windows. The landlady seemed fine, an old and feeble woman. There was a little girl of four or five whom he heard calling "Grandma, grandma"—"just exactly like Hat [Hattie], it made me think of you mother and Hat right away."

He liked the fact that he was the only boarder and was pleased with the "great old yard with grass and some trees back." The sun shone into his room most of the day and it smelled sweet in the clean air. A black girl of twelve or thirteen, Lucy, came and went with water—"she is pretty well the only one I see." His mother had been unloading her family troubles, the overcrowding, an unruly grandchild, and he begged her worriedly, "O my dear mother, you must not think of failing yet—I hope we shall have some comfortable years yet. Mother, don't allow things, troubles to take hold of you."

Walking the hospitals between the long rows of beds, aroused and appalled by the "butcher sights," it was as if the whole of that young America he had imagined himself leading—by the sheer example of his loafing, inviting soul—was laid out around him, writhing and prostrate and dying on cots, some of them broken in mind, wandering mad. By the time the war ended he estimated he had encountered at least a hundred thousand wounded and sick, visiting hospitals a total of six hundred times. Enlarged at first, lifted and transfigured by his "dear boys" and the secret joy of so many poignant ties, he was driven after two hectic years to "sometimes wish I was out of it," frightened by the senselessness of so much death. He was "with more or less all the States, North and South, especially from Maryland and Virginia . . . and thousands of cases from Ohio, Indiana, Illinois, and all the Western States. I was with many rebel officers and men among our wounded . . . and tried to cheer them the same as any. I was among the army teamsters considerably, and indeed always found myself drawn to them. Among the black soldiers, wounded or sick, and in the contraband camps, I also took my way whenever in their neighborhood, and did what I could for them."

In the emotional hothouses of the wards he negotiated friendships that were, on his side, binding. He clung on sometimes to intense attachments after a man was discharged, trying to stay in touch, struggling with the ache of loss. An initial story of troubled love with the handsome Mississippi boy captain ran on to repeat itself in a succession of others. One was Lewis Kirke Brown in the Armory Hospital, lying with a severe leg wound which refused to heal. The affectionate relationship led on to another that flared dangerously. Lewy, a charming country lad from Maryland, had his leg amputated below the knee in late January. Whitman sat by his side during the operation and was there through several night vigils afterward. Taking leave in Brooklyn that summer he urged Lewy to write to him in any fashion he chose. "My darling boy, my comrade, you need never care how you write to me—I never think about literary perfection in letters either, it is the *man* and the *feeling*."

Sergeant Tom Sawyer from Massachusetts, who may have been a patient at Armory but was more likely a friend of Lewy's paying him visits, disturbed Whitman so deeply that he was driven to declare a love which must have baffled the young soldier. We hear of him first in April, when Whitman wrote to give him news of Lewy Brown's progress. "Lew is so good, so affectionate—when I came away he reached up his face and I put my arm around him and we gave each other a long kiss half a minute long." He went on to tell him of his newspaper articles and his clerical work. "I go around some nights when the spirit moves me, sometimes to the gay places just to see the sights. Tom, I wish you was here—Somehow I don't find the comrade that suits me to a dot—and I won't have any other, not for good." We can see again behind this ardent longing the confusion between chaste and unchaste desire which is part of the humiliation running through the Calamus poems.

He and Tom went about briefly in Washington together before the sergeant rejoined his regiment. Whitman wrote to express his hurt feelings. "I was sorry you did not come up to my room to get the shirt and other things you promised to accept from me and take when you went away. I got them all ready, a good strong blue shirt, a pair of drawers and socks, and it would have been a satisfaction to me if you had accepted them. I should have often thought now Tom may be wearing around his body something from me...." Those Army and Navy store love tokens, meant to carry the "feelings of my heart" that would not go in a letter, perhaps found another recipient. Sawyer, who could barely write, got a buddy to copy out a lame apology for his thoughtlessness which he sent through his friend Lewy:

"I want you to give my love to Walter Whitman and tell him I am very sorry that I could not live up to my Prommice because I came away so soon that it slipped my mind and I am very sorry for it."

Somehow this failed to get delivered. In obvious pain, Whitman tried again. "Dear comrade, you must not forget me, for I never shall you. My love you have in life or death forever. I don't know how you feel about it, but it is the wish of my heart to have your friendship, and also that if you should come safe out of this war, we should come together again in some place where we could make our living, and be true comrades and never separated while life lasts—and take Lew Brown too, and never separate from him." The beautiful wild dream of a future together trailed off in an incoherent protestation of eternal love here on earth and "in the world to come."

He tried to reach his "darling brother" by an appeal to Lewy Brown—"you know what to say from me—he is the one I love in my heart"—and then a last cry into the outer cold asked, "Do you wish to shake me off?" Only then did the nonplussed Sawyer write, in his own erratic hand at last: "I hope you will forgive me and in the future I will do better and I hope we may meet again in this world."

Whitman's garret room on the corner of Sixth Street was, as it happened, diagonally across the square from Salmon Chase's splendid residence in Pennsylvania Avenue. John Trowbridge, who had been staying overnight with Chase, came across to look up his Boston-made friend. He stepped into another world.

The first thing to catch his eye was "the thing which should have been under the bed" and wasn't. Nor was it emptied. At after ten in the morning Whitman was only half dressed, his bed unmade, boots in the middle of the floor, a heap of newspapers spilling off the trunk and wobbly pine table. Traipsing up the bleak stairway from the street in poor light, Trowbridge had felt indignant at the realization of his friend's poverty. Not that Whitman seemed bothered or embarrassed. Breakfast was under way, he said, and invited his caller to join him. A chair, buried under the litter of more paper, was recovered for Trowbridge. Whitman cut into a loaf with his jackknife and toasted the slices on a sharpened stick over his little iron stove. The twig went into the stove afterward. He brewed tea in a tin kettle and dipped a spoon in a brown paper bag of sugar. The brown paper sheet used as a butter plate ended in the fire too.

Whitman had made friends with Elijah Allen, the man who ran the Army and Navy store in Washington. Allen had literary interests, was about to marry a poet, Elizabeth Akers—who disapproved of Whitman and soon put an end to the friendship—and was in close touch with John Burroughs, long a passionate admirer of Whitman. Burroughs gave up his schoolteaching in the Catskills and came to Washington to work as a clerk in the Treasury. At first he was too shy to seek out the poet. Whitman was in the habit of strolling into Allen's and dropping down on a camp chair under the awning of the store front; or Allen would see him passing by in a sweat in June, his arms full of bottles and paper sacks of lemons, going to some hospital "to give the boys a good time."

Burroughs was inside one November, lurking hopefully in the rear in case Whitman came by. He came out to find the poet installed on his chair. "Walt, here's the country boy I told you about," Allen said by way of introduction. The two hit it off immediately.

The nature writer would be one of the three luminaries around

Whitman—the other two being O'Connor and Dr. Richard Bucke—
who set about devoting themselves to the poet's promotion with a
fervor he only half discouraged. Generally he was happiest with
Burroughs's sober character. At this first meeting he detected behind
the defensive shyness a young man with a personal problem to solve.
Burroughs was, he thought, "a weak, frail mortal when he first came
down to Washington. I don't think he weighed a hundred pounds
then—was pale, feeble—seemed literally broken up." Nevertheless
he liked this rather wavering country boy at once. Burroughs for his
part found himself bathing gratefully in the older man's depthless
gentleness, and thought his look had something strangely maternal
in it, "as in that of the mother of many children." He left with an
impression of someone who, "with all his frank masculinity," had a
"curious feminine undertone." Later he remarked that Whitman
always had the look of a man who had just taken a bath.

Whitman mused aloud to Horace Traubel in the late 1880s over
what he saw as the tendency in naturalists toward depression, and
wondered if it could be put down to "a withdrawal from human
comradeship." He was thinking of Thoreau. But Burroughs, he
hastened to add, was essentially outgoing. "The world is always open
to him; he likes people." He loved the simplicity of the man's nature
writings, the attractiveness of letters from him, and to demonstrate
read aloud from one: "The bees are working like beavers and there is
a steady stream of golden thighs passing into the hive all the time. I
can do almost anything with them and they won't sting me."
Burroughs, he said, wrote well because he didn't try to write. During
his years in Washington Whitman went up many times for Sunday
breakfasts with him and his wife Ursula. They lived in a small brick
house behind the Capitol, with a potato patch, chickens, and a cow
named Chloe. "Walt was usually late for breakfast," Burroughs
recalled, "and Ursula, who was as punctual as the clock, would get
in a pucker. The coffee would boil, the griddle would smoke, and car
after car would go jingling by, but no Walt. The situation at times
verged on the tragic. But at last a car would stop, and Walt would
roll off it and saunter up to the door—so cheery, and so unaware of
the annoyance he had caused, that we soon forgot our ill-humor."

On other Sundays, turning up at the O'Connors for his roast beef
dinner, he would find Burroughs there too, together with Charley
Eldridge and the Ohio poet and journalist John Piatt. At evening
gatherings the other guests would include William Swinton, a war

correspondent, and a soldier, Aaron Johns. A "very crazy" Polish intellectual dropped by now and then: this was Count Adam Gorowski, who had lost an eye in a duel, so it was said. Whitman knew him as one of the old stagers at Pfaff's. In the near future Gorowski was to lose his government job when he published his libelous *Diary*. In it he indicted everybody except Grant, Stanton, and Whitman himself, who, he wrote, kept a shrine in his heart "for the nameless, for the heroic people," and stood alone because of it.

Tempers flared at these evenings, with Whitman sitting mildly on the sidelines as O'Connor caught fire, raging on about the abomination of slavery and the Civil War as Armageddon, to be won whatever the cost. Whitman would disagree, interjecting that in his opinion the war should be stopped by any means possible. War in his experience was "about nine hundred and ninety-nine parts diarrhea to one part glory; the people who like the wars should be compelled to fight them." He was always shocking the revolutionary O'Connor with his reactionary comments, telling him one time he was "not afraid of conservatism, of being held back. I often wonder if we're not going ahead too swiftly—whether it's not good to have the radicalities, progress, reforms, restrained." Remarks like this had O'Connor frothing at the mouth, outraged in spite of himself. Eldridge was just as shocked to hear Whitman say blithely, after seeing five black regiments marching with Burnside's army in review, "It looked funny to see the President standing with his hat off to them just the same as the rest."

Washington was a dream come true and the culmination of a great effort for Whitman. At the highest point in his aspirations, he began to fail. He had walked into his own book and become his poems, as Paul Zweig truly says. He had never been so close to achieving wholeness, living through acts of frank love with his host of comrades. Yet in the act of embracing them he had to watch them die, or recover and move away, marry and forget him. Never had he been so split. Literally as well as emotionally in two, he longed to be at his mother's side but could not bear to desert his boys. "I was always between two loves at that time. I wanted to be in New York, I had to be in Washington: I was never in one place but I was restless for the other: my heart was distracted."

From Brooklyn where he had gone to rest he wrote to Eldridge, as if his powers were slipping from him, "I feel to devote myself more and more to the work of my life, which is making poems. I must

bring out Drum Taps. I *must* be continually bringing out poems—now
is the heyday. . . . The life here in the cities, and the objects etc of
most, seem to me very flippant and shallow somehow since I returned
this time—

"—My New York boys are good, too good—if I staid here a month
longer I should be killed with kindness—The great recompense of my
journey here is to see my mother so well, and so bravely sailing on
amid many troubles and discouragements like a noble old ship—My
brother Andrew is bound for another world—he is here the greater
part of the time—Charley I think sometimes to be a woman is
greater than to be a man—is more eligible to greatness, not the
ostensible article, but the real one. Dear Comrade, I send you my
love, and to William and Nelly and remember me to Major Hap-
good."

One of his reasons for coming home was to help his mother sort
out her money difficulties. In August Jeff had written to tell him he
thought their mother was following a "mistaken notion of economy."
Andrew and Nancy were sponging off her, and Jesse just sat at the
table vomiting up his meals. Often she was lumbered with Jimmy and
Hattie, Andrew's children. The little girl especially she found bur-
densome—she was so "obstropulus." Mrs. Whitman blamed her son's
drinking on his wife. Andrew was thirty-six, an alcoholic. He lived
in a slum with Nancy, also a heavy drinker. She was pregnant again.
Her two children roamed the streets uncared for, and when Mrs.
Whitman went to see her she was appalled at the conditions she
found there. She had told Walt in several letters that Nancy was
"the lazeyest and dirtiest woman i ever want to see. o walt how
poverty stricken every thing looked, it made me feel bad all night
and so dirty every thing." Andrew was dying in front of her.

When Whitman arrived at this bickering household, he went out
again to vote in the November election—another reason for his
return home. On November 8 he wrote to Lewy Brown, "I went up
to the polls bright and early—I suppose it is not necessary to tell you
how I voted—we have gained a great victory in this city—it went
union this time, though it went democratic strong only a year ago,
and for many years past. . . ." He went to the opera, was conducted
around the water works by Jeff, who was employed there, and kept in
touch with Washington by correspondence.

He tried and failed to take up where he had left off in New York,
seeing the sights, doing his best to enjoy himself in the old ways. On

one jaunt he saw a big regiment of blacks marching in from the country, "all armed and accoutred with the U.S. uniform, muskets etc." On December 1 he prepared to leave. He said goodbye to Andrew, chronically ill now with tuberculosis of the throat. He realized he was seeing his stricken brother for the last time. He traveled back to Washington overnight, and two days later Andrew was dead. A telegram came from Jeff, followed by his letter:

Dear Brother Walt,

I have just telegraphed to you that Andrew was dead. Poor boy he died much easier than one would have supposed. I do hope to God you will come on. I have been with him. Mary, Mother Mat and I, almost all the time since you left. Mary and I watched last night. He has been dying ever since last Wednesday morning— fully 24 hours—Poor Nancy, she takes it woful hard    Mary has acted like the best of Women    It is very affecting to see Nancy and the children    Mattie did everything she possibly could She watched with us till near 3 oclk this morning    Andrew was very desirous of having us all around him when he died. The poor boy seemed to think that that would take nearly all the horror of it away. If you will come on I will try and give you the passage money. Mother and the rest take it very hard. I hope to get an answer by telegraph.

Mary had been summoned from Greenport as Andrew began to die. His children were taken to his mother's house, and the doomed man asked for his mother's rocking chair to sit in during his last hours: he found it impossible to lie down. Jeff and his wife sat with him through Wednesday night "to fan him...and bathe him in brandy." There was an attempt to get him moved to his mother's house, and he seemed to want this, but Nancy kicked up such a scene that his brothers and sisters desisted. He died after a few hours, quietly, "Like any one going to sleep."

There was more squalid quarreling to come. Jesse came out from seeing his brother's body and flew into a rage when Martha's child Hattie did something that annoyed him. He was going to thrash her, he shouted. Martha warned him not to lay a finger on her child, and Jesse called her "very bad names." Jeff, furious over this scene when he heard, threatened to kill his brother. He let out his mad resentment in a letter to Walt. "To think that the wretch should go off and live with an Irish whore, get in the condition he is in by her act and then come and be a source of shortening his mother's life by years    I feel a constant fear for Mother—she says he has these kind of things quite often with her. Calls her everything—and even swears he will keel her over etc.—Ed I don't mind so much because he couldn't help being what he is—but Jess did to himself and made himself what he is—and I think is answerable for it."

Terrible though the death of Andrew was, it was not the only burden Mrs. Whitman had to bear. Jeff was in danger of being drafted, and it was hard to see how the family could survive without his wages. Hannah in Vermont was sick and in her usual turmoil with Charley Heyde, begging to come home and then refusing to be fetched. Jesse's violent behavior had worsened. He hung around the house, unemployable, and sat dangerously in a corner rocking Hattie's cradle compulsively. A year later he went over the edge—he had advanced on his mother a number of times with a raised chair—and Walt had him committed to the Kings County Lunatic Asylum. Jeff believed the root of his insanity was syphilis picked up from a whore. Before he was put away his mother pleaded for him in letters to her worried son in Washington:

> . . . Jeffy must have wrote very strong about him . . . well Walt Jessy is a very great trouble to me to be sure and dont apprecete what i doo for him but he is no more deranged than he has been for the last 3 years    i think it would be very bad for him to be put in the lunatic assilyim. . . . he is very passionate almost to frenzy and always was but of course his brain is very weak    but at the time of his last blow out we had everything to confuse and irritate. . . . i think Walt what a poor unfortunate creature he has been    what a life he has lived    that as long as i can get any thing for him to eat i would rather work and take care of him    that is as long as i seen no danger of harm. . . .

The strain and tension bearing down on Whitman had begun to tell. He was finding the suffering of the wounded in the hospitals almost unbearable. "I feel lately," he wrote to his mother, "as though I must have some intermission, I feel well and hearty enough . . . but my feelings are kept in a painful condition a great part of the time—as to the amount of sufferings of the sick, those who have to do with them are getting more and more callous and indifferent— and then the agony I see every day, I get almost frightened at the world—Mother, I will try to write more cheerfully next time—but I see so much."

In the spring he had seen Burnside's enormous army march through the city—it took four or five hours for them to pass—and in the great throng he spotted his brother, ran out, and fell in step beside him. George was so amazed he forgot to salute the president on the reviewing stand.

One of the bloodiest battles of the war exploded across the Rapidan, continued for eight days, and rolled back its tide of human wreckage. Fifty-four thousand men were killed and wounded in the Virginia Wilderness campaign, and the immense slaughter chilled and sickened the North. Every day steamers at the Sixth Street wharves unloaded their casualties. Ambulances clattered through the city day and night in a stench of wounds as heavy as the flowering magnolia trees.

After this bloody spring he felt homesick, Whitman told his mother, complaining for the first time of ill health: faintness, dizzy attacks, blinding headaches and sore throats, night sweats and nightmares. A physician had taken him aside and warned him of "hospital fatigue" and "hospital fever," pointing out the risks involved in kissing the sick. He went home to Brooklyn at the end of June 1864 and for a fortnight was too ill to leave the house. He stayed there helping his mother and in September was reporting to O'Connor that he was much better, up at Greenport recuperating and at Coney Island swimming. He had even been out on the town. "Last night I was with some of my friends of Fred Gray association, till late wandering the east side of the city first in the lager beer saloons and then elsewhere—one crowded, low, most degraded place we went, a poor blear eyed girl bringing beer... it was one of those places where the air is full of the scent of low thieves, druggies, foul play and prostitution gangrened."

That October, still in Brooklyn, he was rocked by the news of George's capture. His family received two brief messages from him, and then silence. The arrival of his trunk of belongings the day after Christmas drove them all into black gloom. There was no way of telling whether he was alive or dead. Whitman was only too aware of the privations endured by Union prisoners in the Southern prison camps. "Hard, ghastly starvation is the rule. Rags, filth, despair in large open stockades, no shelter, no cooking—such the condition of masses of men, in some places two or three thousand, and in the largest prison as high as thirty thousand confined. The guards are insufficient in numbers, and they make it up by treble severity, shooting the prisoners literally just to keep them under terrorism."

On a wet day of fog, mud, slush, the hard polished ice hanging on in some streets, they delayed several hours before opening the trunk in the front basement at Portland Avenue. Mrs. Whitman took out the uniform, pants, sash, a small diary, books, papers, and carried off her missing boy's shirts to be washed. In February he was released from Libby Prison as part of an amnesty, having survived pneumonia. His luck had held yet again. "I arrived here from the Hotel de Libby," he wrote home wryly from Annapolis, "and if ever a poor devil was glad to get in a Christian Country it was me."

WHITMAN WENT BACK to Washington after an absence of six months to find he had landed a decently paid job at last. Thanks to the intervention of O'Connor and Assistant Secretary of the Interior Ted Otto, he was appointed to a first-class clerkship in the Office of Indian Affairs at a salary of twelve hundred dollars a year. His desk was in the basement of the Patent Office, once packed with war wounded turned away from overflowing hospital wards.

Indian chiefs swathed in vivid blankets, wearing their great nodding headdresses of eagles' feathers, came in to bargain with the Indian commissioner for treaty lands. O'Connor had told him the clerkship would be a sinecure, an easy berth "leaving you time to attend to the soldiers, to your poems, etc, in a word what Archimedes wanted, a place on which to rest the lever." Here was the fulcrum this disgracefully neglected genius needed for his next major move. Whitman wrote to tell Jeff that although he was supposed to get in to work at nine he didn't, and only stayed till four if he had some personal correspondence to finish off for the mail. Jeff wanted to know "What the devil is the Indian dept?" He added his voice to those Washington friends of Whitman who were urging him to go steady for a while, and to ease up on his hospital visiting.

Standing in front of Willard's Hotel one day in February he watched a line of ragged escapees from the Confederate army trudge past. Some of them, seeing a friendly face, nodded to the bearded poet. "Several of the couples trudg'd along with their arms about each other, some probably brothers, as if they were afraid they might somehow get separated. . . . Some of them here and there had fine faces, still it was a procession of misery." A day or two later he approached a crowd of them outside the White House, talked to two brothers from Carolina, and gave one of them his loose change.

On Inauguration Day, March 4, 1865, a furious storm of rain and hail burst against the Capitol, slanting in full of rage and demons. It cleared as suddenly, leaving such an atmosphere of clarity and sweetness that "it showed the stars, long, long before they were due." The president stepped out onto the Capitol portico and as he did so "a curious little white cloud, the only one in that part of the sky, appear'd like a hovering bird, right over him."

For Whitman the very air that day was charged with ambivalence, a mixture of hope and dread. The waiting crowds expected at any moment to hear news of Grant's entry into Richmond, the Confederate capital. Rumors circulated of plots to assassinate the president. In early April Lincoln had dreamed his own death and related it to his wife Mary and his bodyguard Ward Lamon. He had heard muffled sobbing as if from a group of mourners. He got out of his dream bed and wandered downstairs, still hearing the heartbreaking cries. He searched through one lighted room after another but could find no one. Shocked by the endless sounds of grief he came at last to the East Room. A corpse lay on a catafalque in the center of the room. Here was the pitifully weeping group of people. He asked a soldier on guard who it was lying dead and got the answer, "The president." It was a good omen, he insisted. Whomever the assassin had succeeded in killing it wasn't him, since here he was telling of it. No one seemed convinced by his curious logic. And the dream haunted him, he said. He had opened his Bible on waking and came on a passage about dreams and portents. Lamon noticed how sad and pale his chief looked.

In his Inaugural Address Lincoln spoke the words which made Whitman feel more than ever the man's "goodness, tenderness, sadness, and canny shrewdness, underneath the furrows." He delivered the speech in a ringing and rather shrill voice as the sun broke fitfully and a flood of brilliant light bathed the crowd: "With malice toward none; with charity for all; with firmness in the right, as God gives us to see the right, let us strive on to finish the work we are in; to bind up the nation's wounds; to care for him who shall have borne the battle, and for his widow and his orphan—to do all which may achieve and cherish a just and a lasting peace, among ourselves, and with all nations." The sudden burst of sun had made his heart jump, Lincoln said.

That evening at the levee in the White House grounds Whitman let himself be swept in the crush along the passageways and through the various outer rooms to the public reception in the East Room. Someone informed the president that the abolitionist Frederick Douglass was outside, unable to gain entrance because he was a Negro. Lincoln had the man fetched in at once, shook his hand and said he had spotted Douglass in the crowd listening to his address. What did he think of it? Douglass said he had thought it "a sacred effort." Whitman only caught sight of the president in glimpses in the press of people, "drest all in black, with white kid gloves and a claw-hammer coat... looking very disconsolate, and as if he would give anything to be somewhere else."

On consecutive nights following the inauguration the skies over Washington were of an extraordinary beauty. Astronomy was the one branch of science Whitman knew thoroughly. Planets, stars, constellations, and galaxies go spinning through his poetry and prose, and even his journalism. As this succession of blossoming nights went on astonishing him he felt driven to describe them. It was as if the western star, Venus, "teeming maternal orb," was a great drop hung in his heart. He had never seen it so large, so clear. "Five or six nights since, it hung close by the moon, then a little past its first quarter. The star was wonderful, the moon like a young mother. The sky, dark blue, the transparent night, the planets, the moderate west wind, the elastic temperature, the miracle of that great star, and the young and swelling moon swimming in the west, suffused the soul. Then I heard, slow and clear, the deliberate notes of a bugle come up out of the silence, sounding so good through the night's mystery, no hurry, but firm and faithful, floating along, rising, falling leisurely, with here and there a long-drawn note; the bugle, well-played, sounding tattoo in one of the army hospitals near here, where the wounded (some of them personally dear to me) are lying in their cots, and many a sick boy come down to the war from Illinois, Michigan, Wisconsin, Iowa, and the rest."

He heard from his mother that George had arrived safely home, looking thin and drawn but otherwise fine. It was wonderful news, a miracle. Overjoyed, he applied for a fortnight's leave. A few days later he was writing from Brooklyn to tell O'Connor that apart from the rheumatism in George's legs keeping him awake at night, his brother was amazingly well. He had been given an extended furlough and would be there with his family over Easter.

Spring flowers were out. The war had ended at last. General Lee surrendered the Army of Northern Virginia at Appomattox Court House. Lincoln and Secretary of War Stanton threw their arms around each other. Five hundred guns blazed out a victory salute, shattering windows in Lafayette Square. Lincoln's son Tad waved a captured rebel flag from a White House window for the delighted crowd below. A band struck up a cornet-trilling "Dixie," with "Yankee Doodle" for an encore.

On Good Friday evening Lincoln and his wife started out for Ford's Theatre to see an English comedy, *Our American Cousin*. The night was foggy, buildings on either side of their carriage scarcely visible. In the state box Lincoln sat at his ease in a specially provided rocking chair. The play reached its third act. Behind Lincoln a man opened the box door and aimed a derringer at the back of the president's head. When the shot rang out, people in the audience thought it was part of the show. Lincoln slumped over. His assailant slashed out madly at an aide with a dagger, ripping the flesh open clear to the bone. As he leapt from the box his spur caught on a draped flag and he crashed down on the stage, breaking his left shin. In the midst of the commotion and screaming, with people colliding in the aisles on their way to the exits, the assassin hobbled through a backstage door and into the fog.

Next morning the Whitmans opened their Saturday paper in Brooklyn and read the news in sick silence. "Mother prepared breakfast—and other meals afterwards—as usual; but not a mouthful was eaten all day by any of us. We each drank half a cup of coffee: that was all. Little was said. We got every newspaper morning and evening, and the frequent extras of that period, and pass'd them silently to each other."

By noon the darkening sky had begun to drip and then to rain in a slow gloomy downpour, steady rather than hard. As always in times of national crisis or excitement Whitman was drawn to the streets and the crowds. But hardly anyone ventured out. He crossed the East River and walked uptown, past closed-down stores hung with black drapes, under a black sky, the only traffic the Broadway omnibuses jolting over the wet cobbles. The rain went on falling and dripping. Looking up, he stared at "long broad black clouds like great serpents slowly undulating in every direction." Unwilling to leave, he stood in a thickening crowd near the bulletin boards outside the *Tribune* offices.

He was back in Washington in time for the funeral procession as it threaded through the city, led by a detachment of black troops, the funeral car followed by a riderless horse. Ranks of wounded soldiers moved along on crutches. Four thousand blacks in their white gloves and tall silk hats marched in lines stretching from pavement to pavement. In the East Room later that day Lincoln lay in state on a catafalque, exactly as he had dreamed. Everywhere the lilacs were in bloom.

The president's other son, Willie, who had died of a fever three years before, was taken from his grave in Georgetown and placed with his father on the funeral train for its sixteen-hundred-mile trip back to Illinois. A vast throng followed a funeral cortege through the streets in New York, holding up flaming torches. In Albany people came throughout the night to stand by the open coffin. News arrived—the assassin Booth had been trapped and shot dead in Virginia. Crowds stood dumbly in the rain beside bonfires as the train ran past to Indianapolis. There was another huge procession in Chicago. Over the prairies the train puffed south to its final stop, Springfield.

The reverberations from this shocking death went on affecting the nation in "a strange mixture of horror, fury, tenderness, and a stirring wonder brewing." All that spring the threnody Whitman would write gathered and sang in his mind. He rehearsed and discarded lines and chanted them under his breath or out loud on his walks through the woods. He took strolls with John Burroughs and still had the habit from his boyhood of nursing a big stone and tossing it in a rhythm from hand to hand.

The Southern spring breaking in soft waves of blossom and growth all around him, the young grass in shining new spears, the yellowish green clothing the willows, flowered over the flood of the war dead, the white skeletons of countless young men. Out from oblivion heaved the great drooping bloom of a star, a sprig of lilac, a bird singing as though it were immortal. Here were incarnations of the ever-moving flux. Burroughs, a keen ornithologist, drew his friend's attention to the lovely song of the hermit thrush. Whitman, ever the passionate acquirer, claimed it as the missing third symbol he had wanted. His last major poem, the majestic ode for the death of

Lincoln, had begun to root itself in spring among the bones of the dead.

The double trinity which came to him he may have hit on at the outset, or been surprised by, welcoming it as one of those accidents he was always ready to accept. Whitman told Burroughs once he had been searching half his life for the word to express the note struck by a robin. Miracles did happen, if you were patient and could be humble enough. Whitman was a man who waited, armed with a sense of what he called the divine style:

"Nothing will do, not one word or sentence, that is not perfectly *clear*—with positive purpose—harmony with the name, nature, drift of the poem. Also *no ornaments*, especially *no ornamental adjectives*, unless they have come molten hot, and imperiously prove themselves. *No ornamental similes at all—not one: perfect transparent clearness* sanity and health are wanted—that is the Divine Style—O if it can be attained."

First comes the lilac, twined with his memories of the farm dooryard at his grandparents' in West Hills, followed at once by that lustrous star he had seen night after night, large and clear, only to droop like Lincoln and die. He spools out his spontaneously throbbing opening lines:

> When lilacs last in the dooryard bloom'd,
> And the great star early droop'd in the western sky in the night,
> I mourn'd, and yet shall mourn with ever-returning spring.

The thought of his dead captain, a fallen star buried in the black murk of clouds, shakes him to cry out,

> O powerful western fallen star!
> O shades of night! O moody, tearful night!
>
> O harsh surrounding cloud that will not free my soul.

The name of the man for whom he mourns is classically withheld, as if to make room for so much else that Whitman wants us to notice and mourn, and to be gladdened by as well as saddened: the lilac bush growing tall with its "heart-shaped leaves of rich green, with many a pointed blossom rising delicate": the violets peeping among the debris; the blowing white and pink apple blossom in the orchards. We are made aware also, in the midst of these opening organ-notes, of the solitary thrush, hermitlike in its shy seeking to hide itself. In the presence of all this death, here is the "song of the bleeding throat," never stopping, unable to cease or it would itself die.

We go traveling with the coffin, the flags, the dirges,

> Over the breast of spring, the land, amid cities,
> Amid the lanes and through old woods...
> Passing the yellow-spear'd wheat, every grain from its shroud in the
>     dark-brown fields uprisen. . . .

The green branches and blossoms cast on the coffin are meant for all coffins and for all the dead, and in acknowledgment of the mystery of "sane and sacred death," out of which issues the very substance of change, the spark that lights the star and the green fuse, the flame touching the flower. The shy bird to one side comes forward: in all this pomp it has not been forgotten. In the tiny singer in the swamp the poet recognizes his true brother, as he did in "Out of the Cradle" when the mockingbird sang frailly for its lost mate. He hears and understands what the song is telling him, so bashful and tender; what he is being urged toward. Held yet by the dying star, by the "mastering odor" of the lilac reviving memories of lost childhood, by "the large unconscious scenery of the land with its lakes and forests," by the thought of everything going on as it has always done, meals and lives, the oceanlike crowds in the streets and the rising light, the sea's wild heart and the scribbles on the sand, he remembers Easter: the long unraveling black cloud over his head on Broadway as he stood on the cobbles, rained on. The world of the dead has him in thrall. He walks with death as with two comrades, holding them by the hand,

> Then with the knowledge of death as walking one side of me,
> And the thought of death close-walking the other side of me,
> And I in the middle as with companions, and as holding the
>     hands of companions,
> I fled forth to the hiding receiving night that talks not. . . .

He takes the path to the shore and the swamp, shrouded in dimness, haunted by shadowy cedars and ghostly pines, silent and solemn shapes, and hears again the quivering songbird. It pulsates with its carol of death. The song of the bird, tallying with the voice of his soul, frees him to glorify and exalt death. These chantings will henceforth be his message and abiding satisfaction. He sees that the slain can no longer be harmed. At rest, "they suffer'd not." He will retrieve the deathly elements, retrieve sadness and the sad living maimed by grief, the mother, wife, and child, the bereaved lover, the distraught comrade; the shining name on the lips of the people,

> For the sweetest, wisest soul of all my days and lands—and this for
> his dear sake,
> Lilac and star and bird twined with the chant of my soul,
> There in the fragrant pines and the cedars dusk and dim.

Only D. H. Lawrence in our own time, in "The Ship of Death," has written such a great poem of death, so poignant and simple and nude an utterance of a soul concentrated on the self's extinction, as the body slips into the dark and the frail spirit finds an exit for itself, stepping out from the fallen self. Poised on the threshold in the act of foretelling his own death, given up to darkness and the endless patience of the cosmos, his life "only the leavings of a life," snatches of renewal came to him: a flush of yellow, a flush of rose. Whitman too was singing yet again of his own end. A slow, painfully protracted dying it would be, and he would have to pray:

> Come lovely and soothing death,
> Undulate round the world, serenely arriving, arriving,
> In the day, in the night, to all, to each,
> Sooner or later delicate death.

> Dark mother always gliding near with soft feet...
> Lost in the loving floating ocean of thee,
> Laved in the flood of thy bliss O death.

> The night in silence under many a star,
> The ocean shore and the husky whispering wave whose voice I
> know,
> And the soul turning to thee O vast and well-veil'd death,
> And the body gratefully nestling close to thee....

> And the sights of the open landscape and the high-spread sky are
> fitting,
> And life and the fields, and the huge and thoughtful night.

# 10

# The Descent

He had been following a road, and the road stopped, halted before a gaping hole blasted in its path by the war. His great elegy for Lincoln had as counterpoint a lament for his own stalled persona. So many of his comrades, walking out of his book, had died in his arms. He took refuge in the image prepared for him by his disciples. The "good gray poet" raised up by O'Connor was so often now a self-conscious ghost, flapping at a world that refused to take account of him. He wound down, stiffening defensively as he went.

As early as 1863 he had written to Charley Eldridge with a forecast of his own future: "I shall range along the high plateau of my life and capacity for a few years now and then swiftly descend." With a body and psyche dangerously under strain, warning him not to subject himself to more punishment, his health collapsed in the year before the end of the war. He struggled up out of that and was spurred to his final great effort. After that the slope led inexorably downward. He walked the Washington streets in the fierce Southern sun under an umbrella to protect himself from sunstroke. His health was no longer stable. It became less so. He often felt weak, dizzy. His ears buzzed. His old age had begun, at the age of forty-six. In the wards the soldiers had called him "old man." In a way it was what he wanted: to be wise, unruffled, radiant with inner certainty, lifted out of the fray. The faithful watched over him, especially his two cohorts, O'Connor and Burroughs, soon to be joined by a third, Dr.

Bucke. They clamped the mask of prophet on him and he raised no serious objection, only vacillating a little. He had been thrust into the wilderness by his fate, and gradually evolved an exterior to go with it: one photograph he fancied gave him "a sort of Moses in the burning bush look," he said. The poems he produced now were too often programmatic, tedious orations of copybook patriotism that were full of booming and hollow rhetoric. He flickered up emptily from time to time and sank back. Nothing pulsed indomitably as it once did. The sly Zen Buddhist poking fun at his reader's gullibility and presumption seemed to have died—

> To begin with take warning, I am surely different from what you
>     suppose;
> Do you suppose you will find in me your ideal? . . .
> Do you think I am trusty and faithful?
> Do you see no further than this façade, this smooth and tolerant
>     manner of me?
> Do you suppose yourself advancing on real ground toward a real
>     heroic man?

There were resurrections, but they were rare occurrences now. His long meandering poem read out in public at the American Institute in New York for the opening of its industrial arts fair had bits embedded in it that made him sound like a Mayakovsky, hugely delighted and witty as he welcomed over from the Old World that "illustrious emigré the Muse," and saw how she made herself at home,

> Making directly for this rendezvous, vigorously clearing a path
>     for herself, striding through the confusion,
> By thud of machinery and shrill steam-whistle undismay'd,
> Bluff'd not a bit by drain-pipe, gasometers, artificial fertilizers,
> Smiling and pleas'd with palpable intent to stay,
> She's here, install'd amid the kitchen ware!

Immediately after Lincoln's death he found himself in trouble with the new administration. The story goes that James Harlan, the new secretary of the interior, saw or was shown by a "stool pigeon" a copy of Whitman's "evil-smelling" book—a copy he was revising for a fourth edition and had left behind in his desk drawer. The Methodist from Iowa promptly fired his clerk. Whitman carried the note informing him that his services were "dispensed with from and after this date" to O'Connor in a daze. His battling campaigner whirled into action, storming straight in to Assistant Attorney General Ashton to demand the poet's reinstatement.

When Ashton brought up the matter with Harlan, there was the blue paperbound *Leaves of Grass* on Harlan's desk. In Whitman's final years the assiduous Traubel was allowed to inspect it. "This gives a glimpse into the workshop," Whitman said. Nearly all its 456 pages had been attacked in a fury of revision. Colloquialisms were either toned down or defiantly left ("Life is a suck and a sell" became the safe "life is a hollow game"). The whole book was disfigured by crossings-out and additions, ink notes, scrawlings in three colors of pencil, gummed inserts. He had taken heed of Emerson's objections to some "catalogue" passages in long poems but left "Song of Myself" and the permeating sexuality of the whole volume unaltered. Indeed, he underlined the sex in some places. A poem left untitled in the third edition he now called "City of Orgies," from his revised line, "City of orgies, walks and joys." He told O'Connor that most contemporary poetry was nothing but "a few silly fans languidly moved by shrunken fingers," and to tinker with it was useless: it had to be "entirely recreated." Meanwhile, all Ashton could manage was a transfer for Whitman to his own department.

He APPLIED FOR a month's leave so that he could supervise and read proof for his fourth edition, which was to be financed once again by himself. In August 1866 he was in New York and at work with his printers in Beekman Street on his "unkillable work." To be near at hand he stayed with his friends Abby and Helen Price, now at East 55th Street in Manhattan. He had already brought out his *Drum-taps and Sequel* in Washington, including "When Lilacs Last in the Dooryard Bloom'd," and planned to scoop this into his big new edition. It was important for him to be there, breathing down the necks of the printers. They had trouble with his peculiarly irregular lines and made "ridiculous errors." His mother was now seventy-two, living near Brownsville. He went over every day to have his dinner with her.

Back in Washington that October he set about publishing and supplying his book singlehanded, price three dollars; a stopgap arrangement, or so he thought, while he tracked down a commercial publisher. O'Connor and Trowbridge were also on the hunt for possible candidates. George Carleton of New York seemed keen to do it at first, then took fright at the "seminal element." In the same month Carleton—by his own admission "the prize ass of the nineteenth century"—rejected *Leaves* and Mark Twain's first book. To cap it all, the New York firm binding Whitman's edition went broke, and he was lucky to salvage a small number of copies from the wreckage.

O'Connor was determined to change all this. He wrote and published a pamphlet, *The Good Gray Poet*, with the deliberate aim of promoting his friend. Burroughs followed this with his more soberly written *Notes on Walt Whitman as Poet and Person*. O'Connor's effort was embroidered with fanciful touches, including the apocryphal story of Lincoln noticing Whitman at a distance and commenting, "Well, *he* looks like a man!" Apparently the tale originated with Whitman, who was only repeating what a New York admirer had told him in a letter, probably after reading of Goethe's story and Napoleon's supposed exclamation, "Indeed, you are a *Man*."

O'Connor failed to win over the opposition, though he seemed at first to be making headway. He impressed Henry Raymond, editor of the *New York Times*, who thought *The Good Gray Poet* a brilliant exercise in polemics and asked him for a review of Whitman's new edition. The profuse review, spread over four columns of the *Times*, produced an abusive letter from Charley Heyde in Burlington, who identified himself as Whitman's brother-in-law and therefore an authority on the man and his work. His sister Hannah, wrote Charley in his crazy letter, was no more than a "practical version" of Whitman's "offensively vulgar book."

There were stirrings of interest in England. Moncure Conway, Emerson's advance guard back in 1856 when he had sounded Whitman out on a visit to Brooklyn, was now living in England. Quoting fetchingly from *Leaves* he wrote a so-called tribute in the *Fortnightly Review* which mixed good and bad in equal measure, describing the poet as a priapic wild man whose poems introduced "the slop-bucket" to the Victorian drawing room. Whitman was surprised and probably hurt, but held back from direct comment. Allowed space in the *New York Galaxy*, he wrote carefully:

> Personally the author of Leaves of Grass is in no sense or sort whatever the "rough," the "eccentric," "vagabond" or queer person, that the commentators, (always bound for the intensest

possible sensational statement) persist in making him. He has moved, and moves still, along the path of his life's happenings and fortunes, as they befall or have befallen him, with entire serenity and decorum, never defiant even to the conventions, always bodily sweet and fresh, dressed plainly and cleanly, a gait and demeanor of antique simplicity, cheerful and smiling.... All really refined persons, and the women more than the men, take to Walt Whitman. The most delicate and even conventional lady only needs to know him to love him.

Prospects brightened for Whitman in England when William Rossetti, one of the Pre-Raphaelites and a prominent literary figure, entered the lists on the poet's behalf. It was a curious intervention but proved vital in the long run. Years elapsed before Rossetti did anything except spread the word to his friends, though he had been given a copy of the first edition as a Christmas present. His brother Dante Gabriel could see nothing but crudity, and most of Rossetti's friends shared that opinion. Then a Boston author and editor sent him a copy of O'Connor's pamphlet and he began to move.

His idea was to bring out a Selected Poems, with none of the included poems doctored for British readers. The controversial ones would of course be left out. He wrote with considerable tact and grace to Whitman with this proposal, and gave his assurance that none of the poems he reprinted would be tampered with—although he had taken it on himself to alter some of the more cumbersome titles.

Rossetti's *Poems of Walt Whitman* came out in February 1868. His preface to the volume was, like Conway's article, a mix of good and bad, but altogether more intelligent. He criticized the use of "absurd or ill-constructed" words, objected to lapses of style resulting in "obscure, fragmentary and agglomerative" passages, and thought the poet's self-assertion was "boundless"; but he hailed Whitman as, in the main, "a master of words and sounds...the most sonorous poetic and daring voice...of actual democracy...one of the huge forces of our time." Whitman soon came to regret this concession to the taste of "really refined persons," something he had refused to contemplate when it was proposed by Emerson, and he blamed himself as much as Rossetti for what he called the "horrible dismemberment of my book." He had let himself be bowdlerized, and now it was too late. He voiced his shame at this self-betrayal to Traubel.

Twenty years after the event he was still asking why: "Rossetti said expurgate and I yielded—we both made a mistake."

One night he met Pete Doyle, an eighteen-year-old Irish Southerner, an ex-prisoner who was a horsecar conductor in Washington. Whitman had been spending the evening with John and Ursula Burroughs and was making for his bleak room. The December night was cold, stormy. "Walt had his blanket—it was thrown round his shoulder —he seemed like an old sea captain," Doyle remembered. "He was the only passenger, it was a lonely night, so I thought I would go in and talk with him. Something in me made me do it and something in him drew me that way. He used to say there was something in me had the same effect on him. Anyway, I went in the car. We were familiar at once—I put my hand on his knee—we understood. He did not get out at the end of the trip—in fact went all the way back with me. . . . From that time on we were the biggest sort of friends."

His relationship with Doyle was one of combined father-mother to son, and altogether emotional. He knew and accepted that Pete couldn't make head or tail of his book. For intellectual kinship he turned to O'Connor and Burroughs. On a vacation in New York he wrote of his relish at a huge Democratic rally and torchlight procession—he was now staunchly Republican but found the lure of crowds as irresistible as ever. A few days later he was writing to Pete about a hitch in the sale of his new edition, which may have been the refusal of book dealers to stock it:

> There is a pretty strong enmity here towards me and L. of G. among certain classes—not only that it is a great mess of crazy talk and hard words all tangled up without sense or meaning (which, by the way, is I believe your judgment about it)—but others sincerely think that it is a bad book, improper, and ought to be denounced and put down, and its author along with it. There are some venomous but laughable squibs occasionally in the papers. One said that I had received 25 guineas for a piece in an English magazine, but that it was worth all that for any one to read it. Another, the *World*, said: "Walt Whitman was in town yesterday carrying the blue cotton umbrella of the future" (it had been a drizzy forenoon)—so they go at it. When they get off a good squib however I laugh at it just as much as anyone.

He spent a week of this vacation in Providence, Rhode Island, invited there by Thomas Davis, a former member of Congress who had befriended him in Washington. A further attraction was the fact that O'Connor was in Providence, convalescing after a recent illness. Whitman arrived to find himself in a sort of castle standing in its own grounds, a mile and a half out of town. "Pete," he wrote happily, "your old man is in clover." He elaborated on his good fortune with some archly teasing descriptions of the company and his reactions, all elaborately exaggerated for his friend's benefit. "The truth is, Pete, that I am here at present times mainly in the midst of female women, some of them young and jolly—and meet them most every evening in company—and the way in which this aged party comes up to scratch and cuts out the youthful parties and fills their hearts with envy is absolutely a caution. You would be astonished, my son, to see the brass and coolness, and the capacity of flirtation and carrying on with the girls—I would never have believed it of myself. Brought here by destiny, surrounded in this way—sought for, seized upon and ravingly devoured by these creatures—and *so* nice and smart some of them are, and handsome too. . . . Of course, young man, you understand, it is all on the square. . . ."

The following year he was writing from Brooklyn in a very different mood. It was an oppressively hot August and he had begun to feel ill just before leaving Washington. To add to his worries he had left Pete Doyle morbidly depressed with a skin complaint which a doctor had diagnosed as "barber's itch." There had been coldness between them, and Whitman, after three days of feeling "prostrated and deadly weak," wrote asking his friend's forgiveness. Evidently Pete had talked suicidally, shocking the older man. "It seemed indeed to me (for I will talk out plain to you, dearest comrade) that the one I loved, and who has always been so manly and sensible, was gone, and a fool and intentional suicide stood in his place. I spoke so sternly and cutting. But I will say no more of this—for I know such thoughts must have come when you were not yourself but in a moment of derangement—and have passed away like a bad dream. Dearest boy I have no doubt but you will get well and entirely well. . . ." He went on to assure his friend of his loving care. "If you are not well when I come back I will get a good room or two in some quiet place, and we will live together and devote ourselves altogether to the job of curing you, and making you stronger and healthier than ever." He added a term of endearment for a mutual friend by the name of Johnny Lee, "my dear darling boy."

George was about to leave Brooklyn for Camden, New Jersey,

where Walt would eventually join him after being felled by a stroke. George had been offered a post as inspector of pipes in a foundry. He had always been generous to his mother, but marriage seemed to have changed him. As for Jeff and Martha, they were both, according to Mrs. Whitman, heedlessly selfish. "So Walt you see folks changes and Walter I think you and your old mother is about as reliable and good as you can be. . . ." The woes of Hannah were worrying her mother as much as ever—she had had to have her thumb amputated—and Jeff and Martha had been a great trial to her. Martha had been living in Brooklyn with the children until the atmosphere worsened. After she returned to St. Louis with Jeff, Mrs. Whitman described the "seige":

> they pretended to live up stairs but the provisions was prepared
> down    well Walter dear i have lived through it but some things
> i have thought rather hard of    they gave never paid a cent of
> rent nor a cent of gass bill nor given me a dollar when they went
> away    they gave me an allapacca dress when they first came and
> Jeff bought me a little mite of castor    that is all. . . . and matty
> borrowed 50 dollars of george but Jeffy dident settle it    they had
> plenty of money . . . but let everything go. . . . burn this letter. . . .

RECOGNITION IN England was about to produce some strange tributes. Swinburne addressed an ode to Whitman in *Songs Before Sunrise*—though he would later backtrack—and the widow of William Blake's biographer felt reborn when she first read Whitman in 1869. Anne Gilchrist was a woman of considerable intellect who had earned a reputation for herself in the literary world after completing her late husband's biography. She was well respected by many of the famous, Carlyle, Swinburne, and Tennyson among others, and though Whitman was unaware of his breakthrough for several months, he had gained a valuable ally in England.

Through Maddox Brown his new admirer had got hold of a copy of Rossetti's *Poems of Walt Whitman*. She was soon writing to thank Rossetti. "Since I have had it, I can read no other book; it holds me entirely spellbound, and I go through it again and again with deepening delight and wonder." Her pleasure deepened still further when he responded by letting her see his copy of the unexpurgated

*Leaves.* "Anybody who values Whitman as you do ought to read the whole of him." She wrote again in July to express her gratitude and passionate response: "I had not dreamed that words could cease to be words, and become electric streams like these. I do assure you that, strong as I am, I feel sometimes as if I had not bodily strength to read many of these poems." She encountered, she said, "such a weight of emotion; such a tension of the heart, that mine refuses to beat under it—stands quite still—and I am obliged to lay the book down for a while." She mentioned particularly "Voice Out of the Sea," and a poem in "Drum-taps" beginning "Tears, tears,"

> In the night, in solitude, tears,
> On the white shore dripping, dripping, suck'd in by the sand,
> Tears, not a star shining, all dark and desolate,
> Moist tears from the eyes of a muffled head. . . .
>
> Streaming tears, sobbing tears, throes, choked with wild cries. . . .
> But away at night as you fly, none looking—O then the unloosen'd
>    ocean
> Of tears! tears! tears!

Rossetti, gratified by her enthusiasm and by the perceptive critical appreciations of some of the poems, made copies and enclosed them for Whitman, identifying Mrs. Gilchrist only as "a wife and mother." Deeply touched, Whitman wrote back, asked Rossetti to "loan this letter to the lady," and enclosed a photograph of himself. Actual news of Whitman was relayed back to Rossetti and hence to Mrs. Gilchrist through W. J. Stillman, an American painter and art critic friend of Rossetti who had just met the poet in Washington—"had a ride with him in the horse-car up Pennsylvania Avenue (if you are any wiser for that) and a long talk principally about you, whose history (as far as I know it) and that of your family I gave him. . . . He is certainly a man of remarkable qualities—full and harmonious life. . . . He is grey as a badger—white, I should say. . . ."

In the new year Whitman had a visit from a British journalist, Justin McCarthy, who tracked him down "lodged in a room like a garret up several flights of stairs in a thickly populated building." He had been skeptical about reports of Whitman's poverty and wondered if the man liked to act the part of the penniless poet. Here was the reality, "the humble bed, the poor washstand," and the unheated room with its "staggery writing-desk." But "there was an unmistakable dignity about the man despite his poor garb and his utterly careless way of life."

At the time of this visit Whitman was earning sixteen hundred dollars a year as a third-class clerk and paying a small amount of income tax. He sold the occasional poem now and then to periodicals for a decent fee, but he was bringing out the editions of his book at his own expense and usually at a loss. George was contributing much less now to his mother's upkeep, and most of the burden of her and Eddy fell on Walt. Jeff had withdrawn his support. His wife Martha was ill with tuberculosis, and they were living permanently now in St. Louis. It's probable that Whitman gave handouts to Pete Doyle when he was out of work, and to numbers of his friends, ex-soldiers and railroad men, when they were up against it.

Jesse died in March 1870 at Kings County Lunatic Asylum. Whitman was notified of his unfortunate brother's burial in an unmarked grave. Then he had to break the news to his mother. Only a year before he had heard from his mother how Henry Rome, who had been incarcerated with Jesse, "broke out and got away." Since then Henry had been talking a great deal in a deranged way about Jesse, as well as running about the streets "without hat or coat or shoes." Now Mrs. Whitman wrote to say how awful it was "to think the poor soul hadent a friend near him in his last moments     and to think he had a paupers grave     i know it makes no difference but if he could have been buried decently     i was thinking of him more lately than common     i wish Walter you would write Jeff and Hanna that he is dead     i will write to george     i feel very sad of course Walt if he has done ever so wrong he was my first born     but gods will be done     good bie Walter dear."

A few weeks later his spirits were lifted by the appearance of an article in the *Boston Radical*. Rossetti had urged Anne Gilchrist to write one, and to preserve her anonymity for the time being. "A Woman's Estimate of Walt Whitman" was a glowing vindication of everything he had tried to do. There was no carping about this or that; nothing was to be regretted or excused. The abiding strength of his poetry lay in "the grasp laid upon the present." The "Children of Adam" poems, always to be a stumbling block for potential admirers, were supremely necessary, she thought. "It was needed that this silence, this evil spell, should for once be broken, and the daylight let in, that the dark cloud underlying might be scattered to the winds. It was needed that one who could here indicate for us 'the path between reality and the soul' should speak. That is what these beautiful, despised poems...do, read by the light that glows out of the rest of the volume...."

Anne Gilchrist, advised by Rossetti in the autumn of 1871 to approach Whitman directly, wrote her first love letter. Reading his book she had felt "the strong divine soul of the man embracing hers with passionate love...." That was how it had been, she explained shyly, and then came out from behind the third person with her true confession. Mr. Gilchrist was a good man but she hadn't loved him. "I never before dreamed what love meant: not what life meant. Never was alive before—no words but those of 'new birth' can hint the meaning of what then happened to me." As plainly as she could she confronted him with a proposal. The voice coming to her over the Atlantic was "the voice of my mate: it must be so—my love rises up out of the very depths of the grief and tramples upon despair. I can wait—any time, a lifetime, many lifetimes—I can suffer, I can dare, I can learn, grow, toil, but nothing in life or death can tear out of my heart the passionate belief that one day I shall hear that voice say to me, 'My Mate. The one I so much want. Bride, Wife, indissoluble eternal!' It is not happiness I plead with God for—it is the very life of my Soul, my love is its life. Dear Walt...."

It took Whitman two months to work out how to answer this naked letter without giving offense. Only he knew what a pathetic mistake she was making. It must have taken more than one draft to let her down as delicately as he did. Finally he wrote off to Halsted, Essex. Evidently he couldn't make up his mind how to address her, so he left off the salutation and plunged in.

> I have been waiting quite a while for time and the right mood, to answer your letter in a spirit as serious as its own, and in the same unmitigated trust and affection.... I wish to give to it a day, a sort of Sabbath, or holy day, apart to itself, under serene and propitious influences, confident that I could then write you a letter which would do you good, and me too. But I must at least show without further delay that I am not insensible to your love. I too send you my love. And do you feel no disappointment because I now write so briefly. My book is my best letter, my response, my truest explanation of all. In it I have put my body and spirit. You understand this better and fuller and clearer than any one else. And I too fully and clearly understand the loving letter it has evoked.

Then came the cruelty of his "enough," hitting her like a blow on the breast—"Enough that there surely exists so beautiful and delicate a relation, accepted by both of us with joy."

If she could have seen behind his letter and into the turmoil of his notebooks at this time, she might have got the message sooner—unless of course she thought she could reform him—and been spared the unintentional cruelty of his defensiveness. In an effort to cope with his "incessant abnormal perturbation" about Pete and how to respond to him, or about someone else who may have been far more disturbing, he had been forced to analyze himself, and to keep a severe rein on his temptations by means of a series of barely coherent resolutions. Accusing himself of

> cheating... fancying what does not really exist in another, but is all the time in myself alone—utterly deluded and cheated by *myself*, and my own weakness—REMEMBER WHERE I AM MOST WEAK, and most lacking.... Yet always... preserve a kind spirit and demeanor to 16. But PURSUE HER NO MORE....

he resorted to subterfuge, perhaps changing "him" to "her" in case his confessions fell into the wrong hands, steadying his mind with numerals and codes. It would all be more manageable, he told himself tormentedly, if he could adopt

> A cool, gentle (*less demonstrative*) more UNIFORM DEMEANOR—give to poor—help any—be indulgent to the criminal and silly and to low persons generally and the ignorant—but SAY little—make no explanations—*give no confidences*—never attempt puns, or plays upon words, or utter sarcastic comments, or (under ordinary circumstances) hold any discussions or arguments....

and on July 15 he added "good!" But the problem was still there. On the same day he had made up his mind to

> give up absolutely and for good, from this present hour, this FEVERISH, FLUCTUATING, *useless undignified pursuit of* 164 *—too long (much too long), persevered in—so humiliating—It must come at last* and had better come now—(*It cannot possibly be a success*) LET THERE FROM THIS HOUR BE NO FALTERING, NO GETTING—*at all henceforth* (NOT ONCE, *under any circumstances*)—*avoid seeing her, or meeting her, or any talk or explanations*—OR ANY MEETING WHATEVER, FROM THIS HOUR FORTH, FOR LIFE.

Biographers and scholars have got to work to crack the code 16 and 164 used in the frantic agitation of these entries. The simplest theory suggests numbering the letters of the alphabet from 1 to 26. The number 16 would represent P and the 4 stand for D. For all the absoluteness of his injunction to himself, he didn't terminate the relationship, but—if we can believe another entry in which he uses the phrenological jargon for male love—took the heat out of it: "Depress the adhesive nature     It is in excess—making life a torment     All this diseased, feverish disproportionate *adhesiveness.*"

If we need any confirmation that, after three and a half years, the love between the two was still undeclared, there is the letter to his friend shortly after Whitman left Washington—and his notebook agonizing—for Brooklyn in the summer of 1870. He had been "fancying what does not really exist in another" and been happily surprised to find that the reverse was true. "Dear Pete," he wrote,

here I am home again with my mother. . . . We parted there, you know, at the corner of 7th St. Tuesday night. Pete there was something in that hour from 10 to 11 o'clock (parting though it was) that has left me pleasure and comfort for good—I never dreamed that you made so much of having me with you, nor that you could feel so downcast at losing me. I foolishly thought it was all on the other side. But all I will say further on the subject is, I now see clearly that was all wrong.

A month earlier he had written to say how touched he was to hear from Thomas Dixon, an uneducated corkcutter in Sunderland, England, and one of Whitman's most fervent admirers. Dixon was in contact with Ruskin and would be busy in the years ahead placing copies of *Leaves of Grass* in the town libraries of South Shields, Manchester, Newcastle, Warrington, Liverpool, and Plymouth. None of these contacts got a mention in Whitman's letters to Doyle, who would not have been interested anyway. The age difference of nearly thirty years made for a fatherly and at times strangely girlish tone. Ending a letter in August, he signed off, "I believe that is all for tonight, as it is getting late—Goodnight, Peter—goodnight my darling son—here is a kiss for you, dear boy—on the paper here—a good long one. . . . As this is lying here on my table to be sent off tomorrow, I will imagine you with your arm around my neck saying Goodnight, Walt. . . ."

🌿 THE DARK SUBJECTIVITY from which he was struggling to free himself, the onsets of fear and self-deceit, the destructive betrayals, made the task of achieving a new stability—and one that would last—more urgent than ever before. If he could not live from himself as he was, facing the world openly with an unashamed personal life, then he would build "a superb calm character" that would be impervious to inner as well as outer treacheries. Toying with the idea of reconciliation he sketched in outline the personality he wanted to create "by chastity, by elevating the mind through lofty discussions and meditations and themes, and by self-esteem and divine love." After self-castigation, the return to self-making:

his emotions etc are complete in himself irrespective (indifferent) of whether his love, friendship etc are returned or not

He grows, blooms, like some perfect tree or flower, in Nature, whether viewed by admiring eyes, or in some wild wood entirely unknown

His analogy the earth complete in itself enfolding in itself all processes of growth effusing life and power for hidden purposes.

He had gone back to the ideals so forcefully expressed in his 1855 preface, aiming to create a persona for himself that was like a Merlin, "strong and wise and beautiful at 100 years old." In the eyes of many, that was what he became. Somehow his physical infirmity was irrelevant. Only Whitman himself was undeceived, suppressing with difficulty his irritation at the gullibility of those adorers who saw only the outer role. It was a curious dilemma.

Anne Gilchrist, overjoyed to get his letter but pained by its contents, tried again. She reproached him for his refusal to heed the entreaties of her "longing, pining heart." Her subsequent letters had gone unanswered; she had felt relief, buoyant joy, had been cast down, dispirited. It was all too much for Whitman. He wrote a brief note acknowledging her increasingly desperate letters and then, backed into a corner, was forced to tell her bluntly on March 20, 1872, "Let me warn you about myself and about yourself also. You must not construct such an unauthorized and imaginary figure and call it W.W., and so devotedly invest your loving nature in it. The actual W.W. is a very plain personage and entirely unworthy of such devotion."

Impending changes to Mrs. Whitman's old life were making her very unhappy and she was in poor health. George, married now, an inspector of gas pipes in Camden, hardly ever called on her or wrote. He wanted her and Eddy to come and live with them permanently, a formidable arrangement for him and his wife to take on. Walt felt bound to agree. Mrs. Whitman couldn't bear to think of losing her familiar streets and her friends, while Eddy protested at having to give up the church he had been attending most evenings for years, his one pleasure. When she did move, it was a mistake, she felt. She complained to Walt about being resented by George and Louisa— and so was Eddy. Whitman wrote soothingly, "Mother, it is always disagreeable to make a great change, and especially for old folks, but a little time gets things working smoothly, and then one is glad of the change and better off."

Disturbed though Whitman may well have been by love letters from mistaken women, he took semilove letters arriving unsolicited from male strangers in his stride. One was Charles Warren Stoddard, a young journalist and poet living in Hawaii. As an overture, Stoddard launched into a description of his entry into a native village. "I mark one, a lad of eighteen or twenty years who is regarding me. I call him to me, ask his name, giving mine in return. He speaks it over and over, manipulating my body unconsciously, as it were, with bountiful and unconstrained love. . . . I sleep with him on his mats, and at night sometimes waken to find him watching me with earnest, patient looks, his arm over my breast and around me."

Whitman replied, "Those tender and primitive personal relations away off there in the Pacific Islands touched me deeply . . . ," and enclosed a picture of himself as requested. Stoddard went on to publish "A South Sea Idyll" in the *Overland Monthly*, sent his idol a copy, and confided, "I know there is but one hope for me. I must get in amongst people who are not afraid of instincts and who scorn hypocrisy. I am numbed with the frigid manners of the Christians: barbarism has given me the fullest joy of my life and I long to return to it and be satisfied." He was about to sail again for Tahiti. Whitman, touched and a little alarmed, thought he should try to check the young man's overwrought emotionalism. "I received your affectionate letter," he wrote gently, "and presently came your beautiful and soothing South Sea Idyll which I read at once. . . . As to you, I do not of course object to your emotional and adhesive nature, and the outlet thereof, but warmly approve them—but do you know how the hard, pungent, gritty, worldly experiences and qualities in American practical life also serve? how they prevent extravagant sentimentalism? and how they are not without their own great value and even joy?"

Six years later he opened a letter posted in Dublin that so overwhelmed him with its emotional excesses that he was still marveling over it when he was seventy. This "proclamation of comradeship" by Bram Stoker, the future author of *Dracula*, whose name meant nothing to him, had been written "openly because I feel with you one must be open." Stoker enclosed a draft of a letter he had written in 1872 and not mailed. Since then he had been fighting the good fight to secure a hearing for Whitman and "am glad to say that I have been the means of making your work known to many who were scoffers at first."

He went on to describe himself with a good deal of youthful braggadocio: Abraham Stoker, living at 43 Harcourt Street, Dublin, he was twenty-four years of age, a civil service clerk. Was athletic, strong, ugly, winner of a dozen cups at Trinity College, president of the Philosophical Society, and now art and theatre critic of a daily paper. Weight, 168 pounds. Height, six feet two inches. Deep-chested, he had a heavy jaw and big mouth with thick lips, a snub nose and straight hair. He took a delight, he boasted, in letting people he didn't like see his worst side. In 1870 he had seen a derogatory notice of Whitman's poems in the *Temple Bar* magazine. He laughed along with the satire, without bothering to read the work. A year later he got hold of Rossetti's edition and took it home with him. A man who was "of less than half your own age, reared a conservative in a conservative country, and who has always heard your name cried down by the great mass of people who mention it, here felt his heart leap towards you across the Atlantic and his soul swelling at the words or rather the thoughts." He went on for pages with mounting fervor, ending with a declaration of love: "I have said more about myself to you than I have ever said to anyone before. You will not laugh at me for writing this to you. . . . If you ever would care to have more you can imagine, for you have a great heart, how much pleasure it would be to me to write more to you. How sweet a thing it is for a strong healthy man with a woman's eyes and a child's wishes to feel he can speak so to a man who can be if he wishes father, and brother and wife to his soul. . . ."

In old age Whitman was inclined to be indulgent, wary as ever but obviously gratified, telling Horace Traubel dubiously that he never

quite thought himself as the true subject of such utterances. All
the same, one should allow for the fact that his correspondent
was only a boy. Even so he was hit hard, he said, by one sentence
particularly.

Traubel had a try at guessing which one: "I write this openly..."
he suggested.

"That's it," Whitman cried. "That's it: that's me, as I hope I am:
It's *Leaves of Grass* if *Leaves of Grass* is anything."

He mused aloud. Had he been right, he wondered, to accept
Stoker's letter at its face value, or was he being deceived even now
by a pretended spontaneity, something "studied out"? No, he didn't
think so: it wasn't "verbally stiff in the joints anywhere." In any case
he was prepared then, and still was now, "to accept it for just what it
pretends to be."

His reply all those years ago ran as follows:

My dear young man,
Your letters have been most welcome to me—welcome to me as
Person and as Author—I don't know which most—You did well to
write to me so unconventionally, so fresh, so manly and so
affectionate too. I too hope (though it is not probable) that we
shall one day meet each other. Meantime I send you friendship and
thanks.

My physique is entirely shattered—doubtless permanently, from
paralysis and other ailments. But I am up and dressed, and get out
every day a little. Live here quite lonesome, but hearty, and good
spirits. Write to me again.

❧    IN 1873 HE SUFFERED two cataclysmic blows. On a miserable
day in January he had stayed on late in his office at the Treasury
building, his legs up on a sofa in front of the fire, delaying a return to
his own freezing garret room. He dropped the book he was reading as
the wave of faintness submerged him. He lay in a big inert heap
waiting for the weakness to pass. They always did: he had experi-
enced them often enough. Somehow he got downstairs and back to
his room just around the block in Fifteenth Street. A friendly guard
had noticed how drained he looked, how sluggish his movements
were. In the early hours he woke up, found he was unable to move
his left arm or leg, thought little of it, and went back to sleep. The

next morning the doctor who had been called told him he had suffered a paralytic stroke, "a serious attack beyond all cure." Pete Doyle, Charley Eldridge, Nelly O'Connor, and Ursula Burroughs took turns as his nurses. He complained of nausea when he tried to move.

He inched toward a partial recovery, gloomily asking to be left alone. The death of his sister-in-law Martha, Jeff's wife, depressed him further. Then he heard news of his mother's illness. He had been shuffling in to his desk for a couple of hours each day, aided by a stick. With great difficulty he got himself to Camden where his mother had been living so unhappily with George and his wife. Three days later she was dead. After Whitman's own death his executors unearthed an old envelope among his chaotic papers, with the words "Mother's last lines" scrawled across it in his hand. Near the end Louisa Whitman had managed to write: "farewell my beloved sons farewell i have lived beyond all comfort in this world    don't mourn for me my beloved sons and daughters    farewell my dear beloved Walter."

He could not bear his loss. He sat as if frozen by the coffin all night and into the next morning, head bowed, bringing his stick down with mad thudding strokes in a rhythm on the boards, as if hammering out a denial of the death. He wrote to Doyle that it was the great cloud of his life and would never lift from him, and told Abby Price he had been dealt "the only staggering, staying blow and trouble . . . unspeakable—my physical sickness, bad as it is, is nothing to it."

About a week after the funeral he was in Washington, alarming his friends with his condition. Eldridge wrote worriedly to Burroughs how Whitman "was not content to stay in his room so he availed himself of the invitation of the Ashtons and went up there and staid for ten or twelve days. . . . The change to Ashton's was good for him as there were women and a baby, and he had more agreeable surroundings. . . . He still has those distressed spells in the head quite often, and his locomotion is no better. He has two months' leave of absence from June 15. . . . The fact is, I begin to doubt whether Walt is going to recover, and I am very apprehensive of another attack. He is a mere physical wreck to what he was. . . . It is a terrible misfortune, and one of the saddest spectacles I have ever seen. . . ."

On extended leave in Camden, he moved into his mother's room and refused to have anything touched, looking "long and long" at miniatures of her and of Martha. No one was allowed to remove his mother's grey dress hanging in the wardrobe. He was soon desperately lonely in Camden, missing his Washington friends and pleading for a visit from Pete. The bells and whistles and continual rumbling of the trains day and night from the Camden and Amboy Railroad depot tormented him with thoughts of Pete and the "R.R. men living near, around here," men like Pete and his friends, and with useless dreams of travel. Grateful though he was for his brother's kindness, he and George had little to say to each other. George was interested in pipes, he said, not poems. It was George who had said to him once, "Walt, hasn't the world made it plain to you that it'd rather not have your book? Why then don't you call the game off?" Walt had said nothing. George called him "stubborner than a load of bricks." "I said, 'I admit that—but what can I do? I can't surrender. I won't defend myself.' That made him, makes others, madder than if I told them to go to hell."

He allowed a glimpse of the "batter'd, wreck'd old man" he had become to surface in a poem he published in the year following his stroke and his mother's death. In "Prayer of Columbus" he tried to make "one effort more, my altar this bleak sand,"

> My terminus near,
> The clouds already closing in upon me,
> The voyage balk'd, the course disputed, lost. . . .
>
> Thrown on this savage shore, far, far from home,
> Pent by the sea and dark rebellious brows, twelve dreary months,
> Sore, stiff with many toils, sicken'd and nigh to death,
> I take my way along the island's edge,
> Venting a heavy heart. . . .
>
> I am too full of woe!
> Haply I may not live another day. . . .
>
> My hands, my limbs grow nerveless,
> My brain feels rack'd, bewilder'd,
> Let the old timbers part, I will not part,
> I will cling fast to Thee, O God, though the waves buffet me,
> Thee, Thee at least I know.

He confessed to Doyle that "I don't know a soul here—am entirely alone—sometimes sit alone and think for two hours at a stretch—

have not formed a single acquaintance here, in any ways intimate . . . my heart is blank and lonesome utterly."

Pete managed to visit him at least once in Camden, but his work as a brakeman on the Baltimore and Potomac Railroad made visits difficult. The two friends fell silent, the end of their old intimacy clearly in sight. A young replacement would find Walt as pressing in his attentions as he had once been with Pete.

A few months later Whitman was finally discharged from his government post. Stranded in Camden, he dreamed vainly of a "shanty" of his own somewhere, going so far as to pay $450 for a building plot in Royden Street. In February he was felled by another stroke, this time down his right side. Talking in his last years of his paralysis and the blood poisoning he said had led up to it, he seemed convinced that "the trouble at Washington was the culmination of an unusual sympathetic and emotional expenditure of vital energy . . . partly this and perhaps directly from the singular humor of a New York lad there in the hospitals who demanded to have me see him through his trouble—a whim frequently encountered in sick people. I attended to him—bound his wounds—did everything possible for him. He was an extreme case—an awful case—dangerous at any time as a charge. The effect on me was slow. . . ." Then in 1876, slowly recovering some mobility, he met Harry Stafford, a New Jersey farm boy who was working as an office boy at the Camden print shop where a new edition of *Leaves* was going through the press. Taking the emotionally uncertain boy under his wing, he tried to brace the lad up as well as himself, telling him "the real blessings of life are not the fictions generally supposed, but are real, and are mostly within reach of all—you chew on this." The advice came out of bitter years marked by depressions. At least twice he had given up hope of any recovery and burned masses of letters and manuscripts.

Harry took his distinguished old writer friend to meet his mother and father out at Laurel Springs, twelve miles from Camden. George Stafford was a tenant farmer. Here was a family setting which duplicated almost exactly Whitman's early days. Soon he was living as part of the household as a paying guest there, sometimes for weeks at a stretch, making his own laborious way to the marl pit or the little creek where he liked to sit alone. It was spring. Hope stirred in him as the cold earth of winter put out its own flags of hope.

He exercised his half-dead limbs with the aid of a sapling, wrestling it clumsily to the ground. He stretched out naked in the sun, combed and curried himself. He took mud baths. By autumn he had begun to make nature notes for a book which had started to form in his head. One evening as he came in for supper he told Susan and George Stafford that knowing them had done more for him than all the doctors. Out of his times at Timber Creek came his delightfully fresh and random book *Specimen Days*, "free gossip mostly." Other titles, considered and then discarded, were "Idle Days and Nights of a Half Paralytic," "Away from Books—Away from Art," and "Ducks and Drakes." Like the game of ducks and drakes he had played as a boy, he wanted his fragmentary prose to be "a rapid skimming over the pond-surface of my life, thoughts, experiences...an immensely negative book"—by which he meant negative in the Keatsian sense. Hobbling downhill to the creek, a notebook in his pocket, was like taking faltering steps back to health, deliciously entangled in sun and silence and a southwest breeze.

So hanging my clothes on a rail near by, keeping old broadbrim straw on head and easy shoes on feet, haven't I had a good time the last two hours! First with the stiff-elastic bristles rasping arms, breast, sides, till they turn'd scarlet—then partially bathing in the clear waters of a running brook—taking everything very leisurely, with many rests and pauses—stepping about barefooted every few minutes now and then in some neighboring black ooze, for unctuous mud-bath to my feet—a brief second and third rinsing in the crystal running waters—rubbing with the fragrant towel—slow negligent promenades on the turf up and down in the sun, varied with occasional rests, and further frictions of the bristle-brush—sometimes carrying my portable chair with me from place to place, as my range is quite extensive here, nearly a hundred rods, feeling quite secure from intrusion (and that indeed I am not at all nervous about, if it occasionally happens).

As I walked slowly over the grass, the sun shone out enough to show the shadow moving with me. Somehow I seem'd to get identity with each and every thing around me, in its condition. Nature was naked, and I was also.

Enjoying his best summer since boyhood, he must nevertheless have been preoccupied at times with the impending visit of Anne Gilchrist. She had arranged to rent a house in Philadelphia that autumn for herself and her three children. He had protested ineptly, "My dearest friend, I do not approve of your American trans-settlement. I see so many things here you have no idea of—the social, and almost every other kind of crudeness, meagerness, here (at least in appearance).... Don't do anything towards it nor resolve in it nor make any move at all in it without further advice from me. If I should get well enough to voyage, we will talk about it yet in London."

This was a woman hard to hoodwink, and she was determined: nothing was going to stop her now. When she was installed and he went over to see her at her hotel he took John Burroughs along, presumably for moral support, then was relieved to find he genuinely liked the woman and her family. He helped her locate a suitable house to rent. Mrs. Gilchrist was no fool: sizing up the situation she quickly came to terms with her painful disappointment. Generously she set aside a room in her house for Whitman to use whenever he felt inclined. He did stay there a few times, once at least for a whole week. What he liked best was to go over to Philadelphia on the ferry, catch a streetcar, and turn up under his own steam for tea. He sat in a large bamboo rocking chair and either talked or listened. He walked lame, dragging his left leg, leaning heavily on a stick. He looked nearer seventy than sixty. They heard him singing as he bathed or dressed, "for the exercise," he told them.

☙ As EARLY AS last spring he had done his best to get proper training for young Harry Stafford, writing to the Camden printers on the boy's behalf. He was a friend of the family, he explained. "I am anxious Harry should learn the *printer's trade thoroughly—I want him to learn to set type as fast as possible*—want you to give him a chance (less of the mere errands etc)—There is a good deal really in the boy, if he has a chance.... Don't say any thing about this note to him—or in fact to anyone—just tear it up, *and keep the matter to yourself private."*

His intervention was a waste of time. Harry was too restless to stick at anything for long. He worked as a telegraph operator for the railroad company; on the *West Jersey Press*; at the Exposition site in Philadelphia. Whitman provided references and pulled strings whenever he could. It must have been Whitman who got him an appointment as attendant at Dr. Bucke's asylum in London, Ontario. Harry gave that up when the "unearthly noises" of the inmates proved more than he could stand. His mother wrote apologetically to Whitman, "I hope Harry will be ever Greatfull to you fore all your kindness to him."

By then he was more a covert lover than a mentor to this barely literate youth who was liable to attacks of depression—"blue spells" he called them—and swung about in his moods, his own worst enemy. He must have been further confused to find himself in amorous relationship with this complex old man who could never declare unequivocally the truth of what he felt. It was his last serious "perturbation," and he knew only too well the dangers inherent in the situation. He advanced and retreated, cast about for a solution. At one point he seemed to be trying to defuse things, so as to escape Harry's growing possessiveness, by transferring his affection to a farmhand at Laurel Springs by the name of Edward Cattell. A disjointed notebook entry mentions

> the hour (night, June 19 '76, Ed and I) at the front gate by the road saw E.C.
> Sept meetings with Ed C by the pond moonlit nights
> Ed Cattell with me

A crisis blew up, perhaps after he had stirred up responses he could no longer handle, and he wrote in some urgency to Cattell when he was back at Camden:

> Do not call to see me any more at the Stafford family, and do not call there at all any more—Don't ask me why—I will explain to you when we meet. . . . There is nothing in it that I think I do wrong nor am ashamed of, but I wish it kept entirely between you and me—and—I shall feel very much hurt and displeased if you don't keep the whole thing and the present letter entirely to yourself. Mr. and Mrs. Stafford are very near and kind to me, and have been and are like brother and sister to me—and as to Harry, you know how much I love him. Ed, you too have my unalterable love. . . .

A pathetic note from Ed reproached the compromised old man gently. "It seems an age Since i last met With you down at the pond and a lovely time We had of it. . . . I love you walt and Know that my love is returned to."

In the midst of these complications Mrs. Gilchrist suddenly appeared at the Stafford farm on a surprise visit. According to Mrs.

Stafford, Whitman exploded like a volcano. He liked to keep his friends separate, and this was too much. Mrs. Stafford had only seen him so angry once before, when she barged in to clean his room and straighten the mess of his papers. She went on with what she was doing and after a few minutes he was singing to himself.

In Philadelphia in January 1877 he was invited to lecture on Tom Paine. Frank Harris, author of My Life and Loves, was there at Lincoln Hall and reported the event in his book. It was a bitter night, with near-zero temperatures and falling snow. About thirty people turned out in the driving wind to hear Whitman speak in the poorly heated and badly lit hall that would have held a thousand. The poet read slowly from a paper he afterward included in Specimen Days.

He took Harry with him on a few trips, to Esopus in the Catskills where John Burroughs was now living, and to his friends the Johnstons in New York. He informed the Johnstons in advance that he would bring his (adopted) son with him. Another letter told them, "My nephew and I when traveling always share the same room together and the same bed." This casual attempt to disarm his hosts is one more illustration of the innocence of the times. He was a bisexual parent to Harry, as he had been to Pete Doyle and so many others, buying clothes for them if they would let him, but he was also their buddy, tangling with them physically in playful roughhouses now and then—to the annoyance of Burroughs. Seeing Harry and Whitman acting "like two boys" irritated him and exasperated his wife. "Great tribulation in the kitchen in the morning," notes an entry in his journal. "Can't get them up to breakfast in time. Walt takes Harry with him as a kind of foil or refuge from intellectual bores." This was insightful but only part of the story.

It seems that Whitman liked to pledge his affection with the gift of a ring. He had done this naively when writing to Mrs. Gilchrist, enclosing what could have been his mother's wedding ring, "with my love." It may have signified no more than friendship to him, but Anne Gilchrist was bound to interpret it differently. So apparently did Harry when Whitman wanted him to accept a ring. In a notebook entry the ring goes to and fro—

talk with HS and gave him r September 26 '76—(took r back)
Nov 1—Talk with HS in front room (Camden)—gave him r again
Nov 25, 26, 27, 28—Down at White Horse—Memorable talk with HS—settles
the matter

There were jealous scenes, outbursts of temper, stormy accusations. Fearful of what he had aroused, he drew back. His letter from Mrs. Gilchrist's home on June 16 was still heavy with longing, but ahead of the lines lay the termination he had begun to make for: "Dear Harry, not a day or night passes but I think of you. . . . Dear son, how I wish you could come in now, even if but for an hour and take off your coat, and sit down on my lap. . . . I want to see the creek again—and I want to see you, my darling son, and I can't wait any longer—Your old Walt."

Harry would fly off the handle and there would be recriminations, perhaps tears. Then he would ask contritely to be forgiven. "You know how I left you at the station today. . . . I will try by the grace of God to do better. I cannot give you up, and it makes me feel so bad to think how we have spent the last day or two; and all for my temper. I will have to *control* it or it will send me to the states prison or some other bad place. Can't you take me back and me the same—Your lovin but bad tempered Harry."

It took much longer than Whitman would have wished before he was able to disengage himself, or at least shunt the relationship onto a safer track. On July 27, 1877, he wrote in his Commonplace book that he had said "goodbye." Back came a plaintive epistle from Harry the following day. "I heard you was going to Washington and stay and be gon fore some time, is it so? I thought it was strange in you, in not saying anything to me about it, I think of it all the time, I cannot get my mind on my work the best I can do. I should like to come up to Camden next week and stay all night with you if I could, but I suppose I can not do it."

The young man was doing his best after his own fashion to strengthen his masculinity and escape the torment of his ambivalence. Whitman, who had begun by sincerely wanting to help the perplexed Harry, was now no help at all. Harry told his old friend of success in a wrestle with a pal at work, and of mixing with "plenty of girls." His father fell ill and the poet went to Kirkwood to stay a while. The visit only threw Harry back into his turmoil of uncertainty about himself. He wrote on the day Whitman left, "I wish you would put the ring on my finger again, it seems to me ther is something that is wanting to compleet our friendship when I put it on there was but one thing to part it from me and that was death."

He could never quite figure out what Whitman wanted of him, whether the man was a father or mother, a steadfast pal, or a potential husband dreaming of marriage. In fact Whitman was all these and more, reinventing a social bond that Christianity had lost, dodging into and out of identities, forever concealed, always on the point of revealing himself. As for Harry, his flights of fantasy were not plays with illusion but unconscious reactions, throwing him about violently so that he was unable to settle anywhere or at anything for long. He was even haunted and unhappy now at home, where his friend's picture hung on the wall, and "if I go up in my room I always come down feeling worse than I do when I go up, for the first thing I see is your picture, and when I come down in the sitting room there hangs the same, and whenever I do anything, or say anything the picture seems to me is always looking at me."

Whitman at one point seemed to be trying to placate the young man by encouraging him to have a new suit Harry would enjoy wearing, and might even have footed the bill for the outfit himself. "I have been thinking of the suit of cloths which I am to have like yours," Harry wrote pathetically. "I have had myselfe all pictured out with a suit of gray, and a white slouch hat on about fifty times, since you spoke of it; the fellows will call me Walt then. I will have to do something great and good in honor of his name, What will it be?"

Years later they were still tenderly in touch, though by then the intensity of those Timber Creek days had given way to something saner and healthier. Whitman had succeeded in his aim of wrenching himself clear of the "many things, confidences, questions, candid says you would like to have with me, you have never yet broached—me the same," and in the process recovered his supportive paternal role. The days of "perturbation" were over: there would be no more of them now with anyone, ever. He wanted Harry to know how grateful he was for everything.

Dear Hank,

I realize plainly that *if I had not known you*—if it hadn't been for you and our friendship and my going down there summers to the creek with you—and living there with your folks, and the kindness of your mother, and cheering me up—*I believe I should not be a living man today*—I think and remember deeply these things and they comfort me—*and you, my darling boy, are the central figure of them all.*

Of the occasional ridiculous little storms and squalls of the past I have quite discarded them from my memory—and I hope you will too—the other recollections overtop them altogether, and occupy the only permanent place in my heart—as a manly loving friendship for you does also, and will while life lasts—

He would still have the occasional "blue letter" from Harry as he kept drifting from job to job and person to person, slowly drawing nearer to marriage and a settled life. The youngster wrote a jocular and teasing letter after hearing of Whitman's trip to Boston in 1881 to give his Lincoln lecture. "Here I have been waiting in this dry and dusty office for some account of you and your happy trip, and this is the way you serve me is it. Well I have a new *gal* and a mighty nice little thing she is too; just such a one as you would like, and I know if you were to see those pretty rosy lips you would be charmed beyond measure with them, yet you shan't see her now that you used me so. She is a wild rose, plucked from the busom of the forest, pure as a lily and gentle as the summer breez's."

Finally, in 1884, Harry took the plunge and married. Whether or not he found the stability he lacked is unclear. Whitman attended the civil ceremony to wish him well, kept in touch afterward, and visited the couple sporadically.

It was during his absorption in the Staffords that he had met the man who was to assume as much importance in his life as Burroughs and O'Connor. Dr. Richard Maurice Bucke had been reading *Leaves of Grass* for the past ten years. A Canadian, he was an alienist in charge of an insane asylum in London, Ontario. His history was an extraordinary one. Growing up in the backwoods of western Canada he had fought Indians in the United States, attempted a crossing of the Sierra Nevada Mountains in mid-winter, and had a foot amputated after frostbite, then paid his own way through medical school. He had a growing interest in mysticism and would presently fit Whitman into his book *Cosmic Consciousness* as a living example of his ideal being. It is ironic that Maurice Bucke was so impressed by the poet's apparent poise and self-control at a time when Whitman was in the act of reliving through Harry his own troubled young manhood and striving to contain the last of his "Calamus" friendships.

The euphoria Maurice Bucke felt after meeting Whitman for the first time convinced him later that he had had a conversion. From this moment on he was a disciple, the Paul to Whitman's Jesus. He venerated Whitman as avatar rather than as poet. The biography he wrote and published in 1883 was in close collaboration with its subject, so much so that we are never sure whether we are reading Bucke's words or those of the poet. In his book he described Whitman during a visit to him, sitting in his library with a dozen books open before him, his magpie nature pecking here and there. Zweig calls him "not so much a reader as a gleaner."

A passage in Maurice Bucke's biography is a perfect example of the actual life shading into legend:

> Walt Whitman's early years provided the most comprehensive equipment ever attained by a human being, though many things that the schools prescribe were left out. It consisted in absorbing into himself the whole city and country about him, New York and Brooklyn, and their adjacencies; not only their outside shows, but far more their interior heart and meaning.... Then he became thoroughly conversant with the shops, houses, sidewalks, ferries, factories, taverns, gatherings, political meetings, carousings, etc. He was first the absorber of the sunlight, the free air and the open streets, and then of interiors. He knew the hospitals, poorhouses, prisons and their inmates. He passed freely in and about those parts of the city which are inhabited by the worst characters; he knew all their people, and many of them knew him; he learned to tolerate their squalor, vice and ignorance; he saw the good ... and the bad that was in them, and what there was to excuse and justify their lives. It is said that these people, even the worst of them, while entire strangers to Walt Whitman, quite favorably received him without discourtesy and treated him well.... He knew and was sociable with the man that sold peanuts at the corner, and the old woman that dispensed coffee in the market.

From the start Maurice Bucke was a staunch friend and supporter, one of the "hot little prophets" who would gather around him in Camden with pledges of allegiance. Bucke, in due course the recipient of Whitman's running commentary on his ailments, wanted a live saint who would embody his idea of the Cosmic Sense, and in his book *Cosmic Consciousness*, Whitman is it. It was important to have a figure who stepped fully armed straight out of nature, unconscious of his powers—the very picture Whitman sought at times to project for himself. Burroughs hung back, too astute to be taken in, but Bucke eagerly amplified the legend: "Walt Whitman is the best, most perfect example the world has so far had of the

Cosmic Sense, first because he is the man in whom the new faculty has been, probably, most perfectly developed, and especially because he is... the man who in modern times has written distinctly and at large from the point of view of Cosmic Consciousness.... And it is interesting to remark here that Whitman seems to have had as little idea as had Gautama, Paul or Mohammed what it was that gave him the mental power, the moral elevation and the perennial joyousness which are among the characteristics of the state to which he attained and which seem to him subjects of continual wonder. 'Wandering amazed,' he says, 'at my own lightness and glee.'"

This was a far cry from his state of mind shortly before the Canadian's first meeting with him. We have seen how he had always struggled urgently to construct for himself a complete, well-adjusted persona, radiating well-being. Instead he was sick and lonely, racked by a desire for the unattainable, wanting things better and bitterly dissatisfied with the world as it was. Just before meeting Harry Stafford he had written to Pete Doyle, "I get desperate at staying in—not a human soul for cheer, sociability or fun." Spring broke, but not in him. "Pete, the spring finds me pretty much in the same tedious and half way condition I have been."

It was in this bleak spring that he had the idea of a new edition of his work to coincide with the opening of the Centennial Exposition in Philadelphia. All his new work, together with prose such as "Memoranda During the War" and *Democratic Vistas*, would be shoveled into a second volume set up by the New Republic Print Shop in Camden and entitled *Two Rivulets*. The title was meant to emphasize the duality of the contents; not only prose and poetry combined, flowing together as one, but the real and the ideal, night and day, body and spirit, time's ebb and flow, the current of love in men and women. He was hopeful that the Exposition Committee, hearing of his two-volume Centennial edition, would invite him to write and read the official poem for the opening ceremony. The invitation went instead to Bayard Taylor, an ex-friend who had betrayed Whitman more than once with his satirical pieces at Whitman's expense. To add insult to injury, magazines were now regularly rejecting his poems.

He had had enough. The *West Jersey Press* of Camden printed an article on "Walt Whitman's Actual American Position" that he had doubtless written himself, containing biographical details no one else could have known. The poet was now "pretty well at the end of his rope," the piece said. "The real truth is that with the exception of a very few readers (women equally with men), Whitman's poems in their public reception have fallen stillborn in this country. They have been met, and are met today, with the determined denial, disgust and scorn of orthodox American authors, publishers and editors, and, in a pecuniary and worldly sense, have certainly wrecked the life of their author."

He had exaggerated his plight, but it was dire enough. He clipped out the article and mailed it to Rossetti in England, adding the rider, "the plain truth of the situation is here best stated; it is even worse than described in the article."

Rossetti wasted no time. The article was reprinted in the London *Atheneum* on March 11, and two days later Robert Buchanan waded in with a slashing attack on the United States for its shameful neglect of her greatest poet. Politics took over. The British press liked nothing better than a chance to lambast America. Bayard Taylor responded in the *New York Tribune* with a virulent personal attack on Whitman. But the poet was now, if only briefly, a cause célèbre in England. Subscribers began queuing up for his Centennial edition, selling at ten dollars a set. Many paid over the price. On the list were such names as Tennyson, the Rossettis, Edmund Gosse, George Saintsbury, Lord Houghton, and Ford Madox Brown, and the list kept growing. These "deep medicines from the British Isles" were a shot in the arm for Whitman. Even his health improved. He went off gladly to the Stafford farm to see if he could gain extra benefit from this sudden boost to his morale.

❦ HE MADE SLOW but steady progress toward a recovery, but suffered setbacks. He was now permanently lame. He spoke grimly to Anne Gilchrist of his "wounded brain" and his altered inner state. A boon to him in his isolation was the friendship he struck up with Charles Godfrey Leland, author of a book on gypsies and translator of Heine. Walt escaped the constrictions of his brother's household by means of little rambles around the waterfront bars of Market Street in Philadelphia. One port of call was the fruit stall at the end of Market Street, where he sat in a big chair provided by the Italian who kept the stall, chewing peanuts and chatting with the horsecar drivers. Leland met him by chance when he was on one of these little excursions. "He took me into a very common little bar-room where there was a table, and introduced me to several rather shabby common-looking men—not workmen, but looking like Bohemians and bummers. I drank ale and talked, and all easily and naturally enough—I had in my time been *bon compagnon* with Gypsies, tinkers and all kinds of loose fish, and thought nothing of it at all. But when we came forth Whitman complimented me very earnestly on having been so companionable. . . . I had evidently risen greatly in his opinion."

Longfellow crossed the Delaware to visit Whitman in the summer of 1879. With him was George W. Childs, a prominent Philadelphian. Whitman wasn't at home, so the visit must have been unannounced. They returned to the ferry. One of the ferry hands at the dock said they would find Whitman on one of the boats, riding to and fro. When the two men met, nothing memorable was said, and by then Longfellow was out of time. All the same, Whitman was flattered by the visit.

That autumn the chance came up to make the trip of his life, one he had made only on the imaginary journeys of *Leaves of Grass*. Colonel John Forney, publisher of the *Philadelphia Press*, was instrumental in getting him invited as guest of honor and visiting poet at the Kansas Quarter Centennial Celebration. This was small beer compared to the Exposition, but all the same a great opportunity to see the West and at the same time visit Jeff and his family in St. Louis. The party he joined pulled out of West Philadelphia at night, and Whitman relished his first experience of a sleeping car. They were delayed on the journey out by a locomotive crash ahead of them. Because of this, his time with Jeff was cut to one night.

They crossed Missouri in daylight, changed trains at Kansas City, and rattled on to Lawrence, Kansas. En route again, Whitman gave interviews to local papers and provided anonymous ones concocted by himself. He was utterly charmed by Denver, but not by the women, who he thought "do *not* have, either in physique or the mentality appropriate to them, any high native originality of spirit or body. . . . They are 'intellectual' and fashionable, but dyspeptic-looking and generally doll-like; their ambition evidently is to copy their Eastern sisters."

Platte Canyon convinced him that he was gazing at "the law of my own poems." He changed to another railroad at Pueblo, Colorado, and traveled east. Traversing the limitless prairies he took in the thrilling and strange sights, the buffalo grass, cactus, the prairie dogs, herds of antelope and cattle, and the swarms of cowboys, "to me a strangely interesting class, bright-eyed as hawks, with their swarthy complexions and their broad-brimm'd hats."

Back again in St. Louis it was clear he had overtaxed himself. Colonel Forney and the rest of the party left him in the care of his brother. He stayed three months, partly to regain his strength but also because he was strapped. Jeff apparently failed to inquire if Whitman was in funds, and no doubt his brother was too proud to say. He was rescued from acute boredom by an anonymous Christmas present of a hundred dollars which John Burroughs sent on.

Six months later, his appetite for travel whetted by his four-thousand-mile trip, he accepted Maurice Bucke's long-standing invitation and traveled to London, Ontario. On the Sunday after his arrival he went to church on the asylum grounds and paid more attention to the inmates than to the sermon. "I can only say I took long and searching eye-sweeps as I sat there, and it . . . aroused unprecedented thoughts, problems unanswerable." But he was made of sterner stuff than Harry Stafford: the mentally handicapped population were not distressing—or not more so than his afflicted brother Eddy.

He fell ill in the raw January of 1881, his spirits low until an invitation came to deliver his Lincoln lecture in Boston. After he got back to Camden he wrote quite jauntily to John Burroughs, "If I had staid another week I should have been killed with kindness." Probably as a result of this visit he was contacted on his return by a bona fide Boston publisher—and a distinguished one. James Osgood wanted to publish *Leaves of Grass*. Whitman had been along this road before and responded coolly with his proposal for a new expanded edition, giving Osgood "fair warning on one point, the sexuality odes about which the original row was started and kept up so long are all retained and must go in the same as ever." He hadn't forgotten the wretched Thayer and Eldridge experience. The contract he managed to extract was an excellent one: the copyright to remain with him and the book to sell at two dollars, with twenty-five cents for him.

As before, he went up to Boston to supervise the printing and to read proof. He called on Emerson, who was descending into senility and only sat benignly in a corner. Whitman was happy to do the same. Next day he went to dinner with the Emersons, and Mrs. Emerson talked to him about Thoreau.

He might have known that the sex poems would be no more acceptable in Boston in the eighties than they were in 1860. In the reviews the book had a good press and was selling modestly when the district attorney of Boston moved against it on March 1, declaring *Leaves of Grass* obscene literature. Osgood and Company wanted Whitman to allow an edition "lacking the obnoxious features," but the list of changes demanded by the district attorney was more than the poet could take. He took the stand he had taken in 1860. He was owed four hundred dollars in royalties. Taking three hundred of these, Osgood returned the plates, calling at Camden in person with an agreement for Whitman to sign. In the ensuing rumpus the press as a whole came out in support of the poet. So did that old warrior O'Connor, who had been estranged from Whitman for some years after a bitter abolitionist argument. Now their quarrel was forgotten.

The news was not all bad. David McKay in Philadelphia took over *Leaves of Grass* and for a while benefited from the Boston publicity. Being banned in Boston seemed to have its compensations, and for a year the book sold better than it had ever done. Then it slumped again to the usual trickle, with Whitman parceling up and supplying the few orders personally.

Public taste had not changed, nor would it in Whitman's lifetime. A number of visitors to Camden in 1882 included Oscar Wilde, whose lecture tour in America was on the whole a success, though his reception in Philadelphia the day before had been distinctly frosty. Wilde came to pay his respects on his own initiative—he had been an admirer of *Leaves of Grass* since his youth. His mother, Lady Wilde, owned one of the early copies.

Wearing his brown velvet suit he arrived with J. M. Stoddart, the publisher. George's wife offered the two visitors elderberry wine. The two poets were at once delighted with each other. Naturally Whitman was heartened to hear Wilde say that "in England we think there are only two [American] poets—Walt Whitman and Emerson." Whitman made a milk punch for his guests, charmed and flattered by the man of whom "such mocking things are written. . . . He seems to me like a great big, splendid boy. . . . He is so frank, and outspoken, and manly." He was still enlivened by the visit a week later, writing to ask Harry Stafford, "Have you read about Oscar Wilde? He has been to see me and spent an afternoon—He is a fine large handsome youngster—had the *good sense* to take a great fancy to me!—I was invited to reception in Phila. am'g the big bugs and a grand dinner to him by Mr. and Mrs. Childs—but did not go to any—Awful cold here, this is now the third day. . . . (You say you know you are *a great fool*—don't you know every cute fellow secretly knows that about himself—I do)—God bless you my darling boy—Keep a brave heart—"

Longfellow died, and he wrote a memorial tribute to him in the *New York Critic*, drawing attention to the poet's gentleness as the "counteractant most needed for our materialistic, self-assertive, money-worshiping Anglo-Saxon races, and especially for the present age in America. . . ."

🌸 SINCE THE WAR he had shifted to a darker view of American society, indicting it as "canker'd, crude, superstitious and rotten" in his *Democratic Vistas*, his counterblast to Carlyle's attack on democracy ("the Gathering of Men in Swarms" in *Shooting Niagara*). Masked himself—he had a range of disguises—Whitman tore the mask from his nation to reveal the hollowness of heart beneath:

> The spectacle is appalling. We live in an atmosphere of hypocrisy throughout. . . . The depravity of the business classes of our country is not less than has been supposed, but infinitely greater. The official services are . . . saturated in corruption, bribery, falsehood, maladministration, and the judiciary is tainted. . . . The best class we show is but a mob of fashionably dress'd speculators and vulgarians. . . . It is as if we were somehow being endowed with a vast and more and more thoroughly appointed body, and then left with little or no soul.

For all that, he stayed basically and instinctively optimistic about his country in the long term. America, that extraordinary drama, still thrilled him. His fellow Americans were he thought still in the melting pot, a potent stew of half-assimilated nationalities. America had still to achieve a national identity. And so with individuals. To cite Patrick White in his reflections on Australia, "Most of us . . . are still too uncertain *in ourselves*. . . . It is a question of spiritual values and must come from within before it can convince others."

He now saw the nation as blundering but hopeful, its original principles far from realized. Pasternak would look on the New Testament as a gospel which had yet to be tried, and in the same spirit Whitman regarded the word democracy as "a word the real gist of which still sleeps. It is a great word, whose history, I suppose, remains unwritten, because that history has yet to be enacted." *Leaves of Grass* was a language experiment, he insisted, and indeed life itself could be seen as an experiment and "mortality but an exercise." He held firm to his Hegelian vision of democracy as a marriage between the individual and the "aggregate," a contest between paradoxical elements which carried nations forward in an evolving struggle toward an absolute that was "the last, best hope of earth."

It took him until the spring of 1884 to achieve a measure of independence. Life with his brother and sister-in-law he found intolerably dull, grateful though he was for his home comforts. Helped by loans and gifts from friends and donations from admirers in England, selling his books and packing them for dispatch himself as a subscription publisher, he scraped enough together to buy a place of his own in Mickle Street, a working-class district of Camden. The house was run-down, a frame building without a furnace, no more than a hundred yards from the railroad tracks and close to the ferry terminal and the Delaware River. If the wind veered in his direction he was within range of the stinking breath of a fertilizer factory on the far shore.

By the time he was ready to move in under his own roof for the first time ever, with an elderly laborer and his wife for housekeepers—they left within a year, leaving him bereft of furniture—he had dragged his carcass stubbornly and bravely uphill to achieve a life of semi-invalidism which was at any rate endurable. He became acquainted with a kindly widow, Mary Davis, who mended his clothes and cooked him one meal a day. Used to caring for elderly people, she agreed to his proposal to be his housekeeper and moved her furniture into his bare rooms.

Shuffling around in the ice and snow that winter he grew fond of a young railroad worker, Tom Osler. Alas, the youngster was killed soon afterward in a rail accident. Another port of call was at the home of Colonel Johnston, "a great talker, an artist." On most Sunday evenings he took tea with him and his wife, daughter, and son. In his own neighborhood and over in Philadelphia he was helped on and off cars and ferries by the car conductors and drivers, postmen, and ferry men he had come to know.

Until he was stranded in wheelchairs and beached in his bed he hobbled down to the Camden ferry on sticks and enjoyed the Delaware in all weathers—the gulls, the black ocean steamers with their arrogant hulls. He loved his communion with the moving waters, the air, the sky and stars "that speak no word, nothing to the intellect, yet so eloquent. . . . And the ferry men—little they know how much they have been to me, day and night—how many spells of listlessness, ennui, debility they and their hardy ways have dispell'd." He was on name terms with most of them, with Eugene Crosby who helped him aboard "with his strong young arm" hooked around him, with the captains Hand, Walton, and Giberson in the daytime and Captain Olive at night. On spring nights, crossing over from Philadelphia after a visit, he liked to watch the fishermen's little buoy lights—"so pretty, so dreamy—like corpse candles—undulating delicate and lonesome on the surface of the shadowy waters, floating with the current."

One caller at Mickle Street, the homosexual English poet and philosopher Edward Carpenter, was the most acute observer of Whitman in these last years, and indeed of any time. An admirer who wrote his own watered-down Whitmanesque poetry, he was aware from the first of the poet's paradoxical character. He came several times, impressed and alerted each time by Whitman's "infinite tenderness, wistful love, and studied tolerance . . . and a certain artfulness, combined with keen, penetrating and determined candor; the wild-hawk look still there . . . yet with wonderful tenderness at bottom." On a June morning, the day of his final visit, Carpenter found Whitman in a confessional and trusting mood and was given a treat:

> What lies behind *Leaves of Grass* is something that few, very few, only one here and there, perhaps oftenest women, are at all in a position to seize. It lies behind almost every line; but concealed, studiedly concealed; some passages left purposely obscure. There is something in my nature *furtive* like an old hen! . . . I think there are truths which it is necessary to envelop or wrap up.

Reflecting later, Carpenter thought that Whitman had "a great tragic element in his nature" which prevented him ever being "happy in love affairs." He went on, "He celebrates in his poems the fluid, all-solvent disposition, but often was himself less the river than the rock."

Not long before moving into his Mickle Street house he had his last jaunt by the sea. John Burroughs had been in England, meeting most of the writers there who were friendly to Whitman. He joined up with his old friend at a hotel in Ocean Grove, New Jersey, about sixty miles from Camden. For the poet it was like breaking out of prison. Burroughs wrote in his diary: "Long autumn days by the sea with Whitman. Much and copious talk. His presence loosens my tongue. . . . I feel as if under the effects of some rare tonic or cordial all the time. There is something grainy and saline in him, as in the voice of the sea. . . . I leave him and make long loops off down the coast, or back inland, while he moves slowly along the beach, or sits, often with bare head, in some nook sheltered from the wind and sun. . . .'

Burroughs went off to New York and Whitman enjoyed having "the whole performance to myself. . . . Ever that ceaseless sulking gutteral of the sea—ever those muffled distant lion roars. . . . Some vast soul like a planet stopt, arresting, tied. . . ." Before his friend rejoined him he was at work listing adverbs and adjectives suggested by the sounds and sights and smells of the beach. When he left he took away with him his notes for a poem, "With Husky-Haughty Lips, O Sea!," at its core a heart vast as a planet's, and a voice "in huge monotonous rage, of freedom-lover pent."

He ended his days more buoyant and resilient than anyone could have foreseen. Friends hired a nurse as he slowly weakened. Warren Fritzinger, "my sailor-boy nurse," who had run off to sea at fourteen, happened to be the son of a sea captain Mary Davis had taken care of in his last days.

When the old man was totally disabled, an anonymous benefactor presented him with a buggy and safe horse, a sorrel pony by the name of Frank. The gift brought tears to his eyes. In a letter to the Staffords he admitted that he got out most days and had fun but "it is a dwindling business." Winters were hard to bear. "Cold, cold, and snow everywhere outside—bad luck all around—the fire goes out, the clock stops and the water-pipe bursts in the bathroom. But the sun shines, the bird sings away, and Mrs. Davis is in jovial humor. . . ." When his housekeeper moved in she had brought a menagerie with her: a dog, a cat, four birds, and several hens. She bedded the cat down in the shed built onto the kitchen, housed her hens in an outhouse, and allowed the dog to sleep in the parlor.

EDMUND GOSSE, touring the States, came to call. The English poet and critic thought Camden one of the grimiest industrial towns he had ever seen. The melancholy-looking woman who opened the door led him to the stairs, where Whitman was waiting to hoist himself clumsily ahead to his largish room. Gosse took in the small bedstead on the scrubbed planks, a round stove with a stackpipe, and the sort of shoddy wallpaper seen in laborers' cottages in England. Over the whole floor lay the famous Sargasso Sea of paper that every visitor stared at aghast, "swept up here and there into stacks and peaks." Whitman sank into his rocker hung with a wolfskin, the only chair: his guest had to make do with an upturned box. There the poet sat in some splendor in his grey suit and wide-open white collar, his large body scented with soap and *eau de cologne*, hair and beard flowing voluminously, the whole man looking "clean in the highest degree, raised to the nth power of stainlessness, positively blanched with spotlessness like a deal table that has grown old under the scrubbing brush." Before long the conversation sank like the fire in the stove which the poet kept replenishing and "irrigating" from time to time. Sitting there so monumentally he put Gosse in mind of "a great old Angora Tom."

Horace Traubel, a young bank clerk who had known Walt since childhood, running errands and delivering messages for him, undertook the task of recording Whitman's conversations in shorthand. Traubel's socialism sometimes exasperated the poet, though he got on better with the young man's agnosticism. Of the huge quantity of material harvested by this Boswell in the course of eighteen months—a million words published and another million yet to come—much of it is repetitious and banal, the directionless blathering of a trapped man obliged to say something for the reporter's notebook. But the living, breathing, and groaning old man rears up and startles now and then, as live and honest as Whitman would have wished. Like Goethe with Eckerman, you can see him saying things deliberately to shock. It was one way of easing the boredom.

One wonders what Horace said in private about the homespun philosophizing, reminiscence, blurred portraiture, and gossip, the odd blurts of shame and hints of dark secrets, every scrap of which he carted faithfully back home each night and transcribed. Down it all went regardless. He learned to wait for and expect key words to crop up repeatedly—one was "grip." He admired Whitman's grip on his hope. If there was a sin, it was despair, the poet told his questioner. He saw the country drifting, in danger, but still with its youthful quality intact. The intangible dreams of the people would only be realized, he thought, when the New World and the Old were joined in one global embrace. Meanwhile, the world had to be accepted in its reality.

Traubel became accustomed to the artful old devil's evasiveness when backed into a corner, hearing him say one day in self-mockery—or it may have been boastfulness—that he was like a lawyer, always fencing for time. It was the Dutch strain in him, which took naturally to plodding. He arrived eventually, though, after a tussle—and that was the story of his book. "William [O'Connor] used to worry his fur off trying to stir me up." If Traubel ventured to launch into theorizing he would be halted by a growl of impatience and a hand flagging him down. "Tell me things—don't tell me theories. I have theories of my own. Perfumes—rose odors, the flavor of the strawberry—they are a great comfort—they give me dream-hours as I sit here alone."

Traubel mentioned having read somewhere of Huxley saying he didn't hold with evolution as a dogma but as a working hypothesis. Whitman clapped his hands: what a beautiful confession! "Why can't the churches say the same?" He held on to his belief that the universe had its own ends to subserve and the wise thing was to go along with it. O'Connor—and there were others—had got it wrong when they called him a miracle-worker in the hospitals. He had simply found fulfillment there more than anywhere else, "doing miracles for myself."

He sank and rose like a candle flame. On good days he could even joke about his slipping hold on life. "As Miss Nipper says in Dombey and Son, I don't know whether I'm a temporary or a permanency: I don't know whether I'm to stay or move on."

"Hold your horses" was a favorite expression. Traubel understood the old man's optimism to be in some sense a bulwark against something unsupportable waiting in the wings. Peace in spite of fate, Whitman called it, "the feeling that whatever comes is just the thing that ought to come—ought to be welcomed." He lay for hours in a grey stupor and lost track of time, lifting a hand that was too heavy for him. His mind sought ways of escape from this room where he existed "like a rat in a cage day in and day out." He strained to hear the canary singing, the trains puffing and rattling, kids in the neighborhood playing out of doors. He tried to remain present for visitors, languidly drifting off. Giving way to self-pity, relishing the truth if nothing else, he described his wrecked body as a boat tied to the wharf, rotting in the sun. Or as lingering like a dead withered tree ("why cumbereth it on the ground?"). Most touchingly, as an outdoors body serving an indoor sentence. "A little breeze blows into the room and carries me away God knows where."

Horace came in most evenings and became an indispensable caller for the sick poet who knew he would never walk down his beloved open road again. "I'm a prisoner," he said once, managing a smile, "but you are not my jailor. You are in fact my deliverer." After a day or two of no callers except for Traubel he inquired about a deckhand at the ferry who had an ill wife. He gave Horace a quarter to give to Ben Hichens, a newsboy who stood around the ferry quay on the Philadelphia side.

The paradox he presented to his readers and visitors, a celebrity who maintained he was a nobody, he kept up to the end. "The typesetter who sets my book is just as important to cultural life as I am," said B. Traven. It could have been Whitman speaking. The enthusiasm of the self-taught never failed him. Nor did his voraciously assimilative nature. The secret of his great charm lay in a quality of voice, said one admirer. If there was a distinctive Brooklyn accent in his day, it is hard to imagine him refining it. As a poet in the full flood of his powers, during that creative outburst which began in 1854 and was ending only five years later, he had a huge appetite for description. His instinct—one hesitates to call it a strategy—was to move in and occupy an episode, take it over and expand it from the inside, assaulting the reader with its nearness. His ambition was to make himself redundant as an author, to be a leader, a changer of blood, while the gnawing hunger within him clamored to have the world love him. The shy buttonholer, he was always about to depart, delayed only by the suspicion that his manliness had somehow, at the last moment, betrayed him, that his universality was not what it seemed.

One day he told Traubel of a tramp who had been in to see him that morning. The man fancied himself as a poet and read out some of his verse. "Lord pass him, what stuff!" But it was his own work, written on the road. It made Whitman feel bad to think that the fellow could go along in the sun and rain and write while he was housed up in the dust of a dead room "eking out my substance in coalstove words." Next day he confessed he had been sorely jealous of the tramp, so disappointed in fact that he had wanted to cry. "I suppose he's bummin' along somewhere on the road eatin' apples and feelin' drowsy and doin' as he pleases—and here I am in this room growlin' with a bellyache." But it was not all loss and chagrin. "He shook some of his dust off on me."

His mother hadn't seen *Leaves of Grass* as anything wonderful, he confided—how could she? She would shake her head in puzzlement. "God bless her!—But she would put her hand in mine—press my hand—look at me: all as if to say it was all right though beyond her powers to explain."

Sometimes he would be struck by a kind of aphasia, searching for a word and falling silent. One night, holding a cup of water, he went down—caught his foot in a shawl and just bowled over. The worst thing, he said later, was spilling water on a volume of Emerson, "the handsome Emerson." He poked among his sea of papers with his cane and forgot what he was looking for. He opened and closed a pocketknife compulsively as he sat listening to someone. So many of his visitors were literary—when they were not photographers, painters, or sculptors wanting to do portraits—that he got sick of words and longed to repudiate them. "I believe if I met a man who had not written a book I should hug him. . . . Everybody is writing, writing, writing—worst of all, writing poetry. It'd be better if the whole tribe of scribblers—every damn one of us—were sent off somewhere with toolchests to do some honest work."

The joke was on him, as he well knew. He had achieved by sheer will, says Leslie Fiedler, the mask he had dreamed. With Horace Traubel at his elbow he managed to get out a pocket-sized edition of *Leaves*, leather bound, with thin paper, and then a large one-volume edition of his poetry and prose. In 1891 he had composed his swan song, a farewell to the persona he had loved and cherished ever since 1855 and now, playfully and tenderly, had to leave. Or had his phantom self so blended with him that they were now inseparable, even at the point of death? Was it in fact the specter, his own creation as he had thought, that was now shunting him over the threshold for the longest journey, the greatest adventure? His wry humor had not deserted him as he bid

Goodbye, my Fancy!
Farewell, dear mate, dear love!
I'm going away, I know not where,
Or to what fortune, or whether I may ever see you again,
So Goodbye my Fancy.

Now for the last—let me look back a moment;
The slower fainter ticking of the clock is in me,
Exit, nightfall, and soon the heart-thud stopping.

Long have we lived, joy'd, caress'd together;
Delightful!—now separation—Goodbye my Fancy.

You let me not be too hasty,
Long indeed have we lived, slept, filter'd, become really blended
    into one;
Then if we die we die together, (Yes, we'll remain one),
If we go anywhere we'll go together to meet what happens,
May-be it is yourself now really ushering me to the true songs (who
    knows?),
May-be it is you the mortal knob really undoing, turning—so now
    finally,
Goodbye—and hail! my Fancy.

He drew up a will asking for the remains of his mother and father to be buried with him in a small mausoleum he had ordered at Harleigh Cemetery, built to a simple design derived from William Blake. His friend Tom Harned footed the bill.

He left most of his savings and property to Eddy, now fostered out in the country near Camden. Conscious to the end he died on the evening of Saturday, March 26, 1892. Outside a soft rain was falling. Horace Traubel held his right hand. The long drought was over.

# Chronology

| | |
|---|---|
| 1819 | Born May 31 in West Hills, near Huntington, Long Island. |
| 1823 | Whitman family moves to Brooklyn. |
| 1830–1834 | Apprentice printer. |
| 1835 | Printer in New York City until great fire of August 12. |
| 1836–1838 | Pupil-teacher at East Norwich, Long Island. Then teaches at Hempstead, Babylon, Long Swamp, and Smithtown. |
| 1838–1839 | Edits the *Long Islander* at Huntington. Works on *Long Island Democrat*. Teaches at Little Bay Side, near Jamaica. |
| 1840–1841 | Autumn 1840, campaigns for Van Buren. Teaches at Trimming Square, Woodbury, Dix Hills, and Whitestone. |
| 1841 | Begins working as a printer in May in *New World* office. Contributes to *Democratic Review*. |
| 1842 | Edits first New York paper, the *Aurora*, a daily. For a brief period edits *Evening Tattler*. |
| 1845–1846 | Returns to Brooklyn in August. Writes for *Long Island Star* for six months. |
| 1846–1848 | Editor of *Brooklyn Daily Eagle* for nearly two years. Goes south in February 1848 to work on *New Or-* |

|  | *leans Crescent.* Returns via Mississippi and Great Lakes with brother Jeff. |
|---|---|
| 1848–1849 | From September edits "Free Soil" newspaper, the *Brooklyn Freeman.* |
| 1850–1854 | Runs own printing office and stationery store. Freelance writer and real estate speculator. |
| 1855 | *Leaves of Grass* printed by Rome Brothers in Brooklyn and published in July. Father dies July 11. |
| 1856 | Publishes second edition of *Leaves of Grass.* Writes "The Eighteenth Presidency" and contributes to *Life Illustrated.* |
| 1857–1859 | Editor of *Brooklyn Times* for two years. Out of work during winter of 1859–1860. Bohemian phase; frequents Pfaff's restaurant. |
| 1860 | Thayer and Eldridge bring out third edition of *Leaves* in Boston. |
| 1861 | April 12, Fort Sumter attacked by Confederate batteries and Civil War begins. |
| 1862 | Travels to Fredericksburg, Virginia, to search for missing brother George. Stays on in Washington, obtains part-time clerical work in paymaster's office. Hospital visiting begins. |
| 1863–1864 | Continues hospital visits until June 1864, then returns to Brooklyn because of illness. |
| 1865 | January 24, appointed clerk in Department of Interior. Meets Pete Doyle. After witnessing second inauguration of Lincoln, goes home to visit family; Lincoln assassinated April 14. George released from prison in May. Whitman discharged from position in Department of Interior on June 30 and reinstated next day in attorney general's office. In September brings out *Drum-Taps and Sequel,* which contains "When Lilacs Last in the Dooryard Bloom'd." |
| 1866 | William O'Connor's *Good Gray Poet* is published. |
| 1867 | John Burroughs writes first biography of Whitman. In England William Rossetti publishes first article on Whitman's poetry in *London Chronicle.* Fourth edition of *Leaves of Grass* issued. |
| 1868 | William Rossetti's expurgated *Poems of Walt Whitman* is published in London. Second issue of fourth edition contains *Drum-Taps and Sequel.* |

| | |
|---|---|
| 1870 | Whitman suffers depression. Prints *Democratic Vistas*. |
| 1871 | Prints fifth edition of *Leaves of Grass* and receives Anne Gilchrist's first love letter. |
| 1872 | Reads "As a Strong Bird on Pinions Free" at Dartmouth College, June 26. Breaks with O'Connor. Swinburne withdraws support. |
| 1873 | Felled by first paralytic stroke on January 23. Mother dies May 23 at Camden. Whitman permanently disabled, lives with brother George at Camden, New Jersey. |
| 1874 | Sees publication of "Prayer of Columbus" and "Song of the Redwood-Tree." |
| 1875 | Prepares Centennial edition of *Leaves of Grass* and *Two Rivulets*. |
| 1876 | British press accuses America of neglecting Whitman. Recuperates at Stafford Farm. Mrs. Gilchrist arrives in Philadelphia with family. Involvement with Harry Stafford begins. |
| 1879 | Gives first Lincoln lecture in Philadelphia, April 14. Makes Colorado trip and has long visit with brother Jeff in St. Louis. |
| 1880 | Visits Dr. Maurice Bucke at his asylum in London, Ontario. |
| 1881 | After Lincoln lecture in Boston, James Osgood publishes Boston *Leaves of Grass*. |
| 1882 | Action by district attorney forces Osgood to abandon distribution of *Leaves*. Whitman refuses to expurgate. David McKay takes on edition and *Specimen Days* and issues in Philadelphia. |
| 1883 | Dr. Bucke publishes his biography of Whitman in collaboration with the poet. |
| 1884 | Whitman buys a house on Mickle Street in Camden; he is independent at last. |
| 1885 | Anne Gilchrist dies, November 29. |
| 1887 | Portraits and sculptures by Sidney Morse, Herbert Gilchrist, J. W. Alexander, and Thomas Eakins. |
| 1888 | Friends and admirers start fund to pay for medical care. *November Boughs* is published. |
| 1889 | A last birthday dinner. |
| 1890 | Feels compromised by letter from John Addington |

Symonds and counters by claiming six illegitimate children.

1891     Publishes *Goodbye My Fancy.*

1892     Ninth edition of *Leaves of Grass.* Dies March 26 and is buried in Harleigh Cemetery, Camden.

# Notes on Sources

IN THE NOTES that follow, these frequently used sources are cited in abbreviated fashion:

Thomas L. Brasher, ed., *The Collected Writings of Walt Whitman*, New York, 1963. Cited as *Collected Writings*.

Richard M. Bucke, Thomas B. Harned, and Horace L. Traubel, eds., *The Complete Writings of Walt Whitman*, New York and London, 1902. Cited as *Complete Writings*.

Emory Holloway, ed., *Uncollected Poetry and Prose of Walt Whitman*, New York, 1932. Cited as *Uncollected P&P*.

Edwin H. Miller, ed., *The Correspondence*, 6 vols., New York, 1961–1977. Cited as *Correspondence*.

Horace Traubel, *With Walt Whitman in Camden*. Vol. I, Boston, 1906, Vol. II, 1908; Vol. III, 1914; Vol. IV, Philadelphia, 1953; Vol. V, Carbondale, Ill., 1964. Cited as *With WW*.

Walt Whitman, *Leaves of Grass*. Cited as *Leaves*.

Walt Whitman, *Specimen Days*. Cited as *Specimen Days*.

FOREWORD

page xv: "My country is the world..." Thomas Paine, *The Rights of Man*.

page xvi: "his beard full of butterflies..." Federico Garcia Lorca, "Ode to Walt Whitman," *Poet in New York*, New York, 1955.

# NOTES ON SOURCES

CHAPTER 1. THE UNFINISHED COUNTRY

page 5: "the mechanic's wife with her babe..." *Leaves*, "Song of Myself."

pages 5–6: "was founded the most strange settlement..." G. M. Trevelyan, *History of England*, London and New York, 1926.

page 7: "And this need to move speedily..." See Daniel J. Boorstin, *The Americans: The National Experience*, New York, 1965.

page 8: "People were moving from east to west..." See Peter J. Parrish, *The American Civil War*, London, 1975.

pages 8–9: "I was born close to a saw-mill..." Boorstin, *The Americans*.

page 9: "...the New World newspaper served a very different purpose..." See Boorstin, *The Americans*.

page 11: "About the origin of Yankee..." See Boorstin, *The Americans*.

page 13: "The Crockett anecdotes plunged headlong..." Boorstin, *The Americans*.

page 14: "like a great ploughed and sown paddock..." Geoffrey Dutton, *Whitman*, Edinburgh and London, 1961.

CHAPTER 2. MOTHERS

page 15: "How can we forget Darwin?" Traubel, *With WW*.

page 16: "The reality, the simplicity..." Traubel, *With WW*.

page 18: "She spoke in the Tammany Hall..." Traubel, *With WW*.

page 19: "My good daddy used to say..." Traubel, *With WW*.

page 20: "I throw myself on your breast..." *Leaves*, "As I Ebb'd with the Ocean of Life."

page 23: "Epidemics spread rapidly." See Gay Wilson Allen, *The Solitary Singer: A Critical Biography of Walt Whitman*, New York, 1955 (revised 1967).

page 24: "We occupied them one after the other..." *Specimen Days*.

page 24: "so cutely...so shrewdly worded..." Traubel, *With WW*.

page 26: "the sailors marching two by two..." *Collected Writings*.

page 28: "Burr was gentle..." Traubel, *With WW*.

page 29: "He noticed particularly the care..." See *Specimen Days*.

page 30: "rather sedate, not fast..." *Collected Writings*.

page 30: "the pleasing mystery of the different letters..." *Collected Writings*.

page 31: "poverty, quite as strong a force..." *Collected Writings*.

page 32: "Just as Lafayette had done..." See Allen, *The Solitary Singer*.

page 33: "with quick and graceful leaps..." Allen, *The Solitary Singer*.

page 33: "to give America that young maturity..." *Specimen Days*.

page 34: "O what is it in me..." *Leaves*.

page 35: "These became part of that child..." *Leaves*.

page 36: "he felt as though the last float plank..." *Collected Writings*.

CHAPTER 3. PUPIL-TEACHER

page 39: "their sterling sense on most practical subjects..." *Uncollected P&P*.

page 39: "And so he did. And the weakness..." *Uncollected P&P*.

page 39: "Paul Zweig sees in the opening passages..." Paul Zweig, *Walt Whitman: The Making of the Poet*, New York, 1984.

page 41: "He was a muscular young man..." Willis Steell, "Walt Whitman's Early Life on Long Island," *Munsey's Magazine*, January 1909.

page 42: "The sheltering home, if its door..." See *Collected Writings*.

page 42: "unwashed, tangly-haired, rag-covered..." *Collected Writings*.

page 42: "He was like us—yet he was different..." *In Re Walt Whitman*, edited by his literary executors.

page 43: "Then there is George Washington..." See *Collected Writings*.

page 43: "youthful innocence..." *Collected Writings*.

page 44: "Very beautiful was he..." *Collected Writings*.

page 44: "in the predicament of earliest adolescence..." Edgar Z. Friedenberg, *The Vanishing Adolescent*, Boston, 1973.

page 45: "a woman of the noblest make-up..." Traubel, *With WW*.

page 46: "Not only does democracy..." Alexis de Tocqueville, *Democracy in America*, New York, 1945.

page 47: "The study of letters..." Mark Van Doren, ed., *The Portable Emerson*, New York, 1946.

page 47: "There may be reasons for hurrying..." Traubel, *With WW*.

CHAPTER 4. "THIS IS THE CITY"

page 48: "Everything seem'd turning out well..." *Collected Writings*.

page 49: "This breast which now..." Thomas L. Brasher, ed., *The Early Poems and Fiction of Walt Whitman*, New York, 1963.

page 50: "I always was deliberate..." Traubel, *With WW*.

page 51: "How do I love a loafer!" *Uncollected P&P*.

page 52: "Somewhere, back, back..." Traubel, *With WW*.

page 53: "He warn't in his element..." J. Johnston and J. W. Wallace, *Visits to Walt Whitman in 1890–91*, London, 1917.

page 54: "Who should be a better judge..." *Uncollected P&P*.

page 55: "A fellow boarder at 68 Duane..." See Justin Kaplan, *Walt Whitman: A Life*, New York, 1980.

page 57: "The nineteenth century transposed..." Zweig, *Walt Whitman*.

page 59: "judges not as the judge judges..." Walt Whitman, 1855 Preface to *Leaves of Grass*.

page 61: "stacks of furniture upon the sidewalks..." *Uncollected P&P*.

page 62: "one of the painful facts..." Traubel, *With WW*.

page 62: "Mr. Dickens never maligns the poor..." *Uncollected P&P*.

page 63: "possessing little tact..." *Uncollected P&P*.

page 65: "a tow-boat from Philadelphia..." Walt Whitman, *Broadway Journal*, May 31, 1845.

page 65: "The beards of the young men..." *Leaves*, "Song of Myself."

page 66: "A moment's pause..." See Joseph Jay Rubin and Charles H. Brown, eds., *Walt Whitman of the New York Aurora: Editor at Twenty-Two*, State College, Pa., 1950.

page 66: "Looking in at the shop windows..." *Leaves*, "Song of Myself."

page 68: "The prostitute draggles her shawl..." *Leaves*, "Song of Myself."

page 69: "every being with a rational soul..." Rubin and Brown, *Walt Whitman of the New York Aurora*.

page 69: "William Cauldwell, a junior printer..." William Cauldwell, "Walt Whitman as a Young Man," *New York Times*, January 26, 1901.

page 70: "trashy, scurrilous and obscene..." *Uncollected P&P*.

page 70: "so undistinguished from his colleagues..." Zweig, *Walt Whitman*.

page 71: "This is the city..." *Leaves*, "Song of Myself."

page 71: "Tomb Blossoms..." Brasher, *Early Poems and Fiction*.

page 72: "How could I answer the child?" *Leaves*, "Song of Myself."

page 73: "as simple as the falling of a leaf..." Vincent Van Gogh, Letter 411, *The Complete Letters*, London, 1978.

page 74: "with spades and pick axes..." Rubin and Brown, *Walt Whitman of the New York Aurora*.

page 76: "WW: Open it, Horace." Traubel, *With WW*.

page 77: "We consider temperance..." Walt Whitman, *Franklin Evans*, ed. by Emory Holloway, New York, 1929.

CHAPTER 5. REUNION IN BROOKLYN

page 78: "Common interests, and similar vocations..." Thomas Bender, *New York Intellect*, Baltimore, 1987.

page 80: "Where such a litterateur..." Bender, *New York Intellect*.

page 81: "Thomas Bender repeats the story..." See Bender, *New York Intellect*.

page 82: "An essay by a New York critic..." See Bender, *New York Intellect*.

page 83: "the voices of the native-born..." Zweig, *Walt Whitman*.

page 83: "Far away in the distant future..." Allen, *The Solitary Singer*.

page 84: "He is in the forest walks..." Robert E. Spiller and Wallace E. Williams, eds., *The Early Lectures of Ralph Waldo Emerson*, Cambridge, Mass., 1972.

page 85: "When he lifts his great voice..." Spiller and Williams, *Early Lectures of Ralph Waldo Emerson*.

page 86: "One of them featured Mose..." See Allen, *The Solitary Singer*.

page 89: "Why should I be afraid..." *Leaves*, "The Sleepers."

page 90: "The wretched features..." *Leaves*, "The Sleepers."

page 93: "dark, quiet, handsome..." Traubel, *With WW*.

page 94: "Our necessities have been mistaken..." See Julian Symons, *The Tell-tale Heart: The Life and Works of Edgar Allan Poe*, New York, 1978.

page 97: "As he grew a big boy..." *Complete Writings*.

page 98: "He seemed every inch a man..." Kaplan, *Walt Whitman*.

page 100: "made fresher, more natural..." Allen, *The Solitary Singer*.

page 100: "Continuing to hammer..." Allen, *The Solitary Singer*.

page 100: "the stale, second hand foreign method..." Thomas L. Brasher, ed., *Whitman as Editor of the Brooklyn Eagle*, Detroit, 1970.

page 101: "What costly and fashionable dresses!" Emory Holloway and Ralph Adimari, *New York Dissected*, New York, 1936.

page 103: "Some of the wisest and most celebrated..." Floyd Stovall, *The Foreground of "Leaves of Grass,"* Charlottesville, Va., 1974.

pages 103–104: "There is a curious kind of sympathy..." *Uncollected P&P*.

page 104: "alert well-dress'd full-blooded..." Zweig, *Walt Whitman*.

page 105: "Way back, in the Brooklyn days..." Traubel, *With WW*.

page 105: "When the last of the officers..." Cleveland Rodgers and John Black, eds., *The Gathering of the Forces*, New York and London, 1920.

page 106: "My mother and sister would say..." Traubel, *With WW*.

page 108: "Passersby would catch sight of him..." Allen, *The Solitary Singer*.

page 109: "perhaps a few slouches..." *Specimen Days*.

page 111: "It does not follow..." Bender, *New York Intellect*.

page 111: "What suits Great Britain..." Esther Shephard, *Walt Whitman's Pose*, New York, 1938.

page 112: "by all kinds of unnatural and violent..." Allen, *The Solitary Singer*.

page 114: "Though we never acted..." Rodgers and Black, *Gathering of the Forces*.

page 115: "As the water follows the moon..." *Leaves*.

page 115: "I can, from my good seat..." *Collected Writings*.

page 118: "If goodness, charity, faith and love..." Rodgers and Black, *Gathering of the Forces*.

page 118: "With music strong I come..." *Leaves*, "Song of Myself."

page 119: "Her voice is the purest soprano..." Rodgers and Black, *Gathering of the Forces*.

page 120: "The place of the orator..." Clifton J. Furness, ed., *Walt Whitman's Workshop*, Cambridge, Mass., 1928.

page 120: "what an indescribable volume of delight..." *Uncollected P&P*.

page 121: "My younger life was so saturated..." Traubel, *With WW*.

page 122: "The teeming lady comes..." *Leaves*, "Proud Music of the Storm."

page 122: "She was dressed in pink satin..." Kaplan, *Walt Whitman*.

page 124: "Go, blindworm, go..." Van Doren, *The Portable Emerson*.

page 125: "President Polk, baffled by the new issue..." See Stephen B. Oates, *With Malice Toward None: The Life of Abraham Lincoln*, New York, 1977.

page 126: "the half-insane mumblings of a fever-dream..." Oates, *With Malice Toward None*.

page 127: "What has miserable, inefficient Mexico..." Bernard de Voto, *The Year of Decision*, Boston, 1989.

page 129: "It is the fashion of a certain set..." Rodgers and Black, *Gathering of the Forces*.

page 129: "I don't need to find a place..." Traubel, *With WW*.

page 130: "I heard the voice arising..." *Leaves*, "By Blue Ontario's Shore."

page 132: "The great poet absorbs the identity..." Allen, *The Solitary Singer*.

page 134: "At this hour in some part of the earth..." Rodgers and Black, *Gathering of the Forces*.

page 134: "What a gain it would be..." *Uncollected P&P*.

page 136: "reform was a sham..." Traubel, *With WW*.

page 137: "Six considerable Paper-bags..." Thomas Carlyle, *Sartor Resartus*, London, 1908.

page 138: "Who among us has not dreamt..." Quoted in Walter Benjamin, *Charles Baudelaire*, London, 1977.

page 141: "Two conflicting agonistic elements..." *Specimen Days*.

page 141: "Charles Dana the editor..." Traubel, *With WW*.

page 143: "If there are to be States..." Rodgers and Black, *Gathering of the Forces*.

page 144: "with their curious female quality..." D. H. Lawrence, *Studies in Classic American Literature*, New York, 1977.

page 146: "The African race here..." Kaplan, *Walt Whitman*.

page 147: "The negro that drives the long dray..." *Leaves*, "Song of Myself."

page 148: "I think I could turn..." *Leaves*, "Song of Myself."

page 150: "The publisher, in the course..." Rodgers and Black, *Gathering of the Forces*.

page 150: "Mr. W. came here from the *Star* office..." Emory Holloway, "More Light on Whitman," *American Mercury*, February 1924.

CHAPTER 6. SOUTH

page 153: "ten or twelve great strapping drovers..." *Uncollected P&P*.

page 154: "a long, black, ugly roof..." Charles Dickens, *American Notes*, London, 1842.

page 155: "Mother you have no idea..." *Correspondence*, Vol. I.

pages 155–156: "The men get out of the boat first..." Dickens, *American Notes*.

page 156: "In poetry and romance..." *Uncollected P&P*.

page 157: "How solemn! sweeping this dense..." Brasher, *Early Poems and Fiction*.

pages 161–162: "I doubt if there is a city..." Frederick Law Olmsted, "Journey to the Seaboard Slave States," Olmsted Papers, Library of Congress, Washington, D.C.

page 162: "Rude and ignorant man..." Emory Holloway, *Whitman: An Interpretation in Narrative*, New York, 1926.

page 164: "The octoroon was not a whore..." Traubel, *With WW*.

page 168: "I remember it. Such a thing..." Traubel, *With WW*.

page 168: "Not enough to take away..." Traubel, *With WW*.

page 172: "But when the coldness above alluded to..." *Uncollected P&P*.

page 173: "They spent the next two days as tourists..." See Allen, *The Solitary Singer*.

page 174: "Be simple and clear..." *Uncollected P&P*.

page 177: "Hardly any one who takes the trouble..." Joseph Jay Rubin, *The Historic Whitman*, University Park, Pa., 1973.

page 179: "This is unfinished business with me..." *Leaves*, "Song of Myself."

page 179: "Doughfaces, Crawlers, Lice of Humanity..." Brasher, *Early Poems and Fiction*.

page 181: "Don't be so sure about that..." Traubel, *With WW*.

page 183: "The effusion or corporation of the soul..." *Uncollected P&P*.

page 183: "I accept Reality..." *Leaves*, "Song of Myself."

page 185: "Through me forbidden voices..." *Leaves*, "I Sing the Body Electric."

page 186: "I know what Holmes said..." Traubel, *With WW*.

page 187: "This is the lexicographer..." *Leaves*, "Song of Myself."

page 188: "The moth and the fish-eggs..." *Leaves*, "Song of Myself."

page 189: "This man has a grand physical construction..." Madeleine B. Stern, *Heads and Headlines: The Phrenological Fowlers*, Norman, Okla., 1971.

page 189: "The qualities of mind correspond..." Stern, *Heads and Headlines*.

page 190: "The expression of a well-made man..." *Leaves*, "I Sing the Body Electric."

page 191: "One of the real benefits..." Stern, *Heads and Headlines*.

page 193: "Of the terrible doubt of appearances..." *Leaves*, "Of the Terrible Doubt of Appearances."

page 194: "depressed mounds, crumbled and broken stones..." *Specimen Days*.

page 194: "I take the liberty of writing..." *Correspondence*, Vol. I.

## CHAPTER 7. LIFE AS AN ART

pages 196–197: "I would rather hear of natural blasts..." Charles M. Wiltse, ed., *The Papers of Daniel Webster*, Hanover, N.H., 1974–1989.

page 197: "Of olden times, when it came to pass..." Brasher, *Early Poems and Fiction*.

page 198: "some cute fellow who spoke of Jesus..." Traubel, *With WW*.

page 198: "In masses of men..." Traubel, *With WW*.

page 201: "I don't know where to look for a picture..." *Uncollected P&P*.

page 202: "With warm, impulsive souls..." *Uncollected P&P*.

page 204: "Talk not so much, then..." *Uncollected P&P*.

page 205: "Do you ask if he was shiftless?" *In Re Walt Whitman*.

page 206: "I have never been at Washington..." Richard H. Sewell, *John P. Hale and the Politics of Abolition*, Cambridge, Mass., 1965.

page 208: "Pasturelife, foddering, milking..." *Leaves*, "A Song for Occupations."

page 211: "limber-tongued lawyers, very fluent..." Furness, *Walt Whitman's Workshop*.

pages 214–215: "In the country parts were agriculture..." Holloway and Adimari, *New York Dissected*.

page 218: "He regarded me with great love..." Traubel, *With WW*.

page 220: "I will take each man and woman of you..." *Uncollected P&P*.

page 221: "Everything I have done seems to me..." *Uncollected P&P*.

page 221: "Bridal night..." Manuscript Division, Library of Congress, Washington, D.C.

page 222: "Make no quotations and no reference..." *Complete Prose Works* in *Collected Writings*.

page 222: "From the opening of the Oration..." Furness, *Walt Whitman's Workshop*.

page 223: "What is marvelous? What is unlikely?" *Complete Prose Works* in *Collected Writings*.

page 223: "Faith. Becalmed at sea..." Manuscript Division, Library of Congress, Washington, D.C.

page 224: "That I could forget the mockers..." *Leaves*, "Song of Myself."

page 225: "A trance, yet with all the senses alert..." Furness, *Walt Whitman's Workshop*.

page 225: "I dream in my dream..." *Leaves*, "The Sleepers."

## CHAPTER 8. BIRTH OF RAINBOW

page 226: "I saw the book..." *In Re Walt Whitman*.

page 228: "every now and then a woman shows..." Traubel, *With WW*.

page 229: "i sent for jeffy and sent for laura..." Allen, *The Solitary Singer*.

page 230: "that the corpse is slowly borne..." Whitman, 1855 Preface to *Leaves*.

page 230: "I greet you at the beginning of a great career..." *Correspondence*, Vol. I.

page 232: "I can hear his gentle knock still..." Traubel, *With WW*.

page 232: "one cannot leave it about..." Charles Eliot Norton, ed., *Letters of James Russell Lowell*, Boston, 1913.

page 233: "The known universe has one complete lover..." Whitman, 1855 Preface to *Leaves*.

page 233: "The great home of the Soul..." Zweig, *Walt Whitman*.

page 234: "he had barely saved it..." Henry B. Rankin, *Personal Recollections of Abraham Lincoln*, New York, 1916.

page 236: "Such human tenderness at times..." Traubel, *With WW*.

pages 237–238: "Everything in California seems..." Manuscript Division, Library of Congress, Washington, D.C.

page 238: "Poem of passage / the scenes on the river..." Harold W. Blodgett, *1855–56 Notebook Towards the Second Edition of Leaves of Grass*, Carbondale, Ill., 1959.

page 241: "Some don't like my commas..." Traubel, *With WW*.

page 242: "a love of woods, streams and hills..." Herbert Gilchrist, ed., *Anne Gilchrist: Her Life and Writings*, London, 1887.

page 243: "Walt Whitman, the effeminate world..." Holloway and Adimari, *New York Dissected*.

page 244: "Paul Zweig reminds us..." See Zweig, *Walt Whitman*.

pages 244–245: "He sees in the future..." Van Gogh, *The Complete Letters*.

page 248: "He drags the dead out of their coffins..." Whitman, 1855 Preface to *Leaves*.

page 249: "What you give me, I cheerfully accept..." *Leaves*, "To Rich Givers."

page 249: "A noiseless patient spider..." *Leaves*, "A Noiseless Patient Spider."

page 251: "The water itself has a character of its own..." Allen, *The Solitary Singer*.

page 252: "The hounded slave that flags in the race..." *Leaves*, "Song of Myself."

pages 252–253: "one glimpse of real life and nature..." Emory Holloway and Vernolian Schwarz, eds., *I Sit and Look Out: Editorials from the Brooklyn Daily Times*, New York, 1932.

page 253: "O you should see me..." *Correspondence*, Vol. I.

page 254: "Is this then a touch?" *Leaves*, "Song of Myself."

page 255: "any man, a policeman who suddenly looked..." D. H. Lawrence, *Prologue to Women in Love*, Phoenix, Vol. II, London, 1968.

page 256: "in the old tales of mythology..." Richard M. Bucke, *Walt Whitman*, Philadelphia, 1883.

page 258: "Hours continuing long, sore..." *Leaves*, "Calamus VI."

page 260: "In the stillness his face..." *Leaves*, "Calamus III."

page 260: "We imagine a shy circling of the flame..." Zweig, *Walt Whitman*.

page 262: "...The two men I saw today on the pier..." *Leaves*, "Calamus VI."

page 262: "Camerado, this is no book..." *Leaves*, "So Long."

page 266: "While on the walk immediately overhead..." *Leaves*.

page 268: "how he leaned back in his chair..." William Dean Howells, *Literary Friends and Acquaintances*, New York, 1900.

page 269: "We want to be the publishers..." W. S. Kennedy, *The Fight of a Book for the World*, West Yarmouth, Mass., 1926.

page 271: "The dirtiest book in all the world..." Traubel, *With WW.*

page 272: "low ceiling, everything strongly timber'd..." *Complete Writings.*

page 272: "but your letter says you are not..." Josiah Trent Collection, Duke University Library.

page 273: "I was simmering, simmering, simmering..." J. T. Trowbridge, *My Own Story*, Boston, 1903.

page 274: "he is so large and strong..." Jerome Loving, *Walt Whitman's Champion: William Douglas O'Connor*, College Station, Tex., 1978.

page 275: "a mysterious delicious thrill!" Traubel, *With WW.*

page 278: "I fear you took me last night..." Oscar Lion Collection, Rare Book Room, New York Public Library.

page 280: "four sorts of genius...will be needed..." *Complete Writings.*

page 280: "If you don't Resign..." Oates, *With Malice Toward None.*

page 252: "In your hands, dissatisfied fellow countrymen..." Roy P. Basler, Marion D. Pratt, and Lloyd A. Dunlap, *The Collected Works of Abraham Lincoln*, New Brunswick, N.J., 1953.

pages 280–281: "The South was stuck with slavery..." Parrish, *American Civil War.*

pages 281–282: "I had been to the opera on Fourteenth Street..." *Complete Writings.*

page 282: "I have this day, this hour..." Manuscript Division, Library of Congress, Washington, D.C.

page 283: "I often think that I can imagine..." Clarence Ghodes and Rollo G. Silver, eds., *Faint Clews and Indirections: Manuscripts of Walt Whitman and His Family*, Durham, N.C., 1949.

page 284: "Never was such a shambling..." William Pitt Fesenden, quoted in Oates, *With Malice Toward None.*

page 285: "Beautiful that war and all its deeds..." *Leaves*, "Reconciliation."

## CHAPTER 9. LILAC AND STAR AND BIRD

pages 286–287: "The slave pens and auction blocks had been swept away..." See Oates, *With Malice Toward None.*

page 288: "While I was there..." *Complete Writings.*

page 288: "Death is nothing here..." Charles I. Glicksberg, ed., *Walt Whitman and the Civil War*, Philadelphia, 1933.

pages 289–290: "I see before me now..." *Leaves*, "Bivouac on a Mountainside."

pages 290–291: "They are merely tents..." *Complete Writings.*

page 291: "At my feet more distinctly..." *Leaves*, "A March in the Ranks Hard-Prest."

page 292: "O'Connor's Irish landlord had fastened..." Kaplan, *Walt Whitman.*

page 295: "Dear Friend..." *Correspondence*, Vol. I.

page 296: "I said, 'Probably not, my dear...'" Walter Lowenfels, ed., *Walt Whitman's Civil War*, New York, 1961.

pages 296–297: "My idea is a book of the time..." *Correspondence*, Vol. I.

page 297: "The presence of a good middle-aged..." *Correspondence*, Vol. I.

pages 297–298: "Bed 53 wants some licorice..." *Correspondence*, Vol. I.

page 298: "From the stump of the arm..." *Leaves*, "The Wound-Dresser."

pages 299–300: "Dear Friends..." *Correspondence*, Vol. I.

page 301: "Fruit, preserves, pickles..." Kaplan, *Walt Whitman.*
page 302: "as much of a beauty as ever..." *Correspondence,* Vol. I.
page 302: "cut quite a swell." *Correspondence,* Vol. I.
page 303: "The hiss of the surgeon's knife..." *Leaves,* "Song of Myself."
page 304: "I want the battle fought..." Traubel, *With WW.*
pages 304–305: "O my dear mother..." *Correspondence,* Vol. I.
page 305: "with more or less all the States..." *Leaves* (Library of America ed.).
page 306: "Dear comrade..." *Correspondence,* Vol. I.
page 308: "a weak, frail mortal..." Traubel, *With WW.*
page 309: "I was always between two loves..." Traubel, *With WW.*
pages 311–312: "To think that the wretch..." Allen, *The Solitary Singer.*
page 312: "...Jeffy must have wrote..." Trent Collection, Duke University Library.
pages 312–313: "I feel lately as though..." *Correspondence,* Vol. I.
page 313: "Last night I was with..." Holograph in American Literature Collection, Yale University Library, New Haven, Conn.
pages 315–316: "With malice toward none..." Oates, *With Malice Toward None.*
page 316: "Five or six nights since..." *Complete Writings.*
page 317: "Mother prepared breakfast..." *Complete Writings.*
page 319: "Nothing will do..." *Complete Writings.*
page 321: "Come lovely and soothing death..." *Leaves,* "When Lilacs Last in the Dooryard Bloom'd."

CHAPTER 10. THE DESCENT

page 322: "I shall range along the high plateau..." *Correspondence,* Vol. I.
page 323: "To begin with take warning..." *Leaves,* "Song of Myself."
page 323: "Making directly for this rendezvous..." *Leaves,* "Song of the Exposition."
pages 325–326: "Personally the author of Leaves of Grass..." *Correspondence,* Vol. I.
page 327: "Walt had his blanket..." *Complete Writings.*
page 327: "There is a pretty strong enmity here..." *Complete Writings.*
page 328: "The truth is, Pete..." *Correspondence,* Vol. I.
page 328: "If you are not well when I come back..." *Correspondence,* Vol. I.
page 329: "they pretended to live up stairs..." Trent Collection, Duke University Library.
page 329: "Since I have had it, I can read no other book..." Thomas B. Harned, ed., *The Letters of Anne Gilchrist and Walt Whitman,* New York, 1918.
page 330: "had a ride with him in the horse-car..." William Michael Rossetti, *Rossetti Papers, 1862–70,* New York, 1903.
page 331: "to think the poor soul hadent a friend..." Trent Collection, Duke University Library.
page 332: "the voice of my mate: it must be so..." Harned, *Letters of Anne Gilchrist and Walt Whitman.*
page 332: "I have been waiting quite a while..." Harned, *Letters of Anne Gilchrist and Walt Whitman.*
page 333: "cheating...fancying what does not really exist..." Notebook, Library of Congress.
page 334: "here I am home again..." *Correspondence,* Vol. II.

page 335: "his emotions etc are complete..." *Uncollected P&P.*

page 336: "I mark one, a lad of eighteen..." *Correspondence,* Vol. II.

pages 336–337: "I received your affectionate letter..." *Correspondence,* Vol. II.

page 337: "I have said more about myself to you..." *Correspondence,* Vol. II.

page 338: "My dear young man..." *Correspondence,* Vol. II.

page 339: "farewell my beloved sons..." Traubel, *With WW.*

page 339: "was not content to stay in his room..." Clara Barrus, *Whitman and Burroughs, Comrades,* Boston, 1931.

page 340: "Walt, hasn't the world made it plain..." Traubel, *With WW.*

page 341: "the trouble at Washington..." Traubel, *With WW.*

page 342: "So hanging my clothes on a rail..." *Specimen Days.*

pages 342–343: "My dearest friend, I do not approve..." Harned, *Letters of Anne Gilchrist and Walt Whitman.*

page 343: "I am anxious Harry should learn..." *Correspondence,* Vol. III.

page 344: "Do not call to see me..." *Correspondence,* Vol. III.

page 345: "talk with HS and gave him r..." William White, ed., *Daybooks and Notebooks,* in *Collected Writings.*

page 346: "I heard you was going to Washington..." *Correspondence,* Vol. III.

page 347: "if I go up in my room..." *Correspondence,* Vol. III.

pages 347–348: "Dear Hank..." *Correspondence,* Vol. III.

page 349: "Walt Whitman's early years..." Bucke, *Walt Whitman.*

pages 349–350: "Walt Whitman is the best..." Richard M. Bucke, *Cosmic Consciousness: A Study in the Evolution of the Human Mind,* New York, 1923.

page 351: "The real truth is..." Furness, *Walt Whitman's Workshop.*

page 352: "He took me into a very common..." Elizabeth Robins Pennell, *Charles Godfrey Leland,* Boston, 1906.

pages 354–355: "Have you read about Oscar Wilde?" *Correspondence,* Vol. III.

page 355: "Most of us... are still too uncertain..." Patrick White, *Patrick White Speaks,* London, 1990.

page 357: "so pretty, so dreamy—like corpse candles..." *Specimen Days.*

page 357: "What lies behind *Leaves of Grass*..." Edward Carpenter, *Days with Walt Whitman,* London, 1906.

pages 357–358: "a great tragic element in his nature..." Carpenter, *Days with Walt Whitman.*

page 358: "Long autumn days by the sea..." Barrus, *Whitman and Burroughs.*

page 359: "a great old Angora Tom..." Edmund Gosse, *Critical Kit-Kats,* New York, 1896.

page 360: "As Miss Nipper says..." Traubel, *With WW.*

page 362: "I suppose he's bummin' along..." Traubel, *With WW.*

page 363: "Goodbye, my Fancy!" *Leaves,* "Goodbye, My Fancy."

# Selected Bibliography

## I. WHITMAN'S WORKS

### POETRY

*Leaves of Grass*, Brooklyn, 1855. 2nd ed., Brooklyn (Fowler and Wells), 1856. 3rd
  ed., Boston (Thayer and Eldridge), 1860. 4th ed., New York, 1867. 5th ed., and
  *Passage to India*, one volume, Washington, D.C., 1871. 6th ed., Washington, D.C.,
  1872. 7th Centennial ed., Camden, N.J. (reprint of 5th), 1876. 8th ed., Boston
  (James Osgood and Co.), 1881. 9th ed., Philadelphia (David McKay), 1891.
*November Boughs*, Philadelphia (David McKay), 1888.
*Complete Poems and Prose of Walt Whitman, Containing Sands at Seventy and November
  Boughs*, Philadelphia (David McKay), 1892.

### PROSE

*Democratic Vistas*, Washington, D.C., 1871.
*Two Rivulets, prose and verse*, Camden, N.J., 1876.
*Specimen Days and Collect*, Philadelphia (Rees, Welch and Co.), 1882.
*Complete Prose Works*, Philadelphia (David McKay), 1892.

### COLLECTIONS, SELECTIONS, REPRINTS

*The Collected Writings of Walt Whitman*, ed. Thomas L. Brasher, New York University
  Press, 1963.
*The Complete Writings of Walt Whitman*, ed. Richard M. Bucke, Thomas B. Harned,
  and Horace L. Traubel, New York and London, 1902.
*Walt Whitman and the Civil War: A Collection of Original Articles and Manuscripts*, ed.
  Charles I. Glicksberg, Philadelphia, 1933.

## SELECTED BIBLIOGRAPHY

*Faint Clews and Indirections: Manuscripts of Walt Whitman and His Family*, ed. Clarence Gohdes and Rollo G. Silver, Durham, N.C., 1949.

*The Gathering of the Forces: Editorials, Essays, Literary and Dramatic Reviews Written by Walt Whitman as Editor of the Brooklyn Daily Eagle in 1846–47*, ed. Cleveland Rodgers and John Black, New York and London, 1920.

*I Sit and Look Out: Editorials from the Brooklyn Daily Times*, ed. Emory Holloway and Vernolian Schwarz, New York, 1932.

*New York Dissected: A Sheaf of Recently Discovered Newspaper Articles by the Author of Leaves of Grass*, ed. Emory Holloway and Ralph Adimari, New York, 1936.

*Uncollected Poetry and Prose of Walt Whitman*, ed. Emory Holloway, New York, 1932.

Horace Traubel, *With Walt Whitman in Camden*. Vol. I, Boston, 1906; II, 1908; III, 1914; IV, Philadelphia, 1953; V, Carbondale, Ill., 1964.

*The Correspondence*, 6 vols., ed. Edwin Haviland Miller, 1961–1977, New York University Press edition of *The Collected Writings of Walt Whitman*.

*Daybooks and Notebooks*, ed. William White, New York University Press edition, 1978.

*Walt Whitman's Workshop*, ed. Clifton Joseph Furness, Cambridge, Mass., 1928.


## II. BOOKS ABOUT WHITMAN AND STUDIES OF HIS WORK

Gay Wilson Allen, *The Solitary Singer: A Critical Biography of Walt Whitman*, New York, 1955 (revised 1967).

Anonymous, "The Bird of Freedom," essay in the (London) *Times Literary Supplement*, June 2, 1961.

Roger Asselineau, *The Evolution of Walt Whitman*, Cambridge, Mass., and London, 1961.

Henry B. Binns, A Life of Walt Whitman, London, 1905.

Richard M. Bucke, *Walt Whitman*, Philadelphia, 1883.

John Burroughs, *Whitman: A Study*, London, 1894.

Richard V. Chase, *Walt Whitman Reconsidered*, London, 1955.

Henry M. Christman, ed., *Walt Whitman's New York*, New York, 1963.

Malcolm Cowley, "The Guru, the Beatnik and the Good Gray Poet," in *The New Republic*, October 26, 1959.

David Daiches, *Poetry and the Modern World*, Chicago, 1940.

Guy Davenport, "Whitman," essay in *The Geography of the Imagination*, London, 1984.

Geoffrey Dutton, *Walt Whitman*, Edinburgh and London, 1961.

Milton Hindus, ed., *Leaves of Grass, One Hundred Years After*, Stanford and London, 1955.

Emory Holloway, *Whitman: An Interpretation in Narrative*, New York, 1926.

Randall Jarrell, "Some Lines from Whitman," *Poetry and the Age*, New York, 1953.

A. Norman Jeffares, "Walt Whitman: The Barbaric Yawp," in *The Great American Experiment*, ed. Carl Bode, London, 1961.

Justin Kaplan, *Walt Whitman: A Life*, New York, 1980.

# SELECTED BIBLIOGRAPHY

D. H. Lawrence, *Studies in Classic American Literature*, New York, 1923 (reprinted Penguin, London, 1971).

F. R. Leavis, *New Bearings in English Poetry*, London, 1950.

Federico Garcia Lorca, "Ode to Walt Whitman," in *Poet in New York*, New York, 1955.

F. O. Matthiessen, *American Renaissance*, New York, 1941.

Bliss Perry, *Walt Whitman: His Life and Work*, Boston, 1906.

Edith Sitwell, preface to *The American Genius: An Anthology*, London, 1951.

John Addington Symonds, *Walt Whitman: A Study*, London and New York, 1893.

Paul Zweig, *Walt Whitman: The Making of the Poet*, New York, 1984.

# Index

Abbot, Dr. Henry, 214
Adams, John, 27
Adams, John Quincy, 125
Aeschylus, 280
*Age of Reason* (Paine), 5
Alboni, Marietta, 120, 121, 122
Alcott, Bronson, 219, 240, 241, 272
Allen, Elijah, 307
Allen, Gay Wilson, 43, 53, 76, 100
American Institute (New York), 323
*American Notes* (Dickens), 57, 60
*American Review*, 92
Anden, Van, 108, 142, 143, 150
Anderson, Major Robert, 281
"Angel of Tears" (Whitman), 79
*Arabian Nights*, 29
*Arcturus*, 79, 80
*Aristidean*, 92
Arnold, George, 265
Arnold, John, 237, 245
Arnold, Matthew, 199
"Art-Music and Heart-Music"
    (Whitman), 100
"As I Ebb'd with the Ocean of Life"
    ("Bardic Symbols") (Whitman), 263
Ashton, J. Hubley, 324
Astor, John Jacob, 28
Auden, W. H., 260

*Aurora, see New York Aurora*
*Autobiography* (Goethe), 134

Balzac, Honoré de, 82, 117
"Bardic Symbols," *see* "As I Ebb'd with
    the Ocean of Life"
Barnum, P. T., 103, 122
Bartol, Cyrus, 231
Baudelaire, Charles, 90, 138
Beach, Calvin, 276
Beach, Juliette, 276
"Beat, Beat Drums!" (Whitman), 283
Beecher, Henry Ward, 182, 240
Bellini, Vincenzo, 121
Bender, Thomas, 80, 81
Benjamin, Park, 56, 59, 63, 76
Bennett, George C., 249, 250, 252, 264
Benton, Thomas Hart, 179
Béranger, Pierre Jean de, 199
"Bervance: or Father and Son"
    (Whitman), 42
Bettini, Alessandro, 120
Bible, 138, 244, 273, 296, 315, 356
Birkbeck, Morris, 10
Bishop, Anna, 119
Blake, William, 95, 183, 184, 187,
    209, 363

*Blithedale Romance* (Hawthorne), 118
"Blood Money" (Whitman), 197
Boorstin, Daniel, 4, 8, 11, 12
Booth, John Wilkes, 115, 116
Booth, Junius Brutus, 115
Boston, 79, 268–274, 348, 353, 354
*Boston Radical*, 331
Bowery Theatre, 35, 115
"Boy Lover" (Whitman), 149
Bremer, Frederika, 117
Brenton, James P., 51, 52
Brenton, Orvetta, 51
Brisbane, Albert, 83
Broadway Theatre, 151
Brooklyn, 17, 21, 24–35; artists in,
    196, 199, 201, 212, 220;
    expansion of, 32, 195; street life
    in, 22, 23
*Brooklyn Advertiser*, 102, 150, 173, 188
*Brooklyn Daily Eagle*, 61, 76, 93, 102,
    103, 107, 114, 117, 123,
    125–127, 129, 132–134, 136,
    143, 149, 150, 174, 177, 275
*Brooklyn Daily Times*, 234, 249, 250,
    252, 253, 256, 264
*Brooklyn Freeman*, 175–179, 181
*Brooklyn Standard*, 279
Brown, Ford Madox, 329, 351
Brown, Henry Kirke, 199
Brown, John, 168, 268
Brown, Lewis, 305, 306
Brown, Sandford, 53
Brush, Hannah, *see* Whitman, Hannah
    Brush
Bryant, William Cullen, 59, 60, 84,
    128, 182
Bucke, Richard Maurice, 308, 323,
    343, 348, 353
Bull Run, Battle of, 282
Burns, Robert, 265
Burr, Aaron, 28
Burroughs, John, 178, 255, 278, 307,
    308, 318, 327
Burroughs, Ursula, 308, 339, 345,
    348, 349, 358
Byron, George Gordon, Lord, 136

"Calamus" poems (Whitman), 162,
    163, 258, 259, 260, 262
Calhoun, John, 174
Camden, N.J., 81, 275, 339–341, 349,
    350, 354, 363
Carleton, George, 325
Carlyle, Thomas, 85, 133, 135, 136,
    139, 141, 142, 202; on poet as
    hero, 136; on worker-poet, 141
Carpenter, Edward, 357
Cass, Lewis, 149, 176
Cattell, Edward, 344
Cauldwell, 69
*Celestial Wonders of Philosophy*
    (Rafinesque), 212
Centennial Exposition (Philadelphia),
    350
"Chants Democratic" poems
    (Whitman), 255
Chapman, Frederick, 220
Chase, Salmon P., 295, 307
Chateaubriand, François, 147
Cheyneys, 100, 116
"Children of Adam," *see* "Enfans
    d' Adam" poems
Childs, George C., 352
"Child's Champion" (Whitman), 45
"Child's Reminiscence" *see* "Out of the
    Cradle Endlessly Rocking"
Chopin, Frederic, 117
"City of Orgies" (Whitman), 324
Civil War, 281–315; Bull Run, 282;
    Fredericksburg, 284; George
    Whitman wounded in, 284;
    George Whitman taken prisoner
    in, 313
Clapp, Henry, 265–268, 272, 274, 276
Clare, Ada, 265
Clark, Edward, 28, 29
Clark, James, 28
Clark, Lewis Gaylord, 80
Clay, Cassius Marcellus, 196
Clay, Henry, 196
Clemens, Samuel E., 29
Clinton, De Witt, 78
Cobbett, William, 22
Cold Springs, Long Island, 21, 26, 31, 37

Coleridge, Samuel Taylor, 133
"Confession and Warning" (Whitman), 257
Consuelo (Sand), 116, 139
Conway, Moncure D., 230, 231, 235, 325
Cooper, James Fenimore, 29
Cosmic Consciousness (Bucke), 348, 349
Countess of Rudolstadt (Sand), 139, 140
Course of Six Lectures (Mitchel), 212
Crockett, Davy, 13, 14, 56
"Crossing Brooklyn Ferry" (Whitman), 238–240
"Crown" (Lawrence), 244

Dana, Charles, 141, 232–234
Darwin, Charles, 15
Davenport, Guy, 200
Davis, Jefferson, 279
Davis, Mary, 356, 358
Davis, Thomas, 327
"Death in the Schoolroom" (Whitman), 60
"Death Song" (Whitman), 223
Degas, Edgar, 200
Delacroix, Eugene, 117
Democratic Review, 59, 60, 62, 64, 68, 79–82, 92, 98
Democratic Vistas (Whitman), 52, 74, 181, 355
Dewey, John, xiv
Dial, 110, 136
Dickens, Charles, 57, 58, 62, 63, 85, 86, 152, 154–156, 165
Dixon, Thomas, 337
Dostoevsky, Fyodor, 52, 95
Douglas, Stephen A., 252, 316
Douglass, Frederick, 176
Doyle, Peter, 260, 328, 333, 334, 339, 340, 345, 350; first meeting with Whitman, 327
Dracula (Stoker), 337
Drum-Taps (Whitman), 296, 310, 324, 330

"Dumb Kate" (Whitman), 91
Duyckinck, Evert, 79, 80, 98

Eakins, Thomas, 199, 200
Edinburgh Review, 132
"Eighteenth Presidency" (Whitman), 181, 211, 242, 248, 249, 269
Eldridge, Charles, 284, 293, 308, 309, 339; see also Thayer and Eldridge
Eliot, T. S., 228
Emerson, Ralph Waldo, 46, 47, 56, 82, 85, 105, 124, 133, 136, 138, 140, 143, 148, 169, 175, 182, 191, 196, 202–204, 231–236, 253, 267, 271, 273, 295, 301, 326, 353, 354, 362; "Children of Adam" warning, 271; first visit to Whitman by, 231; lecture, "The Poet," New York, 84; letter of greeting to Whitman, 230
"Enfans d'Adam" poems (Whitman), 271, 331
English, Thomas Dunn, 92
Epictetus, 216
"Eris: A Spirit Record" (Whitman), 91
Evening Tattler (New York), 70, 74
Eyre, Ellen, 278

Fellows, Colonel John, 69
Fiedler, Leslie, 362
Finn, Mike, 56
Ford's Theatre, 317
Forrest, Edwin, 112
Fourier, Charles, 83, 143
Fowler, Lorenzo, 185, 189
Fowler, Orson, 185, 189
Fowler and Wells, 185, 186, 243
Fox, George, 141
Franklin, Benjamin, 9
Franklin Evans (Whitman), 55, 75–77, 110, 156, 164
Fredericksburg, Battle of, 284
Free Inquirer, 18
Free Soil movement, 81, 125, 142, 165, 174, 206

Friedenberg, Edgar Z., 44
Fritzinger, Warren, 358
Fuller, Margaret, 82, 110, 111, 118,
    133, 136
Fulton Ferry, 22, 86, 96, 108, 264, 282
Fulton (steam vessel), 26


Garibaldi, Giuseppe, 196
Gauguin, Paul, 147
Giddings, Joshua, 125
Gilchrist, Anne, 329–331, 335, 342,
    344, 345; arrives in America, 343;
    declares love, 332
Godwin, Park, 82
Goethe, Johann Wolfgang von, 133,
    136, 191
"Good-bye My Fancy" (Whitman),
    363
Good Gray Poet (O'Connor), 325
Gorowski, Adam, 309
Gosse, Edmund, 351, 359
Gottschalk, Louis, 266
Graham, Sylvester, 160
Gray, Frederick Schiller, 268, 313
Greeley, Horace, 56, 102, 103, 110,
    126, 240
Greenough, Horatio, 82
Grey, Ellen, 278
Griswold, Rufus, 56
Gunn, John, 54


Hale, Edward Everett, 232, 236
Hale, John Parker, 196, 206
Half-Hours with the Best Authors, 217
Hamlet (Shakespeare), 99
Harlan, James, 323
Harper's Weekly, 283
Harrington (O'Connor), 269, 274
Harris, Frank, 345
Harrison, Gabriel, 227
Harrison, William Henry, 54
Hartshorne, William, 30
Hawthorne, Nathaniel, 60, 82, 93,
    117, 118, 148, 267
Hayes, A. H., 151, 172

Hegel, Georg Wilhelm, 86
Herrick, Nelson, 56, 63, 69, 75
Heyde, Charles, 212, 230
Hicks, Elias, 6, 17, 27, 29, 207, 253
Holloway, Emory, 162
Holmes, Oliver Wendell, 186
Homer, 16
Hospital Sketches (Alcott), 296
House of the Seven Gables
    (Hawthorne), 271
Howells, William Dean, 267, 268
Huene, Frederick, 256
Hughes, Bishop John, 64


"I Saw in Louisiana a Live Oak
    Growing" (Whitman), 163
"I Sing the Body Electric" (Whitman),
    166, 169, 184, 190, 271


Jackson, Andrew, 14, 80
Jefferson, Thomas, 11, 17, 27, 69, 81,
    85
Jesus, 197, 198, 215, 249, 348
Johnson, Judge Samuel, 175
Jones, William Alfred, 82
Julius Caesar (Shakespeare), 109
Jung, Carl, 182


Kaplan, Justin, 44
Kean, Mrs. Charles, 112, 113
Keats, John, 132, 133
Kemble, Fanny, 33
King, Charles, 54
King John (Shakespeare), 107, 112
Knickerbocker Magazine, 80, 83
Kossuth, Louis, 196, 204


La Favorita (Donizetti), 120
Lafayette, Marquis de, 24, 25
Lamon, Ward, 315
Lancaster, Joseph, 25
Laurel Springs, Kirkwood, 341, 344
Lawrence, D. H., 3, 16, 72, 74, 94,

126, 144, 164, 197, 199, 228, 233, 255, 256, 260

*Leaves of Grass* (Whitman), 5, 10, 14, 16, 57, 73, 76, 82, 85, 106, 109, 110, 118, 131, 148, 171, 180, 183, 186, 188, 192, 194, 220, 228, 231–233, 242, 243, 264, 265, 267, 273, 275, 330, 338, 348, 356, 357, 362

   *first edition* (1855), 226, 227, 229, 234, 236, 240, 267, 272

   *second edition* (1856), 238, 243

   *third edition* (1860), 249, 264, 269, 270

   *fourth edition* (1867), 323–325, 327

   *Centennial edition* (1876), 350

   *seventh edition* (1881), 353

   *Complete Poems and Prose* (1888), 362

Lee, Robert E., 317

Leggett, William, 81

Leland, Charles, 351

*Letters on Astronomy* (Olmstead), 212

Libbey, Walter, 201

*Life Illustrated*, 214, 227, 234, 236, 243

Lincoln, Abraham, 106, 142, 149, 166, 169, 174, 196, 280, 281, 283, 304, 315, 316; first seen by Whitman, 279; *Leaves of Grass* and, 234

Lind, Jenny, 122

*Linda de Chamounix* (Donizetti), 119

Liszt, Franz, 117

"Little Bells Last Night" (Whitman), 283

"Little Sleighers" (Whitman), 91

London, Jack, 248

*Long Island Democrat*, 51, 54, 177

*Long Island Farmer*, 54

*Long Island Patriot*, 29, 30

*Long Island Star*, 31, 32, 96, 102, 123

*Long Islander*, 48, 49

Longfellow, Henry Wadsworth, 352, 355

Longfellow, Samuel, 234

Lorca, Federico Garcia, xvi

Lowell, James Russell, 60, 124, 232, 267

*Lucia*, 122

Lucretius, 216

Luther, Martin, 5

Lyell, Charles, 218

Macpherson, James, 137

Macready, Charles, 113

Mann, Horace, 100

*Marginalia* (Poe), 94

Marsh, William, 13, 102

*Martin Chuzzlewit* (Dickens), 58, 59

Marx, Karl, 83, 196

Mathews, Cornelius, 79, 80, 98

Mazzini, Giuseppe, 196, 204

McCarthy, Justin, 330

McClure, Sam, 151, 172

McKay, David, 354

Melville, Herman, 4, 21, 79, 117, 147, 148

*Memoranda During the War* (Whitman), 296, 297

*Memoria Technica*, 217

Menken, Ada, 266

Michelangelo, 280, 304

Michelet, Jules, 133, 140

Miller, Henry, 52

Miller, Perry, 80

Milne, R. M., 132

Mitchell, O. M., 212

*Moby-Dick* (Melville), 148, 202, 271, 272

Montesquieu, Charles de Secondat, 5

Morris, George P., 32

Morris, William, 83

Mount, William Sydney, 199

Murphy, Henry C., 102

Musset, Alfred de, 117

Muybridge, Eadweard, 199, 200

"My Boys and Girls" (Whitman), 43

*My Religion* (Tolstoy), 244

"Nature" (Emerson), 203

*New Era*, 59, 199

*New Orleans Crescent*, 153, 157, 159, 164, 165, 167, 171

*New World* (New York), 56, 59, 70
*New York Advertiser*, 21
*New York Aurora*, 61–70, 74, 75
New York City, 35, 54, 65, 71, 88, 96; boarding houses in, 55, 87, 91; gangs of, 35, 85, 250; opera in, 118, 119, 120, 121, 122; street life of, 60, 66, 67, 85, 109
*New York Daily News*, 193
*New York Democrat*, 91
*New York Evening Post*, 59, 81, 99, 150, 197, 201
*New York Galaxy*, 325
*New York Globe*, 150
*New York Herald*, 284
New York Hospital, 276
*New York Leader*, 283
*New-York Mirror*, 32
*New York Sun*, 76
*New York Sunday Dispatch*, 181
New York Tabernacle, 101
*New York Times*, 267, 294
*New York Tribune*, 109, 110, 150, 171, 174, 179, 226, 227, 234
Newall, James Robinson, 70
Niblo's Gardens, 100, 121, 282
Nietzsche, Friedrich, 171
*Norma*, 121
*North American Review*, 232
*North British Review*, 132
Norton, Charles Eliot, 232
*Notes on Walt Whitman as Poet and Person* (Burroughs), 325
*November Boughs* (Whitman), 12

O'Casey, Sean, 248
O'Connor, Nelly, 44, 292, 293, 304, 324, 339, 360
O'Connor, William, 47, 269, 273, 274, 286, 292, 301, 308, 309, 314, 316, 322, 325, 327, 328, 348
Ogden, William B., 8
"Oh Mother of a Mighty Race" (Bryant), 128
Olmsted, Frederick Law, 161

Osgood, James R., 353, 354
*Ossian* (Macpherson), 137
O'Sullivan, John L., 60, 80, 82, 94, 98
"Our Future Lot" (Whitman), 49, 50
"Out of the Cradle Endlessly Rocking" ("A Word Out of the Sea"/"A Child's Reminiscence") (Whitman), 121, 245, 246, 247, 268
"Out of the Rolling Ocean the Crowd" (Whitman), 276

Paine, Thomas, xv, 5, 17, 27, 69, 93, 207, 253, 345
*Papers on Literature and Art* (Fuller), 110
Park Theatre, 100, 107, 112
Parker, Theodore, 126
Parton, Sara Payson Willis ("Fanny Fern"), 243, 252
Pasternak, Boris, 356
Penn, William, 6
*People* (Michelet), 140
Pfaff, Charles, 266
Pfaff's bar (New York), 265, 267–269, 274, 276–278
*Philadelphia Press*, 352
Phillips, Wendell, 130
Phrenology (Sperzheim and Gall), 185
Piatt, John, 308
Pierce, Franklin, 210, 218
*Pierre* (Melville), 271
Pintard, John, 78
Plato, xiv
Plutarch, 161, 280
Poe, Edgar Allan, 60, 71, 72, 75, 92, 94, 95, 100, 110, 158; publishes article by Whitman, 92; Whitman's verdict on, 95
"Poem of the Proposition of Nakedness" ("Respondez!") (Whitman), 180, 242
*Poems of Walt Whitman* (ed. Rossetti), 326
"Poet" (Emerson), 84

"Poetry for the People" (Jones), 82
Polk, James K., 123, 124, 126, 142
"Prayer of Columbus" (Whitman), 340
Preface (1855) to *Leaves of Grass*, 126, 209, 210, 217, 230, 248
Price, Abby, 235, 236, 245, 256, 266, 270, 324
Price, Edmund, 236
Price, Helen, 237, 245
*Prophetic Books* (Blake), 137, 244
"Protoleaf," see "Starting from Paumanok"
*Putnam's Monthly*, 232

Quakerism, 17, 118

Rabelais, François, 280
Rankin, Henry B., 234
Redpath, James, 269, 296
*Representative Men* (Emerson), 271
"Respondez!" see "Poem of the Proposition of Nakedness"
"Resurgemus" (Whitman), 171
"Revenge and Requittal" (Whitman), 92
*Richard III* (Shakespeare), 33, 109, 112, 113, 115
Richter, Jean Paul, 136
*Rights of Man* (Paine), 5
Roe, Charles, 40, 52, 53
Rome Brothers, 226, 227, 264
Roosa, Dr. St. John, 277
Ropes, John, 56, 63, 69, 75
Rossetti, Dante Gabriel, 266
Rossetti, William, 326, 327, 329, 330, 332; sponsorship and support, 330, 332, 351
Rossini, Giocchino, 121
Rousseau, Jean-Jacques, 52
Ruskin, John, 85, 133, 202, 334
Rynders, Isaiah, 85, 91, 196

Saintsbury, George, 351
Sanborn, Frank, 273

Sand, George, 116, 117, 133, 139
*Sartor Resartus* (Carlyle), 136, 137, 140, 204, 244
*Saturday Press*, 245, 265, 267
Sawyer, Tom, 305–307
*Scarlet Letter* (Hawthorne), 271
Schiller, J. C. F von, 133, 136
Scott, Walter, 29
Severn, J. Milliott, 184
Seward, William H., 146, 197
"Shadow and Light of a Young Man's Soul" (Whitman), 38
Shakespeare, William, 16, 280
Shelley, Percy Bysshe, 136, 224
"Ship of Death" (Lawrence), 74, 321
*Shooting Niagara* (Carlyle), 355
"Sight in Camp in the Daybreak Gray and Dim" (Whitman), 289
"Sleepers" (Whitman), 89, 90, 91, 106, 145
Smith, Susan Garnet, 275
*Social Contract* (Rousseau), 5
*Social Destiny of Man* (Brisbane), 83
Socrates, 204
"Song of Myself" (Whitman), xv, 3, 18, 30, 39, 62, 68, 71, 72, 89, 113, 116, 119, 123, 145, 190, 203, 205, 213, 220, 221, 228, 234, 249, 250, 254
"Song of the Open Road" (Whitman), 220
*Songs Before Sunrise* (Swinburne), 329
"South Sea Idyll" (Stoddard), 336
*Specimen Days* (Whitman), 27, 52, 95, 116, 138, 149, 342
*Spirit of Laws* (Montesquieu), 5
"Spontaneous Me" (Whitman), 271
Spooner, Alden, 31
Spooner, Edwin, 96, 102
*Starry Night* (Van Gogh), 244
"Starting from Paumanok" ("Protoleaf") (Whitman), 271
Stillman, W. J., 330
Stoddard, Charles Warren, 336
Stoker, Bram, 337, 338
Strong, George Templeton, 78, 80, 122, 250

Sutton, Henry, 107, 108
Swedenborg, Emanuel, 237
Swinburne, Algernon, 266
Swinton, John, 294, 301
Swinton, William, 308

Talbot, Jesse, 220
Tammany Hall, New York, 58, 69, 75, 85, 91, 105
Taylor, Edward Thompson, 272
Taylor, General Zachary, 124–126, 167, 177
Tennyson, Alfred, Lord, 329, 351
Thayer and Eldridge, 269, 271, 272, 275, 353
"There Was a Child Went Forth" (Whitman), 34, 44
"This Compost" (Whitman), 215
Thoreau, Henry David, 124, 240, 242, 253, 272, 308, 354; relations with Whitman, 241, 243; rhythmic prose of, 138
Thus Spake Zarathustra (Nietzsche), 244
Timber Creek, Laurel Springs, 342, 347
"To a Common Prostitute" (Whitman), 271
Tocqueville, Alexis de, 31, 171
Tolstoy, Leo, 244
"Tomb Blossoms" (Whitman), 71
Traubel, Horace, 16, 17, 45, 47, 49, 60, 72, 76, 93, 105, 121, 128, 129, 136, 141, 162, 167, 168, 181, 186, 198, 200, 218, 257, 261, 271, 275, 308, 326, 338, 359, 360–363
Tree, Ellen, 112
Trevelyan, G. M., 5
Trowbridge, John Townsend, 272, 295, 307, 325
Turgenev, Ivan, 117
Twain, Mark, 186, 325
Two Rivulets (Whitman), 350
Tyndale, Sarah, 241, 243, 244, 250

Uncle Tom's Cabin (Stowe), 274
"Use of the Body in Relation to the Mind" (Moore), 183

Van Buren, Martin, 45, 54, 80, 176
Van Gogh, Vincent, 72, 73, 83, 161, 244
Van Velsor, Cornelius, 15, 18, 20–22, 32, 277
Vanishing Adolescent (Friedenberg), 44
Verdi, Giuseppe, 120, 121
"Voice Out of the Sea," see "Out of the Cradle Endlessly Rocking"
Voix de Satan (Hugo), 244
Voltaire, 5, 253

Ward, Artemis, 265
Washington, D.C., 82, 283, 286, 287, 292–309, 311, 313, 314, 317, 318, 322, 324–328, 330–339
Washington, George, 9, 24, 105, 106, 125, 204, 287
Webster, Daniel, 144, 182, 196, 197
Wells, Samuel, 233
Wentworth, Horace, 275
West Hills, Long Island, 15, 21, 32, 116
West Jersey Press, 350
Westminster Review, 132, 275
"When Lilacs Last in the Dooryard Bloom'd" (Whitman), 319–321
White, Patrick, 355
White, Sara, 144
Whitman, Andrew (brother), 17, 24, 43, 178, 192, 310; dies, 311
Whitman, Eddy (brother), 36, 38, 43, 97, 192, 212, 219, 237, 257, 336, 363
Whitman, George (brother), 17, 24, 38, 40–43, 48, 49, 65, 75, 97, 108, 123, 168, 177, 196, 205, 226, 229, 234, 254, 282–284, 287, 288, 316, 328, 329, 331, 335, 340; posted missing, 284; taken prisoner, 313

Whitman, Hannah Brush, 18, 19, 37, 212

Whitman, Hannah (sister), 24, 97, 229

Whitman, Hattie (daughter of Andrew), 304, 310, 311

Whitman, Jacob, 20

Whitman, Jesse (brother), 20, 21, 31, 192, 236; committed to asylum, 312; dies, 331

Whitman, Joseph, 18

Whitman, Louisa (mother), 15, 17, 18, 21, 24, 25, 35, 229, 231, 232, 236, 240, 272, 287, 304, 312, 313, 324, 329, 331, 335; Walt's relationship with, 37, 87, 88, 113, 118, 131, 160, 205; death of, 339

Whitman, Martha (Mrs. Jeff Whitman), 255, 284, 293, 311, 339

Whitman, Mary (sister), 43, 97, 181, 229, 311

Whitman, Nancy (Mrs. Andrew Whitman), 310, 311

Whitman, Sara Helen, 274

Whitman, Walt (Walter Whitman, Jr.): apprenticeship in Brooklyn, 29–35; army hospitals, xiv, 293, 295–303, 305, 312; artist friends in Brooklyn, 199, 201, 212, 220; astronomy, 212; as editor of Aurora, 64–70, 74; birthplace on Long Island, 21; boyhood in Brooklyn, 22, 24–34, 83, 146; Brooklyn Art Union speech, 202–204; as editor of Brooklyn Daily Eagle, 76, 93, 102, 103, 107, 109, 114, 117, 123, 125–127, 129, 132–134, 136, 143, 149, 150, 174, 177; Brooklyn Freeman, 175, 176; Bucke's biography of, 348, 349; Burroughs and, 178, 255, 278, 307, 308, 318, 327; "Calamus" poems, 162, 163, 258–260, 262; Camden, 81, 275, 336, 339–341,

349, 350, 354–363; Carlyle's influence on, 133, 135–137; Civil War, 281–315; clerkships in Washington, 293, 314, 324, 331, 341; critics of, 232, 233, 241, 267, 268, 275, 325, 337, 350; cult of old age, 106, 166; Cupid and Psyche, 256, 257; disciples of, 273, 274, 278, 307, 308, 318, 322, 324, 325, 345, 348, 358; "doubleness" of, 72, 123, 163, 192, 208, 262, 263; Eakins's portrait of, 200; Egyptology, 214, 215; Emerson's influence on, 84, 133, 136, 271; Emerson's letter, 230; Epictetus, 216; first publication of, 32; forebears, 15, 18, 19; free-lance journalism, 62, 91, 92, 190, 193; Free Soil movement, 81, 125, 142, 165, 174, 206; Margaret Fuller's influence on, 82, 110, 111, 118; "laziness" of, 51, 52, 70, 150, 178, 205; lecturing, 190, 253; letters from strangers to, 275, 336–338; Lincoln's assassination, its effect on, 317; literary influences on, 29, 33, 93, 116, 133, 137, 138, 140, 186, 187; male friendships of, 161, 162, 181, 208, 209, 305, 306, 341, 343–345; mother's death, its effect on, 16; New Orleans trip, 152–173; New York editor, 9, 61–70, 74, 75, 193; New York's Crystal Palace Exhibition, 218; New York printer, 35, 36; notebooks of 1850s, 174, 202, 222, 223, 261, 264, 333–335; nursing as vocation and therapy, 294, 295–303; O'Connor and, 47, 269, 273, 286, 292, 301, 308, 309, 314, 316; opera, 101, 118–122, 281; oratory as influence on, 34, 55, 104, 105, 115, 118, 120, 196, 222; party politics, 54, 55, 59, 64, 69, 81, 91, 92, 102, 123, 130,

Whitman, Walt (*cont'd.*)
  142, 170, 252; physical
  appearance of, 28, 41, 98, 107,
  128, 139, 188, 198, 218, 227,
  240, 270, 277, 302; phrenology,
  185–192; poetics of, 82–84, 120,
  121, 132, 133, 137, 138, 163,
  187, 221, 319; Quaker influence
  on, 17, 118; real estate speculator,
  177, 178, 195, 207; religion and,
  5, 6, 34, 113, 114, 118, 127,
  183; Rossetti's edition of *Leaves of
  Grass*, 326; Sand's influence on,
  116, 117, 133, 137, 140; sea's
  influence on, 4, 16, 50, 116, 138;
  sexual life of, 48, 257, 258, 260;
  schoolteaching by, 38–41, 44–46,
  53, 54; short stories of, 38, 39,
  41, 42, 44, 45, 60, 71, 90–92;
  slavery issue and, 47, 125, 143,
  149, 168–170, 197, 206, 252,
  309; theatregoing of, 33, 34,
  118; Timber Creek, 342; Western
  trip of, 352, 353; Young
  Americans, 79, 80, 136
Whitman, Walter, Sr. (father), 16, 17,
  19–24, 32, 35; Walt's relationship
  with, 20, 37, 41, 42, 45, 87, 88,
  192, 193, 226; illness and death
  of, 20, 229
Whittier, John Greeleaf, 60, 82, 84,
  196
"Wild Frank's Return" (Whitman), 41,
  60, 88

Wilde, Oscar, 354
Wilkins, Ned, 265, 267
Williams, Naomi, 18, 19
Wilmot, David, 125
Wilmot Proviso, 142, 149, 176
Winter, William, 267
Winton, John, 267
"With Husky-Haughty Lips, O Sea!"
  (Whitman), 358
*Woman and Her Diseases* (Dixon), 117
"Woman's Estimate of Walt Whitman"
  (Gilchrist), 331
Wood, Fernando, 279
"Word Out of the Sea" *see* "Out of the
  Cradle Endlessly Rocking"
Wordsworth, William, 136
Worthington, Erastus, 30
Wright, Frances, 18, 31, 45, 53, 54,
  81, 118
Wright, Silas, 91, 92, 142
*Writer's Notebook* (Dostoevsky), 117

Young Americans, 79, 80, 136
Young, Edward, 141

*Zoopraxia: Men and Animals in Motion*
  (Muybridge), 200
Zweig, Paul, 39, 57, 83, 85, 89, 136,
  158, 202, 222, 244, 252, 260,
  309

Philip Callow was born in Birmingham, England, and studied engineering and the teaching of English before he turned to writing. He has since published twelve novels, several collections of short stories and poems, a volume of autobiography, and two biographies, *Son and Lover: The Young D. H. Lawrence* and *Vincent Van Gogh: A Life,* both of which received critical acclaim. He lives and writes in Evesham, England.

## ELEPHANT PAPERBACKS

**Literature and Letters**

Stephen Vincent Benét, *John Brown's Body*, EL10
Isaiah Berlin, *The Hedgehog and the Fox*, EL21
Robert Brustein, *Dumbocracy in America*, EL421
Anthony Burgess, *Shakespeare*, EL27
Philip Callow, *From Noon to Starry Night*, EL37
Philip Callow, *Son and Lover: The Young D. H. Lawrence*, EL14
Philip Callow, *Vincent Van Gogh*, EL38
James Gould Cozzens, *Castaway*, EL6
James Gould Cozzens, *Men and Brethren*, EL3
Clarence Darrow, *Verdicts Out of Court*, EL2
Floyd Dell, *Intellectual Vagabondage*, EL13
Theodore Dreiser, *Best Short Stories*, EL1
Joseph Epstein, *Ambition*, EL7
André Gide, *Madeleine*, EL8
Gerald Graff, *Literature Against Itself*, EL35
John Gross, *The Rise and Fall of the Man of Letters*, EL18
Irving Howe, *William Faulkner*, EL15
Aldous Huxley, *After Many a Summer Dies the Swan*, EL20
Aldous Huxley, *Ape and Essence*, EL19
Aldous Huxley, *Collected Short Stories*, EL17
Sinclair Lewis, *Selected Short Stories*, EL9
William L. O'Neill, ed., *Echoes of Revolt: The Masses, 1911–1917*, EL5
Budd Schulberg, *The Harder They Fall*, EL36
Ramón J. Sender, *Seven Red Sundays*, EL11
Peter Shaw, *Recovering American Literature*, EL34
Wilfrid Sheed, *Office Politics*, EL4
Tess Slesinger, *On Being Told That Her Second Husband Has Taken His First
      Lover, and Other Stories*, EL12
B. Traven, *The Bridge in the Jungle*, EL28
B. Traven, *The Carreta*, EL25
B. Traven, *The Cotton-Pickers*, EL32
B. Traven, *General from the Jungle*, EL33
B. Traven, *Government*, EL23
B. Traven, *March to the Montería*, EL26
B. Traven, *The Night Visitor and Other Stories*, EL24
B. Traven, *The Rebellion of the Hanged*, EL29
Anthony Trollope, *Trollope the Traveller*, EL31
Ron Warnel, *The Aerodrome*, EL22
Thomas Wolfe, *The Hills Beyond*, EL16

**ELEPHANT PAPERBACKS**

**American History and American Studies**
Stephen Vincent Benét, *John Brown's Body*, EL10
Henry W. Berger, ed., *A William Appleman Williams Reader*, EL126
Andrew Bergman, *We're in the Money*, EL124
Paul Boyer, ed., *Reagan as President*, EL117
Robert V. Bruce, *1877: Year of Violence*, EL102
Philip Callow, *From Noon to Starry Night*, EL37
George Dangerfield, *The Era of Good Feelings*, EL110
Clarence Darrow, *Verdicts Out of Court*, EL2
Floyd Dell, *Intellectual Vagabondage*, EL13
Elisha P. Douglass, *Rebels and Democrats*, EL108
Theodore Draper, *The Roots of American Communism*, EL105
Joseph Epstein, *Ambition*, EL7
Lloyd C. Gardner, *Spheres of Influence*, EL131
Paul W. Glad, *McKinley, Bryan, and the People*, EL119
Daniel Horowitz, *The Morality of Spending*, EL122
Kenneth T. Jackson, *The Ku Klux Klan in the City, 1915–1930*, EL123
Edward Chase Kirkland, *Dream and Thought in the Business Community,
    1860–1900*, EL114
Herbert S Klein, *Slavery in the Americas*, EL103
Aileen S. Kraditor, *Means and Ends in American Abolitionism*, EL111
Leonard W. Levy, *Jefferson and Civil Liberties: The Darker Side*, EL107
Thomas J. McCormick, *China Market*, EL115
Walter Millis, *The Martial Spirit*, EL104
Nicolaus Mills, ed., *Culture in an Age of Money*, EL302
Nicolaus Mills, *Like a Holy Crusade*, EL129
Roderick Nash, *The Nervous Generation*, EL113
William L. O'Neill, ed., *Echoes of Revolt: The Masses, 1911–1917*, EL5
Gilbert Osofsky, *Harlem: The Making of a Ghetto*, EL133
Edward Pessen, *Losing Our Souls*, EL132
Glenn Porter and Harold C. Livesay, *Merchants and Manufacturers*, EL106
John Prados, *Presidents' Secret Wars*, EL134
Edward Reynolds, *Stand the Storm*, EL128
Edward A. Shils, *The Torment of Secrecy*, EL303
Geoffrey S. Smith, *To Save a Nation*, EL125
Bernard Sternsher, ed., *Hitting Home: The Great Depression in Town and
    Country*, EL109
Athan Theoharis, *From the Secret Files of J. Edgar Hoover*, EL127
Nicholas von Hoffman, *We Are the People Our Parents Warned Us Against*,
    EL301
Norman Ware, *The Industrial Worker, 1840–1860*, EL116
Tom Wicker, *JFK and LBJ: The Influence of Personality upon Politics*, EL120
Robert H. Wiebe, *Businessmen and Reform*, EL101
T. Harry Williams, *McClellan, Sherman and Grant*, EL121
Miles Wolff, *Lunch at the 5 & 10*, EL118
Randall B. Woods and Howard Jones, *Dawning of the Cold War*, EL130

## ELEPHANT PAPERBACKS

**Theatre and Drama**
Robert Brustein, *Dumbocracy in America,* EL421
Robert Brustein, *Reimagining American Theatre,* EL410
Robert Brustein, *The Theatre of Revolt,* EL407
Irina and Igor Levin, *Working on the Play and the Role,* EL411
Plays for Performance:
    Aristophanes, *Lysistrata,* EL405
    Pierre Augustin de Beaumarchais, *The Marriage of Figaro,* EL418
    Anton Chekhov, *The Cherry Orchard,* EL420
    Anton Chekhov, *The Seagull,* EL407
    Euripides, *The Bacchae,* EL419
    Euripides, *Iphigenia in Aulis,* EL423
    Euripides, *Iphigenia Among the Taurians,* EL424
    Georges Feydeau, *Paradise Hotel,* EL403
    Henrik Ibsen, *Ghosts,* EL401
    Henrik Ibsen, *Hedda Gabler,* EL413
    Henrik Ibsen, *The Master Builder,* EL417
    Henrik Ibsen, *When We Dead Awaken,* EL408
    Heinrich von Kleist, *The Prince of Homburg,* EL402
    Christopher Marlowe, *Doctor Faustus,* EL404
    *The Mysteries: Creation,* EL412
    *The Mysteries: The Passion,* EL414
    Sophocles, *Electra,* EL415
    August Strindberg, *The Father,* EL406
    August Strindberg, *Miss Julie,* EL422

## ELEPHANT PAPERBACKS

**European and World History**
Mark Frankland, *The Patriots' Revolution,* EL201
Lloyd C. Gardner, *Spheres of Influence,* EL131
Gertrude Himmelfarb, *Darwin and the Darwinian Revolution,* EL207
Gertrude Himmelfarb, *Victorian Minds,* EL205
Thomas A. Idinopulos, *Jerusalem,* EL204
Allan Janik and Stephen Toulmin, *Wittgenstein's Vienna,* EL208
Ronnie S. Landau, *The Nazi Holocaust,* EL203
Clive Ponting, *1940: Myth and Reality,* EL202
Scott Shane, *Dismantling Utopia,* EL206